D1413964

The Undergraduate's Companion to American Writers and Their Web Sites

The Undergraduate's Companion to American Writers and Their Web Sites

James K. Bracken

Larry G. Hinman

2001
Libraries Unlimited, Inc.
Englewood, Colorado

Libraries Unlimited, Inc.
P.O. Box 6633
Englewood, CO 80155-6633
1-800-237-6124
www.lu.com

Library of Congress Cataloging-in-Publication Data

Bracken, James K., 1952-
    The undergraduate's companion to American writers and their web sites / James K.
Bracken, Larry G. Hinman.
        p. cm.
    Includes bibliographical references and index.
    ISBN 1-56308-859-2 (softbound)
        1. American literature--Bibliography. 2. American literature--Research--Computer
network resources. I. Hinman, Larry G. II. Title.

Z1225 .B67 2000
[PS88]
016.8108--dc21
                                                                        00-055848

Contents

Acknowledgments

Several colleagues read different versions and parts of the manuscript as it developed into a book. Their comments helped us focus our efforts and resulted in a more useful companion. In particular, students in English 799: Introduction to Graduate Studies in Literary Bibliography (Summer 1999) reassured us that they (as students) and their own students would profit from a book like this. Professor William Brockman of the University of Illinois Libraries read different sections on several occasions. His advice helped us to trim the variety and number of authors and resources that we proposed to cover. Professor Elizabeth M. Renker of The Ohio State University's English Department also read several sections of the manuscript and provided us with some specific advice about meeting the literary research needs of modern undergraduates.

Dr. William J. Studer and The Ohio State University Libraries' Advisory Committee on Research provided me with a special research leave to work on this project. Colleagues in The Ohio State University Libraries' Main Library deserve thanks. In particular, my colleague in the English, Theater, and Communication Reading Room, Akua Bandele, has been especially supportive and merits special thanks.

—J. K. B.

Mary Flanagan provided the time by releasing me temporarily from my other obligations; and Phil Jensen provided the ongoing computer consulting.

—L. G. H.

Introduction

Welcome to literary research in the 21st century! Never before have so many useful literary research resources in so many different forms been more readily accessible to the literature student—that is, provided you know how and where to find them. This companion will help you take the necessary "first step" in most research on American literature by identifying and describing selected electronic and printed resources (web sites, biographical and critical studies, dictionaries and handbooks, indexes and concordances, journals, and bibliographies) for a selection of American writers. Furthermore, it aims to bridge (in the minds of many modern students and scholars) what appears as a gap between "new and improved" research tools (that is, web sites and other electronic resources accessible by means of the Internet) and what are regarded as literature's more "traditional" tools (printed books and journals contained in libraries). Reality is that Internet resources and printed ones both have appropriate places in a thorough literary research strategy. Effective research on American literature in 2001 and beyond certainly requires the use of both Net and printed resources—and, in fact, often even more than these possibilities. This companion intends to help you know some of the most useful resources that are available to you and when to use them.

What This Guide Does and Doesn't Cover

No single compilation could possibly claim to cover every important American author and the one that most interests you might not be covered in this very selective companion. In fact, this companion only covers a selection of authors whose works are featured in the most recent editions of several widely used literary anthologies, notably *Concise Anthology of American Literature*, 4th ed., ed. George McMichael (Upper Saddle River: Prentice Hall, 1998); *The Harper American Literature*, 2nd ed., ed. Donald McQuade (New York: HarperCollins College, 1996); *The Heath Anthology of American Literature*, 3rd ed., ed. Paul Lauter (Boston: Houghton Mifflin, 1998); and *The Norton Anthology of American Literature*, 5th ed., ed. Nina Baym (New York: W. W. Norton, 1998). The guide's chronological arrangement parallels these anthologies.

One further selection principle should be noted: this guide only covers frequently anthologized American authors who are the subjects of "good" web sites.

The many important and frequently studied American authors not covered in this guide range from Andy Adams and Maya Angelou to Rosanna Warren and Louis Zukofsky. Students who want to identify web sites and references for American authors not found here should consult some of the resources listed in the sections of "Frequently Cited Web Sites" and "Frequently Cited References." Particularly noteworthy are the well-designed and capably maintained metasites *American Literature on the Web*, *American Authors*, and *PAL: Perspectives in American Literature*, as well as the many volumes of the standard *Dictionary of Literary Biography* and Gale's family of encyclopedias of criticism. Both these Internet and printed resources cover more sources for more authors than this or any guide.

For authors' names and dates, this guide references the standard *The Oxford Companion to American Literature*, 6th ed., ed. James D. Hart, with revisions by Phillip W. Leininger (New York: O UP, 1995), along with additions from the *Oxford Companion to African American Literature*, eds. William L. Andrews, Frances Smith Foster, and Trudier Harris (New York: O UP, 1997) and *Oxford Companion to Women's Writing in the United States*, eds. Cathy N. Davidson and Linda Wagner-Martin (New York: O UP, 1995), and other standard sources.

We opened and visited all web sites identified in this guide in March 2000. We have made every effort to identify good web sites for every author covered—and we think that we have succeeded in most instances. From what we regard as the best web sites, you should expect to find biographical sketches of authors, bibliographies of works by and about authors, links to fulltexts of works by and about authors (the latter mostly in the form of online journals), and links to other sites related to authors (if classified, these are often referred to as *webliographies*). On the other hand, this guide should not be regarded as a complete inventory of either Internet or printed resources for any author. When it comes to selectivity, judgment is everything. We regard some web sites and metasites as less useful than others; in fact, in some cases, we consider them useless. In particular, we have excluded web sites related to *Valencia West*, http://valencia.cc.fl.us/lrcwest and *In Marion*, http://hugo.lib.ryerson.ca/MARION/. Our rationale is that these sites provide too little information to help most students. The former makes referrals to reference books without giving complete citations; the latter simply reproduces information from a local online catalog.

To try to find "good" web sites for authors, besides searching the Internet, you should search for citations to resources that describe an author's Internet and printed references in comprehensive literary databases like the *MLA International Bibliography* (*MLA*) and the *Annual Bibliography of English Language and Literature* (*ABELL*); see below for more information on searching these databases. A search phrase linking an author's last name "and Internet" generally identifies likely resources, that is, articles in journals and chapters in books that identify an author's Internet resources. Finally, two printed references are also noteworthy. James L. Harner's *Literary Research Guide: An Annotated Listing of Reference Sources in English Literary Studies*, 3rd ed. (New York: Modern Language Association of America, 1998) describes in great detail the many printed and electronic resources for research on American literature as well as for literature in general. Additions to Harner's standard guide cumulate in a web site, http://www-english.tamu.edu/pubs/lrg/. Resources (mainly printed) available for a wider selection of authors in English are described in detail in James K. Bracken's *Reference Works in British and American Literature*, 2nd ed. (Englewood: Libraries Unlimited, 1998).

A Strategy for Literary Research in the 21st Century

1. Start with the Internet: Looking for Good Web Sites

The best literary researchers efficiently use all of the resources available to them. They consult as many sources of information as they can identify and relentlessly and voraciously seek more and even better ones. In that the Internet promises immediate and abundant rewards (provided you are lucky enough to find "good" web sites, i.e., ones that contain the information that you want), starting with Net searches ("surfing" with search engines, like Yahoo! or Metacrawler) on the names of individual authors is, in fact, no less acceptable a search strategy than looking up those same authors either in a library's card catalog or a periodical index (regardless of whether either is printed or electronic). First steps in research using the Internet—or libraries of printed books and journals—are always fishing expeditions. All that you have to lose is time—life's most precious commodity, to be sure, but in the case of the Internet, time measured in nanoseconds. Your time investment in literary research by means of the Internet will not (and should not) be great. The Net is there for you to search: the best literary researchers must surf to ensure that they have identified all relevant resources.

Finding and Recognizing Good Web Sites and References

The standards for measuring the integrity of any Internet resource are exactly the same (no more or no less) as those used to evaluate any printed reference. Just like the best printed author bibliographies or other literary references, the best literary web sites are ones that are authoritative, that is, they are works that provide reliable and trustworthy information. This companion gives the most attention to resources that can be counted on to provide authoritative information related to individual American authors, whether it is textual, biographical, critical, or bibliographical. Not surprisingly, very few web sites for American authors can be described as exceptional or extraordinary. The promise—and challenge—of literary research on the Internet is that this reality is as changeable as, to paraphrase Mark Twain, the weather in San Francisco: search again in five minutes and you may well discover different web sites.

Domain Searching

The most reliable literary web sites, like the best printed works, derive from authorities, that is, from literary scholars and others (editors, biographers, critics, bibliographers, and the like) as well as from institutions (academic centers and departments, university presses, and professional organizations) for whom interest in a particular author is more than a passing concern, hobby, or assigned term paper topic. Many (but certainly not all) web sites maintained by authorities can be distinguished by the domains *.edu* and *.org* in web addresses (or URLs). You can use this information to focus your Net searches on the most likely authoritative sites by including the domain in a search phrase. For example, the Yahoo! searches (note the quotes around the author's name) for

"Nathanel Hawthorne" domain:edu

or

"Nathanel Hawthorne" domain:org

will limit search results exclusively to web sites originating in colleges and universities or other professional organizations. This is not to disrespect any web site that provides you with exactly the information (reliable and trustworthy) that you want. Rather, it is to help you distinguish between web sites and to help you use your time in the most efficient fashion.

Another way to focus your Net searches is by using authors' dates of birth. For example, the simple search

"Gertrude Stein 1874"

that is, the author's name and birth year enclosed in quotes, will uncover many of the best literary sites in short order.

Keeping Up with Changes

Far and away the most common problem is the changing of a URL. Good web site administrators will transport you to the new site or will provide a link for a certain amount of time. After that time, however, you will almost certainly be on your own. Therefore, the best strategy is to stay connected, "bookmark" good web sites, and update your bookmark as soon as a URL changes.

2. Staying Online: Accessing Proprietary Literary Databases

You have only begun literary research by trying to discover good web sites. Stay online. Presently some of the best literary research resources that cover both works by authors as well as works about them are more often most easily accessible by means of the Internet neither as web sites nor as printed references. Among the major Internet-accessible literary research indexes that identify literary criticism, for example, are the *MLA International Bibliography* (*MLA*) and the *Annual Bibliography of English Language and Literature* (*ABELL*). Comprehensive resources like these identify and cumulate references to the entire world's literature about literature—ranging from scholarly books in the English language and articles and notes published in journals of all varieties to obscure unpublished conference proceedings and academic papers written in foreign languages. Both the *MLA* and *ABELL* identify more research resources than the literary student can hope to read in a lifetime. Likewise accessible by means of the Internet are many general and interdisciplinary indexes, such as *Periodical Abstracts*, *Humanities Index*, and *Arts and Humanities Citation Index*, that routinely and systematically analyze, identify, and cumulate references to articles featured in a wider range of scholarly and popular journals. For many students, articles identified in these indexes will be adequate for literary research.

Still another kind of Internet-accessible literary resource includes the many different fulltext databases, such as the *American Poetry Database*, published by Chadwyck-Healey, and the *Literature Resource Center*, published by Gale. To the confusion of many literary researchers (both novices and veterans), *proprietary, subscription,* or *restricted-access* databases like these might be said to be both on—and off—the Internet. Many libraries and other institutions now subscribe or otherwise contract access to these and many other databases. In short, access to them is not free: your tuition and taxes help to pay for access to them. Moreover, all access to them is typically restricted or limited to particular groups of individuals (enrolled students, community members, and the like). You will not be able to access them unless they admit you. Finally, even though you will access most proprietary databases by means of the Internet (or, at least, from the same computer that you might use for surfing) and many of the databases will look like web sites, you will often be obliged to search these databases in ways more akin to looking up references to books and articles in printed card catalogs and periodical indexes than to Net searching with Yahoo!. Each database is equipped with its own search engine that you will have to learn how to use.

Do not confuse requirements like logging in or searching in prescribed ways with unreasonable impediments to your research. The best literary researchers recognize that conformity and submission to the system (whether that system is a database's or a library's) can pay great dividends. Literary researchers learn to use database and library systems for all that those systems can do for their research. Count yourself lucky to have access to the *MLA* and *ABELL* with functionalities that include "links" to your institution's electronic card catalog, "hot" or linked subject headings, and e-mailable references. You are indeed blessed if you can access the fulltexts of works by and/or about American authors. Earlier researchers were limited to printed resources.

If you are unsure about your access to proprietary databases, ask your instructor or librarian.

3.   Don't Forget about Printed References: You Only Need One Book or Article (If It Is the Right One)

You must expect that many American authors have been the subjects of research long before the advent of the Internet and proprietary databases. Indeed, many major American authors possess their own unique literature, that is, they are the focuses of references that include book- and article-length biographies and critical studies as well as entire journals, dictionaries and handbooks, indexes and concordances, and bibliographies. This companion identifies and, when necessary, briefly describes the best of these printed references for American authors. Prepare yourself to use printed references to identify an author's historical literature (material that predates computers) and, vice versa, to use Internet resources to update printed references. Recognize that web sites and printed references complement each other.

Use printed resources, just like web sites and proprietary databases, for what they can do for you. You should recognize that some widely available printed references, such as the *Dictionary of Literary Biography* (which now includes more than 200 volumes) or Gale's family of encyclopedias of criticism (including *Contemporary Literary Criticism, Twentieth-Century Literary Criticism, Nineteenth-Century Literature Criticism, Literature Criticism from 1400 to 1800, Short Story Criticism, Poetry Criticism, Drama Criticism,* and others, now numbering more than 400 volumes), are most valuable, first, for the information they can provide on a specific author and, second and perhaps more importantly, for identifying in their bibliographies other information resources about an author. Gale's proprietary database, *Literature Resource Center*, now cumulates many of the references offered in these printed series. The best literary references will always lead you to other good resources, both printed and electronic.

4.   Research Isn't Complete Until You Correctly Cite Your Resources

This companion lists citations for all printed references and "most" web sites in a somewhat streamlined version of the style promoted by the Modern Language Association of America as presented in *MLA Style Manual and Guide to Scholarly Publishing*, 2nd ed., ed. Joseph Gibaldi (New York: Modern Language Association of America, 1998); see also "MLA Style" web site at http://www.mla.org/. Entries generally give the site's title, editor, date of creation or last update, sponsor, date visited by us, and URL. Oftentimes, however, especially in the cases of web sites, citing in the MLA style is not merely difficult but seemingly impossible. Many web sites lack identifiable creators, sponsors, and dates of updating. In other instances, some web sites are actually pages within larger sites and, therefore, should be cited in a form more appropriate to a part of a work (like an article in a journal or a chapter in a book) than a separate and complete work (like a book). Although the MLA's citation guidelines attempt to take into account the many possible variations of web sites and references, it is important to remember that even the best literary researchers are sometimes at a loss for the best way to cite a particular resource. Always keep foremost in your mind that the purpose of citation style is to ensure the accurate, complete, and readily intelligible communication of the resources used in research. Your responsibility is to indicate in your reference what can be known about a web site. Do not hesitate to indicate that a web site's editor, updating, or sponsor are unknown; this in fact indicates the present state of the web—and it also perhaps says something about a web site's integrity. When it comes to citing your sources—both Internet and printed—one aspect of your work might be to show that the authors or editors of particular resources have not done their own work particularly well.

We welcome both desiderata as well as corrections or suggestions regarding this work.

Good luck.

Frequently Cited
Web Sites

Academy of American Poets. Ed. unknown. 8 Mar. 2000. The Academy. 9 Mar. 2000, http://www.poets.org/index.html.

Multimedia site includes fulltexts of selected poems, usually with audio of a few; a bibliography of works by the author; a good biographical sketch; and excellent links to other sites. As the site grows, more canonical poets will be added. The expanded list will include Dunbar, Longfellow, Amy Lowell, Masters, Robinson, and others whose absence is now conspicuous. However, the site seems to be reducing the number of poems available for any given author and making some poems available only in downloadable format, even as the site increases the number of poets covered. These practices slightly diminish the value of this otherwise excellent site.

Access Indiana: Teaching & Learning Center. Ed. and update unknown. The Indiana Department of Education and the Indiana State Teachers' Association and the University of Indianapolis. 3 Mar. 2000, http://tlc.ai.org.

An attractively presented and readable site with excellent offsite links. A far-reaching project that goes beyond literature; no index for authors has been found, which means that the site has to be searched by individual author. Mostly useful for links to fulltext and biographical sites.

American Authors. Ed. Donna Campbell. 19 Feb. 2000. Gonzaga U. 3 Mar. 2000, http://www.gonzaga.edu/faculty/campbell/enl311/aufram.html.

A major site. Author pages link to fulltexts of works, biographies, and other sites. Includes offsite links to many sites and extensive bibliographies. In spite of the large number of authors covered, the quality of every page is extremely high.

American Literature on the Web. Ed. Akihito Ishikawa. 4 Apr. 1999. English Dept., Nagasaki C of Foreign Languages. 3 Mar 2000, http://www.nagasaki-gaigo.ac.jp/ishikawa/amlit.

Searchable, classified list sites (fulltexts of works by and about authors and general resources) for the full range of American authors.

American Studies @ the University of Virginia: Hypertexts. Eds. vary. 11 Aug. 1999. U of Virginia. 23 Mar. 2000, http://xroads.virginia.edu/~HYPER/hypertex.html.

Hypertext project from the University of Virginia, using representative works of several authors.

Bohemian Ink. Ed. unknown. 6 Feb. 1999. Sponsor unknown. 24 Mar. 2000, http://www.levity.com/corduroy/.

A site difficult to use in a conventional way because there is no index. The site's lack of conventionality may displease the academic user, but its pages yield much useful information. Most links seem well chosen, but pages for different authors are not alike.

Celebration of Women Writers. Ed. Mary Mark Ockerbloom. 18 Mar. 2000. U of Pennsylvania. 24 Mar. 2000, http://digital.library.upenn.edu/women/.

Comprehensive list of fulltext works by women writers from around the world.

Contemporary Woman Writers. Ed. Anniina Jokinen. 2 Sep. 1999. Luminarium.org. 24 Mar. 2000, http://www.luminarium.org/.

Summaries of a wide range of authors' works and guides for topics; fulltexts of reviews for some of the major works; and links to fulltexts of selected interviews, bibliographies, biographies, and other pages and resources.

Documenting the American South. Ed. unknown. 20 Mar. 2000. Academic Affairs Library, U of North Carolina at Chapel Hill. 24 Mar. 2000, http://metalab.unc.edu/docsouth/index.html.

Site presents the work of the electronic text project that links to fulltexts of works by Southern authors up to 1920 ("Library of Southern Literature" series) and articles about the authors from the *Encyclopedia of Southern Culture*, eds. Charles Reagan Wilson and William Ferris (Chapel Hill: U of North Carolina P, 1989) and other sources. Also available at the site are "First-Person Narratives of the American South" and "North American Slave Narratives."

Domestic Goddesses aka "Scribbling Women." Ed. unknown. 4 Jan. 2000. Sponsor unknown. 23 Mar. 2000, http://www.womenwriters.net/domesticgoddess/.

Disappointing site whose presentation format makes reading difficult. No bibliography in the traditional sense, and even the criticism provided is in the form of links. Onsite photographs abound.

Early American Fiction. Ed. unknown. Copyright 1999. U of Virginia Library. 24 Mar. 2000, http://etext.virginia.edu/eaf/.

A major source for literary 19th-century American literary biography. Pages for authors offer fulltexts of selected 19th-century biographies and works about authors, such as Oscar Fay Adams's *A Dictionary of American Authors* (1901) and Samuel Austin Allibone's *A Critical Dictionary of English Literature* (1900). Access to fulltext works by authors is restricted to subscribing institutions.

EducETH: The English Page. Ed. Hans Fischer. 21 Mar. 2000. EducETH. 24 Mar. 2000, http://educeth.ethz.ch/english/.

Interactive-learning site that tends to overemphasis plot synopses and readers' questions; intended to support classroom instruction. Follow "Reading List" link.

Electronic Poetry Center. Ed. Loss P. Glazier. 9 Mar. 2000. S U of New York at Buffalo. 24 Mar. 2000, http://epc.buffalo.edu/.

Follow "Authors" links to link to online works.

The Glass Ceiling. Ed. unknown. 18 Mar. 2000. TCG Communications. 24 Mar.
2000, http://www.theglassceiling.com/.
  Biographies complete with bibliographies for a number of important women,
writers, and others, many from politics and popular culture.

*Heath Anthology: Syllabus Builder, Version 2.0: Instructor's Guide for the Heath
Anthology of American Literature.* Eds. vary. 15 Nov. 1997. Georgetown U. 24
Mar. 2000, http://www.georgetown.edu/bassr/heath/syllabuild/iguide/.
  Classroom discussion-oriented sites identify major themes, historical perspectives, personal issues, stylistic concerns, original audience, comparisons to contemporaries, study questions, and approaches to expository writing, with selective
annotated bibliographies of works by and about a wide range of authors. Each page
represents the work of a different contributing editor. Consistency has not been maintained: some pages lack bibliographies, some are simply not properly filled out, and at
least one linked page was actually blank (see http://www.georgetown.edu/bassr/
heath/syllabuild/iguide/lee.html for Li-Young Lee).

Historical Lesbian Poetry. Ed. Alexandra North. 22 Nov. 1999. Sappho.com. 24
Mar. 2000, http://www.sappho.com/poetry/historical/index.html.
  Very compact pages offering biographical sketches, fulltexts of poetry repre-
senting the lesbian theme, and bibliographies for further reading.

Howells's Contemporaries: The William Dean Howells Society. Ed. Donna Campbell.
20 Aug. 1999. Gonzaga U. 25 Mar. 2000, http://www.gonzaga.edu/faculty/campbell/
howells/index.html.
  A major site for 19th-century American literature.

Internet Public Library: Native American Authors. Ed. unknown. 13 Jan. 2000. Sponsor unknown. 24 Mar. 2000, http://www.ipl.org/ref/native/.
  Biography and list of awards with a bibliography of online and print resources
for Native American authors.

Knitting Circle: Radclyffe Hall Well of Literature. Eds. vary. 22 Mar. 2000. Lesbian
and Gay Staff Association of South Bank U. 24 Mar. 2000, http://www.sbu.
ac.uk/stafflag/literature.html.
  Contains serious biographical sketches, works by the authors, and works about
the authors. Does a good job incorporating web material with print material.

Literary Kicks. Ed. Levi Asher. Update unknown. Charm.net. 24 Mar. 2000,
http://www.charm.net/~brooklyn/.
  Very complete site with long biographical sketches and very long bibliographies. Includes many excellent links.

Literature & Culture of the American 1950s. Ed. Al Filreis. 22 June 1996. U of Pennsylvania. 24 Mar. 2000, http://www.english.upenn.edu/~afilreis/50s/home.
html.
  Original and encyclopedic site for the 1950s. Course pages of readings include
summaries of works and fulltexts of classic critical works.

Literature Database: Women in Literature. Ed. Bette A. Reagan. 28 May 1998. U of
Kutztown. 24 Mar. 2000, http://www.kutztown.edu/~reagan/lit.html.
  Student-researched and -linked database of selective bibliographies, brief biog-
raphies, and other features for selected American women writers.

Literature Online. Eds. X. J. Kennedy and Dana Gioia. 11 Nov. 1999. Addison Wesley Literature Online. 24 Mar. 2000, http://occ.awlonline.com/bookbind/pubbooks/kennedylfpd_awl.

Encyclopedia-like, authoritative treatment of authors' lives with the works interspersed in the text and also in separate bibliography. Based on Kennedy and Gioia's *Literature: An Introduction to Fiction, Poetry, and Drama,* 7th ed. (New York: Longman, 1999). Students should follow the "Student Resources" link.

Mississippi Writers Page. Ed. John Padgett. 18 Feb. 1999. English Dept., U of Mississippi. 24 Mar. 2000, http://www.olemiss.edu/depts/english/ms-writers/.

Offers excellent authoritative pages containing biographies; bibliographies of works by and about writers, with links to fulltexts; filmographies; and links to other sites.

Nebraska Center for Writers. Ed. Brent Spencer. 1 Nov. 1999. Creighton U. 27 Mar. 2000, http://mockingbird.creighton.edu/NCW/.

Onsite links include biographical sketch, bibliography, selection, quotations, interview, and commentary.

New York State Writers' Institute. Ed. Donald W. Faulkner. 21 Mar. 2000. S U of New York at Albany. 24 Mar. 2000, http://www.albany.edu/writers.

Solid brief biographies, bibliographies of works by and about poets and prose authors, and links to other sites.

The Nobel Prize Internet Archive. Ed. and update unknown. Nobelprizes.com. 23 Mar. 2000, http://nobelprizes.com/nobel/literature/.

Literature page from larger Nobel site. Contains links for all Nobel laureates in literature for every author from 1901 to present.

North American Native Authors Catalog. Ed. "Bowman." Update and sponsor unknown. 24 Mar. 2000, http://www.nativeauthors.com/index.shtml.

A commercial site linking to descriptions of reprints of classic works by Native American authors.

On-Line Books Page. Ed. John Mark Ockerbloom. 24 Mar. 2000. U of Pennsylvania. 24 Mar. 2000, http://digital.library.upenn.edu/books/.

A compilation of 11,000 links to fulltext books available online at various sites.

Online Literature Library. Ed. unknown. 19 Jan. 2000. Knowledge Matters Ltd. 24 Mar. 2000, http://www.literature.org/.

Links to fulltexts of works by American, British, and classical and modern authors.

Outline of American Literature. Ed. Kathryn VanSpanckeren. 28 Apr. 1998. United States Information Agency. 24 Mar. 2000, http://usinfo.org/oal/default.htm.

Written as eight chapters in chronological order. Brief but comprehensive, the site includes one-paragraph entries for 115 American authors. Includes a glossary but no bibliography and no offsite links.

PAL: Perspectives in American Literature. Ed. Paul P. Reuben. 14 Mar. 2000. English Dept., California S U, Stanislaus. 24 Mar. 2000, http://www.csustan.edu/english/reuben/pal/table.html.

Extensive project mainly valuable for bibliographies of works by and about the full range of over 250 American writers with study questions; also includes information on citing pages in MLA style.

Pegasos. Ed. Kuusankosken kaupunginkirjasto. 1 Feb. 2000. Sponsor unknown. 12 Mar. 2000, http://kirjasto.sci.fi/.

Site contains very good, condensed information in the form of a biographical sketch, a list for further reading, and a list of selected works by authors. (Follow "Authors' Calendar" link.) Pages occasionally marred by slight misspellings. No off-site links.

Project Bartleby Archive. Ed. unknown. 25 Mar. 2000. Bartleby.com. 25 Mar. 2000, http://www.bartleby.com/.

Archive of searchable fulltexts of literary works. Indexes for verse, fiction, and nonfiction. Gives biographical sketches and full bibliographical descriptions.

Project Gutenberg. Ed. Pietro Di Micheli. 15 Feb. 2000. Promo.net. 23 Mar. 2000, http://promo.net/pg/pgframed_index.html.

Although Project Gutenberg sites can still be found all over the web, this is the official site of the project.

The Puritans: American Literature Colonial Period (1608-1700). Ed. Inez Ramsey. 21 Nov. 1997. James Madison U. 5 Mar. 2000, http://falcon.jmu.edu/~ramseyil/.

Intended primarily for K-12 educators. Infrequent updating and unmarked restricted links are troublesome. In spite of the intended audience, site is suitable for undergraduate students. Pages for authors include excerpts of texts and biographical and critical studies.

SAC LitWeb. Ed. Roger Blackwell Bailey. 2 Feb. 1998. English Dept., San Antonio C. 28 Feb. 2000, http://www.accd.edu/sac/english/bailey/amerlit1.htm.

Somewhat disappointing site. All pages include major works by authors and works about authors. Many pages do not contain links. Good only for those students seeking brief bibliography.

Twentieth-Century Poetry in English. Ed. Eiichi Hishikawa. 1 Mar. 1999. Faculty of Letters, Kobe U. 25 Mar. 2000, http://www.lit.kobe-u.ac.jp/~hishika/20c_poet.htm.

Fulltexts of selected works, with brief biographies, selected bibliographies of works about the authors, and links to other sites.

UCL Webliography of Twentieth Century Writers of Color. Ed. "jm." "Copyright, 1997." Broward C C. 25 Mar. 2000, http://exodus.broward.cc.fl.us/ucl/writers.htm.

Webliography (or annotated list of web sites) for African American authors.

UTEL Representative Poetry On-line. Ed. Ian Lancashire. 7 Feb. 2000. U of Toronto P. 25 Mar. 2000, http://www.library.utoronto.ca/utel/rp/intro.html.

A model project giving fulltexts of selected poems by American and British writers, with notes on publication history and biography and bibliographies of works by and about each writer. No links provided. A separate "UTEL Prose Database" is also at this site.

Voices and Visions. Ed. William Wargo. 14 Mar. 2000. Annenberg CPB Project. 25 Mar. 2000, http://www.learner.org/collections/multimedia/literature/vvseries/vvspot/.

Attractively presented and user friendly. Includes brief biographical sketch and annotated list of web sites for 13 major American poets, all represented in this guide.

Voices from the Gaps: Women Writers of Color. Eds. vary. 7 Mar. 2000. U of Minnesota. 25 Mar. 2000, http://voices.cla.umn.edu/.

Undergraduate student-authored site for selected major African-American, Asian-American, Chicana/Latina, Indian/Middle Eastern/Arabic, and Indigenous/Native American women writers. Provides fulltexts of selected works by authors as well as biographies, notes, and unannotated bibliographies, with links to other resources.

Writing and Resistance. Ed. Jody F. Kerr. 17 Feb. 1998. Sponsor unknown. 23 Mar. 2000, http://www.public.asu.edu/~metro/aflit/.

Collection of unevenly developed and maintained pages, most giving brief biographies, separate bibliographies of works by and about African-American authors, and links to other sites, many empty.

Frequently Cited References

Ashley, Perry J., ed. *American Newspaper Journalists, 1690-1872* (*Dictionary of Literary Biography* 43). Detroit: Gale, 1985.

———. *American Newspaper Journalists, 1873-1900* (*Dictionary of Literary Biography* 23). Detroit: Gale, 1983.

———. *American Newspaper Journalists, 1926-1950* (*Dictionary of Literary Biography* 29). Detroit: Gale, 1984.

Bain, Robert, and Joseph M. Flora, eds. *Fifty Southern Writers before 1900: A Bio-Bibliographical Sourcebook*. Westport: Greenwood, 1987.

———. *Contemporary Poets, Dramatists, Essayists, and Novelists of the South: A Bio-Bibliographical Sourcebook*. Westport: Greenwood, 1994.

Barstow, Jane Missner. *One Hundred Years of American Women Writing, 1848-1948: An Annotated Bio-Bibliography*. Lanham: Scarecrow, 1997.

Baughman, Ronald, ed. *Contemporary Authors: Bibliographical Series: American Poets: Volume 2*. Detroit: Gale, 1986.

Bruccoli, Matthew J., and Judith S. Baughman, eds. *Modern Classic Writers*. New York: Facts on File, 1994.

———. *Modern Women Writers*. New York: Facts on File, 1994.

———. *Bibliography of American Fiction, 1919-1988*. New York: Facts on File, 1991.

———. *Modern African American Writers*. New York: Facts on File, 1994.

Bryer, Jackson R., ed. *Sixteen Modern American Authors: Volume 2: A Survey of Research and Criticism since 1972*. Durham: Duke UP, 1990.

———. *Sixteen Modern American Authors: A Survey of Research and Criticism*. 3rd ed. Durham: Duke UP, 1974.

Bryfonski, Dedria, [and others], eds. *Twentieth-Century Literary Criticism*. Detroit: Gale, 1978- .

Carpenter, Charles A., ed. *Modern Drama Scholarship and Criticism, 1981-1990: An International Bibliography*. Toronto: U of Toronto P, 1997.

7

Cech, John, ed. *American Writers for Children, 1900-1960* (*Dictionary of Literary Biography* 22). Detroit: Gale, 1983.

Charters, Ann, ed. *The Beats: Literary Bohemians in Postwar America* (*Dictionary of Literary Biography* 16). Detroit: Gale, 1983.

Clark, Randall, Robert E. Morsberger, and Stephen O. Lesser, eds. *American Screenwriters, Second Series* (*Dictionary of Literary Biography* 44). Detroit: Gale, 1986

Conte, Joseph, ed. *American Poets since World War II* (*Dictionary of Literary Biography* 193). Detroit: Gale, 1998.

———. *American Poets since World War II, Fifth Series* (*Dictionary of Literary Biography* 169). Detroit: Gale, 1996.

———. *American Poets since World War II, Fourth Series* (*Dictionary of Literary Biography* 165). Detroit: Gale, 1996.

Cowart, David, and Thomas L. Wymer, eds. *Twentieth-Century American Science-Fiction Writers* (*Dictionary of Literary Biography* 8). Detroit: Gale, 1981.

Cracroft, Richard H., ed. *Twentieth-Century American Western Writers, First Series* (*Dictionary of Literary Biography* 206). Detroit: Gale, 1999.

———. *Twentieth-Century American Western Writers, Second Series* (*Dictionary of Literary Biography* 212). Detroit: Gale, 1999.

Davis, Thadious M., and Trudier Harris, eds. *Afro-American Writers after 1955: Dramatists and Prose Writers* (*Dictionary of Literary Biography* 38). Detroit: Gale, 1985.

———. *Afro-American Fiction Writers after 1955* (*Dictionary of Literary Biography* 33). Detroit: Gale, 1984.

Demastes, William W., ed. *American Playwrights, 1880-1945: A Research and Production Sourcebook*. Westport: Greenwood, 1995.

Duke, Maurice, Jackson R. Bryer, and M. Thomas Inge, eds. *American Women Writers: Bibliographical Essays*. Westport: Greenwood, 1983.

Elliott, Emory, ed. *American Colonial Writers, 1606-1734* (*Dictionary of Literary Biography* 24). Detroit: Gale, 1984.

———. *American Colonial Writers, 1735-1781* (*Dictionary of Literary Biography* 31). Detroit: Gale, 1984.

———. *American Writers of the Early Republic* (*Dictionary of Literary Biography* 37). Detroit: Gale, 1985.

Emerson, Everett. *Major Writers of Early American Literature*. Madison: U of Wisconsin P, 1972.

Erisman, Fred, and Richard W. Etulain, eds. *Fifty Western Writers: A Bio-Bibliographical Sourcebook*. Westport: Greenwood, 1982.

Estes, Glenn E., ed. *American Writers for Children before 1900* (*Dictionary of Literary Biography* 42). Detroit: Gale, 1985.

———. *American Writers for Children since 1960: Fiction* (*Dictionary of Literary Biography* 52). Detroit: Gale, 1986.

Etulain, Richard W., and N. Jill Howard, eds. *Bibliographical Guide to the Study of Western American Literature.* 2nd ed. Albuquerque: U of New Mexico P, 1995.

Evans, Robert C., Anne C. Little, and Barbara Wiedemann. *Short Fiction: A Critical Companion.* West Cornwall: Locust Hill, 1997.

Flora, Joseph M., and Robert Bain, eds. *Contemporary Fiction Writers of the South: A Bio-Bibliographical Sourcebook.* Westport: Greenwood, 1993.

———. *Fifty Southern Writers after 1900: A Bio-Bibliographical Sourcebook.* Westport: Greenwood, 1987.

Gale, Robert L., ed. *Nineteenth-Century American Western Writers* (*Dictionary of Literary Biography* 186). Detroit: Gale, 1998.

Giles, James R., and Wanda Giles, eds. *American Novelists since World War II, Third Series* (*Dictionary of Literary Biography* 143). Detroit: Gale, 1994.

———. *American Novelists since World War II, Fourth Series* (*Dictionary of Literary Biography* 152). Detroit: Gale, 1995.

Glitsch, Catherine. *American Novel Explication, 1991-1995.* North Haven: Archon, 1998.

Greiner, Donald J., ed. *American Poets since World War II, First Series* (*Dictionary of Literary Biography* 5). Detroit: Gale, 1980.

Gwynn, R. S., ed. *American Poets since World War II, Third Series* (*Dictionary of Literary Biography* 120). Detroit: Gale, 1992.

———. *American Poets since World War II, Second Series* (*Dictionary of Literary Biography* 105). Detroit: Gale, 1991.

Harbert, Earl N., and Robert A. Rees, eds. *Fifteen American Authors before 1900: Bibliographical Essays on Research and Criticism.* Rev. ed. Madison: U of Wisconsin P, 1984.

Harris, Laurie Lanzen, and Sheila Fitzgerald, [and others], eds. *Short Story Criticism.* Detroit: Gale, 1988- .

———, [and others], eds. *Nineteenth-Century Literature Criticism.* Detroit: Gale, 1981- .

Harris, Trudier, ed. *Afro-American Writers before the Harlem Renaissance* (*Dictionary of Literary Biography* 50). Detroit: Gale, 1986.

———. *Afro-American Writers from the Harlem Renaissance to 1940* (*Dictionary of Literary Biography* 51). Detroit: Gale, 1987.

————. *Afro-American Writers, 1940-1955* (*Dictionary of Literary Biography* 76). Detroit: Gale, 1988.

————, and Thadious M. Davis, eds. *Afro-American Poets since 1955* (*Dictionary of Literary Biography* 41). Detroit: Gale, 1985.

Helterman, Jeffrey, and Richard Layman, eds. *American Novelists since World War II, First Series* (*Dictionary of Literary Biography* 2). Detroit: Gale, 1978.

Inge, Thomas M., Maurice Duke, and Jackson R. Bryer, eds. *Black American Writers: Bibliographical Essays. Volume 1: The Beginnings through the Harlem Renaissance and Langston Hughes; Volume 2: Richard Wright, Ralph Ellison, James Baldwin, and Amiri Baraka.* New York: St. Martin's, 1978.

Jason, Philip K. *Nineteenth Century American Poetry: An Annotated Bibliography.* Pasadena: Salem, 1989.

————. *Vietnam War in Literature: An Annotated Bibliography of Criticism.* Pasadena: Salem, 1992.

Jay, Gregory S., ed. *Modern American Critics since 1955* (*Dictionary of Literary Biography* 67). Detroit: Gale, 1988.

Kaul, Arthur J., ed. *American Literary Journalists, 1945-1995, First Series* (*Dictionary of Literary Biography* 185). Detroit: Gale, 1998.

Kellman, Steven G. *Modern American Novel: An Annotated Bibliography.* Pasadena: Salem, 1991.

Kibler, James E., Jr., ed. *American Novelists since World War II, Second Series* (*Dictionary of Literary Biography* 6). Detroit: Gale, 1980.

Kimbel, Bobby Ellen, ed. *American Short-Story Writers, 1910-1945, Second Series* (*Dictionary of Literary Biography* 102). Detroit: Gale, 1991.

————. *American Short-Story Writers, 1910-1945, First Series* (*Dictionary of Literary Biography* 86). Detroit: Gale, 1989.

————, and William E. Grant, eds. *American Short-Story Writers before 1880* (*Dictionary of Literary Biography* 74). Detroit: Gale, 1988.

————. *American Short-Story Writers, 1880-1910* (*Dictionary of Literary Biography* 78). Detroit: Gale, 1988.

King, Kimball. *Ten Modern American Playwrights: An Annotated Bibliography.* New York: Garland, 1982.

Knight, Denise D. *Nineteenth-Century American Women Writers: A Bio-Bibliographical Critical Sourcebook.* Westport: Greenwood, 1997.

Kolin, Philip C., ed. *American Playwrights since 1945: A Guide to Scholarship, Criticism, and Performance.* New York: Greenwood, 1989.

Kopley, Richard, ed. *Prospects for the Study of American Literature: A Guide for Scholars and Students.* New York: New York UP, 1997.

Lawlor, William. *Beat Generation: A Bibliographical Teaching Guide*. Lanham: Scarecrow, 1998.

Leo, John R. *Guide to American Poetry Explication: Volume 2: Modern and Contemporary*. Boston: G. K. Hall, 1989.

Lindfors, Bernth, and Reinhard Sander, eds. *Twentieth-Century Caribbean and Black African Writers, Third Series* (*Dictionary of Literary Biography* 157). Detroit: Gale, 1995.

———. *Twentieth-Century Caribbean and Black African Writers* (*Dictionary of Literary Biography* 117). Detroit: Gale, 1992.

Ljungquist, Kent P., ed. *Bibliography of American Fiction through 1865*. New York: Facts on File, 1994.

Lomelí, Francisco, and Carl R. Shirley, eds. *Chicano Writers, First Series* (*Dictionary of Literary Biography* 82). Detroit: Gale, 1989.

———. *Chicano Writers, Second Series* (*Dictionary of Literary Biography* 122). Detroit: Gale, 1992.

MacNicholas, John, ed. *Twentieth-Century American Dramatists* (*Dictionary of Literary Biography* 7). Detroit: Gale, 1981.

Martine, James J., ed. *American Novelists, 1910-1945* (*Dictionary of Literary Biography* 9). Detroit: Gale, 1981.

———. *Contemporary Authors: Bibliographical Series: American Novelists: Volume 1*. Detroit: Gale, 1986.

McCaffery, Larry, ed. *Postmodern Fiction: A Bio-Bibliographical Guide*. Westport: Greenwood, 1986.

Meanor, Patrick, ed. *American Short-Story Writers since World War II* (*Dictionary of Literary Biography* 130). Detroit: Gale, 1993.

Morsberger, Robert E., Stephen O. Lesser, and Randall Clark, eds. *American Screenwriters* (*Dictionary of Literary Biography* 26). Detroit: Gale, 1984.

Mulford, Carla, Angela Vietto, and Amy E. Winans, eds. *American Women Prose Writers to 1820* (*Dictionary of Literary Biography* 200). Detroit: Gale, 1999.

Myerson, Joel, ed. *Antebellum Writers in New York and the South* (*Dictionary of Literary Biography* 3). Detroit: Gale, 1979.

———. *The American Renaissance in New England* (*Dictionary of Literary Biography* 1). Detroit: Gale, 1978.

———. *Transcendentalists: A Review of Research and Criticism*. New York: Modern Language Association of America, 1984.

Nagel, James, Gwen L. Nagel, and Judith S. Baughman, eds. *Bibliography of American Fiction, 1866-1918*. New York: Facts on File, 1993.

Nelson, Emmanuel S., ed. *African American Authors, 1745-1945: A Bio-Bibliographical Critical Sourcebook.* Westport: Greenwood, 2000.

Pearlman, Mickey, ed. *American Women Writing Fiction: Memory, Identity, Family, Space.* Lexington: UP of Kentucky, 1989.

Perry, Margaret. *Harlem Renaissance: An Annotated Bibliography and Commentary.* New York: Garland, 1982.

Peterson, Jane T., and Suzanne Bennett. *Women Playwrights of Diversity: A Bio-Bibliographical Sourcebook.* Westport: Greenwood, 1997.

Pizer, Donald, and Earl N. Harbert, eds. *American Realists and Naturalists (Dictionary of Literary Biography* 12). Detroit: Gale, 1982.

Pollack, Sandra, and Denise D. Knight, eds. *Contemporary Lesbian Writers of the United States: A Bio-Bibliographical Critical Sourcebook.* Westport: Greenwood, 1993.

Poupard, Dennis, [and others], eds. *Literature Criticism from 1400 to 1800.* Detroit: Gale, 1984- .

Quartermain, Peter, ed. *American Poets, 1880-1945, Second Series (Dictionary of Literary Biography* 48). Detroit: Gale, 1986.

——. *American Poets, 1880-1945, Third Series (Dictionary of Literary Biography* 54). Detroit: Gale, 1987.

——. *American Poets, 1880-1945, First Series (Dictionary of Literary Biography* 45). Detroit: Gale, 1986.

Rathbun, John W., and Monica M. Grecu, eds. *American Literary Critics and Scholars, 1800-1850 (Dictionary of Literary Biography* 59). Detroit: Gale, 1987.

——. *American Literary Critics and Scholars, 1850-1880 (Dictionary of Literary Biography* 64). Detroit: Gale, 1988.

——. *American Literary Critics and Scholars, 1880-1900 (Dictionary of Literary Biography* 71). Detroit: Gale, 1988.

Reisman, Rosemary M. Canfield, and Christopher J. Canfield. *Contemporary Southern Women Fiction Writers: An Annotated Bibliography.* Metuchen: Scarecrow, 1994.

——, and Suzanne Booker-Canfield. *Contemporary Southern Men Fiction Writers: An Annotated Bibliography.* Lanham: Scarecrow, 1998.

Riley, Carolyn, [and others], eds. *Contemporary Literary Criticism.* Detroit: Gale, 1973- .

Riley, Sam G., ed. *American Magazine Journalists, 1741-1850 (Dictionary of Literary Biography* 73). Detroit: Gale, 1988.

——. *American Magazine Journalists, 1850-1900 (Dictionary of Literary Biography* 79). Detroit: Gale, 1988.

———. *American Magazine Journalists, 1900-1960, First Series* (*Dictionary of Literary Biography* 91). Detroit: Gale, 1990.

———. *American Magazine Journalists, 1900-1960* (*Dictionary of Literary Biography* 137). Detroit: Gale, 1994.

Roemer, Kenneth M., ed. *Native American Writers of the United States* (*Dictionary of Literary Biography* 175). Detroit: Gale, 1997.

Rood, Karen Lane, ed. *American Writers in Paris, 1920-1939* (*Dictionary of Literary Biography* 4). Detroit: Gale, 1980.

Rosenblum, Joseph, ed. *American Book-Collectors and Bibliographers* (*Dictionary of Literary Biography* 140). Detroit: Gale, 1994.

Ross, Donald, and James J. Schramer, eds. *American Travel Writers, 1850-1915* (*Dictionary of Literary Biography* 189). Detroit: Gale, 1998.

Roudane, Matthew C., ed. *Contemporary Authors: Bibliographical Series American Dramatists: Volume 3*. Detroit: Gale, 1989.

Ruppert, James. *Guide to American Poetry Explication: Volume 1: Colonial and Nineteenth-Century*. Boston: G. K. Hall, 1989.

Saar, Doreen Alvarez, and Mary Anne Schofield, eds. *Eighteenth-Century Anglo-American Women Novelists: A Critical Reference Guide*. New York: G. K. Hall, 1996.

Schramer, James J., and Donald Ross, eds. *American Travel Writers, 1776-1864* (*Dictionary of Literary Biography* 183). Detroit: Gale, 1997.

Shapiro, Ann R. *Jewish American Women Writers: A Bio-Bibliographical and Critical Sourcebook*. Westport: Greenwood, 1994.

Shatzky, Joel, and Michael Taub, eds. *Contemporary Jewish-American Novelists: A Bio-Critical Sourcebook*. Westport: Greenwood, 1997.

Shuman, R. Baird. *American Drama, 1918-1960: An Annotated Bibliography*. Pasadena: Salem, 1992.

Trachtenberg, Stanley, ed. *American Humorists, 1800-1950* (*Dictionary of Literary Biography* 11). Detroit: Gale, 1982.

Trudeau, Lawrence J., [and others], eds. *Drama Criticism*. Detroit: Gale, 1991- .

Walden, Daniel, ed. *Twentieth-Century American-Jewish Fiction Writers* (*Dictionary of Literary Biography* 28). Detroit: Gale, 1984.

Williams, Dana A. *Contemporary African American Female Playwrights: An Annotated Bibliography*. Westport: Greenwood, 1998.

Wilson, Clyde N., ed. *American Historians, 1607-1865* (*Dictionary of Literary Biography* 30). Detroit: Gale, 1984.

———. *American Historians, 1866-1912* (*Dictionary of Literary Biography* 47). Detroit: Gale, 1986.

————. *Twentieth-Century American Historians* (*Dictionary of Literary Biography* 17). Detroit: Gale, 1983.

Woodress, James, ed. *Eight American Authors: A Review of Research and Criticism.* Rev. ed. New York: Norton, 1971.

Young, Robyn V., [and others], eds. *Poetry Criticism.* Detroit: Gale, 1991- .

Web Sites and References for American Authors

John Smith, 1580-1631

Web Sites

"The Puritans: American Literature Colonial Period (1608-1700)." *American Literature*. 13 Mar. 2000, http://falcon.jmu.edu/~ramseyil/amlitcol.htm.

Biographies and Criticism

"(Captain) John Smith." Poupard, *Literature Criticism from 1400 to 1800* 9:347-89.
    Excerpts of comments and criticism on Smith from 1624-1986, with an annotated bibliography.

Emerson, Everett H. *Captain John Smith*. Rev. ed. New York: Twayne, 1993.

Fleming, Thomas. "John Smith." Wilson, *American Historians, 1607-1865* (*Dictionary of Literary Biography* 30) 285-90.

Leary, Lewis. "John Smith." Elliott, *American Colonial Writers, 1606-1734* (*Dictionary of Literary Biography* 24) 289-93.

Bibliographies

Goodman, Jennifer R. "Captain John Smith." Bain and Flora, *Fifty Southern Writers before 1900* 427-34.

Hayes, Kevin J. *Captain John Smith: A Reference Guide*. Boston: G. K. Hall, 1991.
    Describes about 1,000 popular, literary, and historical references to Smith since 1613, with a brief list of Smith's writings.

John Winthrop, 1588-1649

Web Sites

"The Puritans: American Literature Colonial Period (1608-1700)." *American Literature*. 13 Mar. 2000, http://falcon.jmu.edu/~ramseyil/amlitcol.htm.

Biographies and Criticism

Bremer, Francis J. "John Winthrop." Wilson, *American Historians, 1607-1865* (*Dictionary of Literary Biography* 30) 341-46.

Emerson, Everett. "John Winthrop." Elliott, *American Colonial Writers, 1606-1734* (*Dictionary of Literary Biography* 24) 353-63.

"John Winthrop." Poupard, *Literature Criticism from 1400 to 1800* 31:308-99.
   Excerpts of comments and criticism on Winthrop from 1630-1992, with an annotated bibliography.

Schweninger, Lee. *John Winthrop*. Boston: Twayne, 1990.

William Bradford, 1590-1657

Web Sites

"The Puritans: American Literature Colonial Period (1608-1700)." *American Literature*. 13 Mar. 2000, http://falcon.jmu.edu/~ramseyil/amlitcol.htm.

Biographies and Criticism

Calhoon, Robert M. "William Bradford." Wilson, *American Historians, 1607-1865* (*Dictionary of Literary Biography* 30) 38-44.

Shuffelton, Frank. "William Bradford." Elliott, *American Colonial Writers, 1606-1734* (*Dictionary of Literary Biography* 24) 19-28.

Bibliographies

Gallagher, Edward J., and Thomas Werge. *Early Puritan Writers: A Reference Guide: William Bradford, John Cotton, Thomas Hooker, Edward Johnson, Richard Mather, Thomas Shepard*. Boston: G. K. Hall, 1976.
   Briefly describes about 150 works on Bradford since 1669.

Levin, David. "William Bradford." Emerson, *Major Writers of Early American Literature* 11-32.
   Survey of research.

Anne (Dudley) Bradstreet, c. 1612-1672

Web Sites

Ms. Fye's Resource Page: General Information on Anne Bradstreet. 13 Mar. 2000, http://www.glasgow-ky.com/fye/ms_fye/anne_bradstreet.htm.

"The Puritans: American Literature Colonial Period (1608-1700)." *American Literature*. 13 Mar. 2000, http://falcon.jmu.edu/~ramseyil/amlitcol.htm.

"Selected Poetry of Anne Bradstreet." *Representative Poetry On-line*. 13 Mar. 2000, http://www.library.utoronto.ca/utel/rp/authors/abrad.html.

Biographies and Criticism

"Anne Bradstreet." Poupard, *Literature Criticism from 1400 to 1800* 30:112-55.
   Excerpts of criticism on Bradstreet from 1970-1991, with an annotated bibliography.

"Anne (Dudley) Bradstreet." Poupard, *Literature Criticism from 1400 to 1800* 4:81-114.
Excerpts of comments and criticism on Bradstreet from 1650-1985, with an annotated bibliography.

"Anne Bradstreet." Young, *Poetry Criticism* 10:1-66.
Excerpts of comments and criticism on Bradstreet from 1951-1990, with an annotated bibliography.

Martin, Wendy. "Anne Bradstreet." Elliott, *American Colonial Writers, 1606-1734* (*Dictionary of Literary Biography* 24) 29-36.

Rosenmeier, Rosamond. *Anne Bradstreet Revisited.* Boston: Twayne, 1991.

Bibliographies

Dolle, Raymond F. *Anne Bradstreet: A Reference Guide.* Boston: G. K. Hall, 1990.
Describes about 400 works on Bradstreet since 1650.

Ruppert, James. "Bradstreet, Anne." *Guide to American Poetry Explication* 3-7.

Stanford, Ann. "Three Puritan Women: Anne Bradstreet, Mary Rowlandson, and Sarah Kemble Knight." Duke, Bryer, and Inge, *American Women Writers* 3-20.
Survey of research.

———. "Anne Bradstreet." Emerson, *Major Writers of Early American Literature* 33-58.
Survey of research.

Michael Wigglesworth, 1631-1705

Web Sites

About Michael Wigglesworth and His Poetry. 13 Mar. 2000, http://ourworld. compuserve.com/homepages/wcarson/wigglife.htm.

"Michael Wigglesworth." *Heath Anthology.* 13 Mar. 2000, http://www.georgetown. edu/bassr/heath/syllabuild/iguide/wigglesw.html.
Notes on themes in texts, with study questions and brief bibliography of criticism.

"The Michael Wigglesworth Page." *SAC LitWeb.* 13 Mar. 2000, http://www.accd. edu/sac/english/bailey/wigglesw.htm.

Biographies and Criticism

Bosco, Ronald A. "Michael Wigglesworth." Elliott, *American Colonial Writers, 1606-1734* (*Dictionary of Literary Biography* 24) 337-42.

Bibliographies

Ruppert, James. "Wigglesworth, Michael." *Guide to American Poetry Explication* 238-39.

Mary (White) Rowlandson, c. 1635-c. 1678

Web Sites

"The Puritans: American Literature Colonial Period (1608-1700)." *American Literature*. 13 Mar. 2000, http://falcon.jmu.edu/~ramseyil/amlitcol.htm.

Biographies and Criticism

Lang, Amy Schrager. "Mary Rowlandson." Mulford, Vietto, and Winans, *American Women Prose Writers to 1820* (*Dictionary of Literary Biography* 200) 304-12.

VanDerBeets, Richard. "Mary Rowlandson." Elliott, *American Colonial Writers, 1606-1734* (*Dictionary of Literary Biography* 24) 266-67.

Bibliographies

Stanford, Ann. "Three Puritan Women: Anne Bradstreet, Mary Rowlandson, and Sarah Kemble Knight." Duke, Bryer, and Inge, *American Women Writers* 3-20. Survey of research.

Edward Taylor, c. 1644-1729

Web Sites

"Edward Taylor." *Heath Anthology*. 13 Mar. 2000, http://www.georgetown.edu/bassr/heath/syllabuild/iguide/taylor.html.
    Notes on themes with study questions. Contains a good bibliography that gives brief information for works about Taylor (including chapters in books).

"The Puritans: American Literature Colonial Period (1608-1700)." *American Literature*. 13 Mar. 2000, http://falcon.jmu.edu/~ramseyil/amlitcol.htm.

Biographies and Criticism

"Edward Taylor." Poupard, *Literature Criticism from 1400 to 1800* 11:340-404.
    Excerpts of comments and criticism on Taylor from 1701-1988, with an annotated bibliography.

Grabo, Norman S. *Edward Taylor*. Rev. ed. Boston: Twayne, 1988.

Stanford, Donald E. "Edward Taylor." Elliott, *American Colonial Writers, 1606-1734* (*Dictionary of Literary Biography* 24) 310-21.

Indexes and Concordances

Craig, Raymond A. *A Concordance to the Minor Poetry of Edward Taylor (1642?-1729), American Colonial Poet*. Lewiston: Edwin Mellen, 1992.
    Keyed to Thomas M. Davis and Virginia L. Davis's *Edward Taylor's Minor Poetry* (Boston: Twayne, 1981).

Russell, Gene. *A Concordance to the Poems of Edward Taylor*. Washington: Microcard Editions, 1973.
    Based on Donald E. Stanford's *The Poems* (New Haven: Yale UP, 1960).

Bibliographies

Gefvert, Constance J. *Edward Taylor: An Annotated Bibliography, 1668-1970*. Kent: Kent State UP, 1971.
Complete descriptions for Taylor's writings, brief entries for about 250 critical works, and a thorough survey of modern research.

Grabo, Norman S., and Jane Wainwright. "Edward Taylor." Harbert and Rees, *Fifteen American Authors before 1900* 439-67.
Survey of research.

Ruppert, James. "Taylor, Edward." *Guide to American Poetry Explication* 179-90.

Stanford, Donald E. "Edward Taylor." Emerson, *Major Writers of Early American Literature* 59-92.
Survey of research.

Cotton Mather, 1663-1728

Web Sites

The Cotton Mather Home Page. Ed. Philip R. Johnson. 1998. Spurgeon Archive. 13 Mar. 2000, http://www.gty.org/~phil/mather.htm.
Links to texts of selected works by Mather from unspecified editions.

Increase & Cotton Mather. Ed. Margo Burns. 18 Feb. 2000. Sponsor unknown. 13 Mar. 2000, http://www.ogram.org/17thc/mathers.shtml.
Links to sites for texts of works by the Mathers and articles about them as well as information about the Salem witchcraft trials.

"The Puritans: American Literature Colonial Period (1608-1700)." *American Literature*. 13 Mar. 2000, http://falcon.jmu.edu/~ramseyil/amlitcol.htm.

Biographies and Criticism

Arndt, Murray. "Cotton Mather." Wilson, *American Historians, 1607-1865 (Dictionary of Literary Biography* 30) 169-75.

"Cotton Mather." Poupard, *Literature Criticism from 1400 to 1800* 38:146-248.
Excerpts of comments and criticism on Mather from 1693-1991, with an annotated bibliography.

Hayes, Kevin J. "Cotton Mather." Rosenblum, *American Book-Collectors and Bibliographers (Dictionary of Literary Biography* 140) 153-58.

Lowance, Mason I., Jr. "Cotton Mather." Elliott, *American Colonial Writers, 1606-1734 (Dictionary of Literary Biography* 24) 200-211.

Bibliographies

Bercovitch, Sacvan. "Cotton Mather." Emerson, *Major Writers of Early American Literature* 93-150.
Survey of research.

Holmes, Thomas James. *Cotton Mather: A Bibliography of His Works*. Cambridge: Harvard UP, 1940.
　　Complete descriptions of Mather's works and fragments.

Sarah Kemble Knight, 1666-1727

Web Sites

"The Puritans: American Literature Colonial Period (1608-1700)." *American Literature*. 13 Mar. 2000, http://falcon.jmu.edu/~ramseyil/amlitcol.htm.

Biographies and Criticism

Dietrich, Deborah. "Sarah Kemble Knight." Mulford, Vietto, and Winans, *American Women Prose Writers to 1820* (*Dictionary of Literary Biography* 200) 221-27.

"Sarah Kemble Knight." Poupard, *Literature Criticism from 1400 to 1800* 7:218-31.
　　Excerpts of comments and criticism on Knight from 1825-1980, with an annotated bibliography.

Bibliographies

Stanford, Ann. "Three Puritan Women: Anne Bradstreet, Mary Rowlandson, and Sarah Kemble Knight." Duke, Bryer, and Inge, *American Women Writers* 3-20.
　　Survey of research.

William Byrd, 1674-1744

Web Sites

"The Puritans: American Literature Colonial Period (1608-1700)." *American Literature*. 13 Mar. 2000, http://falcon.jmu.edu/~ramseyil/amlitcol.htm.

Biographies and Criticism

Hayes, Kevin J. "William Byrd II." Rosenblum, *American Book-Collectors and Bibliographers* (*Dictionary of Literary Biography* 140) 32-39.

Preston, Richard M. "William Byrd II." Elliott, *American Colonial Writers, 1606-1734* (*Dictionary of Literary Biography* 24) 44-50.

Bibliographies

Bain, Robert. "William Byrd of Westover." Bain and Flora, *Fifty Southern Writers before 1900* 55-74.

Cutting, Rose Marie. *John and William Bartram, William Byrd II, and St. John de Crevecoeur: A Reference Guide*. Boston: G. K. Hall, 1976.
　　Describes about 150 works on Byrd since 1817.

Davis, Richard Beale. "William Byrd." Emerson, *Major Writers of Early American Literature* 151-78.
　　Survey of research.

Hayes, Kevin J. *The Library of William Byrd of Westover*. Madison: Madison House, 1996.

John Bartram, 1699-1777

Web Sites

Bartram, John 1699-1777. Ed. Freeman S. Howlett. Update unknown. Horticulture Dept., Ohio State U. 13 Mar. 2000, http://hortwww-2.ag.ohio-state.edu/hort/history/145.html.
Article on Bartram linked to the fulltext of Bartram's son's account book.

Biographies and Criticism

Scheick, William J. "John Bartram." Elliott, *American Colonial Writers, 1735-1781* (*Dictionary of Literary Biography* 31) 22-32.

Bibliographies

Cutting, Rose Marie. *John and William Bartram, William Byrd II, and St. John de Crevecoeur: A Reference Guide*. Boston: G. K. Hall, 1976.
Describes about 150 works on John Bartram since 1715.

Jonathan Edwards, 1703-1758

Web Sites

The Christian Hall of Fame Portrait: Jonathan Edwards. 28 Feb. 2000, http://www.chof.org/edwards.htm.

Edwards, Jonathan. Ed. unknown. 2000. Versaware. 13 Mar. 2000, http://www.fwkc.com/encyclopedia/low/articles/e/e007000360f.html.
Encyclopedia article.

"Edwards, Jonathan (1703-1758)." *Evangelical Dictionary of Theology*. Ed. M. A. Noll. Update and sponsor unknown. 13 Mar. 2000, http://www.jonathanedwards.com/text/edot.htm.
Scholarly article with a good bibliography.

Eschatology. Ed. Jonathan Barlow and Ed Walsh. Update unknown. Center for Reformed Theology and Apologetics (CRTA). 13 Mar. 2000, http://www.reformed.org/eschaton/eschatology.html.
Links to texts of Edwards's *Humble Attempt* and *Work of Redemption* from unspecified editions.

Jonathan Edwards on the Web. Ed. Don Westblade. 17 Aug. 1998. Dept. of Philosophy and Religion, Hillsdale C. 13 Mar. 2000, http://www.hillsdale.edu/academics/Phil&Rel/JE/Links.html.
Includes list of Edwards's works, with links to fulltexts, and essays on topics related to Edwards.

Jonathan Edwards.com. Ed. Mark Trigsted. Update unknown. Dallas Theological Seminary. 13 Mar. 2000, http://WWW.JonathanEdwards.com/.
Claims to be the "world's largest Edwards web site." Links to texts of Edwards's sermons, theological and scientific works, and works on revival (from unspecified editions) and texts on his life and ministry, with a classified bibliography of works by and about him.

"The Puritans: American Literature Colonial Period (1608-1700)." *American Literature.* 13 Mar. 2000, http://falcon.jmu.edu/~ramseyil/amlitcol.htm.

Sinners in the Hands of an Angry God by Jonathan Edwards. Ed. and update unknown. Christian Classics Ethereal Library, Wheaton C. 13 Mar. 2000, http://www.reformed.org/documents/sinners.html.
Text of work by Edwards from unspecified edition.

Biographies and Criticism

"Jonathan Edwards." Poupard, *Literature Criticism from 1400 to 1800* 7:88-132.
Excerpts of comments and criticism on Edwards from 1764-1986, with an annotated bibliography.

Lesser, M. X. *Jonathan Edwards.* Boston: Twayne, 1988.

Lowance, Mason I., Jr. "Jonathan Edwards." Elliott, *American Colonial Writers, 1606-1734 (Dictionary of Literary Biography* 24) 95-108.

Bibliographies

Emerson, Everett. "Jonathan Edwards." Harbert and Rees, *Fifteen American Authors before 1900* 230-49.
Survey of research.

Johnson, Thomas H. *The Printed Writings of Jonathan Edwards, 1703-1758: A Bibliography.* Princeton: Princeton UP, 1940.
Complete descriptions of Edwards's works.

Lesser, M. X. *Jonathan Edwards: An Annotated Bibliography, 1979-1993.* Westport: Greenwood, 1994.
Updates Lesser, below, with 700 works on Edwards.

———. *Jonathan Edwards: A Reference Guide.* Boston: G. K. Hall, 1981.
Describes about 1,800 works on Edwards since 1729.

Shea, Daniel B., Jr. "Jonathan Edwards." Emerson, *Major Writers of Early American Literature* 179-204.
Survey of research.

Benjamin Franklin, 1706-1790

Web Sites

The Autobiography of Benjamin Franklin. Ed. and update unknown. Archiving Early America. 13 Mar. 2000, http://earlyamerica.com/lives/franklin/index.html.
Fulltext of Franklin's work (apparently from 1793 edition) with an introduction.

"Benjamin Franklin." *Access Indiana: Teaching & Learning Center.* 13 Mar. 2000, http://tlc.ai.org/franklin.htm.
Encyclopedic links to texts of works by and about Franklin.

"Benjamin Franklin." *American Literature on the Web.* 13 Mar. 2000, http://www.nagasaki-gaigo.ac.jp/ishikawa/amlit/f/franklin1718.htm.

Benjamin Franklin: An Enlightened American. Ed. and update unknown. Thinkquest. 13 Mar. 2000, http://library.advanced.org/22254/mainframe.htm.
Franklin trivia with a good chronology, brief annotated bibliography (indicating reading level difficulty of the books), and list of other works and multimedia works about Franklin.

Ben Franklin: Glimpses of the Man. 13 Mar. 2000, http://www.fi.edu/franklin/rotten.html.

Benjamin Franklin Web Sites. 13 Mar. 2000, http://www.ttl98.dsu.edu/eyema/benjamin_franklin_web_sites.htm.

"Chapter 2: Early American Literature: Benjamin Franklin." *PAL: Perspectives in American Literature.* 13 Mar. 2000, http://www.csustan.edu/english/reuben/pal/chap2/franklin.html.

"The Puritans: American Literature Colonial Period (1608-1700)." *American Literature.* 13 Mar. 2000, http://falcon.jmu.edu/~ramseyil/amlitcol.htm.

The Way to Wealth. Ed. and update unknown. Havill Publishing. 13 Mar. 2000, http://www.havillnet.com/wealth.htm.
Fulltext of work by Franklin from an unspecified edition.

Biographies and Criticism

Amacher, Richard E. "Benjamin Franklin." Elliott, *American Colonial Writers, 1606-1734 (Dictionary of Literary Biography* 24) 125-47.

"Benjamin Franklin." Poupard, *Literature Criticism from 1400 to 1800* 25:99-190.
Excerpts of comments and criticism on Franklin from 1811-1990, with an annotated bibliography.

Duhadaway, Donald A., Jr. "Benjamin Franklin." Schramer and Ross, *American Travel Writers, 1776-1864 (Dictionary of Literary Biography* 183) 103-14.

Kirkhorn, Michael. "Benjamin Franklin." Ashley, *American Newspaper Journalists, 1690-1872 (Dictionary of Literary Biography* 43) 192-212.

Pratte, Alf. "Benjamin Franklin." Riley, *American Magazine Journalists, 1741-1850 (Dictionary of Literary Biography* 73) 101-11.

Zall, P. M. *Franklin's Autobiography: A Model Life.* Boston: Twayne, 1989.

Indexes and Concordances

Barbour, Frances M. *A Concordance to the Sayings in Franklin's Poor Richard.* Detroit: Gale, 1974.
  Keyed to Paul Leicester Ford's edition of *The Sayings of Poor Richard* (New York: Putnam, 1890) and *Poor Richard: The Almanacks* (New York: Heritage, 1964).

Humes, James C. *The Wit & Wisdom of Benjamin Franklin: A Treasury of More Than 900 Quotations and Anecdotes.* New York: HarperCollins, 1995.

Bibliographies

Buxbaum, Melvin H. *Benjamin Franklin, 1721-1906: A Reference Guide.* Boston: G. K. Hall, 1983.
  Describes about 1,800 writings on Franklin, in particular early anonymous notices and reviews.

———. *Benjamin Franklin, 1907-1983: A Reference Guide.* Boston: G. K. Hall, 1988.
  Continues Buxbaum, above, adding about 4,000 entries.

Ford, Paul Leicester. *Franklin Bibliography: A List of Books Written by, or Relating to Benjamin Franklin.* 1889; New York: Burt Franklin, 1968.
  Standard guide to Franklin's works, with complete descriptions.

Granger, Bruce. "Benjamin Franklin." Harbert and Rees, *Fifteen American Authors before 1900* 250-80.
  Survey of research.

LeMay, J. A. Leo. "Benjamin Franklin." Emerson, *Major Writers of Early American Literature* 205-44.
  Survey of research.

———. *The Canon of Benjamin Franklin, 1722-1776: New Attributions and Reconsiderations.* Newark: U of Delaware P, 1986.

Jupiter Hammon, c. 1720-c. 1800

Web Sites

"Jupiter Hammon." *Heath Anthology.* 13 Mar. 2000, http://www.georgetown.edu/bassr/heath/syllabuild/iguide/hammon.html.

A Slave and a Poet: Jupiter Hammon. 13 Mar. 2000, http://www.lihistory.com/4/hs423a.htm.

Biographies and Criticism

"Jupiter Hammon." Harris, *Nineteenth-Century Literature Criticism* 5:260-66.
  Excerpts of comments and criticism on Hammon from 1915-1977, with an annotated bibliography.

"Jupiter Hammon." Young, *Poetry Criticism* 16:175-92.
Excerpts of comments and criticism on Hammon from 1915-1992, with an annotated bibliography.

O'Neale, Sondra A. "Jupiter Hammon." Elliott, *American Colonial Writers, 1735-1781* (*Dictionary of Literary Biography* 31) 107-12.

———. "Jupiter Hammon." Harris, *Afro-American Writers before the Harlem Renaissance* (*Dictionary of Literary Biography* 50) 156-63.

Bibliographies

Johnson, Lonnell E. "Jupiter Hammon." Nelson, *African American Authors, 1745-1945* 209-12.
Survey of research.

Klinkowitz, Jerome. "Early Writers: Jupiter Hammon, Phillis Wheatley, and Benjamin Banneker." Inge, Duke, and Bryer, *Black American Writers* I, 1-20.
Survey of research.

John Woolman, 1720-1772

Web Sites

"John Woolman." *Heath Anthology*. 13 Mar. 2000, http://www.georgetown.edu/bassr/heath/syllabuild/iguide/woolman.html.

Biographies and Criticism

Werge, Thomas. "John Woolman." Elliott, *American Colonial Writers, 1735-1781* (*Dictionary of Literary Biography* 31) 274-90.

Samson Occom, 1723-1792

Web Sites

"Samson Occom." *Heath Anthology*. 13 Mar. 2000, http://www.georgetown.edu/bassr/heath/syllabuild/iguide/occom.html.

Biographies and Criticism

Rosenberg, Ruth. "Samson Occom." Roemer, *Native American Writers of the United States* (*Dictionary of Literary Biography* 175) 203-07.

Benjamin Banneker, 1731-1806

Web Sites

Banneker, Benjamin. Ed. Wolfgang Dick. 4 Mar. 1999. U of Bonn. 12 Mar. 2000, http://www.astro.uni-bonn.de/~pbrosche/persons/pers_banneker.html.
German site; simple in design but comprehensive.

"Benjamin Banneker." *Africans in America: Revolution: People and Events.* 12 Mar. 2000, http://web-cr05.pbs.org/wgbh/aia/part2/2p84.html.

"Benjamin Banneker." *Mathematicians of the African Diaspora.* 12 Mar. 2000, http://newton.math.buffalo.edu/mad/special/banneker-benjamin.html.

Bibliographies

Klinkowitz, Jerome. "Early Writers: Jupiter Hammon, Phillis Wheatley, and Benjamin Banneker." Inge, Duke, and Bryer, *Black American Writers* I, 1-20.

Michel-Guillaume Jean de Crèvecoeur (J. Hector St. John de Crevecoeur), 1735-1813

Web Sites

"J. Hector St. John de Crèvecoeur." *Heath Anthology.* 13 Mar. 2000, http://www.georgetown.edu/bassr/heath/syllabuild/iguide/crevecoe.html.

Bibliographies

Cutting, Rose Marie. *John and William Bartram, William Byrd II, and St. John de Crevecoeur: A Reference Guide.* Boston: G. K. Hall, 1976.
Describes about 150 works on Crevecoeur since 1782.

Thomas Paine, 1737-1809

Web Sites

The American Crisis. Ed., update, and sponsor unknown. 13 Mar. 2000, http://libertyonline.hypermall.com/Paine/Crisis/Crisis-TOC.html.
Fulltext of Paine's work from an unspecified edition.

Common Sense. Ed. and update unknown. Archiving Early America. 13 Mar. 2000, http://www.earlyamerica.com/earlyamerica/milestones/commonsense/index.html.
Facsimile and transcription of 1791 edition.

Friends of Thomas Paine. 13 Mar. 2000, http://userweb.interactive.net/~phila/.

Historical Writings: Thomas Paine. Ed. Cliff Walker. 1999. Positive Atheism. 13 Mar. 2000, http://www.aracnet.com/~atheism/tochpain.htm.
Includes links to fulltexts of a small fraction of Paine's writings available on the web.

Thomas Paine. Ed. and update unknown. World Union of Deists. 13 Mar. 2000, http://www.deism.com/paine.htm.
Fulltexts of works included in *Life and Writings of Thomas Paine,* ed. Daniel Edwin Wheeler (New York: Vincent Parke, 1980).

Thomas Paine National Historical Association. Ed. Kenneth Burchell. Update unknown. The Association. 13 Mar. 2000, http://www.dpipc.com/cdadesign/
paine/home.html.
Links to fulltexts of Paine's works (in unspecified editions) with other information about him.

Biographies and Criticism

Burriss, Larry L. "Thomas Paine." Gary Kelly and Edd Applegate, eds. *British Re-
form Writers, 1789-1832 (Dictionary of Literary Biography* 158). Detroit: Gale,
1995. 266-74.

Goldman, Maureen. "Thomas Paine." Elliott, *American Colonial Writers, 1735-1781
(Dictionary of Literary Biography* 31) 186-202.

Price, Henry T. "Thomas Paine." Ashley, *American Newspaper Journalists,
1690-1872 (Dictionary of Literary Biography* 43) 338-47.

Stovall, James Glen. "Thomas Paine." Riley, *American Magazine Journalists,
1741-1850 (Dictionary of Literary Biography* 73) 225-34.

"Thomas Paine." Harris, *Nineteenth-Century Literature Criticism* 62:243-397.
Excerpts of comments and criticism on Paine from 1859-1994, with an annotated bibliography.

Wilson, Jerome D., and William F. Ricketson. *Thomas Paine.* Updated ed. Boston:
Twayne, 1989.

Bibliographies

Gimbel, Richard. *The Resurgence of Thomas Paine: With the Catalogue of an Exhibi-
tion: Thomas Paine Fights for Freedom in Three Worlds.* Worcester: American
Antiquarian Society, 1961.
Descriptive guide to Paine's works.

———. *Thomas Paine: A Bibliographical Check List of Common Sense: With an Account of Its Publication.* New Haven: Yale UP, 1956.
Includes a list of contemporary works related to *Common Sense.*

William Bartram, 1739-1823

Web Sites

"William Bartram: Links to Related Sites." 12 Mar. 2000, http://www.icad.uga.
edu/products/Teacher/bartramLinks.shtml.

Biographies and Criticism

Seavey, Ormond. "William Bartram." Elliott, *American Writers of the Early Republic (Dictionary of Literary Biography* 37) 31-38.

Bibliographies

Cutting, Rose Marie. *John and William Bartram, William Byrd II, and St. John de Crevecoeur: A Reference Guide*. Boston: G. K. Hall, 1976.
Describes about 150 works on Bartram since 1792.

Thomas Jefferson, 1743-1826

Web Sites

The Declaration of Independence. Ed. unknown. April 15, 1998. National Archives and Records Administration. 13 Mar. 2000, http://www.nara.gov/exhall/charters/declaration/decmain.html.
Facsimile of *Declaration of Independence* with notes on Jefferson's authorship and links to related sources.

Monticello. Ed. unknown. 27 Jan. 2000. Thomas Jefferson Memorial Foundation. 13 Mar. 2000, http://www.monticello.org/.
Authoritative site.

"Thomas Jefferson." *A Hypertext on American History*. 13 Mar. 2000, http://odur.let.rug.nl/~usa/P/tj3/tj3.htm.

Thomas Jefferson. 13 Mar. 2000, http://history.hanover.edu/19th/jefferso.htm.

Thomas Jefferson. Ed. and update unknown. Jefferson Soc., U of Virginia. 28 Feb. 2000, http://scs.student.virginia.edu/~jefflds/jefferson.html.
Links to fulltexts of selected works by and about Jefferson.

Thomas Jefferson: Comprehensive, Annotated Bibliographies of Writings about Him, 1826-1992. Ed. Frank Shuffelton. 1999. Electronic Text Center, U of Virginia Library. 13 Mar. 2000, http://etext.virginia.edu/jefferson/bibliog/.
Contains separately and cumulatively searchable texts of Shuffelton's 1984 and 1992 bibliographies, below, and update and supplement, "Jefferson in the Nineties: An Annotated Bibliography" covering works about Jefferson after 1991.

Biographies and Criticism

Le Beau, Bryan F. "Thomas Jefferson." Schramer and Ross, *American Travel Writers, 1776-1864* (*Dictionary of Literary Biography* 183) 187-96.

Richardson, Robert D., Jr. "Thomas Jefferson." Elliott, *American Colonial Writers, 1735-1781* (*Dictionary of Literary Biography* 31) 136-49.

"Thomas Jefferson." Harris, *Nineteenth-Century Literature Criticism* 11:134-216.
Excerpts of comments and criticism on Jefferson from 1776-1983, with an annotated bibliography.

Indexes and Concordances

Kaminski, John P. *Citizen Jefferson: The Wit and Wisdom of an American Sage*. Madison: Madison House, 1994.
Based on Julian P. Boyd, Charles T. Cullen, and John Catanzariti's *The Papers of Thomas Jefferson* (Princeton: Princeton UP, 1950-).

Bibliographies

Huddleston, Eugene L. *Thomas Jefferson: A Reference Guide.* Boston: G. K. Hall, 1982.
Describes about 1,400 works on Jefferson since 1837.

Peden, William. "Thomas Jefferson." Bain and Flora, *Fifty Southern Writers before 1900* 268-76.

Shuffelton, Frank. *Thomas Jefferson: A Comprehensive Annotated Bibliography of Writings about Him (1826-1980).* New York: Garland, 1984.
International in scope with 3,447 entries.

———. *Thomas Jefferson, 1981-1990: An Annotated Bibliography.* New York: Garland, 1992.
Continues Shuffelton, above, adding 642 items.

Abigail (Smith) Adams, 1744-1818

Web Sites

Abigail Adams. 12 Mar. 2000, http://www.whitehouse.gov/WH/glimpse/firstladies/html/aa2.html.

"John Adams and Abigail Adams." *Heath Anthology.* 13 Mar. 2000, http://www.georgetown.edu/bassr/heath/syllabuild/iguide/adamsaj.html.

Biographies and Criticism

Gelles, Edith Belle. *First Thoughts: Life and Letters of Abigail Adams.* New York: Twayne, 1998.

———, and Angela Vietto. "Abigail Adams." Mulford, Vietto, and Winans, *American Women Prose Writers to 1820* (*Dictionary of Literary Biography* 200) 3-15.

Perry, Dennis R. "John Adams and Abigail Adams." Schramer and Ross, *American Travel Writers, 1776-1864* (*Dictionary of Literary Biography* 183) 3-17.

Philip (Morin) Freneau, 1752-1832

Web Sites

"Philip Freneau." *Heath Anthology.* 13 Mar. 2000, http://www.georgetown.edu/bassr/heath/syllabuild/iguide/freneau.html.

Biographies and Criticism

"Philip Morin Freneau." Harris, *Nineteenth-Century Literature Criticism* 1:312-25.
Excerpts of comments and criticism on Freneau from 1807-1977, with an annotated bibliography.

Stovall, James Glen. "Philip Morin Freneau." Ashley, *American Newspaper Journalists, 1690-1872* (*Dictionary of Literary Biography* 43) 218-26.

Vitzthum, Richard C. "Philip Freneau." Elliott, *American Writers of the Early Republic* (*Dictionary of Literary Biography* 37) 163-81.

Bibliographies

Hiltner, Judith R. *The Newspaper Verse of Philip Freneau: An Edition and Bibliographical Survey*. Troy: Whitston, 1986.

Leary, Lewis. "Philip Freneau." Emerson, *Major Writers of Early American Literature* 245-72.

Paltsits, Victor Hugo. *A Bibliography of the Separate and Collected Works of Philip Freneau: Together with an Account of His Newspapers*. New York: Dodd, Mead, 1903.
Complete descriptions.

Ruppert, James. "Freneau, Philip." *Guide to American Poetry Explication* 122-26.

Phillis Wheatley, 1753?-1784

Web Sites

"Phillis Wheatley." *American Women in Literature Database*. 13 Mar. 2000, http://www.kutztown.edu/~reagan/wheatley.html.

"Phillis Wheatley." *Voices from the Gaps: Women Writers of Color*. 13 Mar. 2000, http://voices.cla.umn.edu/authors/PhillisWheatley.html.

"The Phillis Wheatley Page." *SAC LitWeb*. 13 Mar. 2000, http://www.accd.edu/sac/english/bailey/wheatley.htm.

Phillis Wheatley: Precursor of American Abolitionism. 13 Mar. 2000, http://www.forerunner.com/forerunner/X0214_Phillis_Wheatley.html.

"Selected Poetry of Phillis Wheatley." *Representative Poetry On-line*. 19 Mar. 2000, http://www.library.utoronto.ca/utel/rp/authors/wheat.html.

Biographies and Criticism

O'Neale, Sondra A. "Phillis Wheatley." Elliott, *American Colonial Writers, 1735-1781* (*Dictionary of Literary Biography* 31) 260-67.

"Phillis Wheatley." Poupard, *Literature Criticism from 1400 to 1800* 3:406-38.
Excerpts of comments and criticism on Wheatley from 1773-1984, with an annotated bibliography.

"Phillis Wheatley." Young, *Poetry Criticism* 3:330-64.
Excerpts of comments and criticism on Wheatley from 1773-1989, with an annotated bibliography.

Williams, Kenny J. "Phillis Wheatley." Harris, *Afro-American Writers before the Harlem Renaissance* (*Dictionary of Literary Biography* 50) 245-59.

Bibliographies

Choucair, Mona M. "Phillis Wheatley." Nelson, *African American Authors, 1745-1945* 463-68.
Survey of research.

Klinkowitz, Jerome. "Early Writers: Jupiter Hammon, Phillis Wheatley, and Benjamin Banneker." Inge, Duke, and Bryer, *Black American Writers* I, 1-20.
Survey of research.

Robinson, William H. *Phillis Wheatley: A Bio-Bibliography*. Boston: G. K. Hall, 1981.
Evaluative descriptions of about 600 works on Wheatley since 1761 with a checklist of Wheatley's works.

Ruppert, James. "Wheatley, Phillis." *Guide to American Poetry Explication* 198-99.

Joel Barlow, 1754-1812

Web Sites

"Joel Barlow." *Heath Anthology*. 13 Mar. 2000, http://www.georgetown.edu/bassr/heath/syllabuild/iguide/barlow.html.

Biographies and Criticism

"Joel Barlow." Harris, *Nineteenth-Century Literature Criticism* 23:1-46.
Excerpts of comments and criticism on Barlow from 1788-1982, with an annotated bibliography.

Tichi, Cecelia. "Joel Barlow." Elliott, *American Writers of the Early Republic* (*Dictionary of Literary Biography* 37) 18-31.

Bibliographies

Ruppert, James. "Barlow, Joel." *Guide to American Poetry Explication* 1-3.

Royall Tyler, 1757-1826

Web Sites

"Royall Tyler." *Heath Anthology*. 13 Mar. 2000, http://www.georgetown.edu/bassr/heath/syllabuild/iguide/tyler.html.

Biographies and Criticism

Gaston, James C. "Royall Tyler." Elliott, *American Writers of the Early Republic* (*Dictionary of Literary Biography* 37) 279-89.

"Royall Tyler." Harris, *Nineteenth-Century Literature Criticism* 3:570-79.
Excerpts of comments and criticism on Tyler from 1787-1978, with an annotated bibliography.

Bibliographies

Hull, William E. "Royall Tyler." Ljungquist, *Bibliography of American Fiction through 1865* 264-65.

Hannah Webster Foster, 1759-1840

Web Sites

"Hannah Webster Foster." *Heath Anthology*. 13 Mar. 2000, http://www.georgetown.edu/bassr/heath/syllabuild/iguide/foster.html.

Biographies and Criticism

Davidson, Cathy N. "Hannah Webster Foster." Elliott, *American Writers of the Early Republic* (*Dictionary of Literary Biography* 37) 161-63.

Verhoeven, W. M. "Hannah Webster Foster." Mulford, Vietto, and Winans, *American Women Prose Writers to 1820* (*Dictionary of Literary Biography* 200) 122-31.

Bibliographies

Glitsch, Catherine. "Foster, Hannah Webster." *American Novel Explication, 1991-1995* 90.

Millsaps, Ellen M. "Hannah Webster Foster." Ljungquist, *Bibliography of American Fiction through 1865* 112-13.

Saar, Doreen Alvarez. "Foster, Hannah Webster (1758-1840)." Doreen Alvarez Saar and Mary Anne Schofield, eds. *Eighteenth-Century Anglo-American Women Novelists*. New York: G. K. Hall, 1996. 221-37.
Describes about 75 studies since 1901.

William Dunlap, 1766-1839

Web Sites

"EAF Authors: William Dunlap." *Early American Fiction*. 12 Mar. 2000, http://etext.lib.virginia.edu/eaf/authors/second/wd.html.

Biographies and Criticism

Grimsted, David. "William Dunlap." Wilson, *American Historians, 1607-1865* (*Dictionary of Literary Biography* 30) 77-84.

Harvey, Robert D. "William Dunlap." Rathbun and Grecu, *American Literary Critics and Scholars, 1800-1850* (*Dictionary of Literary Biography* 59) 101-7.

Johnson, Claudia. "William Dunlap." Elliott, *American Writers of the Early Republic* (*Dictionary of Literary Biography* 37) 117-27.

"William Dunlap." Harris, *Nineteenth-Century Literature Criticism* 2:207-18.
Excerpts of comments and criticism on Dunlap from 1789-1977, with an annotated bibliography.

Bibliographies

Wegelin, Oscar. *A Bibliographical Checklist of the Plays and Miscellaneous Writings of William Dunlap (1766-1839)*. New York: Charles F. Heartman, 1916.
Complete descriptions.

Anne Newport Royall, 1769-1854

Web Sites

"EAF Authors: Anne Newport Royall." *Early American Fiction*. 12 Mar. 2000,
http://etext.lib.virginia.edu/eaf/authors/second/anr.html.

Biographies and Criticism

Fleener, Nickieann. "Anne Royall." Ashley, *American Newspaper Journalists, 1690-1872 (Dictionary of Literary Biography 43)* 402-08.

Charles Brockden Brown, 1771-1810

Web Sites

"Charles Brockden Brown." *Heath Anthology*. 13 Mar. 2000, http://www.georgetown.edu/bassr/heath/syllabuild/iguide/brownc.html.

Biographies and Criticism

"Charles Brockden Brown." Harris, *Nineteenth-Century Literature Criticism* 22:1-59.
Excerpts of comments and criticism on Brown from 1798-1983, with an annotated bibliography.

———. Harris, *Nineteenth-Century Literature Criticism* 74:1-205.
Excerpts of criticism on Brown from 1902-1996, with an annotated bibliography.

Cleman, John. "Charles Brockden Brown." Rathbun and Grecu, *American Literary Critics and Scholars, 1800-1850 (Dictionary of Literary Biography 59)* 26-35.

Ringe, Donald A. *Charles Brockden Brown*. Rev. ed. Boston: Twayne, 1991.

Rosenthal, Bernard. "Charles Brockden Brown." Elliott, *American Writers of the Early Republic (Dictionary of Literary Biography 37)* 69-81.

Schaefermeyer, Mark J. "Charles Brockden Brown." Riley, *American Magazine Journalists, 1741-1850 (Dictionary of Literary Biography 73)* 21-28.

Bibliographies

Glitsch, Catherine. "Brown, Charles Brockden." *American Novel Explication, 1991-1995* 35-36.

Parker, Patricia L. *Charles Brockden Brown: A Reference Guide*. Boston: G. K. Hall, 1980.
Describes about 650 works on Brown since 1796.

Ringe, Donald A. "Charles Brockden Brown." Emerson, *Major Writers of Early American Literature* 273-94.
Survey of research.

Stewart, E. Kate. "Charles Brockden Brown." Ljungquist, *Bibliography of American Fiction through 1865* 65-67.

Washington Irving, 1783-1859

Web Sites

"Chapter 3: Early Nineteenth Century: Washington Irving." *PAL: Perspectives in American Literature*. 13 Mar. 2000, http://www.csustan.edu/english/reuben/pal/chap3/irving.html.

"Washington Irving." *American Literature on the Web*. 13 Mar. 2000, http://www.nagasaki-gaigo.ac.jp/ishikawa/amlit/i/irving_w19ro.htm.

Washington Irving. 13 Mar. 2000, http://www.geocities.com/Athens/Parthenon/6672/.

"Washington Irving." *Pegasos*. 13 Mar. 2000, http://www.kirjasto.sci.fi/wirving.htm.

"Washington Irving (1783-1859)." *Studies in American Literature Sources*. 13 Mar. 2000, http://www.shsu.edu/~eng_wpf/amlitchron_18th.html#irving.

Washington Irving Resources. 13 Mar. 2000, http://www.uni-freiburg.de/philfak3/eng/irving.html.

Biographies and Criticism

Baron, Xavier. "Washington Irving." Schramer and Ross, *American Travel Writers, 1776-1864* (*Dictionary of Literary Biography* 183) 168-86.

Bowden, Mary Weatherspoon. *Washington Irving*. Boston: Twayne, 1981.

Clark, William Bedford. "Washington Irving." Trachtenberg, *American Humorists, 1800-1950* (*Dictionary of Literary Biography* 11) 224-37.

Kime, Wayne R. "Washington Irving." Gale, *Nineteenth-Century American Western Writers* (*Dictionary of Literary Biography* 186) 166-80.

———. "Washington Irving." Wilson, *American Historians, 1607-1865* (*Dictionary of Literary Biography* 30) 147-55.

Myers, Andrew B. "Washington Irving." Myerson, *Antebellum Writers in New York and the South* (*Dictionary of Literary Biography* 3) 166-87.

Pancost, David W. "Washington Irving." Rathbun and Grecu, *American Literary Critics and Scholars, 1800-1850* (*Dictionary of Literary Biography* 59) 175-85.

Rust, Richard D. "Washington Irving." Kimbel and Grant, *American Short-Story Writers before 1880* (*Dictionary of Literary Biography* 74) 171-88.

Steck, Jacqueline. "Washington Irving." Riley, *American Magazine Journalists, 1741-1850* (*Dictionary of Literary Biography* 73) 197-206.

"Washington Irving." Harris, *Nineteenth-Century Literature Criticism* 2:364-93.
    Excerpts of comments and criticism on Irving from 1819-1981, with an annotated bibliography.

———. Harris, *Nineteenth-Century Literature Criticism* 19:325-52.
    Excerpts of comments and criticism on Irving from 1820-1981, with an annotated bibliography.

"Washington Irving." Harris and Fitzgerald, *Short Story Criticism* 2:236-70.
    Excerpts of criticism on Irving from 1819-1981, with an annotated bibliography.

Bibliographies

Bowden, Edwin T. *Washington Irving Bibliography*. Boston: Twayne, 1989.
    Complete descriptions of Irving's works.

Etulain, Richard W., and N. Jill Howard. "Washington Irving." *Bibliographical Guide to the Study of Western American Literature* 262-65.

Hayes, Edmund M., and Mary Jo Tate. "Washington Irving." Ljungquist, *Bibliography of American Fiction through 1865* 149-54.

Springer, Haskell. *Washington Irving: A Reference Guide*. Boston: G. K. Hall, 1976.
    Describes about 1,000 comments and criticisms since 1807; continued by Springer and Raylene Penner's "Washington Irving: A Reference Guide Updated," *Resources for American Literary Study* 11 (1981): 257-79.

Tuttleton, James W. "Washington Irving." Harbert and Rees, *Fifteen American Authors before 1900* 330-56.
    Survey of research.

Seattle, Chief, 1786-1866

Web Sites

Chief Seattle's Letter to All the People. 13 Mar. 2000, http://www.nidlink.com/~bobhard/seattle.html.

Chief Seattle on Internet. 13 Mar. 2000, http://www.geocities.com/Athens/2344/chiefs3.htm.
    Site contains material about the now-controversial speech of 1854 and a link to the oldest known version of that speech. Site's author tends to obfuscate rather than to clarify the controversy that has stemmed from the fact that the original version of the speech was simply not recorded. Contains useful bibliography of works about Chief Seattle. Offsite links provided.

A Few References to Chief Seattle. Ed. Patrick Jennings. 1996. Sponsor unknown. 13
Mar. 2000, http://www.synaptic.bc.ca/ejournal/seattle2.htm.
Site gives a fair appraisal that leads to a clear understanding of the speech of
1854 controversy. Both offsite and onsite links, some broken.

The Original Chief Seattle Statement. 13 Mar. 2000, http://magna.com.au/
~prfbrown/thchief2.html.

James Fenimore Cooper, 1789-1851

Web Sites

"Chapter 3: Early Nineteenth Century: James Fenimore Cooper." *PAL: Perspectives
in American Literature.* 13 Mar. 2000, http://www.csustan.edu/english/reuben/
pal/chap3/cooper.html.

"EAF Authors: James Fenimore Cooper." *Early American Fiction.* 13 Mar. 2000,
http://etext.lib.virginia.edu/eaf/authors/first/jfc.html.

James Fenimore Cooper. 13 Mar. 2000, http://www.cwrl.utexas.edu/~maria/cooper/
jfc_home.htm.

James Fenimore Cooper Society. Ed. Hugh C. MacDougall. Update unknown. The
Society. 13 Mar. 2000, http://library.cmsu.edu/cooper/COOPER.HTM.
Includes excellent offsite links and onsite links to "Cooper on Film," "Cooper
on Stage," and Works "by Cooper, and contents and titles of the Occasional Papers"
of the Society. Unfortunately, the site contains no other bibliography of literary
criticism.

Romancing the Indian. 13 Mar. 2000, http://xroads.virginia.edu/~HYPER/HNS/
Indians/main.html.

Biographies and Criticism

Gardner, Jared. "James Fenimore Cooper." Schramer and Ross, *American Travel
Writers, 1776-1864* (*Dictionary of Literary Biography* 183) 48-67.

"James Fenimore Cooper." Harris, *Nineteenth-Century Literature Criticism*
1:193-229.
Excerpts of comments and criticism on Cooper from 1822-1978, with an annotated bibliography.

———. Harris, *Nineteenth-Century Literature Criticism* 27:122-90.
Excerpts of comments and criticism on Cooper's "Leatherstocking" novels
(*The Pioneers, The Last of the Mohicans, The Prairie, The Pathfinder,* and *The
Deerslayer*) from 1823-1988, with an annotated bibliography.

———. Harris, *Nineteenth-Century Literature Criticism* 54:246-303.
Excerpts of comments and criticism on Cooper from 1849-1990, with an annotated bibliography.

McWilliams, John. *The Last of the Mohicans: Civil Savagery and Savage Civility.*
New York: Twayne, 1995.

Railton, Stephen. "James Fenimore Cooper." Myerson, *Antebellum Writers in New York and the South* (*Dictionary of Literary Biography* 3) 74-93.

Ringe, Donald A. *James Fenimore Cooper*. Updated ed. Boston: Twayne, 1988.

Dictionaries, Encyclopedias, and Handbooks

Summerlin, Mitchell Eugene. *A Dictionary to the Novels of James Fenimore Cooper*. Greenwood: Penkevill, 1987.

Walker, Warren S. *Plots and Characters in the Fiction of James Fenimore Cooper*. Hamden: Archon Books, 1978.

Bibliographies

Beard, James Franklin. "James Fenimore Cooper." Harbert and Rees, *Fifteen American Authors before 1900* 63-127.
Survey of research.

Dyer, Alan Frank. *James Fenimore Cooper: An Annotated Bibliography of Criticism*. New York: Greenwood, 1991.
Describes 1,943 works since 1820.

Etulain, Richard W., and N. Jill Howard. "James Fenimore Cooper." *Bibliographical Guide to the Study of Western American Literature* 200-205.

Glitsch, Catherine. "Cooper, James Fenimore." *American Novel Explication, 1991-1995* 52-53.

Spiller, Robert E., and Philip C. Blackburn. *A Descriptive Bibliography of the Writings of James Fenimore Cooper*. 1903. New York: Burt Franklin, 1968.
Complete descriptions.

Wallace, James D. "James Fenimore Cooper." Ljungquist, *Bibliography of American Fiction through 1865* 88-94.

Catharine Maria Sedgwick, 1789-1867

Web Sites

"Catharine Maria Sedgwick." *Heath Anthology*. 13 Mar. 2000, http://www.georgetown.edu/bassr/heath/syllabuild/iguide/sedgwick.html.

Biographies and Criticism

"Catharine Maria Sedgwick." Harris, *Nineteenth-Century Literature Criticism* 19:423-53.
Excerpts of comments and criticism on Sedgwick from 1822-1974, with an annotated bibliography.

"Catharine Maria Sedgwick." Myerson, *The American Renaissance in New England* (*Dictionary of Literary Biography* 1) 162.

Tingley, Stephanie A. "Catharine Maria Sedgwick." Schramer and Ross, *American Travel Writers, 1776-1864* (*Dictionary of Literary Biography* 183) 278-84.

Zaidman, Laura M. "Catharine Maria Sedgwick." Kimbel and Grant, *American Short-Story Writers before 1880* (*Dictionary of Literary Biography* 74) 323-29.

Bibliographies

Glitsch, Catherine. "Sedgwick, Catherine Maria." *American Novel Explication, 1991-1995* 225-26.

Saulsbury, Rebecca R. "Catharine Maria Sedgwick." Knight, *Nineteenth-Century American Women Writers* [351]-60.
Includes a brief survey of Sedgwick's critical reception and a selective list of studies.

Westbrook, Perry D. "Catharine Maria Sedgwick." Ljungquist, *Bibliography of American Fiction through 1865* 215-16.

Lydia Huntley Sigourney, 1791-1865

Web Sites

"Lydia Howard Huntley Sigourney." *Heath Anthology*. 13 Mar. 2000, http://www.georgetown.edu/bassr/heath/syllabuild/iguide/sigourney.html.

Biographies and Criticism

Bowles, Dorothy A. "Lydia H. Sigourney." Riley, *American Magazine Journalists, 1741-1850* (*Dictionary of Literary Biography* 73) 264-74.

Delaney, Laurie. "Lydia H. Sigourney." Schramer and Ross, *American Travel Writers, 1776-1864* (*Dictionary of Literary Biography* 183) 285-91.

Gay, Carol. "Lydia Huntley Sigourney." Estes, *American Writers for Children before 1900* (*Dictionary of Literary Biography* 42) 322-28.

"Lydia Sigourney." Harris, *Nineteenth-Century Literature Criticism* 21:288-316.
Excerpts of comments and criticism on Sigourney from 1815-1987, with an annotated bibliography.

Stern, Madeleine B. "Lydia Howard (Huntley) Sigourney." Myerson, *The American Renaissance in New England* (*Dictionary of Literary Biography* 1) 163-64.

Bibliographies

Kilcup, Karen L. "Lydia Howard Huntley Sigourney." Knight, *Nineteenth-Century American Women Writers* [361]-67.

William Cullen Bryant, 1794-1878

Web Sites

"EAF Authors: William Cullen Bryant." *Early American Fiction*. 13 Mar. 2000, http://etext.lib.virginia.edu/eaf/authors/first/wcb.html.

"Poems / William Cullen Bryant." *Humanities Text Initiative American Verse Collection*. 13 Mar. 2000, http://www.hti.umich.edu/bin/amv-idx.pl?type=header&id=BryanPoems.
Text of New York: Harper and Brothers, 1840 edition.

"William Cullen Bryant." *American Literature on the Web*. 13 Mar. 2000, http://www.nagasaki-gaigo.ac.jp/ishikawa/amlit/19ro/f_authors19ro.htm.
Good set of links, mostly for texts of works by Bryant.

Biographies and Criticism

Boylan, James. "William Cullen Bryant." Ashley, *American Newspaper Journalists, 1690-1872* (*Dictionary of Literary Biography* 43) 79-90.

Free, William J. "William Cullen Bryant." Rathbun and Grecu, *American Literary Critics and Scholars, 1800-1850* (*Dictionary of Literary Biography* 59) 43-50.

Harrington, Kristine. "William Cullen Bryant." Ross and Schramer, *American Travel Writers, 1850-1915* (*Dictionary of Literary Biography* 189) 49-54.

McLean, Albert F. *William Cullen Bryant*. Updated ed. Boston: Twayne, 1989.

Tomlinson, David. "William Cullen Bryant." Myerson, *Antebellum Writers in New York and the South* (*Dictionary of Literary Biography* 3) 30-43.

"William Cullen Bryant." Harris, *Nineteenth-Century Literature Criticism* 6:156-94.
Excerpts of comments and criticism on Bryant from 1808-1971, with an annotated bibliography.

———. Harris, *Nineteenth-Century Literature Criticism* 46:1-57.
Excerpts of criticism on Bryant from 1905-1991, with an annotated bibliography.

"William Cullen Bryant." Young, *Poetry Criticism* 20:1-49.
Excerpts of comments and criticism on Bryant from 1916-1989, with an annotated bibliography.

Bibliographies

Boswell, Jeanetta. *The Schoolroom Poets: A Bibliography of Bryant, Holmes, Longfellow, Lowell, and Whittier with Selective Annotation*. Metuchen: Scarecrow, 1983.
Describes about 400 works on Bryant since 1900.

Jason, Philip K. "William Cullen Bryant." *Nineteenth Century American Poetry* 26-34.
Describes 45 studies.

Phair, Judith Turner. *A Bibliography of William Cullen Bryant and His Circle, 1808-1972*. Troy: Whitston, 1975.
Describes about 750 works.

Rocks, James E. "William Cullen Bryant." Harbert and Rees, *Fifteen American Authors before 1900* 37-79.
Survey of research.

Ruppert, James. "Bryant, William Cullen." *Guide to American Poetry Explication* 7-11.

John Pendleton Kennedy, 1795-1870

Web Sites

"EAF Authors: John Pendleton Kennedy." *Early American Fiction*. 13 Mar. 2000, http://etext.lib.virginia.edu/eaf/authors/second/jpk.html.
Texts of selected 19th-century works about Pendleton.

Biographies and Criticism

"John Pendleton Kennedy." Harris, *Nineteenth-Century Literature Criticism* 2:427-35.
Excerpts of comments and criticism on Kennedy from 1833-1966, with an annotated bibliography.

Ridgely, J. V. "John Pendleton Kennedy." Myerson, *Antebellum Writers in New York and the South* (*Dictionary of Literary Biography* 3) 188-94.

Bibliographies

Tomlinson, David O. "John Pendleton Kennedy." Bain and Flora, *Fifty Southern Writers before 1900* 286-95.

Wills, Jack C. "John Pendleton Kennedy." Ljungquist, *Bibliography of American Fiction through 1865* 158-59.

William Apess, 1798-?

Web Sites

"William Apess." *North American Native Authors Catalog*. 13 Mar. 2000, http://nativeauthors.com/search/bio/bioapess.html.

"William Apess." *Internet Public Library: Native American Authors Project*. 13 Mar. 2000, http://www.ipl.org/cgi/ref/native/browse.pl/A11.

Biographies and Criticism

O'Connell, Barry. "William Apess." Roemer, *Native American Writers of the United States* (*Dictionary of Literary Biography* 175) 21-29.

"William Apess." Harris, *Nineteenth-Century Literature Criticism* 73:1-35.
Excerpts of criticism on Apess from 1977-1997, with an annotated bibliography.

Lydia Maria Child, 1802-1880

Web Sites

"Lydia Maria Child." *Heath Anthology*. 13 Mar. 2000, http://www.georgetown.edu/bassr/heath/syllabuild/iguide/child.html.

Biographies and Criticism

Karcher, Carolyn L. "Lydia Maria Child." Kimbel and Grant, *American Short-Story Writers before 1880* (*Dictionary of Literary Biography* 74) 43-53.

"Lydia Maria Child." Harris, *Nineteenth-Century Literature Criticism* 6:195-209.
Excerpts of comments and criticism on Child from 1824-1980, with an annotated bibliography.

———. Harris, *Nineteenth-Century Literature Criticism* 73:36-139.
Excerpts of comments and criticism on Child from 1833-1994, with an annotated bibliography.

Myerson, Joel. "Lydia Maria Child." Myerson, *The American Renaissance in New England* (*Dictionary of Literary Biography* 1) 26-27.

Bibliographies

Hoeller, Hildegard. "Lydia Maria Child." Knight, *Nineteenth-Century American Women Writers* [42]-49.

Holland, Patricia G. "Lydia Maria Child." Ljungquist, *Bibliography of American Fiction through 1865* 79-82.

Ralph Waldo Emerson, 1803-1882

Web Sites

"Ralph Waldo Emerson." *Academy of American Poets*. 8 Mar. 2000, http://www.poets.org/lit/poet/rwemefst.htm.

Ralph Waldo Emerson. 13 Mar. 2000, http://www.tombtown.com/bios/emerson.htm.

Ralph Waldo Emerson. 13 Mar. 2000, http://history.hanover.edu/19th/emerson.htm.
Solid list of links to fulltexts of Emerson's works.

Ralph Waldo Emerson. Ed. James Gagne. Update and sponsor unknown. 13 Mar. 2000, http://members.xoom.com/RWEmerson/.
Cluttered and annoying site that offers little information about Emerson's life or his work.

The Works of Ralph Waldo Emerson. Ed. Jim Manley. 2000. Sponsor unknown. 13 Mar. 2000, http://www.rwe.org/.
Excellent site. Contains links to texts of works by and about Emerson with a chronology and other information and a list of resources.

Biographies and Criticism

Avery, Donald R. "Ralph Waldo Emerson." Riley, *American Magazine Journalists, 1741-1850* (*Dictionary of Literary Biography* 73) 85-92.

Buell, Lawrence. "Ralph Waldo Emerson." Myerson, *The American Renaissance in New England* (*Dictionary of Literary Biography* 1) 48-60.

Harvey, Bruce A. "Ralph Waldo Emerson." Schramer and Ross, *American Travel Writers, 1776-1864* (*Dictionary of Literary Biography* 183) 96-102.

"Ralph Waldo Emerson." Harris, *Nineteenth-Century Literature Criticism* 1:274-311.
Excerpts of comments and criticism on Emerson from 1837-1981, with an annotated bibliography.

————. Harris, *Nineteenth-Century Literature Criticism* 38:141-232.
Excerpts of criticism on Emerson from 1952-1989, with an annotated bibliography.

"Ralph Waldo Emerson." Young, *Poetry Criticism* 18:64-122.
Excerpts of comments and criticism on Emerson from 1844-1993, with an annotated bibliography.

Richardson, Robert D., Jr. "Ralph Waldo Emerson." Rathbun and Grecu, *American Literary Critics and Scholars, 1800-1850* (*Dictionary of Literary Biography* 59) 108-29.

Yannella, Donald. *Ralph Waldo Emerson.* Boston: Twayne, 1982.

Dictionaries, Encyclopedias, and Handbooks

Carpenter, Frederick Ives. *Emerson Handbook.* New York: Hendricks House, 1953.

Porte, Joel, and Saundra Morris. *Cambridge Companion to Ralph Waldo Emerson.* New York: Cambridge UP, 1999.

Von Frank, Albert J. *An Emerson Chronology.* New York: G. K. Hall, 1994.
Exemplary in detail.

Indexes and Concordances

Frome, Keith Weller. *Hitch Your Wagon to a Star and Other Quotations from Ralph Waldo Emerson.* New York: Columbia UP, 1996.

Hubbell, George Shelton. *A Concordance to the Poems of Ralph Waldo Emerson.* New York: H. W. Wilson, 1932.
Based on *Complete Works* (Boston: Houghton Mifflin, 1903-1904).

Ihrig, Mary Alice. *Emerson's Transcendental Vocabulary: A Concordance.* New York: Garland, 1982.

Irey, Eugene F. *A Concordance to Five Essays of Ralph Waldo Emerson: Nature, The American Scholar, The Divinity School, Self-Reliance, Fate.* New York: Garland, 1981.

Journals

ESQ: A Journal of the American Renaissance. Pullman: Washington State U, 1955- .
Formerly *Emerson Society Quarterly* (1955-68); featured "Current Bibliography" from 1972-77.

Bibliographies

Burkholder, Robert E., and Joel Myerson. *Emerson: An Annotated Secondary Bibliography*. Pittsburgh: U of Pittsburgh P, 1985.
Comprehensive guide to comments and criticism since 1816.

———. "Ralph Waldo Emerson." Myerson, *Transcendentalists* 135-66.
Survey of research.

———. *Ralph Waldo Emerson: An Annotated Bibliography of Criticism, 1980-1991*. Westport: Greenwood, 1994.
Updates Burkholder and Myerson's 1985 guide, above, adding entries for 1,055 items.

Cameron, Kenneth Walter. *The Emerson Tertiary Bibliography with Researcher's Index*. Hartford: Transcendental Books, 1986.

———. *The Emerson Tertiary Bibliography with Researcher's Index: Supplement One*. Hartford: Transcendental Books, 1995.

Myerson, Joel. "Ralph Waldo Emerson." Kopley, *Prospects for the Study of American Literature* 6-20.
The most up-to-date and authoritative survey of research.

———. *Ralph Waldo Emerson: A Descriptive Bibliography*. Pittsburgh: U of Pittsburgh P, 1982.
Exhaustive; gives complete descriptions of Emerson's works.

Putz, Manfred. *Ralph Waldo Emerson: A Bibliography of Twentieth-Century Criticism*. Frankfurt am Main: Verlag Peter Lang, 1986.

Ruppert, James. "Emerson, Ralph Waldo." *Guide to American Poetry Explication* 110-21.

Stovall, Floyd. "Ralph Waldo Emerson." Woodress, *Eight American Authors* 37-83.
Survey of research.

Nathaniel Hawthorne, 1804-1864

Web Sites

"Nathaniel Hawthorne." *American Literature on the Web*. 13 Mar. 2000, http://www.nagasaki-gaigo.ac.jp/ishikawa/amlit/h/hawthorne19ro.htm.
Extensive list of online texts of Hawthorne's works.

"Nathaniel Hawthorne." *Malaspina Great Books Home Page*. 13 Mar. 2000, http://www.mala.bc.ca/~mcneil/haw.htm.

Nathaniel Hawthorne. Ed. Eric Eldred. 20 Jan. 2000. Eldritch Press. 1 Mar. 2000, http://eldred.ne.mediaone.net/nh/.
Considered the best Hawthorne web site. Contains fulltexts of selected Hawthorne major (*Scarlet Letter*, *House of the Seven Gables*, *Blithedale Romance*, *Twice-Told Tales*, *Mosses from an Old Manse*, *Life of Franklin Pierce*) and minor

works; selected texts of documents, letters, journals, and other substantial biographical information (under "Life of Nathaniel Hawthorne [1804-1864]") as well as a "Hawthorne Timeline"; texts of selected early and recent criticism; and a bibliography of works about Hawthorne. Other useful pages included selected quotes from the works; indexes of names and places; FAQs for Hawthorne; and links to other sites.

Nathaniel Hawthorne Homepage. 13 Mar. 2000, http://www.english.uiuc.edu/ kofkeedurfee/.

Nathaniel Hawthorne Society. Ed. Lee Person. 4 Jan. 2000. U of Alabama at Birmingham. 13 Mar. 2000, http://www.uab.edu/english/nhsoc/nhspage.html.

In addition to society news and information, the site gives contents of recent issues of *Nathaniel Hawthorne Review* (1996-).

Biographies and Criticism

Baym, Nina. *The Scarlet Letter: A Reading.* Boston: Twayne, 1986.

Buitenhuis, Peter. *The House of Seven Gables: Severing Family and Colonial Ties.* Boston: Twayne, 1991.

Bunge, Nancy L. *Nathaniel Hawthorne: A Study of the Short Fiction.* New York: Twayne, 1993.

Carton, Evan. *The Marble Faun: Hawthorne's Transformations.* New York: Twayne, 1992.

Grant, William E. "Nathaniel Hawthorne." Kimbel and Grant, *American Short-Story Writers before 1880* (*Dictionary of Literary Biography* 74) 143-63.

Martin, Terence. *Nathaniel Hawthorne.* Rev. ed. Boston: Twayne, 1983.

"Nathaniel Hawthorne." Harris, *Nineteenth-Century Literature Criticism* 2:290-337.
     Excerpts of comments and criticism on Hawthorne from 1837-1964, with an annotated bibliography.

———. Harris, *Nineteenth-Century Literature Criticism* 10:267-319.
     Excerpts of comments and criticism on *The Scarlet Letter* from 1850-1983, with an annotated bibliography.

———. Harris, *Nineteenth-Century Literature Criticism* 17:107-60.
     Excerpts of comments and criticism on *The Blithedale Romance* from 1841-1982, with an annotated bibliography.

———. Harris, *Nineteenth-Century Literature Criticism* 23:166-223.
     Excerpts of comments and criticism on *The Marble Faun* from 1859-1983, with an annotated bibliography.

———. Harris, *Nineteenth-Century Literature Criticism* 39:165-252.
     Excerpts of comments and criticism on *The House of the Seven Gables* from 1851-1991, with an annotated bibliography.

"Nathaniel Hawthorne." Harris and Fitzgerald, *Short Story Criticism* 3:152-97.
     Excerpts of criticism on Hawthorne from 1842-1978, with an annotated bibliography.

Pennell, Melissa McFarland. *Student Companion to Nathaniel Hawthorne*. Westport: Greenwood Press, 1999.

Sterling, Laurie A. "Nathaniel Hawthorne and Sophia Peabody Hawthorne." Schramer and Ross, *American Travel Writers, 1776-1864* (*Dictionary of Literary Biography* 183) 148-61.

Turner, Arlin. "Nathaniel Hawthorne." Myerson, *The American Renaissance in New England* (*Dictionary of Literary Biography* 1) 80-101.

" 'Young Goodman Brown': Nathaniel Hawthorne." Harris and Fitzgerald, *Short Story Criticism* 29:233-313.
  Excerpts of criticism on Hawthorne's short story from 1952-1996, with an annotated bibliography.

Dictionaries, Encyclopedias, and Handbooks

Gale, Robert L. *A Nathaniel Hawthorne Encyclopedia*. New York: Greenwood, 1991.

———. *Plots and Characters in the Fiction and Sketches of Nathaniel Hawthorne*. Hamden: Archon, 1968.

Newman, Lea Bertani Vozar. *A Reader's Guide to the Short Stories of Nathaniel Hawthorne*. Boston: G. K. Hall, 1979.

Indexes and Concordances

Byers, John R., and James Jarratt Owen. *A Concordance to the Five Novels of Nathaniel Hawthorne*. New York: Garland, 1980.
  Based on the standard *Centenary Edition of the Works of Nathaniel Hawthorne* (Columbus: Ohio State UP, 1962-).

Journals

Nathaniel Hawthorne Review. Pittsburgh: Nathaniel Hawthorne Society, 1974- .
  Formerly *Hawthorne Society Newsletter* (1974-85).

Bibliographies

Blair, Walter. "Nathaniel Hawthorne." Woodress, *Eight American Authors* 85-128.
  Survey of research.

Boswell, Jeanetta. *Nathaniel Hawthorne and the Critics: A Checklist of Criticism, 1900-1978*. Metuchen: Scarecrow, 1982.
  Comprehensive coverage with about 2,800 annotated entries.

Clark, C. E. Frazer, Jr. *Nathaniel Hawthorne: A Descriptive Bibliography*. Pittsburgh: U of Pittsburgh P, 1978.
  Comprehensive, with complete descriptions of Hawthorne's works.

Glitsch, Catherine. "Hawthorne, Nathaniel." *American Novel Explication, 1991-1995* 107-11.

Idol, John L., Jr. "Nathaniel Hawthorne." Ljungquist, *Bibliography of American Fiction through 1865* 122-29.

Little, Anne C. "Nathaniel Hawthorne: 'Rappaccini's Daughter'." Evans, Little, and Wiedemann, *Short Fiction* 73-82.
Describes 12 studies.

———. "Nathaniel Hawthorne: 'Young Goodman Brown'." Evans, Little, and Wiedemann, *Short Fiction* 83-91.
Describes 12 studies.

Myerson, Joel. "Nathaniel Hawthorne." Myerson, *Transcendentalists* 328-35.
Survey of research.

Scharnhorst, Gary. *Nathaniel Hawthorne: An Annotated Bibliography of Comment and Criticism before 1900*. Metuchen: Scarecrow, 1988.
Describes 2,586 items on Hawthorne since 1828.

William Gilmore Simms, 1806-1870

Web Sites

"EAF Authors: William Gilmore Simms." *Early American Fiction*. 13 Mar. 2000, http://etext.lib.virginia.edu/eaf/authors/first/wgs.html.
Texts of 19th-century biographies of Simms and a guide to the William Gilmore Simms Collection at the University of Virginia.

"The Life of Francis Marion by William Gilmore Simms." *The On-Line Books Page*. 13 Mar. 2000, http://tom.cs.cmu.edu/cgi-bin/book/lookup?num=843.
Project Gutenberg Release #843 (March 1997) text of Simms's work.

"William Gilmore Simms, 1806-1870. The Yemassee. A Romance of Carolina." *Documenting the American South*. 13 Mar. 2000, http://metalab.unc.edu/docsouth/simms/menu.html.
Fulltext of New York: Harper, 1844 edition of Simms's work with link to a brief biography and list of further readings by Mary Ann Wimsatt from *Encyclopedia of Southern Culture*.

Biographies and Criticism

Butterworth, Keen. "William Gilmore Simms." Myerson, *Antebellum Writers in New York and the South* (*Dictionary of Literary Biography* 3) 306-18.

Kibler, James Everett, Jr. "William Gilmore Simms." Riley, *American Magazine Journalists, 1741-1850* (*Dictionary of Literary Biography* 73) 275-92.

Shillingsburg, Miriam J. "William Gilmore Simms." Rathbun and Grecu, *American Literary Critics and Scholars, 1800-1850* (*Dictionary of Literary Biography* 59) 297-308.

"William Gilmore Simms." Harris, *Nineteenth-Century Literature Criticism* 3:498-515.
Excerpts of comments and criticism on Simms from 1834-1976, with an annotated bibliography.

Wilson, Clyde N. "William Gilmore Simms." Wilson, *American Historians, 1607-1865* (*Dictionary of Literary Biography* 30) 277-85.

Bibliographies

Butterworth, Keen. "William Gilmore Simms." Ljungquist, *Bibliography of American Fiction through 1865* 218-25.

————, and James E. Kibler, Jr. *William Gilmore Simms: A Reference Guide*. Boston: G. K. Hall, 1980.
Describes about 1,200 comments and criticisms since 1825.

Glitsch, Catherine. "Simms, William Gilmore." *American Novel Explication, 1991-1995* 227-28.

Kibler, James E. *The Poetry of William Gilmore Simms: An Introduction and Bibliography*. Spartanburg: Southern Studies Program, U of South Carolina, 1979.
Listings for anthologies, poems, and attributed poems.

Wegelin, Oscar. *A Bibliography of the Separate Writings of William Gilmore Simms of South Carolina, 1806-1870*. 3rd ed. Hattiesburg: Book Farm, 1941.
Complete descriptions of 86 books.

Wimsatt, Mary Ann. "William Gilmore Simms." Bain and Flora, *Fifty Southern Writers before 1900* 395-415.

Henry Wadsworth Longfellow, 1807-1882

Web Sites

"EAF Authors: Henry Wadsworth Longfellow." *Early American Fiction*. 13 Mar. 2000, http://etext.lib.virginia.edu/eaf/authors/first/hwl.html.
Excellent for fulltexts of selected 19th-century biographies of Longfellow.

"Henry Wadworth Longfellow." *American Literature on the Web*. 13 Mar. 2000, http://www.nagasaki-gaigo.ac.jp/ishikawa/amlit/l/longfellow19ro.htm.

Henry Wadsworth Longfellow: Biography. 13 Mar. 2000, http://www.auburn.edu/~vestmon/longfellow_bio.html.

Longfellow in the Atlantic Monthly. 13 Mar. 2000, http://www.theatlantic.com/unbound/poetry/longfel/hwlindex.htm.
Fulltexts of three poems by Longfellow.

Selected Poetry of Henry Wadsworth Longfellow." *Representative Poetry On-line*. 19 Mar. 2000, http://www.library.utoronto.ca/utel/rp/authors/longfel.html.

Biographies and Criticism

Allaback, Steven. "Henry Wadsworth Longfellow." Myerson, *The American Renaissance in New England* (*Dictionary of Literary Biography* 1) 117-24.

Griffith, John. "Henry Wadsworth Longfellow." Rathbun and Grecu, *American Literary Critics and Scholars, 1800-1850* (*Dictionary of Literary Biography* 59) 207-19.

"Henry Wadsworth Longfellow." Harris, *Nineteenth-Century Literature Criticism* 2:468-500.
Excerpts of comments and criticism on Longfellow from 1833-1971, with an annotated bibliography.

———. Harris, *Nineteenth-Century Literature Criticism* 45:95-192.
Excerpts of comments and criticism on Longfellow from 1842-1993, with an annotated bibliography.

Bibliographies

Boswell, Jeanetta. *The Schoolroom Poets: A Bibliography of Bryant, Holmes, Longfellow, Lowell, and Whittier with Selective Annotation*. Metuchen: Scarecrow, 1983.
Describes about 550 works on Longfellow since 1900.

Jason, Philip K. "Henry Wadsworth Longfellow." *Nineteenth Century American Poetry* 58-69.
Describes about 50 studies.

Livingston, Luther S. *A Bibliography of the First Editions in Book Form of the Writings of Henry Wadsworth Longfellow*. 1908. New York: Burt Franklin, 1968.
Complete descriptions but dated.

Ruppert, James. "Longfellow, Henry Wadsworth." *Guide to American Poetry Explication* 132-37.

Rust, Richard Dilworth. "Henry Wadsworth Longfellow." Harbert and Rees, *Fifteen American Authors before 1900* 357-78.
Survey of research.

John Greenleaf Whittier, 1807-1892

Web Sites

[*John Greenleaf Whittier*]. 13 Mar. 2000, http://home.erols.com/kfraser/whittier.html.

John Greenleaf Whittier. 13 Mar. 2000, http://www.haverhill.com/library/hpl2jgw.html.

"The John Greenleaf Whittier Page." *SAC LitWeb*. 13 Mar. 2000, http://www.accd.edu/sac/english/bailey/whittier.htm.

"Selected Poetry of John Greenleaf Whittier." *Representative Poetry On-line*. 19 Mar. 2000, http://www.library.utoronto.ca/utel/rp/authors/whitti.html.

Biographies and Criticism

"John Greenleaf Whittier." Harris, *Nineteenth-Century Literature Criticism* 8:482-534.
  Excerpts of comments and criticism on Whittier from 1831-1984, with an annotated bibliography.

———. Harris, *Nineteenth-Century Literature Criticism* 59:346-93.
  Excerpts of criticism on Whittier from 1902-1993, with an annotated bibliography.

von Frank, Albert J. "John Greenleaf Whittier." Myerson, *The American Renaissance in New England* (*Dictionary of Literary Biography* 1) 191-200.

Journals

Whittier Newsletter. Amesbury and Haverhill: Whittier Clubs and Homes, 1966-88.
  Published an annual "Whittier Bibliography."

Bibliographies

Boswell, Jeanetta. *The Schoolroom Poets: A Bibliography of Bryant, Holmes, Longfellow, Lowell, and Whittier with Selective Annotation*. Metuchen: Scarecrow, 1983.
  Describes about 400 works on Whittier since 1900.

Currier, Thomas F. *A Bibliography of John Greenleaf Whittier*. Cambridge: Harvard UP, 1937.
  Standard (albeit dated) descriptive bibliography of Whittier's works.

Jason, Philip K. "John Greenleaf Whittier." *Nineteenth Century American Poetry* 70-77.
  Describes 35 studies.

Keller, Karl. "John Greenleaf Whittier." Harbert and Rees, *Fifteen American Authors before 1900* 468-500.
  Survey of research.

Ruppert, James. "Whittier, John Greenleaf." *Guide to American Poetry Explication* 234-38.

Von Frank, Albert J. *Whittier: A Comprehensive Bibliography*. New York: Garland, 1976.
  Describes works by and about Whittier.

Harriet Wilson, 1808-c. 1870

Web Sites

"*Our Nig; or, Sketches from the Life of a Free Black*." 13 Mar. 2000, http://xroads.virginia.edu/~HYPER/hwilson/title.htm.
  Fulltext of Boston: Rand and Avery, 1859 edition with page facsimiles from a copy in the "University of Virginia Special Collections Department in Alderman Library" and editor's introduction.

Biographies and Criticism

Gates, Henry Louis, Jr. "Harriet E. Adams Wilson." Harris, *Afro-American Writers before the Harlem Renaissance* (*Dictionary of Literary Biography* 50) 268-71.

Bibliographies

Barstow, Jane Missner. "Harriet Wilson." *One Hundred Years of American Women Writing, 1848-1948* 287-90.
Describes selected editions, biographies, and criticism.

Davis, Cynthia J. "Harriet E. Wilson." Knight, *Nineteenth-Century American Women Writers* [484]-89.

Glitsch, Catherine. "Wilson, Harriet E." *American Novel Explication, 1991-1995* 271-72.

Nelson, Emanuel S. "Harriet E. Wilson." Nelson, *African American Authors, 1745-1945* 483-87.
Survey of research.

Trimbur, John. "Harriet E. Wilson." Ljungquist, *Bibliography of American Fiction through 1865* 282.

Oliver Wendell Holmes, 1809-1894

Web Sites

"Oliver Wendell Holmes." *Poetry Archives*. Ed. Kevin Howard and others. Update unknown. emule.com. 25 Mar. 2000, http://www.emule.com/poetry/works.cgi?author=73.
Page contains links to 28 fulltext poems by Holmes.

"Selected Poetry of Oliver Wendell Holmes." *Representative Poetry On-line*. 19 Mar. 2000, http://www.library.utoronto.ca/utel/rp/authors/holmes.html.
Ten poems in fulltext: "Cacoethes Scribendi," "The Chambered Nautilus," "Contentment," "Daily Trials by a Sensitive Man," "The Deacon's Masterpiece," "The Flâneur," "The Last Leaf," "The Living Temple," "Old Ironsides," "The Two Streams."

Biographies and Criticism

Canacci, James E. "Oliver Wendell Holmes." Ross and Schramer, *American Travel Writers, 1850-1915* (*Dictionary of Literary Biography* 189) 160-65.

"Oliver Wendell Holmes." Harris, *Nineteenth-Century Literature Criticism* 14:96-153.
Excerpts of comments and criticism on Holmes from 1837-1985, with an annotated bibliography.

Menikoff, Barry. "Oliver Wendell Holmes." Myerson, *The American Renaissance in New England* (*Dictionary of Literary Biography* 1) 106-13.

Bibliographies

Boswell, Jeanetta. *The Schoolroom Poets: A Bibliography of Bryant, Holmes, Longfellow, Lowell, and Whittier with Selective Annotation.* Metuchen: Scarecrow, 1983.
Describes about 500 works on Holmes since 1900.

Currier, Thomas Franklin, and Eleanor M. Tilton. *A Bibliography of Oliver Wendell Holmes.* New York: New York UP, 1953.
Complete descriptions of Holmes's works, with listings for about 1,200 works on Holmes.

Jason, Philip K. "Oliver Wendell Holmes." *Nineteenth Century American Poetry* 103-07.
Describes about 25 studies.

Menikoff, Barry. "Oliver Wendell Holmes." Harbert and Rees, *Fifteen American Authors before 1900* 281-305.
Survey of research.

Ruppert, James. "Holmes, Oliver Wendell." *Guide to American Poetry Explication* 126-27.

Abraham Lincoln, 1809-1865

Web Sites

Abraham Lincoln Online. Ed. unknown. 2000. Sponsor unknown. 13 Mar. 2000, http://www.netins.net/showcase/creative/lincoln.html.
Most comprehensive page for Lincoln, containing texts of selected speeches and letters; classified bibliography of works about him (under "Lincoln Bookshelf"); photo tour of historical places associated with him; lists of other printed and online resources; and information on current news and events related to Lincon. Useful "Educational Links" contain FAQs for Lincoln; texts and selections from of his writings and from his autobiographies and biographies; and list of "Writings about Lincoln."

Abraham Lincoln Research Site. Ed. Roger Norton. 2000. Sponsor unknown. 13 Mar. 2000, http://members.aol.com/RVSNorton/Lincoln2.html.
Texts of biographies; quotes from Lincoln's speeches and other works; many contributed essays on his life, death, family, politics, and other topics; and links to other resources.

Books by and about Abraham Lincoln: A Selected Bibliography of Illinois State Library Holdings. Ed. unknown. 9 Feb. 1996. S Library of Illinois. 13 Mar. 2000, http://www.sos.state.il.us/special/lincoln/bib_isl.html.
Useful annotated bibliography.

Biographies and Criticism

"Abraham Lincoln." Harris, *Nineteenth-Century Literature Criticism* 18:206-84.
Excerpts of comments and criticism on Lincoln from 1858-1980, with an annotated bibliography.

Lang, H. Jack. *Lincoln's Fireside Reading: The Books That Made the Man: The Story of the Five Basic Books Which Served as the Foundation for Abraham Lincoln's Remarkable Self-education*. Cleveland: World, 1965.

Dictionaries, Encyclopedias, and Handbooks

Miers, Earl Schenck, ed. *Lincoln Day by Day: A Chronology, 1809-1865*. 1960. Dayton: Morningside, 1991.

Neely, Mark E., Jr. *Abraham Lincoln Encyclopedia*. New York: McGraw-Hill, 1982.

Winn, Ralph B., ed. *Concise Lincoln Dictionary: Thoughts and Statements*. New York: Philosophical Library, 1959.

Indexes and Concordances

Ayres, Alex, ed. *Wit and Wisdom of Abraham Lincoln*. New York: Meridian, 1992.

Boritt, Gabor S., ed. *Of the People, By the People, For the People: And Other Quotations*. New York: Columbia UP, 1996.

Fehrenbacher, Don E., and Virginia Fehrenbacher, eds. *Recollected Words of Abraham Lincoln*. Stanford: Stanford UP, 1996.

Gross, Anthony, ed. *Wit and Wisdom of Abraham Lincoln*. New York: Barnes & Noble, 1994.

Humes, James C. *Wit & Wisdom of Abraham Lincoln: A Treasury of More Than 650 Quotations and Anecdotes*. New York: HarperCollins, 1996.

Bibliographies

Angle, Paul M. *A Shelf of Lincoln Books: A Critical, Selective Bibliography of Lincolniana*. 1946. Westport: Greenwood, 1972.

Matthews, Elizabeth W. *Lincoln as a Lawyer: An Annotated Bibliography*. Carbondale: Southern Illinois UP, 1991.

Edgar Allan Poe, 1809-1849

Web Sites

"Edgar Allan Poe." *Online Literature Library*. 13 Mar. 2000, http://www.literature.org/authors/poe-edgar-allan/.
Fulltexts of selected works from unspecified editions.

Edgar Allan Poe. Ed. Stefan Gmoser. 5 Feb. 2000. Sponsor unknown. 13 Mar. 2000, http://bau2.uibk.ac.at/sg/poe/poe.html.
Question and answer format that links to fulltexts of Poe's works (from unspecified editions) and *Edgar Allan Poe Home*. 13 Mar. 2000, http://www.gothic.net/poe/.

Edgar Allan Poe Society of Baltimore. Ed. unknown. 2 Mar. 2000. Edgar Allan Poe Soc. of Baltimore. 13 Mar. 2000, http://www.eapoe.org/index.htm.
The most authoritative and useful web site for Poe. "Information about Poe" and "The Works" link to the "Canon of Poe's Works" listing Poe's poems, tales,

Bibliographies

Carlson, Eric W. "Edgar Allan Poe." Bain and Flora, *Fifty Southern Writers before 1900* 365-88.

Casale, Ottavio M. "Edgar Allan Poe." Myerson, *Transcendentalists* 362-71.
Survey of research.

Dameron, J. Lasley, and Irby B. Cauthen, Jr. *Edgar Allan Poe: A Bibliography of Criticism, 1827-1967*. Charlottesville: UP of Virginia, 1974.
Evaluative descriptions of 3,000 items.

Heartman, Charles F., and James R. Canny. *A Bibliography of First Printings of the Writings of Edgar Allan Poe: Together with a Record of First and Contemporary Later Printings of His Contributions to Annuals, Anthologies, Periodicals, and Newspapers Issued during His Lifetime: Also Some Spurious Poeana and Fakes*. Rev. ed. Hattiesburg: The Book Farm, 1943.
Complete descriptions, but badly dated.

Hubbell, Jay B. "Edgar Allan Poe." Woodress, *Eight American Authors* 3-36.
Survey of research.

Hyneman, Esther F. *Edgar Allan Poe: An Annotated Bibliography of Books and Articles in English, 1827-1973*. Boston: G. K. Hall, 1974.
Slightly more up-to-date than Dameron and Cauthen, above.

Jason, Philip K. "Edgar Allan Poe." *Nineteenth Century American Poetry* 78-102.
Describes about 130 studies.

Little, Anne C. "Edgar Allan Poe: 'The Cask of Amontillado'." Evans, Little, and Wiedemann, *Short Fiction* 211-17.
Describes 12 studies.

———. "Edgar Allan Poe: 'The Fall of the House of Usher'." Evans, Little, and Wiedemann, *Short Fiction* 218-27.
Describes 12 studies.

Ljungquist, Kent P. "Edgar Allan Poe." Kopley, *Prospects for the Study of American Literature* 39-57.
The most up-to-date survey of research.

———. "Edgar Allan Poe." Ljungquist, *Bibliography of American Fiction through 1865* 200-208.

Ruppert, James. "Poe, Edgar Allan." *Guide to American Poetry Explication* 154-64.

(Sarah) Margaret Fuller, 1810-1850

Web Sites

"Margaret Fuller." *American Literature on the Web*. 13 Mar. 2000, http://www.nagasaki-gaigo.ac.jp/ishikawa/amlit/19ro/f_authors19ro.htm.
Good list of Fuller pages.

Margaret Fuller Homepage. Ed. and update unknown. Eastern Kentucky U. 13 Mar.
    2000, http://www.arh.eku.edu/eng/KOPACZ/Fuller.htm.
    Although frequently cited and linked, web site is badly maintained; operable
contents limited to the text of *Fuller's Woman in the Nineteenth Century*, ed. Arthur
B. Fuller (Boston: Jewett, 1855).

Margaret Fuller Society. Ed. unknown. 26 Mar. 1999. Dept. of English, Texas A & M
    U. 13 Mar. 2000, http://www-english.tamu.edu/fuller/.
    Offers selected bibliography of works by and about Fuller compiled by Larry
J. Reynolds, society news, and a Fuller listserv; most links to other Fuller pages
inoperable.

Biographies and Criticism

Baker, Nora. "Sarah Margaret Fuller, Marchesa D'Ossoli." Riley, *American Maga-
    zine Journalists, 1741-1850* (*Dictionary of Literary Biography* 73) 112-23.

George, Sharon K. "Sarah Margaret Fuller, Marchesa D'Ossoli." Rathbun and Grecu,
    American Literary Critics and Scholars, 1800-1850 (*Dictionary of Literary
    Biography* 59) 142-53.

"Margaret Fuller." Harris, *Nineteenth-Century Literature Criticism* 5:153-74.
    Excerpts of comments and criticism on Fuller from 1844-1980, with an anno-
tated bibliography.

———. Harris, *Nineteenth-Century Literature Criticism* 50:215-61.
    Excerpts of comments and criticism on Fuller from 1845-1994, with an anno-
tated bibliography.

Myerson, Joel. "Sarah Margaret Fuller, Marchesa D'Ossoli." Myerson, *The Ameri-
    can Renaissance in New England* (*Dictionary of Literary Biography* 1) 66-72.

Steele, Jeffrey. "Margaret Fuller." Schramer and Ross, *American Travel Writers,
    1776-1864* (*Dictionary of Literary Biography* 183) 126-38.

Indexes and Concordances

James, Laurie. *The Wit & Wisdom of Margaret Fuller Ossoli*. New York: Golden
    Heritage, 1988.

Bibliographies

Hudspeth, Robert N. "Margaret Fuller." Myerson, *Transcendentalists* 175-88.
    Survey of research.

Myerson, Joel. *Margaret Fuller: A Descriptive Bibliography*. Pittsburgh: U of Pitts-
    burgh P, 1978.
    Complete descriptions of Fuller's works.

———. *Margaret Fuller: An Annotated Secondary Bibliography*. New York: Burt
    Franklin, 1977.
    Critically describes 1,245 criticisms and comments since 1834; updated by
Myerson's "Supplement to Margaret Fuller: An Annotated Secondary Bibliography," *Studies in the American Renaissance* (1984): 331-85.

———. *Margaret Fuller: An Annotated Bibliography of Criticism, 1983-1995*. Westport: Greenwood, 1998.
Updates Myerson, above.

Smith, Susan Belasco. "Margaret Fuller." Knight, *Nineteenth-Century American Women Writers* [150]-59.
Contains brief survey of Fuller's critical reception and selective list of studies.

Harriet (Elizabeth) Beecher Stowe, 1811-1896

Web Sites

"Harriet Beecher Stowe." *Domestic Goddesses*. 14 Mar. 2000, http://www.womenwriters. net/domesticgoddess/stowe1.htm.
Good content, only slightly marred by the overall appearance.

"Harriet Beecher Stowe." *Mothers in Uncle Tom's America*. 14 Mar. 2000, http://xroads.virginia.edu/~MA97/riedy/hbs.html.

Harriet Beecher Stowe. 14 Mar. 2000, http://www.cs.cmu.edu/People/mmbt/women/ StoweHB.html.

Biographies and Criticism

Adams, John R. *Harriet Beecher Stowe*. Updated ed. Boston: Twayne, 1989.

Donovan, Josephine. *Uncle Tom's Cabin: Evil, Affliction, and Redemptive Love*. Boston: Twayne, 1991.

"Harriet Beecher Stowe." Harris, *Nineteenth-Century Literature Criticism* 3:535-69.
Excerpts of comments and criticism on Stowe from 1852-1974, with an annotated bibliography.

"Harriet Beecher Stowe: *Uncle Tom's Cabin; or, Life among the Lowly*." Harris, *Nineteenth-Century Literature Criticism* 50:327-407.
Excerpts of criticism on *Uncle Tom's Cabin* from 1971-1992, with an annotated bibliography.

Hovet, Theodore R. "Harriet Beecher Stowe." Kimbel and Grant, *American Short-Story Writers before 1880 (Dictionary of Literary Biography* 74) 348-55.

Lenz, Millicent. "Harriet Beecher Stowe." Estes, *American Writers for Children before 1900 (Dictionary of Literary Biography* 42) 338-50.

Stern, Madeleine B. "Harriet Beecher Stowe." Myerson, *The American Renaissance in New England (Dictionary of Literary Biography* 1) 168-69.

———. "Harriet Beecher Stowe." Pizer and Harbert, *American Realists and Naturalists (Dictionary of Literary Biography* 12) 425-33.

Wright, Sarah Bird. "Harriet Beecher Stowe." Ross and Schramer, *American Travel Writers, 1850-1915 (Dictionary of Literary Biography* 189) 305-20.

Bibliographies

Ashton, Jean W. *Harriet Beecher Stowe: A Reference Guide*. Boston: G. K. Hall, 1977.
  Describes about 800 comments and criticisms since 1843, with appendixes of fiction and dramas based on *Uncle Tom's Cabin* and Stowe's life.

Barstow, Jane Missner. "Harriet Beecher Stowe." *One Hundred Years of American Women Writing, 1848-1948* 60-68.
  Describes selected editions, biographies, and criticism.

Glitsch, Catherine. "Stowe, Harriet Beecher." *American Novel Explication, 1991-1995* 234-36

Hedrick, Joan D. "Harriet Beecher Stowe." Kopley, *Prospects for the Study of American Literature* 112-32.
  The most up-to-date survey of research.

Hildreth, Margaret Holbrook. *Harriet Beecher Stowe: A Bibliography*. Hamden: Archon, 1976.
  Brief descriptions of Stowe's works, with listings for creative and critical writings about or inspired by her; updated by John D. Haskell, Jr.'s "Addenda to Hildreth: Harriet Beecher Stowe," *PBSA* 72 (1978): 348.

Kirkham, E. Bruce. "Harriet Beecher Stowe." Ljungquist, *Bibliography of American Fiction through 1865* 238-44.

Knight, Denise D. "Harriet Beecher Stowe." Knight, *Nineteenth-Century American Women Writers* [406]-13.
  Includes survey of critical reception.

Martin R(obinson) Delany, 1812-1885

Web Sites

"Martin Robinson Delany." *American Literature on the Web*. 12 Mar. 2000, http://www.nagasaki-gaigo.ac.jp/ishikawa/amlit/d/delany19re.htm.

Biographies and Criticism

Marsh-Lockett, Carol P. "Martin Robinson Delany." Harris, *Afro-American Writers before the Harlem Renaissance* (*Dictionary of Literary Biography* 50) 74-80.

Bibliographies

Davidson, Adenike Marie. "Martin Robinson Delany." Nelson, *African American Authors, 1745-1945* 101-07.
  Survey of research.

Ellison, Curtis W., and E. W. Metcalf, Jr. *William Wells Brown and Martin R. Delany: A Reference Guide*. Boston: G. K. Hall, 1978.
  Describes about 350 works on Delany since 1838.

Etulain, Richard W., and N. Jill Howard. "Marin R. Delany." *Bibliographical Guide to the Study of Western American Literature* 223.

Miller, Ruth, and Peter J. Katopes. "Modern Beginnings: William Wells Brown, Charles Waddell Chesnutt, Martin R. Delany, Paul Laurence Dunbar, Sutton E. Griggs, Frances Ellen Watkins Harper, and Frank J. Webb." Inge, Duke, and Bryer, *Black American Writers* I, 133-60.
Survey of research.

Harriet Jacobs (Linda Brent), 1813-1897

Web Sites

"Harriet Ann Jacobs." *Heath Anthology*. 13 Mar. 2000, http://www.georgetown.edu/bassr/heath/syllabuild/iguide/jacobs.html.

Biographies and Criticism

"Harriet Jacobs." Harris, *Nineteenth-Century Literature Criticism* 67:117-203.
Excerpts of comments and criticism on Jacobs from 1861-1996, with an annotated bibliography.

Bibliographies

Barstow, Jane Missner. "Harriet Ann Jacobs." *One Hundred Years of American Women Writing, 1848-1948* 276-79.
Describes selected editions, biographies, and criticism.

Martin, Terry J. "Harriet A. Jacobs (Linda Brent)." Knight, *Nineteenth-Century American Women Writers* [262]-69.

Novak, Terry. "Harriet Ann Jacobs." Nelson, *African American Authors, 1745-1945* 275-79.
Survey of research.

T(homas) B(angs) Thorpe, 1815-1878

Web Sites

"EAF Authors: Thomas Bangs Thorpe." *Early American Fiction*. 14 Mar. 2000, http://etext.lib.virginia.edu/eaf/authors/second/tbt.html.
Links to fulltexts of selected 19th-century criticism.

Biographies and Criticism

Bain, Robert. "Thomas Bangs Thorpe." Myerson, *Antebellum Writers in New York and the South* (*Dictionary of Literary Biography* 3) 335-39.

Keller, Mark A. "Thomas Bangs Thorpe." Trachtenberg, *American Humorists, 1800-1950* (*Dictionary of Literary Biography* 11) 497-505.

Bibliographies

Current-Garcia, Eugene. "Thomas Bangs Thorpe." Bain and Flora, *Fifty Southern Writers before 1900* 452-63.

Estes, David C. "Thomas Bangs Thorpe." Ljungquist, *Bibliography of American Fiction through 1865* 256-57.

William Wells Brown, 1816?-1884

Web Sites

"Chapter 3: Early Nineteenth Century: William Wells Brown." *PAL: Perspectives in American Literature*. 14 Mar. 2000, http://www.csustan.edu/english/reuben/pal/chap3/brown.html.

"The William Wells Brown Page." *SAC LitWeb*. 3 Mar. 2000, http://www.accd.edu/sac/english/bailey/wwbrown.htm.
This site links to the PAL site above, which is more complete.

Biographies and Criticism

Candela, Gregory L. "William Wells Brown." Harris, *Afro-American Writers before the Harlem Renaissance (Dictionary of Literary Biography* 50) 18-31.

Katopes, Peter J. "William Wells Brown." Myerson, *Antebellum Writers in New York and the South (Dictionary of Literary Biography* 3) 27-29.

Reed, Brian D. "William Wells Brown." Schramer and Ross, *American Travel Writers, 1776-1864 (Dictionary of Literary Biography* 183) 35-42.

"William Wells Brown." Harris, *Nineteenth-Century Literature Criticism* 2:45-56.
Excerpts of comments and criticism on Brown from 1847-1979, with an annotated bibliography.

"William Wells Brown." Trudeau, *Drama Criticism* 1:30-48.
Excerpts of criticism on Brown in general and on *The Escape* from 1858-1974, with an annotated bibliography.

Bibliographies

Ellison, Curtis W., and E. W. Metcalf, Jr. *William Wells Brown and Martin R. Delany: A Reference Guide*. Boston: G. K. Hall, 1978.
Describes about 800 works on Brown since 1844.

Hull, William E. "William Wells Brown." Ljungquist, *Bibliography of American Fiction through 1865* 70-71.

Miller, Ruth, and Peter J. Katopes. "The Polemicists: David Walker, Frederick Douglass, Booker T. Washington, and W. E. B. Du Bois." Inge, Duke, and Bryer, *Black American Writers* I, 133-60.
Survey of research.

Sekora, John. "William Wells Brown." Bain and Flora, *Fifty Southern Writers before 1900* 44-54.

Woodard, Loretta G. "William Wells Brown." Nelson, *African American Authors, 1745-1945* 64-72.
Survey of research.

Frederick Douglass, 1817-1895

Web Sites

"Chapter 3: Early Nineteenth Century: Frederick Douglass." *PAL: Perspectives in American Literature.* 14 Mar. 2000, http://www.csustan.edu/english/reuben/pal/chap3/douglass.html.

"Frederick Douglass." *Heath Anthology.* 13 Mar. 2000, http://www.georgetown.edu/bassr/heath/syllabuild/iguide/douglass.html.

Biographies and Criticism

Chiasson, Lloyd E., and Philip B. Dematteis. "Frederick Douglass." Riley, *American Magazine Journalists, 1850-1900* (*Dictionary of Literary Biography* 79) 139-43.

"Frederick Douglass." Harris, *Nineteenth-Century Literature Criticism* 7:118-48.
Excerpts of comments and criticism on Douglass from 1841-1982, with an annotated bibliography.

———. Harris, *Nineteenth-Century Literature Criticism* 55:84-129.
Excerpts of comments and criticism on Douglass from 1845-1991, with an annotated bibliography.

"Frederick Douglass." Myerson, *The American Renaissance in New England* (*Dictionary of Literary Biography* 1) 46-47.

Hively, Russell K. "Frederick Douglass." Harris, *Afro-American Writers before the Harlem Renaissance* (*Dictionary of Literary Biography* 50) 80-91.

Murphy, Sharon M. "Frederick Douglass." Ashley, *American Newspaper Journalists, 1690-1872* (*Dictionary of Literary Biography* 43) 160-68.

Bibliographies

Chander, Harish. "Frederick Douglass." Nelson, *African American Authors, 1745-1945* 108-20.
Survey of research.

Davis, Mary Kemp. "Frederick Douglass." Bain and Flora, *Fifty Southern Writers before 1900* 190-204.

Moses, Wilson J. "Frederick Douglass." Kopley, *Prospects for the Study of American Literature* 91-111.
The most up-to-date survey of research.

Turner, W. Burghardt. "The Polemicists: David Walker, Frederick Douglass, Booker T. Washington, and W. E. B. Du Bois." Inge, Duke, and Bryer, *Black American Writers* I, 47-132.
Survey of research.

Henry David Thoreau, 1817-1862

Web Sites

Cybersaunter: Henry David Thoreau. 14 Mar. 2000, http://www.umsa.umd.edu:80/ thoreau/.

Henry David Thoreau. 14 Mar. 2000, http://www.mcelhearn.com/thoreau/thoreaulinks. html.

Henry David Thoreau. 14 Mar. 2000, http://member.aol.com/Jonaslit/Thoreau.html.

Henry David Thoreau. 14 Mar. 2000, http://usmh12.usmd.edu/thoreau/history.html.
Biographical site.

Henry David Thoreau (1817-1862). Ed. Dirk H. Kelder. 19 Jan. 1999. Sponsor not known. 14 Mar. 2000, http://www.chebucto.ns.ca/~ac230/thoreau.html.
Best and most useful links include the texts of Thoreau's writings; comprehensive list of other Thoreau links (under "Related Links"); and FAQs about Thoreau; also includes quotations, images (mostly of Walden Pond) and journal entries of both Thoreau and Emerson for 25 May 1853, after the two had walked together.

Thoreau Home Page. Ed. and update unknown. Thoreau Institute and Thoreau Soc. 14 Mar. 2000, http://www.walden.org/.
In addition to organizational information, contains a helpful "Overviews" link with a bibliography; "Life and Writings" link that offers topical introductions for Thoreau's writings, life, contemporaries, times, country (read Thoreau country), scholars who publish on him, and legacies; and related links.

The Writings of Henry D. Thoreau. Eds. Elizabeth Witherell and Lihong Xie. 24 Aug. 1999. Northern Illinois U. 14 Mar. 2000, http://libws66.lib.niu.edu/thoreau/.
Information on standard edition of Thoreau's works as well as featured pages on Thoreau's life, handwriting, manuscripts, and the like, with links to other sites.

Biographies and Criticism

Adams, Stephen. "Henry David Thoreau." Schramer and Ross, *American Travel Writers, 1776-1864* (*Dictionary of Literary Biography* 183) 305-11.

Bickman, Martin. *Walden: Volatile Truths.* New York: Twayne, 1992.

Harding, Walter. "Henry David Thoreau." Myerson, *The American Renaissance in New England* (*Dictionary of Literary Biography* 1) 170-82.

"Henry David Thoreau." Harris, *Nineteenth-Century Literature Criticism* 7:346-414.
Excerpts of comments and criticism on Thoreau from 1848-1983, with an annotated bibliography.

──────. Harris, *Nineteenth-Century Literature Criticism* 21:317-73.
Excerpts of comments and criticism on Thoreau from 1928-1987, with an annotated bibliography.

"Walden; or, Life in the Woods: Henry David Thoreau." Harris, *Nineteenth-Century Literature Criticism* 61:278-390.
Excerpts of comments and criticism on *Walden* from 1854-1993, with an annotated bibliography.

Schneider, Richard J. *Henry David Thoreau*. Boston: Twayne, 1987.

Dictionaries, Encyclopedias, and Handbooks

Borst, Raymond R. *Thoreau Log: A Documentary Life of Henry David Thoreau, 1817-1862*. New York: G. K. Hall, 1992.
Comprehensive day-by-day (and often hour-by-hour) record of Thoreau's life based on primary documents.

Harding, Walter, and Michael Meyer. *New Thoreau Handbook*. New York: New York UP, 1980.

Myerson, Joel. *Cambridge Companion to Henry David Thoreau*. Cambridge: Cambridge UP, 1995.

Indexes and Concordances

Karabatsos, James. *Word-Index to "A Week on the Concord and Merrimack Rivers."* Hartford: Transcendental Books, 1971.

Ogden, Marlene A., and Clifton Keller. *Walden: A Concordance*. New York: Garland, 1985.
Based on *Walden* in vol. 1 of *Writings of Henry D. Thoreau* (Princeton: Princeton UP, 1971).

Stowell, Robert F. *Thoreau Gazeteer*. Princeton: Princeton UP, 1970.

Van Anglen, Kevin P. *Simplify, Simplify and Other Quotations from Henry David Thoreau*. New York: Columbia UP, 1996.

Journals

Concord Saunterer. Concord: Thoreau Lyceum, orig. ser., 1966-1988; new ser., 1993- .

Thoreau Quarterly: A Journal of Literary and Philosophic Studies. Minneapolis: U of Minnesota, 1969-85.

Thoreau Society Bulletin. Concord: Thoreau Society, 1941- .
Features "Additions to the Thoreau Bibliography"; cumulated in Jean C. Advena's *Bibliography of the Thoreau Society Bulletin Bibliographies, 1941-1969* (Troy: Whitston, 1971).

Bibliographies

Borst, Raymond R. *Henry David Thoreau: A Descriptive Bibliography*. Pittsburgh: U of Pittsburgh P, 1982.
Comprehensive guide to Thoreau's works with complete descriptions.

Boswell, Jeanetta, and Sarah Crouch. *Henry David Thoreau and the Critics: A Checklist of Criticism, 1900-1978*. Metuchen: Scarecrow, 1981.
Largely unannotated listing of 2,150 works about Thoreau.

Cameron, Kenneth Walter. *Toward a Thoreau Tertiary Bibliography (1833-1899)*. Hartford: Transcendental Books, 1988.

———. *Thoreau Secondary Bibliography: Supplement Two (1836-1940)*. Hartford: Transcendental Books, 1997.
Identifies 1,513 items.

Leary, Lewis. "Henry David Thoreau." Woodress, *Eight American Authors* 129-71.
Survey of research.

Ljungquist, Kent P. "Additions to Nineteenth-Century Comment on Thoreau," *Thoreau Society Bulletin* 211 (Spring-Summer 1995): 12-13.
Supplements Scharnhorst, below.

Meyer, Michael. "Henry David Thoreau." Myerson, *Transcendentalists* 260-85.
Survey of research.

Ruppert, James. "Thoreau, Henry David." *Guide to American Poetry Explication* 191-93.

Sattelmeyer, Robert. *Thoreau's Reading: A Study in Intellectual History with a Bibliographical Catalogue*. Princeton: Princeton UP, 1988.

Scharnhorst, Gary. *Henry David Thoreau: An Annotated Bibliography of Comment and Criticism before 1900*. New York: Garland, 1992.
Describes 2,087 items since 1840.

Witherell, Elizabeth Hall. "Henry David Thoreau." Kopley, *Prospects for the Study of American Literature* 21-38.
The most up-to-date survey of research.

Julia Ward Howe, 1819-1910

Web Sites

"Julia Ward Howe." *Women's History*. 12 Mar. 2000, http://womenshistory.miningco.com/education/womenshistory/blhowe1.htm.

"Selected Poetry of Julia Ward Howe." *Representative Poetry On-line*. 19 Mar. 2000, http://www.library.utoronto.ca/utel/rp/authors/howejulia.html.

Biographies and Criticism

"Julia Ward Howe." Bryfonski, *Twentieth-Century Literary Criticism* 21:104-15.
Excerpts of comments and criticism on Howe from 1853-1962, with an annotated bibliography.

Logan, Lisa. "Julia Ward Howe." Ross and Schramer, *American Travel Writers, 1850-1915* (*Dictionary of Literary Biography* 189) 166-71.

Stern, Madeleine B. "Julia Ward Howe." Myerson, *The American Renaissance in New England* (*Dictionary of Literary Biography* 1) 114-15.

Bibliographies

Barstow, Jane Missner. "Julia Ward Howe." *One Hundred Years of American Women Writing, 1848-1948* 223-24.
Describes selected editions, biographies, and criticism.

Wurzel, Nancy R. "Julia Ward Howe." Knight, *Nineteenth-Century American Women Writers* [247]-52.

James Russell Lowell, 1819-1891

Web Sites

James Russell Lowell. 14 Mar. 2000, http://www.lib.rochester.edu/camelot/auth/lowell.htm.
Brief biographical sketch only.

Biographies and Criticism

Berthold, Dennis. "James Russell Lowell." Rathbun and Grecu, *American Literary Critics and Scholars, 1850-1880* (*Dictionary of Literary Biography* 64) 148-71.

Hitchcock, Bert. "James Russell Lowell." Riley, *American Magazine Journalists, 1850-1900* (*Dictionary of Literary Biography* 79) 225-31.

"James Russell Lowell." Harris, *Nineteenth-Century Literature Criticism* 2:501-23.
Excerpts of comments and criticism on Lowell from 1841-1977, with an annotated bibliography.

Rapple, Brendan A. "James Russell Lowell." Ross and Schramer, *American Travel Writers, 1850-1915* (*Dictionary of Literary Biography* 189) 247-54.

Wortham, Thomas. "James Russell Lowell." Myerson, *The American Renaissance in New England* (*Dictionary of Literary Biography* 1) 126-31.

———. "James Russell Lowell." Trachtenberg, *American Humorists, 1800-1950* (*Dictionary of Literary Biography* 11) 291-303.

Bibliographies

Boswell, Jeanetta. *Schoolroom Poets: A Bibliography of Bryant, Holmes, Longfellow, Lowell, and Whittier with Selective Annotation.* Metuchen: Scarecrow, 1983.
    Describes about 400 works on Lowell since 1900.

Cooke, George Willis. *Bibliography of James Russell Lowell.* Boston: Houghton Mifflin, 1906.
    Comprehensive guide to Lowell's works.

Jason, Philip K. "James Russell Lowell." *Nineteenth Century American Poetry* 121-27.
    Describes about 30 studies.

Rees, Robert A. "James Russell Lowell." Harbert and Rees, *Fifteen American Authors before 1900* 379-401.
    Survey of research.

Ruppert, James. "Lowell, James Russell." *Guide to American Poetry Explication* 137-38.

Wortham, Thomas. "James Russell Lowell." Myerson, *Transcendentalists* 336-42.
    Survey of research.

Herman Melville, 1819-1891

Web Sites

"Herman Melville." *Academy of American Poets.* 8 Mar. 2000, http://www.poets.org/lit/poet/hmelvfst.htm.

"Herman Melville." *American Authors.* 14 Mar. 2000, http://www.gonzaga.edu/faculty/campbell/enl311/melville.htm.
    Good selected bibliographies and study questions for *Moby-Dick* and "Bartleby, the Scrivener," with links to other sites.

"Herman Melville." *American Literature on the Web.* 14 Mar. 2000, http://www.nagasaki-gaigo.ac.jp/ishikawa/amlit/19ro/f_authors19ro.htm.
    Good list of Melville pages and fulltexts.

"Herman Melville." *Great Books Index.* 14 Mar. 2000, http://books.mirror.org/gb.melville.html.

"Herman Melville." *Knitting Circle.* 18 Mar. 2000, http://www.sbu.ac.uk/stafflag/hermanmelville.html.

Life and Works of Herman Melville. Ed. "jmadden." 17 Aug. 1999. Melville.org and Multiverse. 14 Mar. 2000, http://www.melville.org/.
    Excellent site for texts of works by Melville (under "Herman Melville Online") and descriptions of their publishing histories, with excerpts from early criticism and reviews. Also contains substantial biographical and background information, including a bibliography of Melville biographies and excerpts from journals and letters on Melville and Nathaniel Hawthorne; observations on Melville by friends, family

members, and celebrities; Melville's reflections on his works, life, and other topics; and Melville's obituary notices, with links to other sites for Melville, other authors, and related topics (like whaling).

Biographies and Criticism

" 'Bartleby, the Scrivener': Herman Melville." Harris, *Nineteenth-Century Literature Criticism* 49:375-430.
   Excerpts of criticism on "Bartleby, the Scrivener" from 1962-1987, with an annotated bibliography.

" 'Bartleby, the Scrivener': Herman Melville." Harris and Fitzgerald, *Short Story Criticism* 17:326-92.
   Excerpts of criticism on Melville's short story from 1953-1987, with an annotated bibliography.

Cohen, Hennig. "Herman Melville." Myerson, *Antebellum Writers in New York and the South* (*Dictionary of Literary Biography* 3) 221-45.

"Herman Melville." Harris, *Nineteenth-Century Literature Criticism* 3:324-86.
   Excerpts of comments and criticism on Melville from 1846-1982, with an annotated bibliography.

―――. Harris, *Nineteenth-Century Literature Criticism* 12:247-325.
   Excerpts of comments and criticism on *Moby Dick* from 1850-1981, with an annotated bibliography.

―――. Harris, *Nineteenth-Century Literature Criticism* 29:314-83.
   Excerpts of criticism on *Billy Budd* from 1924-1989, with an annotated bibliography.

"Herman Melville." Harris and Fitzgerald, *Short Story Criticism* 1:292-332.
   Excerpts of criticism on Melville from 1854-1983, with an annotated bibliography.

Lee, A. Robert. "Herman Melville." Kimbel and Grant, *American Short-Story Writers before 1880* (*Dictionary of Literary Biography* 74) 249-67.

McSweeney, Kerry. *Moby-Dick: Ishmael's Mighty Book*. Boston: Twayne, 1986.

Selby, Nick. *Herman Melville: Moby-Dick*. New York: Columbia UP, 1999.

"*Typee*: Herman Melville." Harris, *Nineteenth-Century Literature Criticism* 45:193-257.
   Excerpts of criticism on *Typee* from 1921-1990, with an annotated bibliography.

Dictionaries, Encyclopedias, and Handbooks

Bercaw, Mary K. *Melville's Sources*. Evanston: Northwestern UP, 1987.

Bryant, John. *Companion to Melville Studies*. Westport: Greenwood, 1986.
   Authoritative essays, with extensive bibliographies.

Gale, Robert L. *Herman Melville Encyclopedia*. Westport: Greenwood, 1995.

———. *Plots and Characters in the Fiction and Narrative Poetry of Herman Melville.* Hamden: Archon, 1969.

Gidmark, Jill B. *Melville Sea Dictionary: A Glossed Concordance and Analysis of the Sea Language in Melville's Nautical Novels.* Westport: Greenwood, 1982.

Kier, Kathleen E. *Melville Encyclopedia: The Novels.* 2nd ed. Troy: Whitston, 1994.

Levine, Robert S. *Cambridge Companion to Herman Melville.* New York: Cambridge UP, 1998.

Leyda, Jay. *Melville Log: A Documentary Life of Herman Melville, 1819-1891.* 1951. New York: Gordian, 1969.
Extensive excerpts from Melville's works and other documents.

Miller, James E., Jr. *Reader's Guide to Herman Melville.* New York: Farrar, Straus, Cudahy, 1962.

Indexes and Concordances

Irey, Eugene F. *Concordance to Herman Melville's Moby Dick.* New York: Garland, 1982.
Based on Luther S. Mansfield and Howard P. Vincent's 1952 Hendricks House edition.

Maeno, Shigeru, and Kaneaki Inazumi. *Melville Lexicon.* Tokyo: Kaibunsha, 1984.

Murray, Charles J. *Concordance to Melville's Billy Budd.* Ph.D. dissertation, Oxford: Miami U, 1979.
Keyed to Harrison Hayford and Merton M. Sealts, Jr.'s edition of *Billy Budd, Sailor* (Chicago: U of Chicago P, 1962).

Richardson, William D. *Melville's "Benito Cereno": An Interpretation, with Annotated Text and Concordance.* Durham: Carolina Academic P, 1987.
Indexes text in *The Piazza Tales* (New York: Dix and Edwards, 1856).

Wegener, Larry Edward. *Concordance to Herman Melville's Clarel: A Poem and Pilgrimage in the Holy Land.* Glassboro: Melville Society, 1979.
Based on 1876 (New York: G. P. Putnam) edition; reprinted (Lewiston: Edwin Mellen, 1997).

———. *Concordance to Herman Melville's Mardi, and A Voyage Thither.* New York: Garland, 1991.
Indexes Northwestern-Newberry edition (1970).

———. *A Concordance to Herman Melville's Pierre; Or, The Ambiguities.* New York: Garland, 1985.
References Northwestern-Newberry edition (1971).

———. *A Concordance to Herman Melville's The Confidence-Man, His Masquerade.* New York: Garland, 1987.
Indexes Northwestern-Newberry edition (1984).

Journals

Leviathan: A Journal of Melville Studies. Hempstead: Melville Soc. of America, 1999- .

Melville Society Extracts. Hempstead: Melville Soc. of America, 1969- .

Bibliographies

Boswell, Jeanetta. *Herman Melville and the Critics: A Checklist of Criticism, 1900-1978.* Metuchen: Scarecrow, 1981.

Bryant, John. "Herman Melville." Kopley, *Prospects for the Study of American Literature* 58-90.
The most up-to-date survey of research.

Glitsch, Catherine. "Melville, Herman." *American Novel Explication, 1991-1995* 172-74.

Higgins, Brian. "Herman Melville." Myerson, *Transcendentalists* 348-61.
Survey of research.

———. *Herman Melville: An Annotated Bibliography, Volume I: 1846-1930.* Boston: G. K. Hall, 1979.
Extensive descriptions of about 1,500 works on Melville, with valuable coverage of contemporary responses; supplemented by Gary Scharnhorst's "More Uncollected Melville Reviews and Notices," *Melville Society Extracts* 106 (1996): 12-14,

———. *Herman Melville: A Reference Guide, 1931-1960.* Boston: G. K. Hall, 1987.
Continues Higgin's 1979 guide, above.

Jason, Philip K. "Herman Melville." *Nineteenth Century American Poetry* 128-45.
Describes about 100 studies.

Little, Anne C. "Herman Melville: 'Bartleby the Scrivener'." Evans, Little, and Wiedemann, *Short Fiction* 165-72.
Describes 16 studies.

Marovitz, Sanford E. "Herman Melville." Ljungquist, *Bibliography of American Fiction through 1865* 175-84.

Phelps, Leland R., and Kathleen McCullough. *Herman Melville's Non-English Reputation: A Research Guide.* Boston: G. K. Hall, 1983.

Ruppert, James. "Melville, Herman." *Guide to American Poetry Explication* 139-53.

Wright, Nathalia. "Herman Melville." Woodress, *Eight American Authors* 173-224.
Survey of research.

Susan Bogert Warner
(Elizabeth Wetherell), 1819-1885

Web Sites

"Wide Wide World (1850)." *Celebration of Women Writers*. 14 Mar. 2000, http://www.cs.cmu.edu/afs/cs.cmu.edu/user/mmbt/www/women/warner-susan/wide/wide.html.
Fulltext of Warner's novel (Philadelphia: J. B. Lippincott, 1850).

Biographies and Criticism

MacDonald, Ruth K. "Susan Bogert Warner (Elizabeth Wetherell)." Estes, *American Writers for Children before 1900* (*Dictionary of Literary Biography* 42) 362-67.

Stern, Madeleine B. "Susan (Bogert) Warner." Myerson, *Antebellum Writers in New York and the South* (*Dictionary of Literary Biography* 3) 348-49.

"Susan Warner." Harris, *Nineteenth-Century Literature Criticism* 31:331-56.
Excerpts of comments and criticism on Warner from 1850-1988, with an annotated bibliography.

Bibliographies

Barstow, Jane Missner. "Susan Warner." *One Hundred Years of American Women Writing, 1848-1948* 68-71.
Describes selected editions, biographies, and criticism.

De Jong, Mary G. "Susan Bogert Warner." Ljungquist, *Bibliography of American Fiction through 1865* 272-74.

Glitsch, Catherine. "Warner, Susan Bogert." *American Novel Explication, 1991-1995* 259.

Sanderson, Dorothy Hurlbut. *They Wrote for a Living: A Bibliography of the Works of Susan Bogert Warner and Anna Bartlett Warner*. West Point: Constitution Island Association, 1976.
Lists works by and about the Warners.

Weiss, Jane. "Susan Warner." Knight, *Nineteenth-Century American Women Writers* [452]-62.
Surveys biography, major works and themes, and critical reception, with a selective list of studies.

Walt(er) Whitman, 1819-1892

Web Sites

"Poet at Work: Recovered Notebooks from the Thomas Biggs Harned Walt Whitman Collection." *American Memory*. 14 Mar. 2000, http://lcweb2.loc.gov/wwhome.html.

"Selected Poetry of Walt Whitman." *Representative Poetry On-line.* 19 Mar. 2000, http://www.library.utoronto.ca/utel/rp/authors/whitmn.html.

"Walt Whitman." *Academy of American Poets.* 9 Mar. 2000, http://www.poets.org/lit/poet/wwhitfst.htm.

The Walt Whitman Hypertext Archive. Ed. Charles B. Green. 10 Aug. 1999. Institute for Advanced Technology in the Humanities, U of Virginia. 14 Mar. 2000, http://jefferson.village.Virginia.edu/whitman/.
An excellent and authoritative site offering fulltexts of works by Whitman as well as other information about him, including fulltexts of early reviews of his works. Cumulates bibliographies of works about Whitman compiled by William White through Winter 1986 and by Ed Folsom thereafter (through 1998) in *Walt Whitman Review* and *Walt Whitman Quarterly Review.*

Biographies and Criticism

Miller, James E., Jr. *Leaves of Grass: America's Lyric-Epic of Self and Democracy.* New York: Twayne, 1992.

———. *Walt Whitman.* Updated ed. Boston: Twayne, 1990.

Myerson, Joel. "Walt Whitman." Myerson, *Antebellum Writers in New York and the South* (*Dictionary of Literary Biography* 3) 350-71.

"Walt Whitman." Harris, *Nineteenth-Century Literature Criticism* 4:534-606.
Excerpts of comments and criticism on Whitman from 1855-1975, with an annotated bibliography.

———. Harris, *Nineteenth-Century Literature Criticism* 31:357-448.
Excerpts of comments and criticism on *Leaves of Grass* from 1855-1990, with an annotated bibliography.

"Walt Whitman." Young, *Poetry Criticism* 3:365-424.
Excerpts of comments and criticism on Whitman from 1855-1989, with an annotated bibliography.

Yamauchi, Hisako. "Walt Whitman." Rathbun and Grecu, *American Literary Critics and Scholars, 1850-1880* (*Dictionary of Literary Biography* 64) 274-87.

Dictionaries, Encyclopedias, and Handbooks

Allen, Gay Wilson. *New Walt Whitman Handbook.* New York: New York UP, 1975.

———. *Reader's Guide to Walt Whitman.* New York: Farrar, Straus & Giroux, 1970.

Greenspan, Ezra. *Cambridge Companion to Walt Whitman.* Cambridge: Cambridge UP, 1995.

Krieg, Joann P. *Whitman Chronology.* Iowa City: U of Iowa P, 1998.

Indexes and Concordances

Eby, Edwin H. *Concordance of Walt Whitman's Leaves of Grass and Selected Prose Writings.* Seattle: U of Washington P, 1949-1955.
References Whitman's Camden edition (1876).

Journals

Mickle Street Review. Camden: Walt Whitman Association, 1979-1990.

Walt Whitman Quarterly Review. Iowa City: U of Iowa P, 1955- .
   Formerly *Walt Whitman Newsletter* (1955-1958) and *Walt Whitman Review* (1959-1982); includes "Whitman: A Current Bibliography."

Bibliographies

Asselineau, Roger. "Walt Whitman." Woodress, *Eight American Authors* 225-72.
   Survey of research.

Boswell, Jeanetta. *Walt Whitman and the Critics: A Checklist of Criticism, 1900-1978*. Metuchen: Scarecrow, 1980.

Etulain, Richard W., and N. Jill Howard. "Walt Whitman." *Bibliographical Guide to the Study of Western American Literature* 419-20.

Folsom, Ed. "Walt Whitman." Kopley, *Prospects for the Study of American Literature* 133-54.
   The most up-to-date survey of research.

Giantvalley, Scott. *Walt Whitman, 1838-1939: A Reference Guide*. Boston: G. K. Hall, 1981.
   Extensive descriptions of English-language works about Whitman; addenda in *Walt Whitman Quarterly Review* 4 (1986): 24-40.

Jason, Philip K. "Walt Whitman." *Nineteenth Century American Poetry* 146-88.
   Describes over 200 studies.

Kummings, Donald G. *Walt Whitman, 1940-1975: A Reference Guide*. Boston: G. K. Hall, 1982.
   Describes 3,172 works on Whitman in all languages.

Loving, Jerome. "Walt Whitman." Myerson, *Transcendentalists* 375-83.
   Survey of research.

Myerson, Joel. *Walt Whitman: A Descriptive Bibliography*. Pittsburgh: U of Pittsburgh P, 1993.
   An outstanding example of modern descriptive bibliography; comprehensive guide to Whitman's works, with complete descriptions.

Ruppert, James. "Whitman, Walt." *Guide to American Poetry Explication* 199-234.

Mary Boykin (Miller) Chesnut, 1823-1886

Web Sites

"Mary Boykin Chesnut." *The Glass Ceiling*. 14 Mar. 2000, http://www.theglassceiling.com/biographies/bio10.htm.
   Extremely well-written, although unsigned, biography of Chesnut, including quotations by Chesnut about Jefferson Davis, Robert E. Lee, and Abraham Lincoln, and also a list of books for further reading.

"Mary Boykin Miller Chesnut." *Documenting the American South*. 14 Mar. 2000, http://metalab.unc.edu/docsouth/chesnut/menu.html.
Fulltext of Chesnut's *A Diary from Dixie* (New York: D. Appleton and Company, 1905), with an authoritative biography of Chesnut by Elizabeth Muhlenfeld.

Biographies and Criticism

DeCredico, Mary A. *Mary Boykin Chesnut: A Confederate Woman's Life*. Madison: Madison House, 1996.

Muhlenfeld, Elisabeth. *Mary Boykin Chesnut: A Biography*. Baton Rouge: Louisiana S UP, 1981.

Francis Parkman, 1823-1893

Web Sites

Francis Parkman. 12 Mar. 2000, http://etext.lib.virginia.edu/railton/projects/rissetto/parkman.html.

The Oregon Trail. (by Francis Parkman) 12 Mar. 2000, http://promo.net/cgi-promo/pg/t9.cgi?author=Parkman,%20Francis&whole=yes&ftpsi.

Biographies and Criticism

Connelly, Thomas L. "Francis Parkman, Jr." Myerson, *The American Renaissance in New England* (*Dictionary of Literary Biography* 1) 151-52.

"Francis Parkman." Harris, *Nineteenth-Century Literature Criticism* 12:326-81.
Excerpts of comments and criticism on Parkman from 1849-1983, with an annotated bibliography.

Gray, James L. "Francis Parkman." Schramer and Ross, *American Travel Writers, 1776-1864* (*Dictionary of Literary Biography* 183) 231-42.

Mullin, Michael J. "Francis Parkman." Gale, *Nineteenth-Century American Western Writers* (*Dictionary of Literary Biography* 186) 283-95.

Vitzthum, Richard C. "Francis Parkman." Wilson, *American Historians, 1607-1865* (*Dictionary of Literary Biography* 30) 202-14.

Bibliographies

Etulain, Richard W., and N. Jill Howard. "Francis Parkman." *Bibliographical Guide to the Study of Western American Literature* 332-33.

Henry Timrod, 1828-1867

Web Sites

The Project Gutenberg Etext of the Poems of Henry Timrod. 12 Mar. 2000, http://cdrom1.lima.ohio-state.edu/cd/guten069/etext97/htimr10.txt.

Biographies and Criticism

Green, Claud B. "Henry Timrod." Myerson, *Antebellum Writers in New York and the South* (*Dictionary of Literary Biography* 3) 339-42.

"Henry Timrod." Harris, *Nineteenth-Century Literature Criticism* 25:358-89.
Excerpts of comments and criticism on Timrod from 1860-1981, with an annotated bibliography.

Bibliographies

Boswell, Jeanetta. *Spokesmen for the Minority: A Bibliography of Sidney Lanier, William Vaughan Moody, Frederick Goddard Tuckerman, and Jones Very: With Selective Annotations.* Metuchen: Scarecrow, 1987.
Selective descriptions of about 200 works on Timrod.

DeBellis, Jack. "Henry Timrod." Bain and Flora, *Fifty Southern Writers before 1900* 464-72.

———. *Sidney Lanier, Henry Timrod, and Paul Hamilton Hayne: A Reference Guide.* Boston: G. K. Hall, 1978.
Describes works about Timrod since 1860.

Emily (Elizabeth) Dickinson, 1830-1886

Web Sites

Dickinson Electronic Archives. Ed. Martha Nell Smith. 7 Jan. 1999. Institute for Advanced Technology in the Humanities, U of Virginia. 14 Mar. 2000, http://jefferson.village.virginia.edu/dickinson/.
Offers a tantalizing view of a feminist approach to Dickinson's writing in its "Writings by Susan Dickinson" pages, emphasizing Emily's relationship with her sister-in-law, Susan Huntington Dickinson. Includes the texts of some important letters and documents, such as editor Thomas Higginson's letter to Emily and Emily's obituary, written by Susan, but offers no letters between Emily and Susan. Features fulltext of the conference proceedings of the MLA Emily Dickinson International Society Roundtable and "Works Cited and Bibliography" page. Restricted access to some pages.

"Emily Dickinson." *Academy of American Poets.* 8 Mar. 2000, http://www.poets.org/lit/poet/edickfst.htm.

"Emily Dickinson." *American Women in Literature Database.* 14 Mar. 2000, http://www.kutztown.edu/faculty/reagan/dickinson.html.

"Emily Dickinson." 14 Mar. 2000, http://metalab.unc.edu/cheryb/women/Emily-Dickinson.html.
Essentially a biographical site.

"Emily Dickinson." Ed. Kris Selander. 3 July 3 1999. Sponsor unknown. 14 Mar. 2000, http://userweb.interactive.net/~krisxlee/emily/.
Link-oriented site that accesses a Dickinson biography and fulltexts of approximately 500 poems, letters, pictures, and also an essential link to the Emily Dickinson

International Society. The downside is that there is too much information on the site, and much of it is extremely trivial.

Emily Dickinson International Society. Ed. Gary Lee Stonum. 1 Oct. 1999. Case Western Reserve U. 14 Mar. 2000, http://www.cwru.edu/affil/edis/edisindex. html.
Includes original photographs of family members and distant relatives; impressive international Dickinson Scholars Registry (with names, street and e-mail addresses, and sometimes photographs); informational links to *Emily Dickinson Journal* and *Emily Dickinson Bulletin*; moderated listserv; and links to *Dickinson Electronic Archives* at the University of Virginia, *Paul's Black's Emily Dickinson Page*, and page called *Virtual Emily*.

Emily Dickinson on the Web. 14 Mar. 2000, http://www.amherstcommon.com/ demo/walking_tour/emily.html.
Links to other sites.

"Selected Poetry of Emily Dickinson." *Representative Poetry On-line*. 19 Mar. 2000, http://www.library.utoronto.ca/utel/rp/authors/dickn.html.

Biographies and Criticism

"Emily Dickinson." Harris, *Nineteenth-Century Literature Criticism* 21:1-86.
Excerpts of comments and criticism on Dickinson from 1862-1985, with an annotated bibliography.

"Emily Dickinson." Young, *Poetry Criticism* 1:76-119.
Excerpts of comments and criticism on Dickinson from 1890-1988, with an annotated bibliography.

Miller, Ruth. "Emily Dickinson." Myerson, *The American Renaissance in New England* (*Dictionary of Literary Biography* 1) 34-45.

Dictionaries, Encyclopedias, and Handbooks

Eberwein, Jane Donahue. *Emily Dickinson Encyclopedia*. Westport: Greenwood, 1998.

Grabher, Gudrun, Roland Hagenbuchle, and Cristanne Miller, eds. *Emily Dickinson Handbook*. Amherst: U of Massachusetts P, 1998.
Collection of original essays.

Indexes and Concordances

Bennett, Fordyce R. *A Reference Guide to the Bible in Emily Dickinson's Poetry*. Lanham: Scarecrow, 1997.

Rosenbaum, S. P. *Concordance to the Poems of Emily Dickinson*. Ithaca: Cornell UP, 1964.
Based on Thomas H. Johnson's *Poems of Emily Dickinson* (Cambridge: Harvard UP, 1955).

Journals

Dickinson Studies: Emily Dickinson (1830-86), U.S. Poet. Brentwood: Emily Dickinson International Society, 1968-1993.
    Formerly *Emily Dickinson Bulletin* (1968-1978); irregularly featured "Current Bibliography."

Emily Dickinson Journal. Niwot: Emily Dickinson International Soc., 1992- .

Single Hound: The Poetry and Image of Emily Dickinson. Newmarket: Andrew Leibs, 1989-1990.

Bibliographies

Barstow, Jane Missner. "Emily Dickinson." *One Hundred Years of American Women Writing, 1848-1948* 146-53.
    Describes selected editions, biographies, and criticism.

Boswell, Jeanetta. *Emily Dickinson: A Bibliography of Secondary Sources, with Selective Annotations, 1890 through 1987.* Jefferson: McFarland, 1989.
    Describes about 2,500 English-language items.

Duchac, Joseph. *Poems of Emily Dickinson: An Annotated Guide to Commentary Published in English, 1890-1977.* Boston: G. K. Hall, 1979.
    Continued by Duhac, below.

———. *Poems of Emily Dickinson: An Annotated Guide to Commentary Published in English, 1978-1989.* New York: G. K. Hall, 1993.
    With Duhac's 1979 guide, above, describes about 8,000 commentaries (in approximately 1,400 books and articles).

Ferlazzo, Paul J. "Emily Dickinson." Myerson, *Transcendentalists* 320-27.
    Survey of research.

Loeffelholz, Mary. "Prospects for the Study of Emily Dickinson." *Resources for American Literary Study* 25.1 (1999): [1]-25.
    Up-to-date survey of research.

Myerson, Joel. *Emily Dickinson: A Descriptive Bibliography.* Pittsburgh: U of Pittsburgh P, 1984.
    Complete descriptions of Dickinson's works; updated by Myerson's "Supplement to Emily Dickinson: A Descriptive Bibliography," *Emily Dickinson Journal* 4.2 (1995): 87-127.

Ruppert, James. "Dickinson, Emily." *Guide to American Poetry Explication* 16-108.

Walker, Nancy A. "Emily Dickinson." Knight, *Nineteenth-Century American Women Writers* [99]-110.
    Surveys Dickinson's biography, major works and themes, and critical reception, with a selective list of studies.

Woodress, James. "Emily Dickinson." Harbert and Rees, *Fifteen American Authors before 1900* 185-229.
    Survey of research.

Rebecca Harding (Blaine) Davis, 1831-1910

Web Sites

"Life in the Iron Mills." *The On-Line Books Page*. 14 Mar. 2000, http://tom.cs.cmu.edu/cgi-bin/book/lookup?num=876.
Fulltext of Project Gutenberg Release #876 (April 1997).

"Rebecca Harding Davis." *American Authors*. 14 Mar. 2000, http://www.gonzaga.edu/faculty/campbell/enl311/davis.htm.
Biography of Davis with links to fulltexts of her works.

"Rebecca Harding Davis." *A Guide to Classic Mystery and Detection*. 14 Mar. 2000, http://members.aol.com/MG4273/melville.htm#Davis.

Biographies and Criticism

Buchanan, Laurie, and Laura Ingram. "Rebecca Harding Davis." Kimbel and Grant, *American Short-Story Writers before 1880* (*Dictionary of Literary Biography* 74) 92-96.

"Rebecca Harding (Blaine) Davis." Bryfonski, *Twentieth-Century Literary Criticism* 6:147-57.
Excerpts of comments and criticism on Davis from 1862-1977, with an annotated bibliography.

Rose, Jane Atteridge. *Rebecca Harding Davis*. New York: Twayne, 1993.

Bibliographies

Barstow, Jane Missner. "Rebecca Harding Davis." *One Hundred Years of American Women Writing, 1848-1948* 39-43.
Describes selected editions, biographies, and criticism.

Glitsch, Catherine. "Davis, Rebecca Harding." *American Novel Explication, 1991-1995* 58-59.

Harris, Sharon M. "Rebecca Harding Davis: A Bibliography of Secondary Criticism, 1958-1986." *Bulletin of Bibliography* 45.4 (1988): 233-46.

Long, Lisa A. "Rebecca Harding Davis." Knight, *Nineteenth-Century American Women Writers* [88]-98.
Includes a brief survey of Davis's critical reception and a selective list of studies.

Rose, Jane Atteridge. "Rebecca Harding Davis." Nagel, Nagel, and Baughman, *Bibliography of American Fiction, 1866-1918* 145-46.

Louisa May Alcott, 1832-1888

Web Sites

About the Author [Louisa May Alcott]. 14 Mar. 2000, http://xroads.virginia.edu/~hyper/ALCOTT/ABOUTLA.html.

Alcott Web.com. 14 Mar. 2000, http://www.alcottweb.com/.

"Chapter 5: Late Nineteenth Century: Louisa May Alcott." *PAL: Perspectives in American Literature.* 14 Mar. 2000, http://www.csustan.edu/english/reuben/pal/chap5/lalcott.html.

"Louisa May Alcott." 14 Mar. 2000, http://www.empirezine.com/spotlight/alcott/alcott.htm.

Welcome to Orchard House. Ed. unknown. 1997. Louisa May Alcott Memorial Association. 14 Mar. 2000, http://www.louisamayalcott.org/.
    Web site of the Alcotts' home, a museum owned and operated by the Association.

Biographies and Criticism

Jolliffe, Lee. "Louisa May Alcott." Riley, *American Magazine Journalists, 1850-1900* (*Dictionary of Literary Biography* 79) 12-17.

Keyser, Elizabeth Lennox. *Little Women: A Family Romance.* New York: Twayne, 1999.

"Louisa May Alcott." Harris, *Nineteenth-Century Literature Criticism* 6:11-26.
    Excerpts of comments and criticism on Alcott from 1865-1975, with an annotated bibliography.

———. Harris, *Nineteenth-Century Literature Criticism* 58:1-92.
    Excerpts of criticism on Alcott from 1979-1995, with an annotated bibliography.

"Louisa May Alcott." Harris and Fitzgerald, *Short Story Criticism* 27:1-63.
    Excerpts of criticism on Alcott from 1943-1995, with an annotated bibliography.

MacDonald, Ruth K. "Louisa May Alcott." Estes, *American Writers for Children before 1900* (*Dictionary of Literary Biography* 42) 18-36.

———. *Louisa May Alcott.* Boston: Twayne, 1983.

Stern, Madeleine B. "Louisa May Alcott." Myerson, *The American Renaissance in New England* (*Dictionary of Literary Biography* 1) 4-6.

Bibliographies

Barstow, Jane Missner. "Louisa May Alcott." *One Hundred Years of American Women Writing, 1848-1948* 25-31.
    Describes selected editions, biographies, and criticism.

Eiselein, Gregory. "Louisa May Alcott." Knight, *Nineteenth-Century American Women Writers* [1]-10.
    Includes a brief survey of Alcott's critical reception and a selective list of studies.

Glitsch, Catherine. "Alcott, Louisa May." *American Novel Explication, 1991-1995* 12-13.

Gulliver, Lucile. *Louisa May Alcott: A Bibliography.* Boston: Little, Brown, 1932.
    Brief descriptions of Alcott's works.

Myerson, Joel. "Louisa May Alcott." Nagel, Nagel, and Baughman, *Bibliography of American Fiction 1866-1918* 38-41.

Payne, Alma J. *Louisa May Alcott: A Reference Guide.* Boston: G. K. Hall, 1980. Describes about 400 works on Alcott.

Shealy, Daniel. "Prospects for the Study of Louisa May Alcott." *Resources for American Literary Study* 24.2 (1998): [157]-76. Survey of research.

Samuel Langhorne Clemens (Mark Twain), 1835-1910

Web Sites

Mark Twain. Ed. Jim Zwick. 3 Mar. 2000 About.com, Inc. 14 Mar. 2000, http://marktwain.miningco.com.
Links to both scholarly and popular resources, including association sites, on-line biographies, criticism, texts of Twain's novels and journalism, correspondence, shorter works, 14 historical magazines, historical maps, manuscripts, and online exhibits. Lists online teaching resources. Does not shy away from controversial topics—like *Huckleberry Finn* today—but tries to place Twain into his own historical context.

"Mark Twain (Samuel Clemens)." *Malaspina Great Books Home Page.* 14 Mar. 2000, http://mala.bc.ca/~mcneil/twain.htm.

Mark Twain and His Times. Ed. Stephen Railton. 1998. U of Virginia 14 Mar. 2000, http://etext.lib.virginia.edu/railton/index2.html.
A handsomely illustrated site that combines originality and organization. Separately treats five major works (*Innocents Abroad, Tom Sawyer, Huckleberry Finn, A Connecticut Yankee in King Arthur's Court,* and *Pudd'nhead Wilson*), giving texts, illustrations, and valuable contemporary reviews. "Archive bibliography" (68 items) is somewhat disappointing. Also includes a "memory builder game."

Mark Twain Quest. 14 Mar. 2000, http://www.wms-arl.org/twmision.htm.

Samuel Clemens "Mark Twain." 14 Mar. 2000, http://www.tamu-commerce.edu/coe/shed/espinoza/s/ham-p-657.html.

TwainWeb. Eds. Taylor Roberts and Kevin Bochynski. 24 February 2000. Mark Twain Forum. 14 Mar. 2000, http://web.mit.edu/linguistics/www/forum/.
Highly unusual site that dares to break new ground, thereby rising above the blandness and sameness of other web sites, but lacks participation of major Twain scholars. Among the best features are a survival guide that anticipates questions and gives advice that points students to the standard reference sources (for example, letters as good sources for seeing if Twain ever met someone, or a catalog of his library as a source for discovering if a certain book may have interested Twain) and an admonishment to students not to use the listserv as a substitute for their own research; signed book reviews (edited by graduate student Roberts); and a fully searchable archive that includes controversial topics, like the so-called culture wars and racial or same-sex relationships in the life and work of Twain.

Biographies and Criticism

"*The Adventures of Tom Sawyer*: Mark Twain." Bryfonski, *Twentieth-Century Literary Criticism* 59:158-212.
Excerpts of comments and criticism on Twain's novel from 1876-1988, with an annotated bibliography.

Baetzhold, Howard G. "Samuel Langhorne Clemens (Mark Twain)." Rathbun and Grecu, *American Literary Critics and Scholars, 1850-1880* (*Dictionary of Literary Biography* 64) 34-47.

Covici, Pascal, Jr. "Mark Twain (Samuel Langhorne Clemens)." Trachtenberg, *American Humorists, 1800-1950* (*Dictionary of Literary Biography* 11) 526-55.

Gerber, John C. *Mark Twain*. Boston: Twayne, 1988.

Gribben, Alan. "Samuel Langhorne Clemens (Mark Twain)." Kimbel and Grant, *American Short-Story Writers before 1880* (*Dictionary of Literary Biography* 74) 54-83.

Hill, Hamlin. "Samuel Langhorne Clemens (Mark Twain)." Gale, *Nineteenth-Century American Western Writers* (*Dictionary of Literary Biography* 186) 55-70.

———. "Samuel Langhorne Clemens (Mark Twain)." Pizer and Harbert, *American Realists and Naturalists* (*Dictionary of Literary Biography* 12) 71-94.

Hutchinson, Stuart. *Mark Twain: Tom Sawyer and Huckleberry Finn*. New York: Columbia UP, 1999.

"Mark Twain." Bryfonski, *Twentieth-Century Literary Criticism* 6:452-88.
Excerpts of comments and criticism on Clemens from 1867-1980, with an annotated bibliography.

———. Bryfonski, *Twentieth-Century Literary Criticism* 12:423-55.
Excerpts of comments and criticism on Clemens from 1869-1982, with an annotated bibliography.

———. Bryfonski, *Twentieth-Century Literary Criticism* 19:349-417.
Excerpts of comments and criticism on *Huckleberry Finn* from 1885-1985, with an annotated bibliography.

———. Bryfonski, *Twentieth-Century Literary Criticism* 36:350-420.
Excerpts of comments and criticism on *A Connecticut Yankee in King Arthur's Court* from 1889-1987, with an annotated bibliography.

"Mark Twain: *The Prince and the Pauper*." Bryfonski, *Twentieth-Century Literary Criticism* 48:326-62.
Excerpts of comments and criticism on Twain's work from 1880-1988, with an annotated bibliography.

"Mark Twain." Harris and Fitzgerald, *Short Story Criticism* 6:291-356.
Excerpts of criticism on Twain from 1900-1988, with an annotated bibliography.

Melton, Jeffrey Alan. "Samuel Langhorne Clemens (Mark Twain)." Ross and Schramer, *American Travel Writers, 1850-1915* (*Dictionary of Literary Biography* 189) 65-78.

" 'The Mysterious Stranger': Mark Twain." Harris and Fitzgerald, *Short Story Criticism* 26:317-65.
Excerpts of criticism on Twain's work from 1938-1991, with an annotated bibliography.

Quirk, Tom. *Mark Twain: A Study of the Short Fiction.* New York: Twayne, 1997.

Sloane, David E. E. *Adventures of Huckleberry Finn: American Comic Vision.* Boston: Twayne, 1988.

Stovall, James Glen. "Samuel Langhorne Clemens (Mark Twain)." Ashley, *American Newspaper Journalists, 1873-1900* (*Dictionary of Literary Biography* 23) 31-46.

Dictionaries, Encyclopedias, and Handbooks

Gale, Robert L. *Plots and Characters in the Works of Mark Twain.* Hamden: Archon, 1973.

LeMaster, J. R., James D. Wilson, and Christie Graves Hamric. *Mark Twain Encyclopedia.* New York: Garland, 1993.

Long, E. Hudson, and J. R. LeMaster. *New Mark Twain Handbook.* New York: Garland, 1985.

Ramsay, Robert L., and Frances Guthrie Emberson. *Mark Twain Lexicon.* 1938. New York: Russell and Russell, 1963.

Rasmussen, R. Kent. *Mark Twain A to Z: The Essential Reference to His Life and Writings.* New York: Facts on File, 1995.

Wilson, James D. *Reader's Guide to the Short Stories of Mark Twain.* Boston: G. K. Hall, 1987.

Journals

Mark Twain Circular: Newsletter of the Mark Twain Circle of America. Charleston: The Citadel, 1987- .
Features "Current Books and Articles."

Mark Twain Journal. Charleston: College of Charleston, 1936- .

Twainian. Hannibal: Mark Twain Research Foundation, 1939-1989, 1993- .

Bibliographies

Carpenter, Charles A. "Twain, Mark." *Modern Drama Scholarship and Criticism, 1981-1990* 88.

Clark, Harry Hayden. "Mark Twain." Woodress, *Eight American Authors* 273-320.
Survey of research.

Emerson, Everett. "Samuel Langhorne Clemens [Mark Twain]." Bain and Flora, *Fifty Southern Writers before 1900* 144-64.

Etulain, Richard W., and N. Jill Howard. "Samuel L. Clemens." *Bibliographical Guide to the Study of Western American Literature* 188-98.

Evans, Robert C. "Mark Twain: 'The Celebrated Jumping Frog of Calaveras County'." Evans, Little, and Wiedemann, *Short Fiction* 246-51.
Describes 11 studies.

Glitsch, Catherine. "Twain, Mark." *American Novel Explication, 1991-1995* 245-49.

Gribben, Alan. *Mark Twain's Library: A Reconstruction.* Boston: G. K. Hall, 1980.

———. " Samuel Langhorne Clemens." Nagel, Nagel, and Baughman, *Bibliography of American Fiction, 1866-1918* 121-31.

Johnson, Merle. *A Bibliography of the Works of Mark Twain (Samuel Langhorne Clemens): A List of First Editions in Book Form and of First Printings in Periodicals and Occasional Publications of His Varied Literary Activities.* Rev. ed. New York: Harper, 1935.
Standard guide to works by Twain.

Kinch, J. C. B. *Mark Twain's German Critical Reception, 1875-1986: An Annotated Bibliography.* New York: Greenwood, 1989.

Rodney, Robert M. *Mark Twain International: A Bibliography and Interpretation of His Worldwide Popularity.* Westport: Greenwood, 1982.
Identifies more than 5,300 editions in 73 languages from 55 countries.

Sloane, David E. E., and Michael J. Kiskis. "Mark Twain." Kopley, *Prospects for the Study of American Literature* 155-76.
The most up-to-date survey of research.

Tenney, Thomas Asa. *Mark Twain: A Reference Guide.* Boston: G. K. Hall, 1977.
Describes about 4,900 works on Twain since 1858.

(Francis) Bret(t) Harte, 1836-1902

Web Sites

"The Bret Harte Page." *SAC LitWeb.* 14 Mar. 2000, http://www.accd.edu/Sac/english/bailey/harte.htm.

"Chapter 5: Late Nineteenth Century: Bret Harte." *PAL: Perspectives in American Literature.* 14 Mar. 2000, http://www.csustan.edu/english/reuben/pal/chap5/harte.html.
Includes bibliographies of works by and about Harte.

Francis Bret Harte. 14 Mar. 2000, http://home.erols.com/kfraser/harte.html.

Biographies and Criticism

"Bret Harte." Harris and Fitzgerald, *Short Story Criticism* 8:207-61.
Excerpts of criticism on Harte from 1870-1980, with an annotated bibliography.

Fleming, Charles A. "Bret Harte." Riley, *American Magazine Journalists, 1850-1900* (*Dictionary of Literary Biography*) 181-90.

"(Francis) Bret(t) Harte." Bryfonski, *Twentieth-Century Literary Criticism* 1:339-44. Excerpts of criticism on Harte from 1921-1973.

———. Bryfonski, *Twentieth-Century Literary Criticism* 25:187-227. Excerpts of comments and criticism on Harte from 1868-1980, with an annotated bibliography.

Golemba, Henry L. "Bret Harte." Kimbel and Grant, *American Short-Story Writers before 1880* (*Dictionary of Literary Biography* 74) 134-42.

Scharnhorst, Gary. *Bret Harte*. New York: Twayne, 1992.

———. "Bret Harte." Gale, *Nineteenth-Century American Western Writers* (*Dictionary of Literary Biography* 186) 154-65.

Sloane, David E. E. "Bret Harte." Rathbun and Grecu, *American Literary Critics and Scholars, 1850-1880* (*Dictionary of Literary Biography* 64) 91-99.

Vorpahl, Ben Merchant. "Bret Harte." Pizer and Harbert, *American Realists and Naturalists* (*Dictionary of Literary Biography* 12) 226-39.

Bibliographies

Barnett, Linda Diz. *Bret Harte: A Reference Guide*. Boston: G. K. Hall, 1980. Critical descriptions for more than 2,300 works about Harte since 1865.

Bendixen, Alfred. "Bret Harte." Nagel, Nagel, and Baughman, *Bibliography of American Fiction, 1866-1918* 214-17.

Etulain, Richard W., and N. Jill Howard. "Bret Harte." *Bibliographical Guide to the Study of Western American Literature* 250-52.

Morrow, Patrick D. "Bret Harte." Erisman and Etulain, *Fifty Western Writers* 172-82.

Scharnhorst, Gary. *Bret Harte: A Bibliography*. Lanham: Scarecrow, 1995. Brief descriptions of Harte's published and unpublished writings.

William Dean Howells, 1837-1920

Web Sites

"William Dean Howells." *American Literature on the Web*. 14 Mar. 2000, http://www.nagasaki-gaigo.ac.jp/ishikawa/amlit/h/howells19re.htm.

William Dean Howells. 14 Mar. 2000, http://chuma.cas.usf.edu/~devore/howells.html.

"William Dean Howells Society." *Howells's Contemporaries*. 14 Mar. 2000, http://www.gonzaga.edu/faculty/campbell/howells/.
Excellent site that includes a somewhat disappointing annotated bibliography of criticism about Howells in addition to an unannotated list of recent books and articles about him, archived listserv postings, and five issues of online journal, *Howellsian*;

list of 15 contemporaries of Howells; society announcements, calls for papers, and membership directory. Links to other Howells's sites, commentary by contemporaries, letters from Twain, scholarship and teaching, pictures, and articles by Howells in *Atlantic Monthly*, *Harper's*, and *Harper's New Monthly Magazine*. "No frames" version recommended for speed.

Biographies and Criticism

Baron, Xavier. "William Dean Howells." Ross and Schramer, *American Travel Writers, 1850-1915* (*Dictionary of Literary Biography* 189) 172-92.

Eble, Kenneth Eugene. *William Dean Howells*. Boston: Twayne, 1982.

Ferlazzo, Paul J. "William Dean Howells." Kimbel and Grant, *American Short-Story Writers before 1880* (*Dictionary of Literary Biography* 74) 164-70.

Kaul, A. J. "William Dean Howells." Riley, *American Magazine Journalists, 1850-1900* (*Dictionary of Literary Biography* 79) 196-204.

Martin, Gloria. "William Dean Howells." Rathbun and Grecu, *American Literary Critics and Scholars, 1850-1880* (*Dictionary of Literary Biography* 64) 114-30.

"William Dean Howells." Bryfonski, *Twentieth-Century Literary Criticism* 7:362-401.
Excerpts of comments and criticism on Howells from 1860-1980, with an annotated bibliography.

———. Bryfonski, *Twentieth-Century Literary Criticism* 17:160-93.
Excerpts of comments and criticism on Howells from 1971-1984, with an annotated bibliography.

———. Bryfonski, *Twentieth-Century Literary Criticism* 41:231-87.
Excerpts of comments and criticism on *The Rise of Silas Lapham* from 1985-1989, with an annotated bibliography.

Woodress, James. "William Dean Howells." Pizer and Harbert, *American Realists and Naturalists* (*Dictionary of Literary Biography* 12) 270-97.

Dictionaries, Encyclopedias, and Handbooks

Carrington, George C., Jr., and Ildiko de Papp Carrington. *Plots and Characters in the Fiction of William Dean Howells*. Hamden: Archon, 1976.

Bibliographies

Brenni, Vito J. *William Dean Howells: A Bibliography*. Metuchen: Scarecrow, 1973.
Brief information for Howell's works and descriptions of about 800 works on him.

Carpenter, Charles A. "Howells, William Dean." *Modern Drama Scholarship and Criticism, 1981-1990* 61.

Dock, Julie Bates. "William Dean Howells." Demastes, *American Playwrights, 1880-1945* [183]-95.

Eichelberger, Clayton L. *Published Comment on William Dean Howells through 1920: A Research Bibliography*. Boston: G. K. Hall, 1976.
Covers Howells's contemporary critical reception.

Etulain, Richard W., and N. Jill Howard. "William Dean Howells." *Bibliographical Guide to the Study of Western American Literature* 259.

Gibson, William M., and George Arms. *A Bibliography of William Dean Howells*. New York: New York Public Library, 1948.
Complete descriptions of Howells's works; updated by Ulrich Halfmann's "Addenda to Gibson and Arms: Twenty-Three New Howell Items," *PBSA* 66 (1972): 174-77.

Glitsch, Catherine. "Howells, William Dean." *American Novel Explication, 1991-1995* 124-26.

Nordloh, David J. "William Dean Howells." Nagel, Nagel, and Baughman, *Bibliography of American Fiction, 1866-1918* 232-39.

———. "William Dean Howells." Harbert and Rees, *Fifteen American Authors before 1900* 306-29.
Survey of research.

Henry (Brooks) Adams, 1838-1918

Web Sites

Biography of Henry Adams. 14 Mar. 2000, http://www.anova.org/henry-adams.html.

The Education of Henry Adams. 14 Mar. 2000, http://xroads.virginia.edu/~HYPER/HADAMS/ha_home.html.
Contains text of *The Education of Henry Adams*.

"Henry Adams." *Heath Anthology*. 13 Mar. 2000, http://www.georgetown.edu/bassr/heath/syllabuild/iguide/adamsh.html.

Biographies and Criticism

"*The Education of Henry Adams*: Henry Adams." Bryfonski, *Twentieth-Century Literary Criticism* 52:1-49.
Excerpts of comments and criticism on Adams's work from 1918-1984, with an annotated bibliography.

Harbert, Earl N. "Henry Adams." Pizer and Harbert, *American Realists and Naturalists* (*Dictionary of Literary Biography* 12) 3-14.

"Henry (Brooks) Adams." Bryfonski, *Twentieth-Century Literary Criticism* 4:1-22.
Excerpts of comments and criticism on Adams from 1879-1970, with an annotated bibliography.

Inness, Sherrie A. "Henry Adams." Ross and Schramer, *American Travel Writers, 1850-1915* (*Dictionary of Literary Biography* 189) 3-11.

O'Brien, Michael. "Henry Adams." Wilson, *American Historians, 1866-1912 (Dictionary of Literary Biography* 47) 17-27.

Bibliographies

Harbert, Earl N. "Henry Adams." Harbert and Rees, *Fifteen American Authors before 1900* 3-54.
Survey of research.

———. *Henry Adams: A Reference Guide.* Boston: G. K. Hall, 1978.
Describes about 500 studies of Adams since 1879.

Ambrose (Gwinett) Bierce, 1842-1914?

Web Sites

Ambrose Bierce. 14 Mar. 2000, http://www.bnl.com/shorts/bios/biobierc.html.

Ambrose Bierce. 14 Mar. 2000, http://stommel.tamu.edu/~baum/bierce.html.

Ambrose Bierce. Ed. Alan Gullette. 21 July 1999. Sponsor not known. 14 Mar. 2000, http://www.creative.net/~alang/lit/horror/abierce.sht.
Most useful and up-to-date site for Bierce, with links to texts of Bierce's works, biographies of Bierce, reviews of works by and about him, and other Bierce sites.

Don Swaim's Ambrose Bierce. Ed. Don Swaim. Update not known. Sponsor not known. 14 Mar. 2000, http://pwp.usa.pipeline.com/~donswa/index.html.
Mainly useful for links to text of *Devil's Dictionary* (New York: Boni, 1911) and works by Bierce and links to other Bierce pages.

"Selected Poetry of Ambrose Bierce." *Representative Poetry On-line.* 19 Mar. 2000, http://www.library.utoronto.ca/utel/rp/authors/bierce.html.

Biographies and Criticism

"Ambrose Bierce." Bryfonski, *Twentieth-Century Literary Criticism* 1:83-96.
Excerpts of criticism on Bierce from 1927-1968.

"Ambrose (Gwinett) Bierce." Bryfonski, *Twentieth-Century Literary Criticism* 7:87-98.
Excerpts of criticism on Bierce from 1891-1980, with an annotated bibliography.

———. Bryfonski, *Twentieth-Century Literary Criticism* 44:1-53.
Excerpts of criticism on Bierce from 1911-1990, with an annotated bibliography.

"Ambrose Bierce." Harris and Fitzgerald, *Short Story Criticism* 9:48-101.
Excerpts of criticism on Bierce from 1892-1990, with an annotated bibliography.

Grenander, M. E. "Ambrose Bierce." Gale, *Nineteenth-Century American Western Writers (Dictionary of Literary Biography* 186) 28-39.

———. "Ambrose Bierce." Pizer and Harbert, *American Realists and Naturalists (Dictionary of Literary Biography* 12) 23-36.

———. "Ambrose Bierce." Rathbun and Grecu, *American Literary Critics and Scholars, 1880-1900* (*Dictionary of Literary Biography* 71) 27-37.

Mundt, Whitney R. "Ambrose Bierce." Ashley, *American Newspaper Journalists, 1873-1900* (*Dictionary of Literary Biography* 23) 16-25.

O'Brien, Matthew. "Ambrose Bierce." Trachtenberg, *American Humorists, 1800-1950* (*Dictionary of Literary Biography* 11) 38-48.

Bibliographies

Etulain, Richard W., and N. Jill Howard. "Ambrose Bierce." *Bibliographical Guide to the Study of Western American Literature* 156-58.

Evans, Robert C. "Ambrose Bierce: 'An Occurrence at Owl Creek Bridge'." Evans, Little, and Wiedemann, *Short Fiction* 7-12.
Describes 11 studies.

Fortenberry, George F. "Ambrose Bierce (1842-1914?): A Critical Bibliography of Secondary Comment." *American Literary Realism* 4 (1971): 11-56.

Gaer, Joseph. *Ambrose Gwinett Bierce: Bibliography and Biographical Data.* [s.l.: s.n., 1935].
Brief information for Bierce's works; updated by George Monteiro's "Addenda to Gaer: Bierce in The Anti-Philistine," *PBSA* 66 (1972): 71-72; and "Addenda to Gaer: Reprintings of Bierce's Stories," *PBSA* 68 (1974): 330-31; William L. Andrews's "Some New Ambrose Bierce Fables," *American Literary Realism* 8 (1975): 349-52; and John C. Stubbs's "Ambrose Bierce's Contributions to Cosmopolitan: An Annotated Bibliography," *American Literary Realism* 4 (1971): 57-59.

Grenander, M. E. "Ambrose Bierce." Nagel, Nagel, and Baughman, *Bibliography of American Fiction 1866-1918* 72-75.

Joshi, S. T., and David E. Schultz. *Ambrose Bierce: An Annotated Bibliography of Primary Sources.* Westport: Greenwood, 1999.

Rubens, Philip M., and Robert Jones. "Ambrose Bierce: A Bibliographic Essay and Bibliography." *American Literary Realism* 16 (1983): 73-91.
Review of research.

Sidney Lanier, 1842-1881

Web Sites

About Sidney Lanier. 14 Mar. 2000, http://www.erols.com/kfraser/lanier.htm.

"Sidney Lanier, 1842-1881." *Documenting the American South.* 14 Mar. 2000, http://metalab.unc.edu/docsouth/lanier/menu.html.
Text of Poems of Sidney Lanier (New York: Scribner's, 1884).

Biographies and Criticism

De Bellis, Jack. "Sidney Lanier." Rathbun and Grecu, *American Literary Critics and Scholars, 1850-1880* (*Dictionary of Literary Biography* 64) 136-47.

"Sidney Lanier." Harris, *Nineteenth-Century Literature Criticism* 6:230-82.
Excerpts of comments and criticism on Lanier from 1867-1975, with an annotated bibliography.

Indexes and Concordances

Graham, Philip, and Joseph Jones. *Concordance to the Poems of Sidney Lanier, Including the Poem Outlines and Certain Uncollected Items.* Austin: U of Texas P, 1939.
Based on Mary Day Lanier's *Poems of Sidney Lanier* (New York: Scribner's, 1929), H. W. Lanier's *Poem Outlines* (New York: Scribner's, 1908), and uncollected poems.

Bibliographies

Boswell, Jeanetta. *Spokesmen for the Minority: A Bibliography of Sidney Lanier, William Vaughan Moody, Frederick Goddard Tuckerman, and Jones Very: With Selective Annotations.* Metuchen: Scarecrow, 1987.
Describes 906 works about Lanier, with a list of his works.

DeBellis, Jack. *Sidney Lanier, Henry Timrod, and Paul Hamilton Hayne: A Reference Guide.* Boston: G. K. Hall, 1978.
Describes works about Lanier since 1868.

Gabin, Jane S. "Sidney Lanier." Bain and Flora, *Fifty Southern Writers before 1900* 303-11.

Jason, Philip K. "Sidney Lanier." *Nineteenth Century American Poetry* 232-37.
Describes about 25 studies.

Leo, John R. "Lanier, Sidney." *Guide to American Poetry Explication* 233.

Ruppert, James. "Lanier, Sidney." *Guide to American Poetry Explication* 129-32.

Henry James, (Jr.), 1843-1916

Web Sites

"Chapter 5: Late Nineteenth Century: Henry James." *PAL: Perspectives in American Literature.* 14 Mar. 2000, http://www.csustan.edu/english/reuben/pal/chap5/james.html.
Useful selected bibliography and study questions emphasizing *The Portrait of a Lady*.

Cher Maitre: The Other Sides of Henry James. 14 Mar. 2000, http://www.bookpage.com/themerc/henryjames.html.

"Henry James." *American Literature on the Web.* 14 Mar. 2000, http://www.nagasaki-gaigo.ac.jp/ishikawa/amlit/j/james19re.htm.
Extensive classified list of links to pages for James, particularly texts of his works.

"Henry James." *Knitting Circle.* 18 Mar. 2000, http://www.sbu.ac.uk/stafflag/henryjames.html.

Henry James. 14 Mar. 2000, http://history.hanover.edu/19th/james.htm.

Henry James: Online Works. 14 Mar. 2000, http://www.anova.org/h-james.html.

Henry James Review. Ed. Susan M. Griffin. Update unknown. Project Muse. 14 Mar. 2000, http://calliope.jhu.edu/journals/hjr/.
Contains text of vol. 16- (1995-).

Henry James Scholar's Guide to Web Sites. Ed. Richard D. Hathaway. 1 Mar. 2000. SUNY New Paltz. 14 Mar. 2000, http://www.newpaltz.edu/~hathaway/.
Extensive authoritative classified list of links to James resources. Especially valuable for links to texts of clearly identified standard editions of James's works as well as selected works about James (with emphasis on film reviews). Other features include "JamesF-L," a discussion group; *Henry James Review*; and society and conference information.

"Selected Bibliography: Portrait of a Lady." *American Authors.* 14 Mar. 2000, http://www.gonzaga.edu/faculty/campbell/engl462/portbib.html.
Selected unannotated bibliography of works about *The Portrait of a Lady.*

Biographies and Criticism

Bell, Ian F. A. *Washington Square: Styles of Money.* New York: Twayne, 1993.

"*Daisy Miller*: Henry James." Bryfonski, *Twentieth-Century Literary Criticism* 64:133-96.
Excerpts of comments and criticism on *Daisy Miller* from 1909-1993, with an annotated bibliography.

Daugherty, Sarah B. "Henry James." Rathbun and Grecu, *American Literary Critics and Scholars, 1880-1900* (*Dictionary of Literary Biography* 71) 102-28.

Fogel, Daniel Mark. *Daisy Miller: A Dark Comedy of Manners.* Boston: Twayne, 1990.

Gale, Robert L. "Henry James." Kimbel and Grant, *American Short-Story Writers before 1880* (*Dictionary of Literary Biography* 74) 189-207.

———. "Henry James." Pizer and Harbert, *American Realists and Naturalists* (*Dictionary of Literary Biography* 12) 297-326.

Heller, Terry. *The Turn of the Screw: Bewildered Vision.* Boston: Twayne, 1989.

"Henry James." Bryfonski, *Twentieth-Century Literary Criticism* 2:243-76.
Excerpts of comments and criticism on James from 1903-1975.

———. Bryfonski, *Twentieth-Century Literary Criticism* 24:313-65.
Excerpts of comments and criticism on *The Turn of the Screw* from 1898-1984, with an annotated bibliography.

———. Bryfonski, *Twentieth-Century Literary Criticism* 40:97-172.
Excerpts of comments and criticism on *The Portrait of a Lady* from 1881-1986, with an annotated bibliography.

———. Bryfonski, *Twentieth-Century Literary Criticism* 47:147-209.
Excerpts of comments and criticism on James from 1905-1991, with an annotated bibliography.

"Henry James." Harris and Fitzgerald, *Short Story Criticism* 8:262-353.
Excerpts of criticism on James from 1879-1986, with an annotated bibliography.

"Henry James (Jr.)." Bryfonski, *Twentieth-Century Literary Criticism* 11:314-49.
Excerpts of comments and criticism on James from 1876-1983, with an annotated bibliography.

Hocks, Richard A. *The Ambassadors: Consciousness, Culture, Poetry.* New York: Twayne, 1997.

———. *Henry James: A Study of the Short Fiction.* Boston: Twayne, 1990.

Long, Robert Emmet. *Henry James: The Early Novels.* Boston: Twayne, 1983.

Macnaughton, William R. *Henry James: The Later Novels.* Boston: Twayne, 1987.

Powers, Lyall H. *The Portrait of a Lady: Maiden, Woman, and Heroine.* Boston: Twayne, 1991.

White, Craig. "Henry James." Ross and Schramer, *American Travel Writers, 1850-1915* (*Dictionary of Literary Biography* 189) 199-221.

Dictionaries, Encyclopedias, and Handbooks

Albers, Christina E. *Reader's Guide to the Short Stories of Henry James.* New York: G. K. Hall, 1997.

Fogel, Daniel Mark. *Companion to Henry James Studies.* Westport: Greenwood, 1993.

Freedman, Jonathan. *Cambridge Companion to Henry James.* New York: Cambridge UP, 1998.

Gale, Robert L. *Henry James Encyclopedia.* New York: Greenwood, 1989.

———. *Plots and Characters in the Fiction of Henry James.* Hamden: Archon Books, 1965.

Leeming, Glenda. *Who's Who in Henry James.* New York: Taplinger, 1976.

Putt, S. Gorley. *Henry James: A Reader's Guide.* Ithaca: Cornell UP, 1966.

Indexes and Concordances

Auchincloss, Louis. *Quotations from Henry James.* Charlottesville: UP of Virginia, 1985.

Bender, Claire E., and Todd K. Bender. *Concordance to Henry James's The Turn of the Screw.* New York: Garland, 1988.
References *Aspern Papers, The Turn of the Screw, The Liar, The Two Faces* (New York: Scribner's, 1908).

Bender, Todd K. *Concordance to Henry James's Daisy Miller*. New York: Garland, 1987.
Based on *Daisy Miller, The Patagonian, and Other Tales* (New York: Scribner's, 1909).

———. *Concordance to Henry James's The Awkward Age*. New York: Garland, 1989.
Indexes 1908 (New York: Scribner's) edition.

———, and D. Leon Higdon. *Concordance to Henry James's The Spoils of Poynton*. New York: Garland, 1988.
Based on *Spoils of Poynton, A London Life, The Chaperon* (New York: Scribner's, 1908).

Higdon, David Leon, and Todd K. Bender. *Concordance to Henry James's The American*. New York: Garland, 1985.
Based on 1907 (New York: Scribner's) edition.

Hulpke, Erika. *Concordance to Henry James's What Maisie Knew*. New York: Garland, 1989.
Based on 1908 (New York: Scribner's) edition.

Journals

Henry James Review. Louisville: Henry James Soc., 1979- .

Bibliographies

Bradbury, Nicola. *Annotated Critical Bibliography of Henry James*. New York: St. Martin's, 1987.
Describes 367 major critical studies.

Budd, John. *Henry James: A Bibliography of Criticism, 1975-1981*. Westport: Greenwood, 1983.
Largely superseded by Funston, below.

Carpenter, Charles A. "James, Henry." *Modern Drama Scholarship and Criticism, 1981-1990* 62.

Edel, Leon, and Dan H. Laurence. *Bibliography of Henry James*. 3rd ed. Oxford: Clarendon, 1982.
Complete descriptions of James's works.

Fogel, Daniel Mark. "Henry James." Kopley, *Prospects for the Study of American Literature* 177-200.
The most up-to-date survey of research.

Funston, Judith E. *Henry James: A Reference Guide, 1975-1987*. Boston: G. K. Hall, 1991.
About 2,300 annotated entries; with the guides of McColgan, Scura, and Taylor, below, collectively offer the best critical guidance to works about James.

Gale, Robert L. "Henry James." Woodress, *Eight American Authors* 321-75.
Survey of research.

Glitsch, Catherine. "James, Henry." *American Novel Explication, 1991-1995* 131-36.

Kirby, David. "Henry James." Nagel, Nagel, and Baughman, *Bibliography of American Fiction, 1866-1918* 242-50.

Little, Anne C. "Henry James: 'The Beast in the Jungle'." Evans, Little, and Wiedemann, *Short Fiction* 120-27.
Describes 15 studies.

McColgan, Kristin Pruitt. *Henry James, 1917-1959: A Reference Guide*. Boston: G. K. Hall, 1979.
About 1,700 annotated entries.

Ricks, Beatrice. *Henry James: A Bibliography of Secondary Works*. Metuchen: Scarecrow, 1975.
Offers less critical guidance than Funston, McColgan, Scura, and Taylor (see above and below).

Scura, Dorothy McInnis. *Henry James, 1960-1974: A Reference Guide*. Boston: G. K. Hall, 1979.
About 2,000 annotated entries.

Taylor, Linda J. *Henry James, 1866-1916: A Reference Guide*. Boston: G. K. Hall, 1982.
About 2,600 annotated entries.

Tucker, Jackie. "Henry James." Demastes, *American Playwrights, 1880-1945* [214]-23.

George Washington Cable, 1844-1925

Web Sites

"Cable, George Washington, 1844-1925, Writer and Critic." *Documenting the American South*. 14 Mar. 2000, http://metalab.unc.edu/docsouth/cablecreole/about.html.
Brief biography of Cable excerpted from *Encyclopedia of Southern Culture*, eds. Charles Reagan Wilson and William Ferris (Chapell Hill: U of North Carolina P), with links to fulltexts of *Grandisimmes*, *John March, Southerner*, and *Old Creole Days*.

Cable Reminiscences. 14 Mar. 2000, http://etext.virginia.edu/railton/huckfinn/cablemem.html.

"Chapter 5: Late Nineteenth Century: 1865-1890: George Washington Cable." *PAL: Perspectives in American Literature*. 14 Mar. 2000, http://www.csustan.edu/english/reuben/pal/chap5/cable.html.

George W. Cable: Old Creole Days. Ed. not known. 15 Sept. 1995. Sponsor not known. 14 Mar. 2000, http://english-www.hss.cmu.edu/fiction/old-creole-days.txt.
Text of unidentified edition of Cable's work.

"George Washington Cable." *American Literature on the Web*. 14 Mar. 2000, http://www.nagasaki-gaigo.ac.jp/ishikawa/amlit/c/cable19re.htm.

Biographies and Criticism

Cleman, John. *George Washington Cable Revisited.* New York: Twayne, 1996.

"George Washington Cable." Bryfonski, *Twentieth-Century Literary Criticism* 4:23-38.
Excerpts of comments and criticism on Cable from 1877-1975, with an annotated bibliography.

"George Washington Cable." Harris and Fitzgerald, *Short Story Criticism* 4:46-80.
Excerpts of criticism on Cable from 1881-1982, with an annotated bibliography.

Kreyling, Michael. "George Washington Cable." Pizer and Harbert, *American Realists and Naturalists* (*Dictionary of Literary Biography* 12) 42-50.

Longest, George C. "George Washington Cable." Kimbel and Grant, *American Short-Story Writers before 1880* (*Dictionary of Literary Biography* 74) 30-42.

Bibliographies

Cleman, John Lawrence. "George Washington Cable." Nagel, Nagel, and Baughman, *Bibliography of American Fiction, 1866-1918* 97-99.

Roberson, William H. *George Washington Cable: An Annotated Bibliography.* Metuchen: Scarecrow, 1982.
Describes works by Cable and 891 works about him.

Stephens, Robert O. "George Washington Cable." Bain and Flora, *Fifty Southern Writers before 1900* 75-85.

Sarah Winnemucca (Hopkins) (Thocmetony), 1844-1891

Web Sites

Sarah Winnemucca. 14 Mar. 2000, http://www.twostar.com/oracle/library/hera/spirit8.html.

Sarah Winnemucca. 14 Mar. 2000, http://www.blastbooks.com/RAWDEAL/Winnemucca/fr2winn.htm.

"Sarah Winnemucca Hopkins." *American Women in Literature Database.* 14 Mar. 2000, http://www.kutztown.edu/faculty/reagan/hopkins.html.

Biographies and Criticism

Rosenberg, Ruth. "Sarah Winnemucca." Roemer, *Native American Writers of the United States* (*Dictionary of Literary Biography* 175) 316-21.

Bibliographies

Bryant, Shelle C. Wilson, and Patrick W. Bryant. "Sarah Winnemucca Hopkins." Knight, *Nineteenth-Century American Women Writers* [241]-46.

Joel Chandler Harris, 1848-1908

Web Sites

Biography. 14 Mar. 2000, http://xroads.virginia.edu/~UG97/remus/bio.html. Includes bibliography.

Joel Chandler Harris. 14 Mar. 2000, http:// falcon.jmu.edu/~ramseyil/harris.htm.

Wren's Nest. 14 Mar. 2000, http://www.accessatlanta.com/community/groups/ wrensnest/.

Biographies and Criticism

Bickley, R. Bruce, Jr. "Joel Chandler Harris." Trachtenberg, *American Humorists, 1800-1950* (*Dictionary of Literary Biography* 11) 189-201.

Hale, Doty. "Joel Chandler Harris." Kimbel and Grant, *American Short-Story Writers, 1880-1910* (*Dictionary of Literary Biography* 78) 205-19.

Hoskins, Robert L. "Joel Chandler Harris." Riley, *American Magazine Journalists, 1900-1960* (*Dictionary of Literary Biography* 91) 139-48.

"Joel Chandler Harris." Bryfonski, *Twentieth-Century Literary Criticism* 2:209-16. Excerpts of comments and criticism on Harris from 1897-1968.

Keenan, Hugh T. "Joel Chandler Harris." Estes, *American Writers for Children before 1900* (*Dictionary of Literary Biography* 42) 222-40.

Stonecipher, Harry W. "Joel Chandler Harris." Ashley, *American Newspaper Journalists, 1873-1900* (*Dictionary of Literary Biography* 23) 160-76.

Bibliographies

Bickley, R. Bruce, Jr. "Joel Chandler Harris." Nagel, Nagel, and Baughman, *Bibliography of American Fiction, 1866-1918* 209-12.

———. *Joel Chandler Harris: A Reference Guide.* Boston: G. K. Hall, 1978. Extensive descriptions of 1,442 works on Harris since 1862.

———, and Hugh T. Keenan. *Joel Chandler Harris: An Annotated Bibliography of Criticism, 1977-1996: With Supplement, 1892-1976.* Westport: Greenwood, 1997.
Updates Bickley's 1978 guide, above.

MacKethan, Lucinda H. "Joel Chandler Harris." Bain and Flora, *Fifty Southern Writers before 1900* 227-39.

Sarah Orne Jewett, 1849-1909

Web Sites

"Sarah Orne Jewett." *Domestic Goddesses.*14 Mar. 2000, http://www.womenwriters.net/ domesticgoddess/jewett1.htm.

Sarah Orne Jewett Text Project. Ed. Terry Heller. June 1999. Coe C. 14 Mar. 2000, http://www.public.coe.edu/~theller/soj/sj-index.htm.

Exemplary web-text project presenting texts of short stories published in Jewett's lifetime, poems, letters, and uncollected short stories in a pleasant readable format, with informative cover pages authored by Heller (Hall Professor of English at Coe), illustrations, notes, and complete citations to bibliographic sources. Other important links describe the project and study and research ideas, with bibliographic references, and give a brief biographical sketch of Jewett. External links to research ideas.

Biographies and Criticism

Anderson, David D. "Sarah Orne Jewett." Kimbel and Grant, *American Short-Story Writers before 1880* (*Dictionary of Literary Biography* 74) 208-31.

Nagel, Gwen L. "Sarah Orne Jewett." Pizer and Harbert, *American Realists and Naturalists* (*Dictionary of Literary Biography* 12) 326-37.

"Sarah Orne Jewett." Bryfonski, *Twentieth-Century Literary Criticism* 1:359-69.
Excerpts of criticism on Jewett from 1922-1973.

"(Theodora) Sarah Orne Jewett." Bryfonski, *Twentieth-Century Literary Criticism* 22:114-51.
Excerpts of comments and criticism on Jewett from 1877-1980, with an annotated bibliography.

"(Theodora) Sarah Orne Jewett." Harris and Fitzgerald, *Short Story Criticism* 6:148-83.
Excerpts of criticism on Jewett from 1877-1989, with an annotated bibliography.

Bibliographies

Barstow, Jane Missner. "Sarah Orne Jewett." *One Hundred Years of American Women Writing, 1848-1948* 50-54.
Describes selected editions, biographies, and criticism.

Eppard, Philip B. "Local Colorists: Sarah Orne Jewett, Mary E. Wilkins Freeman, and Mary N. Murfree." Duke, Bryer, and Inge, *American Women Writers* 21-46.

Glitsch, Catherine. "Jewett, Sarah Orne." *American Novel Explication, 1991-1995* 136-37

Nagel, Gwen L. "Sarah Orne Jewett." Nagel, Nagel, and Baughman, *Bibliography of American Fiction, 1866-1918* 250-52.

———, and James Nagel. *Sarah Orne Jewett: A Reference Guide*. Boston: G. K. Hall, 1977.
Helpful descriptions of about 800 works on Jewett since 1873; supplemented by the Nagels' "Sarah Orne Jewett: A Reference Guide: An Update," *American Literary Realism* 17 (1984): 228-63.

Weber, Clara Carter, and Carl J. Weber. *A Bibliography of the Published Writings of Sarah Orne Jewett*. Waterville: Colby College , 1949.
Standard guide to Jewett's works, but with limited bibliographic information.

Westbrook, Perry D. "Sarah Orne Jewett." Knight, *Nineteenth-Century American Women Writers* [270]-80.
Includes a brief survey of Jewett's critical reception and a selective list of studies.

Wiedemann, Barbara. "Sarah Orne Jewett: 'A White Heron'." Evans, Little, and Wiedemann, *Short Fiction* 128-34.
Describes 10 studies.

Lafcadio Hearn, 1850-1904

Web Sites

A Brief Biography of Lafcadio Hearn. 14 Mar. 2000, http://www.imasy.or.jp/~daichi/Lafcadio/life.htm.

Lafcadio Hearn. 3 Mar. 2000, http://www.lafcadiohearn.com/.

The Lafcadio Hearn Page. 14 Mar. 2000, http://www.wolfenet.com/~sfbrown/Koizumi.html.

Webliography of Lafcadio Hearn. 3 Mar. 2000, http://www.toyama-u.ac.jp/tya/library/lhurl.html.
By mixing Japanese and English in the text, the authors have created a site that is most appropriate for students fluent in both languages. English-speaking students may still want to follow the English-language links.

Biographies and Criticism

Célestin, Roger. "Lafcadio Hearn." Ross and Schramer, *American Travel Writers, 1850-1915* (*Dictionary of Literary Biography* 189) 144-59.

Hakutani, Yoshinobu. "Lafcadio Hearn." Kimbel and Grant, *American Short-Story Writers, 1880-1910* (*Dictionary of Literary Biography* 78) 220-25.

Kreyling, Michael. "Lafcadio Hearn." Pizer and Harbert, *American Realists and Naturalists* (*Dictionary of Literary Biography* 12) 245-53.

"(Patricio) Lafcadio (Tessima Carlos) Hearn." Bryfonski, *Twentieth-Century Literary Criticism* 9:117-40.
Excerpts of comments and criticism on Hearn from 1887-1978, with an annotated bibliography.

Bibliographies

Kibbe, Kristi. "Lafcadio Hearn." Nagel, Nagel, and Baughman, *Bibliography of American Fiction, 1866-1918* 217-20.

Perkins, P. D., and Ione Perkins. *Lafcadio Hearn: A Bibliography of His Writings.* Boston: Houghton Mifflin, 1934.
Complete descriptions of works by Hearn, with lists of works about him.

Kate (O'Flaherty) Chopin, 1851-1904

Web Sites

Guide to Internet Resources for Kate Chopin's The Awakening (1899). Ed. Sharon Masturzo. Update unknown. U of Southern Florida. 14 Mar. 2000, http://soleil.acomp.usf.edu/~smasturz/index.html.
An ambitious library school student project mainly useful for an annotated bibliography, biography, and web links.

"Kate Chopin." *Domestic Goddesses.* 14 Mar. 2000, http://www.womenwriters.net/domesticgoddess/chopin1.htm.

"Kate Chopin." *On-line Texts.* 14 Mar. 2000, http://www.inform.umd.edu/EdRes/ReadingRoom/Fiction/Chopin/.

Kate Chopin: A Re-Awakening. Ed. John Shortess. "Copyright 1998." Public Broadcasting Service. 14 Mar. 2000, http://www.pbs.org/katechopin/.
An offshoot of a PBS television program, the strong site provides a wealth of texts and biographical detail. Contains a brief but useful chronology of Chopin's life; an excellent electronic library; very good web links; lists of recent editions of Chopin's work, bibliographies, and criticism; and descriptions of the contents of Chopin collections in historical societies and the Library of Congress (letters, legal documents, manuscripts, newspaper articles, and magazine articles).

Kate Chopin: The Story of an Hour (1894). 14 Mar. 2000, http://www.wsu.edu:8080/~wldciv/world_civ_reader/world_civ_reader_2/chopin.html.

Biographies and Criticism

Davis, Sara deSaussure. "Katherine Chopin." Pizer and Harbert, *American Realists and Naturalists* (*Dictionary of Literary Biography* 12) 59-71.

Dyer, Joyce. *The Awakening: A Novel of Beginnings.* New York: Twayne, 1993.

Inge, Tonette Bond. "Katherine Chopin." Kimbel and Grant, *American Short-Story Writers, 1880-1910* (*Dictionary of Literary Biography* 78) 90-110.

"Kate Chopin." Harris and Fitzgerald, *Short Story Criticism* 8:63-115.
Excerpts of criticism on Chopin from 1894-1986, with an annotated bibliography.

"Kate (O'Flaherty) Chopin." Bryfonski, *Twentieth-Century Literary Criticism* 5:141-61.
Excerpts of comments and criticism on Chopin from 1891-1977, with an annotated bibliography.

———. Bryfonski, *Twentieth-Century Literary Criticism* 14:55-84.
Excerpts of comments and criticism on Chopin from 1894-1982, with an annotated bibliography.

Koloski, Bernard. *Kate Chopin: A Study of the Short Fiction.* New York: Twayne; London: Prentice Hall, 1996.

Skaggs, Peggy. *Kate Chopin.* Boston: Twayne, 1985.

Dictionaries, Encyclopedias, and Handbooks

Bonner, Thomas, Jr. *Kate Chopin Companion: With Chopin's Translations from French Fiction.* New York: Greenwood, 1988.
"Bibliographic Essay," pp. 233-45, reviews research.

Bibliographies

Ballard, Sandra L. "Kate Chopin." Nagel, Nagel, and Baughman, *Bibliography of American Fiction, 1866-1918* 117-18.

———. "Kate Chopin." Bruccoli and Baughman, *Modern Women Writers* 15-19.

Barstow, Jane Missner. "Kate Chopin." *One Hundred Years of American Women Writing, 1848-1948* 34-39.
Describes selected editions, biographies, and criticism.

Boynton, Victoria. "Kate Chopin." Knight, *Nineteenth-Century American Women Writers* [50]-60.
Includes brief survey of Chopin's critical reception, emphasizing *The Awakening*, and selective list of studies.

Glitsch, Catherine. "Chopin, Kate." *American Novel Explication, 1991-1995* 48-49.

Inge, Tonette Bond. "Kate Chopin." Duke, Bryer, and Inge, *American Women Writers* 47-69.
Survey of research.

Rowe, Anne E. "Kate Chopin." Bain and Flora, *Fifty Southern Writers before 1900* 132-43.

Springer, Marlene. *Edith Wharton and Kate Chopin: A Reference Guide.* Boston: G. K. Hall, 1976.
Describes about 240 critical studies since 1890; supplemented by Springer's "Kate Chopin: A Reference Guide Updated," *Resources for American Literary Study* 11 (Autumn 1981): 280-303; and Barbara C. Gannon's "Kate Chopin: A Secondary Bibliography," *American Literary Realism* 17 (Spring 1984): 124-29.

Mary E(leanor) Wilkins Freeman, 1852-1930

Web Sites

"Freeman, Mary Eleanor Wilkins." *Project Gutenberg.* 14 Mar. 2000, http://promo.net/pg/.
Texts of five works by Wilkins based on unknown editions. Use search engine to search for author.

"Mary E. Wilkins Freeman." *American Literature on the Web.* 14 Mar. 2000, http://www.nagasaki-gaigo.ac.jp/ishikawa/amlit/f/freeman19re.htm.
List of links to texts of works by Freeman.

"Mary E. Wilkins Freeman." *Heath Anthology*. 13 Mar. 2000, http://www.georgetown. edu/bassr/heath/syllabuild/iguide/freeman.htm.

Mary Wilkins Freeman. 14 Mar. 2000, http://www.siue.edu/~jvoller/Authors/ f.html#freeman.

"Mary Eleanor Wilkins Freeman." *Howells's Contemporaries*. 14 Mar. 2000, http://www.gonzaga.edu/faculty/campbell/howells/freeman.htm.
Contains texts of works by Freeman and illustrations, but lacks texts or a bibliography of works about the author.

Biographies and Criticism

Boren, Lynda S. "Mary Wilkins Freeman." Pizer and Harbert, *American Realists and Naturalists* (*Dictionary of Literary Biography* 12) 183-91.

"Mary Wilkins Freeman." Bryfonski, *Twentieth-Century Literary Criticism* 9:59-80.
Excerpts of comments and criticism on Freeman from 1887-1980, with an annotated bibliography.

"Mary Wilkins Freeman." Harris and Fitzgerald, *Short Story Criticism* 1:189-203.
Excerpts of criticism on Freeman from 1887-1983, with an annotated bibliography.

Reichardt, Mary R. *Mary Wilkins Freeman: A Study of the Short Fiction*. New York: Twayne, 1997.

Westbrook, Perry D. "Mary E. Wilkins Freeman." Kimbel and Grant, *American Short-Story Writers, 1880-1910* (*Dictionary of Literary Biography* 78) 159-73.

———. *Mary Wilkins Freeman*. Rev. ed. Boston: Twayne, 1988.

Bibliographies

Barstow, Jane Missner. "Mary Wilkins Freeman." *One Hundred Years of American Women Writing, 1848-1948* 43-48.
Describes selected editions, biographies, and criticism.

Eppard, Philip B. "Local Colorists: Sarah Orne Jewett, Mary E. Wilkins Freeman, and Mary N. Murfree." Duke, Bryer, and Inge, *American Women Writers* 21-46. Survey of research.

Glitsch, Catherine. "Freeman, Mary Wilkins." *American Novel Explication, 1991-1995* 90-91.

Marchalonis, Shirley. " Mary E. Wilkins Freeman." Nagel, Nagel, and Baughman, *Bibliography of American Fiction, 1866-1918* 178-80.

Westbrook, Perry D. "Mary Eleanor Wilkins Freeman." Knight, *Nineteenth-Century American Women Writers* [139]-49.
Includes a brief survey of Freeman's critical reception and a selective list of studies.

Harold Frederic, 1856-1898

Web Sites

The Damnation of Theron Ware. 14 Mar. 2000, http://www.ofcn.org/cyber.serv/
resource/bookshelf/dware10/.

"Harold Frederic 1856-1898." *Howells's Contemporaries.* 14 Mar. 2000, http://www.
gonzaga.edu/faculty/campbell/howells/frederic.htm.
Mainly useful for links to selected texts of Frederic's works, including two editions of *Damnation of Theron Ware* (Chicago: Stone and Kimball, 1896; and New
York: D. Appleton, 1896); and an unannotated bibliography of works about Frederic
from 1958 through 1997.

Biographies and Criticism

"Harold Frederic." Harris, *Nineteenth-Century Literature Criticism* 10:181-222.
Excerpts of comments and criticism on Frederic from 1887-1976, with an annotated bibliography.

Thorn, William J., and Philip B. Dematteis. "Harold Frederic." Ashley, *American
Newspaper Journalists, 1873-1900* (*Dictionary of Literary Biography* 23)
125-31.

Woodward, Robert H. "Harold Frederic." Pizer and Harbert, *American Realists and
Naturalists* (*Dictionary of Literary Biography* 12) 173-83.

Bibliographies

Garner, Stanton. "Harold Frederic." Nagel, Nagel, and Baughman, *Bibliography of
American Fiction, 1866-1918* 175-77.

Glitsch, Catherine. "Frederic, Harold." *American Novel Explication, 1991-1995* 90.

O'Donnell, Thomas F., Stanton Garner, and Robert H. Woodward. *Bibliography of
Writings by and about Harold Frederic.* Boston: G. K. Hall, 1975.
Lists Frederic's works and about 1,000 works on him.

Booker T(aliaferro) Washington, 1856-1915

Web Sites

Booker T. Washington. 14 Mar. 2000, http://minerva.acc.virginia.edu/~history/
courses/fall.97/hius323/btw.html.

Booker T. Washington. 14 Mar. 2000, http://ushistory.net/washington.html.

Booker T. Washington. 14 Mar. 2000, http://lcweb2.loc.gov/ammem/aap/bookert.
html.

Booker T. Washington. 14 Mar. 2000, http://library.advanced.org/10320/Washngtn.
htm.

Booker T. Washington. 14 Mar. 2000, http://www.gatewayva.com/pages/bhistory/washingt.htm.

"Booker T. Washington, 1856-1915, Educator." *Documenting the American South.* 14 Mar. 2000, http://metalab.unc.edu/docsouth/washington/about.html.
Includes a signed article on Washington by Louis R. Harlan, links to texts of three works by Washington (*Up from Slavery*, *An Autobiography*, and *My Larger Education*). Better organization of the links at the bottom of the page would reduce unnecessary clicking.

Booker Taliaferro Washington. Ed. Julie Minter. Update unknown. West Virginia Archives and History. 3 Mar. 2000, http://www.wvlc.wvnet.edu/history/wvhsl331.html.
Good starting point for biographical information on Washington, but not a scholarly site. Offers only the most general links, and the "Works Cited" section needs updating in that it fails to cite major recent works such as the five-volume *Reference Library of Black America* (Detroit: Gale, 1994) and Louis Harlan's biography *Booker T. Washington: The Wizard of Tuskegee* (New York: Oxford UP, 1983).

Biographies and Criticism

"Booker T(aliaferro) Washington." Bryfonski, *Twentieth-Century Literary Criticism* 10:512-45.
Excerpts of comments and criticism on Washington from 1895-1981, with an annotated bibliography.

Bibliographies

Olson, Ted. "Booker T. Washington." Nelson, *African American Authors, 1745-1945* 440-47.
Survey of research.

O'Neale, Sondra. "Booker T. Washington." Bain and Flora, *Fifty Southern Writers before 1900* 502-13.

Turner, W. Burghardt. "The Polemicists: David Walker, Frederick Douglass, Booker T. Washington, and W. E. B. Du Bois." Inge, Duke, and Bryer, *Black American Writers* I, 47-132.
Survey of research.

Wovoka, c. 1856-1932

Web Sites

"Wovoka (Jack Wilson)." 12 Mar. 2000, http://www.pbs.org/weta/thewest/wpages/wpgs400/w4wovoka.htm.

"Wovoka's Message: The Promise of the Ghost Dance." 12 Mar. 2000, http://www.pbs.org/weta/thewest/wpages/wpgs680/gdmessg.htm.

Charles W(addell) Chesnutt, 1858-1932

Web Sites

"The Charles Chestnutt Page." *SAC LitWeb*. 14 Mar. 2000, http://www.accd.edu/Sac/english/bailey/chesnutt.htm.

"Charles W. Chesnutt (1858-1932)." *Howells's Contemporaries*. 3 Mar. 2000, http://www.gonzaga.edu/faculty/campbell/howells/chesnutt.htm.
Includes a very good selected bibliography with links to the Charles W. Chesnutt Association and to texts of works by Chesnutt and the *Encylopedia of Southern Culture*'s article on Chesnutt from *Documenting the American South*. Editor Donna Campbell has also managed to find a site called English Server Fiction Collection for three of Chesnutt's short stories.

David's Neckliss. 14 Mar. 2000, http://english-www.hss.cmu.edu/fiction/chesnutt/daves-neckliss.txt.

March of Progress by Charles W. Chesnutt. 14 Mar. 2000, http://www.toptags.com/aama/books/book1.htm.

Biographies and Criticism

Andrews, William L. "Charles Waddell Chesnutt." Harris, *Afro-American Writers before the Harlem Renaissance* (*Dictionary of Literary Biography* 50) 36-51.

"Charles Waddell Chesnutt." Bryfonski, *Twentieth-Century Literary Criticism* 5:129-40.
Excerpts of comments and criticism on Chesnutt from 1899-1974, with an annotated bibliography.

———. Bryfonski, *Twentieth-Century Literary Criticism* 39:68-111.
Excerpts of comments and criticism on Chesnutt from 1901-1988, with an annotated bibliography.

"Charles Waddell Chesnutt." Harris and Fitzgerald, *Short Story Criticism* 7:1-46.
Excerpts of criticism on Chesnutt from 1900-1987, with an annotated bibliography.

Render, Sylvia Lyons. "Charles Waddell Chesnutt." Kimbel and Grant, *American Short-Story Writers, 1880-1910* (*Dictionary of Literary Biography* 78) 68-82.

Scruggs, Charles W. "Charles Waddell Chesnutt." Pizer and Harbert, *American Realists and Naturalists* (*Dictionary of Literary Biography* 12) 51-59.

Wonham, Henry B. *Charles W. Chesnutt: A Study of the Short Fiction*. New York: Twayne, 1998.

Bibliographies

Andrews, William L. "Charles W. Chesnutt." Bain and Flora, *Fifty Southern Writers before 1900* 107-17.

Ellison, Curtis W., and E. W. Metcalf, Jr. *Charles W. Chesnutt: A Reference Guide*. Boston: G. K. Hall, 1977.
Describes about 700 works on Chesnutt since 1887.

Glitsch, Catherine. "Chesnutt, Charles Waddell." *American Novel Explication, 1991-1995* 47-48.

Guzzio, Tracie Church. "Charles Waddell Chesnutt." Nelson, *African American Authors, 1745-1945* 73-79.
Survey of research.

Kinnamon, Keneth. "Charles W. Chesnutt." Nagel, Nagel, and Baughman, *Bibliography of American Fiction, 1866-1918* 113-15.

———. "Charles Waddell Chesnutt." Bruccoli and Baughman, *Modern African American Writers* 12-18.

Miller, Ruth, and Peter J. Katopes. "The Polemicists: David Walker, Frederick Douglass, Booker T. Washington, and W. E. B. Du Bois." Inge, Duke, and Bryer, *Black American Writers* I, 133-60.

Charles Alexander Eastman (Ohiyesa), 1858-1939

Web Sites

"Chapter 6: Charles Alexander Eastman." *PAL: Perspectives in American Literature.* 14 Mar. 2000, http://www.csustan.edu/english/reuben/pal/chap6/eastman.html.

"Charles Alexander Eastman." *Heath Anthology.* 13 Mar. 2000, http://www.hmco.com/college/english/heath/syllabuild/iguide/eastman.html.

The Soul of an Indian. 3 Mar. 2000, http://magna.com.au/~prfbrown/eastman7.html. An overemphasis on graphics detracts from this site.

Biographies and Criticism

Copeland, Marion W. *Charles Alexander Eastman (Ohiyesa).* Boise: Boise State U, 1978.

"Charles Alexander Eastman." Bryfonski, *Twentieth-Century Literary Criticism* 55:160-89.
Excerpts of comments and criticism on Eastman from 1930-1992, with an annotated bibliography.

Wilson, Raymond. "Charles A. Eastman (Ohiyesa)." Roemer, *Native American Writers of the United States* (*Dictionary of Literary Biography* 175) 75-83.

———. *Ohiyesa: Charles Eastman, Santee Sioux.* Urbana: U of Illinois P, 1983.

(Hannibal) Hamlin Garland,
1860-1940

Web Sites

"Hamlin Garland." *American Authors*. 14 Mar. 2000, http://www.gonzaga.edu/ faculty/campbell/engl462/garland.htm.

Hamlin Garland. Ed. Keith Newlin. Update unknown. U of North Carolina at Wilmington. 14 Mar. 2000, http://www.uncwil.edu/people/newlink/garland/.
    More scholarly of two Garland sites maintained by Newlin emphasizing biography, especially correspondence, with annotated lists of critical studies under "Selected Letters" and "Bibliography." No fulltexts of Garland's works, aside from his famous essay on French Impressionism and a sample page from a manuscript and its transcription (under "Editing Hamlin Garland") .

Hamlin Garland Project. 14 Mar. 2000, http://www.usc.edu/isd/locations/doheny/ref/ ERC/pro5.html.

Hamlin Garland Society. Ed. Keith Newlin. 27 July 1999. U of North Carolina at Wilmington. 14 Mar. 2000, http://www.uncwil.edu/garland/.
    Good site for undergraduates studying Garland by the leading expert on Hamlin bibliography and biography. Special features include an excellent gallery of nicely scanned photographs of Garland, his wife, and home. Link to "Resources" contains bibliographies, most notably Paul Reuben's Garland guide and bibliography in *PAL: Perspectives in American Literature*. Also links to selected texts of Garland's works and archival collections. Membership link includes an online membership application and listserv subscription form. "Biography" and "Newsletter" links still under development.

Biographies and Criticism

"Hamlin Garland." Bryfonski, *Twentieth-Century Literary Criticism* 3:189-205.
    Excerpts of comments and criticism on Garland from 1891-1976, with an annotated bibliography.

"Hamlin Garland." Harris and Fitzgerald, *Short Story Criticism* 18:140-95.
    Excerpts of criticism on Garland from 1891-1982, with an annotated bibliography.

McCullough, Joseph B. "Hamlin Garland." Gale, *Nineteenth-Century American Western Writers* (*Dictionary of Literary Biography* 186) 124-36.

———. "Hamlin Garland." Kimbel and Grant, *American Short-Story Writers, 1880-1910* (*Dictionary of Literary Biography* 78) 179-94.

Silet, Charles L. P. "Hamlin Garland." Rathbun and Grecu, *American Literary Critics and Scholars, 1880-1900* (*Dictionary of Literary Biography* 71) 71-81.

Stronks, James B. "Hamlin Garland." Pizer and Harbert, *American Realists and Naturalists* (*Dictionary of Literary Biography* 12) 203-12.

Bibliographies

Bryer, Jackson R., and Eugene Harding. *Hamlin Garland and the Critics: An Annotated Bibliography*. Troy: Whitston, 1973.
Describes more than 1,200 reviews and critical studies; updated by Charles L. P. Silet and Robert E. Welch's "Further Additions to Hamlin Garland and the Critics," *American Literary Realism* 9 (1976): 268-75; and "Corrections to Hamlin Garland and the Critics," *PBSA* 72 (1978): 106-09.

Carpenter, Charles A. "Garland, Hamlin." *Modern Drama Scholarship and Criticism, 1981-1990* 56.

Etulain, Richard W., and N. Jill Howard. "Hamlin Garland." *Bibliographical Guide to the Study of Western American Literature* 235-38.

McCullough, Joseph. "Hamlin Garland." Erisman and Etulain, *Fifty Western Writers* 131-41.

Nagel, James. "Hamlin Garland." Nagel, Nagel, and Baughman, *Bibliography of American Fiction, 1866-1918* 185-87.

Newlin, Keith. *Hamlin Garland: A Bibliography, with a Checklist of Unpublished Letters*. Troy: Whitston, 1998.

———. "Hamlin Garland: A Bibliography (1896-1940)." *Bulletin of Bibliography* 54.1 (1997): 11-20.

Silet, Charles L. P. *Henry Blake Completeer and Hamlin Garland: A Reference Guide*. Boston: G. K. Hall, 1977.
Describes works about Garland since 1891.

Charlotte Perkins Gilman, 1860-1935

Web Sites

Charlotte Perkins Gilman. 14 Mar. 2000, http://us.history.wisc.edu/hist102/bios/19.html.

Charlotte Perkins Gilman Bibliography. 14 Mar. 2000, http://hubcap.clemson.edu/~sparks/gilmbib.html.

The Yellow Wallpaper. 14 Mar. 2000, http://www.media.mit.edu/people/davet/yp/wallpaper.html.

The Yellow Wall-Paper Site. Ed. unknown. 3 Sept. 1996. U of Texas. 14 Mar. 2000, http://www.cwrl.utexas.edu/~daniel/amlit/wallpaper/wallpaper.html.
Texts of "The Yellow Wall-Paper" and Gilman's explanation of why she wrote it, with an archive of student discussions of the text.

Biographies and Criticism

"Charlotte Perkins Gilman." Bryfonski, *Twentieth-Century Literary Criticism* 9:95-116.
Excerpts of comments and criticism on Gilman from 1895-1981, with an annotated bibliography.

———. Bryfonski, *Twentieth-Century Literary Criticism* 37:173-218.
Excerpts of comments and criticism on Gilman from 1899-1988, with an annotated bibliography.

"Charlotte Perkins Gilman." Harris and Fitzgerald, *Short Story Criticism* 13:116-76.
Excerpts of criticism on Gilman from 1920-1991, with an annotated bibliography.

Knight, Denise D. *Charlotte Perkins Gilman: A Study of the Short Fiction.* New York: Twayne, 1997.

Scharnhorst, Gary. *Charlotte Perkins Gilman.* Boston: Twayne, 1985.

Bibliographies

Barstow, Jane Missner. "Charlotte Perkins Gilman." *One Hundred Years of American Women Writing, 1848-1948* 209-17.
Describes selected editions, biographies, and criticism.

Etulain, Richard W., and N. Jill Howard. "Charlotte Perkins Gilman." *Bibliographical Guide to the Study of Western American Literature* 240.

Golden, Catherine J. "Charlotte Perkins Gilman." Knight, *Nineteenth-Century American Women Writers* [160]-67.
Includes a brief survey of Gilman's critical reception and a selective list of studies.

Launspach, Sonja. "Charlotte Perkins Gilman." Nagel, Nagel, and Baughman, *Bibliography of American Fiction 1866-1918* 189-91.

Scharnhorst, Gary. *Charlotte Perkins Gilman: A Bibliography.* Metuchen: Scarecrow, 1985.
Brief information for works by Gilman and a list of selected critical works about her since 1883.

Wiedemann, Barbara. "Charlotte Perkins Gilman: 'The Yellow Wallpaper'." Evans, Little, and Wiedemann, *Short Fiction* 64-72.
Describes nine studies.

William Sydney Porter (O. Henry), 1862-1910

Web Sites

"O. Henry." *American Literature on the Web.* 14 Mar. 2000, http://www.nagasaki-gaigo. ac.jp/ishikawa/amlit/o/ohenry19re.htm.

William Sydney Porter. 14 Mar. 2000, http://www.ils.unc.edu/nc/WilliamPorter. html.

Biographies and Criticism

Cline, Carolyn Garrett. "William Sydney Porter (O. Henry)." Riley, *American Magazine Journalists, 1850-1900* (*Dictionary of Literary Biography* 79) 242-51.

Current-Garcia, Eugene. *O. Henry: A Study of the Short Fiction*. New York: Twayne, 1993.

———. "William Sydney Porter (O. Henry)." Pizer and Harbert, *American Realists and Naturalists* (*Dictionary of Literary Biography* 12) 409-16.

Luedtke, Luther S., and Keith Lawrence. "William Sydney Porter (O. Henry)." Kimbel and Grant, *American Short-Story Writers, 1880-1910* (*Dictionary of Literary Biography* 78) 288-307.

"O. Henry." Bryfonski, *Twentieth-Century Literary Criticism* 1:345-52.
Excerpts of criticism on Porter from 1907-1974.

———. Bryfonski, *Twentieth-Century Literary Criticism* 19:166-202.
Excerpts of criticism on Porter from 1905-1981, with an annotated bibliography.

"O. Henry." Harris and Fitzgerald, *Short Story Criticism* 5:153-203.
Excerpts of criticism on Porter from 1909-1988, with an annotated bibliography.

Bibliographies

Clarkson, Paul S. *Bibliography of William Sydney Porter (O. Henry)*. Caldwell: Caxton Printers, 1938.
Complete descriptions of Porter's writings.

Current-Garcia, Eugene. "William Sydney Porter [O. Henry]." Flora and Bain, *Fifty Southern Writers after 1900* 368-81.

Etulain, Richard W., and N. Jill Howard. "William Sidney Porter." *Bibliographical Guide to the Study of Western American Literature* 339.

Harris, Richard C. *William Sydney Porter (O. Henry): A Reference Guide*. Boston: G. K. Hall, 1980.
Describes works about Porter since 1904.

Luedtke, Luther S. "William Sydney Porter." Nagel, Nagel, and Baughman, *Bibliography of American Fiction, 1866-1918* 307-09.

Edith (Newbold Jones) Wharton, 1862-1937

Web Sites

Edith Wharton Society. 9 Jan. 2000. Ed. Donna Campbell. 14 Mar. 2000, http://www.gonzaga.edu/faculty/campbell/wharton/index.html.
Excellent site containing authoritative information for students and teachers of all levels and representing Professor Campbell's best effort to date. Contains fulltexts of Wharton's fiction, poetry, essays, and nonfiction; lengthy unannotated bibliography as well as selected bibliography of recommended works, and lists of new editions of Wharton's works and new books about her; index for *Edith Wharton Review*

(1984-); lists of recent conference programs and calls for papers for upcoming conferences; society membership directory; links to teaching Wharton to high school and college students; and a query form.

Biographies and Criticism

"*The Age of Innocence*: Edith Wharton." Bryfonski, *Twentieth-Century Literary Criticism* 53:360-414.
  Excerpts of comments and criticism on Wharton's novel from 1920-1991, with an annotated bibliography.

"Edith Wharton." Bryfonski, *Twentieth-Century Literary Criticism* 3:550-82.
  Excerpts of comments and criticism on Wharton from 1899-1977, with an annotated bibliography.

"Edith (Newbold Jones) Wharton." Bryfonski, *Twentieth-Century Literary Criticism* 9:539-55.
  Excerpts of comments and criticism on Wharton from 1899-1980, with an annotated bibliography.

————. Bryfonski, *Twentieth-Century Literary Criticism* 27:381-417.
  Excerpts of comments and criticism on *Ethan Frome* from 1911-1984, with an annotated bibliography.

"Edith (Newbold Jones) Wharton." Harris and Fitzgerald, *Short Story Criticism* 6:411-44.
  Excerpts of criticism on Wharton from 1903-1987, with an annotated bibliography.

Lawson, Richard H. "Edith Wharton." Kimbel and Grant, *American Short-Story Writers, 1880-1910* (*Dictionary of Literary Biography* 78) 308-23.

McDowell, Margaret B. "Edith Wharton." Rood, *American Writers in Paris, 1920-1939* (*Dictionary of Literary Biography* 4) 408-13.

————. *Edith Wharton*. Rev. ed. Boston: Twayne, 1990.

Springer, Marlene. *Ethan Frome: A Nightmare of Need*. New York: Twayne, 1993.

Tuttleton, James W. "Edith Wharton." Pizer and Harbert, *American Realists and Naturalists* (*Dictionary of Literary Biography* 12) 433-50.

Wagner-Martin, Linda. *The Age of Innocence: A Novel of Ironic Nostaglia*. New York: Twayne, 1996.

————. *The House of Mirth: A Novel of Admonition*. Boston: Twayne, 1990.

White, Barbara Anne. *Edith Wharton: A Study of the Short Fiction*. Boston: Twayne, 1991.

Wolff, Cynthia Griffin. "Edith Wharton." Martine, *American Novelists, 1910-1945* (*Dictionary of Literary Biography* 9) 126-42.

Wright, Sarah Bird. "Edith Wharton." Ross and Schramer, *American Travel Writers, 1850-1915* (*Dictionary of Literary Biography* 189) 336-52.

Dictionaries, Encyclopedias, and Handbooks

Wright, Sarah Bird. *Edith Wharton A to Z: The Essential Guide to the Life and Work*. New York: Facts on File, 1998.

Journals

Edith Wharton Review. Brooklyn: Edith Wharton Soc., 1984- . Formerly *Edith Wharton Newsletter* (1984-89).

Bibliographies

Barstow, Jane Missner. "Edith Wharton." *One Hundred Years of American Women Writing, 1848-1948* 113-22.
Describes selected editions, biographies, and criticism.

Bendixen, Alfred. "Edith Wharton." Bruccoli and Baughman, *Modern Women Writers* 76-84.

———. "Edith Wharton." Nagel, Nagel, and Baughman, *Bibliography of American Fiction, 1866-1918* 347-50.

Garrison, Stephen. *Edith Wharton: A Descriptive Bibliography*. Pittsburgh: U of Pittsburgh P, 1990.
The standard guide to Wharton's works, with complete descriptions.

Glitsch, Catherine. "Wharton, Edith." *American Novel Explication, 1991-1995* 263-67.

Kellman, Steven G. "Edith Wharton." *Modern American Novel* 136-44.
Describes about 40 critical works.

Lauer, Kristin O., and Margaret P. Murray. *Edith Wharton: An Annotated Secondary Bibliography*. New York: Garland, 1990.
Describes about 1,200 comments, criticisms, and other works.

Tuttleton, James W. "Edith Wharton." Duke, Bryer, and Inge, *American Women Writers* 71-107.
Survey of research.

Wagner-Martin, Linda. "Edith Wharton." Kopley, *Prospects for the Study of American Literature* 201-18.
The most up-to-date survey of research.

(Nicholas) Black Elk, 1863-1950

Web Sites

"Black Elk." *North American Native Authors Catalog*. 14 Mar. 2000, http://www.nativeauthors.com/search/bio/bioblackelk.html.

Biographies and Criticism

"Black Elk." Bryfonski, *Twentieth-Century Literary Criticism* 33:1-23.
Excerpts of comments and criticism on Black Elk and John G. Neihardt from 1932-1984, with an annotated bibliography.

Bibliographies

Etulain, Richard W., and N. Jill Howard. "Nicholas Black Elk." *Bibliographical Guide to the Study of Western American Literature* 159.

Mary (Hunter) Austin, 1868-1934

Web Sites

Mary Austin's The Land of Little Rain. Eds. vary. 21 May 1996. U of Delaware. 14 Mar. 2000, http://odin.english.udel.edu/gweight/prof/web/austin/template2.html.
Student site includes a brief biography of Austin; textual analysis and publication history of *Land of Little Rain*, with texts of selected reviews; and a selected bibliography.

Biographies and Criticism

Ballard, Rae Galbraith. "Mary Austin." Martine, *American Novelists, 1910-1945* (*Dictionary of Literary Biography* 9) 51-57.

Graulich, Melody. "Mary Austin." Kimbel and Grant, *American Short-Story Writers, 1880-1910* (*Dictionary of Literary Biography* 78) 13-20.

Hoyer, Mark T. "Mary Austin." Cracroft, *Twentieth-Century American Western Writers, First Series* (*Dictionary of Literary Biography* 206) 20-32.

"Mary (Hunter) Austin." Bryfonski, *Twentieth-Century Literary Criticism* 25:15-46.
Excerpts of comments and criticism on Austin from 1903-1982, with an annotated bibliography.

Pearce, T. M. *Mary Hunter Austin.* New York: Twayne, 1965.

Bibliographies

Carpenter, Charles A. "Austin, Mary." *Modern Drama Scholarship and Criticism, 1981-1990* 50.

Etulain, Richard W., and N. Jill Howard. "Mary Austin." *Bibliographical Guide to the Study of Western American Literature* 150-52.

Gaer, Joseph. *Mary Austin: Bibliography and Biographical Data.* [s. l.: s. n., 1934].
Brief information for Austin's works and 14 works about her.

Leo, John R. "Austin, Mary." *Guide to American Poetry Explication* 18.

Pearce, T. M. "Mary Hunter Austin." Erisman and Etulain, *Fifty Western Writers* 21-31.

Schiller, Emily. "Mary Austin." Nagel, Nagel, and Baughman, *Bibliography of American Fiction, 1866-1918* 58-60.

W(illiam) E(dward) B(urghardt) Du Bois, 1868-1963

Web Sites

"Chapter 9: Harlem Renaissance—William Edward Burghardt Du Bois." *PAL: Perspectives in American Literature*. 14 Mar. 2000, http://www.csustan.edu/english/reuben/pal/chap9/dubois.html.
   A very good, reliable site for students wanting basic information about the writing of Du Bois, with very brief biographical information and unannotated bibliographies of works by and about Du Bois.

"W. E. B. Du Bois." *Access Indiana: Teaching & Learning Center*. 14 Mar. 2000, http://tlc.ai.org/dubois.htm.
   Includes some biographical links and links to the texts of Du Bois's most important works, including *The Evolution of Negro Leadership* and *The Talented Tenth* (through Indiana University) and *The Souls of Black Folks* (through Project Bartleby). The offsite biographical links are somewhat disappointing, and the page is not signed. Broken link to the W. E. B. Du Bois Learning Center indicates that the site needs better updating.

W.E.B. Du Bois. 14 Mar. 2000, http://www.kcpl.org/sc/exhibits/autographs/dubois.htm.

W. E. B. Du Bois Virtual University. Ed. Jennifer Wager. Update unknown. Tripod.com. 14 Mar. 2000, http://members.tripod.com/~DuBois/index.html.
   The most complete scholarly W. E. B. Du Bois site. Contains major links for an overview of the site (under "About"); annotated bibliographies of books, dissertations, and critical articles; four biographical essays (including one for Martin Luther King, Jr.); conferences, with a list of international scholars; and library and classroom (both needing development). Wager is a graduate student at Georgetown U.

Biographies and Criticism

Arndt, Murray. "W. E. B. Du Bois." Wilson, *American Historians, 1866-1912* (*Dictionary of Literary Biography* 47) 86-92.

Gayle, Addison, Jr. "W. E. B. Du Bois." Harris, *Afro-American Writers before the Harlem Renaissance* (*Dictionary of Literary Biography* 50) 92-105.

Moore, Jack B. *W. E. B. Du Bois*. Boston: Twayne, 1981.

Snorgrass, J. William. "W. E. B. Du Bois." Riley, *American Magazine Journalists, 1900-1960* (*Dictionary of Literary Biography* 91) 95-105.

"W. E. B. Du Bois." Riley, *Contemporary Literary Criticism* 64:101-35.
   Excerpts of criticism on Du Bois from 1909-1989, with an annotated bibliography.

———. Riley, *Contemporary Literary Criticism* 96:125-63.
Excerpts of criticism on Du Bois from 1972-1994, with an annotated bibliography.

Indexes and Concordances

Weinberg, Meyer. *World of W. E. B. Du Bois: A Quotation Sourcebook*. Westport: Greenwood, 1992.

Bibliographies

Aptheker, Herbert. *Annotated Bibliography of the Published Writings of W. E. B. Du Bois*. Millwood: Kraus-Thomson, 1973.
Detailed summaries and contents of Du Bois's works.

Carpenter, Charles A. "Du Bois, W. E. B." *Modern Drama Scholarship and Criticism, 1981-1990* 54.

Dudley, David L. "W. E. B. Du Bois." Nelson, *African American Authors, 1745-1945* 121-31.
Survey of research.

Glitsch, Catherine. "Du Bois, W. E. B." *American Novel Explication, 1991-1995* 68.

Partington, Paul G. *W. E. B. Du Bois: A Bibliography of His Published Writings*. Rev. ed. Whittier: Partington, 1979.
More complete bibliographic descriptions of Du Bois's writings than given in Aptheker, above.

———. *W. E. B. DuBois: A Bibliography of His Published Writings: Supplement*. Whittier: Partington, 1984.
Continues Partington's 1979 guide, above.

Perry, Margaret. "DuBois, W[illiam] E[dward] B[urghardt]." *Harlem Renaissance* 75-77.

Ruppert, James. "Du Bois, W. E. B." *Guide to American Poetry Explication* 108-09.

Turner, W. Burghardt. "The Polemicists: David Walker, Frederick Douglass, Booker T. Washington, and W. E. B. Du Bois." Inge, Duke, and Bryer, *Black American Writers* I, 47-132.
Survey of research.

Edgar Lee Masters, 1868?-1950

Web Sites

"Edgar Lee Masters." *Anti-Imperialism in the United States 1898-1935*. 14 Mar. 2000, http://www.boondocksnet.com/masters/.

"Edgar Lee Masters." *Pegasos*. 14 Mar. 2000, http://www.kirjasto.sci.fi/emasters.htm.

Edgar Lee Masters. 14 Mar. 2000, http://www.outfitters.com/illinois/fulton/masters. html.

"The Edgar Lee Masters Page." *SAC LitWeb*. 14 Mar. 2000, http://www.accd.edu/ sac/english/bailey/masters.htm.
Reliable site containing an excellent link to the first chapter of a memoir by Masters's son, Hilary; a valuable chronological list of Masters's work; and an interesting link to a pictorial site, "Virtual Spoon River Scenic Drive." Otherwise, somewhat disappointing, with many inoperable links (including to selections from *Spoon River Anthology*, which Bailey calls indispensable) and others restricted in access.

"Spoon River Anthology." *Project Gutenberg*. 14 Mar. 2000, http://promo.net/cgi-promo/pg/t9.cgi.

Biographies and Criticism

"Edgar Lee Masters." Bryfonski, *Twentieth-Century Literary Criticism* 2:460-80.
Excerpts of comments and criticism on Masters from 1915-1968.

——. Bryfonski, *Twentieth-Century Literary Criticism* 25:281-318.
Excerpts of comments and criticism on Masters from 1915-1983, with an annotated bibliography.

"Edgar Lee Masters." Young, *Poetry Criticism* 1:319-50.
Excerpts of comments and criticism on Masters from 1915-1980, with an annotated bibliography.

Russell, Herbert K. "Edgar Lee Masters." Quartermain, *American Poets, 1880-1945, Third Series* (*Dictionary of Literary Biography* 54) 293-312.

Wrenn, John H., and Margaret M. Wrenn. *Edgar Lee Masters*. Boston: Twayne, 1983.

Bibliographies

Carpenter, Charles A. "Masters, Edgar Lee." *Modern Drama Scholarship and Criticism, 1981-1990* 66.

William Vaughn Moody, 1869-1910

Web Sites

"Anti-Imperialist Poems by William Vaughn Moody." *Anti-Imperialism in the United States, 1898-1935*. 14 Mar. 2000, http://www.boondocksnet.com/lit/index.html.

"William Vaughn Moody." *Humanities Text Initiative American Verse Collection*. 14 Mar. 2000, http://www.hti.umich.edu/bin/amv-idx.pl?type=header&id= MoodWPoems.
Text of Moody's *Poems* (New York; Boston: Houghton, Mufflin [sic], 1901).

Biographies and Criticism

Partridge, Colin. "William Vaughn Moody." Quartermain, *American Poets, 1880-1945, Third Series* (*Dictionary of Literary Biography* 54) 320-28.

Zaidman, Laura M. "William Vaughn Moody." MacNicholas, *Twentieth-Century American Dramatists* (*Dictionary of Literary Biography* 7) 120-25.

Bibliographies

Boswell, Jeanetta. *Spokesmen for the Minority: A Bibliography of Sidney Lanier, William Vaughn Moody, Frederick Goddard Tuckerman, and Jones Very: With Selective Annotations*. Metuchen: Scarecrow, 1987.
Selective descriptions of about 360 works on Moody.

Carpenter, Charles A. "Moody, William Vaughn." *Modern Drama Scholarship and Criticism, 1981-1990* 69.

Konkle, Lincoln. "William Vaughn Moody." Demastes, *American Playwrights, 1880-1945* [302]-309.

Edwin Arlington Robinson, 1869-1935

Web Sites

"The Edwin Arlington Robinson Homepage." *SAC Litweb*. 14 Mar. 2000, http://www.accd.edu/sac/english/bailey/robinson.htm.

Etexts by Author Robinson, Edwin Arlington, 1869-1935. Ed. unknown. Copyright 1999. Promonet for Project Gutenberg. 14 Mar. 2000, http://promo.net/cgi-promo/pg/t9.cgi.
Includes texts of four different versions of each of the following three poems: "Children of the Night," "The Man Against the Sky," and "The Three Taverns."

"Selected Poetry of Edwin Arlington Robinson (1869-1935)." *Representative Poetry On-line*. 14 Mar. 2000, http://www.library.utoronto.ca/utel/rp/authors/robnea.html.
Mainly useful for links to the text of 11 poems by Robinson, including "Richard Corey" and "Miniver Cheevy Entertains a Man from Stratford." Also includes a very brief biography, annotated bibliography, photograph, discussion of editorial conventions. A good beginning for students wishing to get access to Arlington's poetry.

Biographies and Criticism

"Edwin Arlington Robinson." Bryfonski, *Twentieth-Century Literary Criticism* 5:399-419.
Excerpts of comments and criticism on Robinson from 1897-1979, with an annotated bibliography.

"Edwin Arlington Robinson." Young, *Poetry Criticism* 1:457-98.
Excerpts of comments and criticism on Robinson from 1897-1969, with an annotated bibliography.

Joyner, Nancy Carol. "Edwin Arlington Robinson." Quartermain, *American Poets, 1880-1945, Third Series* (*Dictionary of Literary Biography* 54) 366-87.

Indexes and Concordances

Sundermeir, Michael William. *Concordance to the Poetry of Edwin Arlington Robinson.* Ph.D. dissertation, Lincoln: U of Nebraska, 1972.
References *Collected Poems of Edwin Arlington Robinson* (New York: Macmillan, 1937).

Bibliographies

Barnard, Ellsworth. "Edwin Arlington Robinson." Bryer, *Sixteen Modern American Authors* 473-98.
Survey of research; supplemented by Barnard in Bryer's *Sixteen Modern American Authors: Volume 2* 558-81.

Hogan, Charles Beecher. *Bibliography of Edwin Arlington Robinson.* New Haven: Yale UP, 1936.
Standard guide to Robinson's works, with complete descriptions; updated and corrected by Hogan's "Edwin Arlington Robinson: New Bibliographical Notes," *PBSA* 35 (1941): 115-44; and William White's *Edwin Arlington Robinson: A Supplementary Bibliography* (Kent: Kent State UP, 1971).

Joyner, Nancy Carol. *Edwin Arlington Robinson: A Reference Guide.* Boston: G. K. Hall, 1978.
Describes about 1,400 works on Robinson since 1894.

Ruppert, James. "Robinson, Edwin A." *Guide to American Poetry Explication* 164-78.

(Benjamin) Frank(lin) Norris, 1870-1902

Web Sites

"Frank Norris." *American Literature on the Web.* 14 Mar. 2000, http://www.nagasaki-gaigo.ac.jp/ishikawa/amlit/n/norris19re.htm.

"Frank Norris (1870-1902)." *Howells's Contemporaries.* 14 Mar. 2000, http://www.gonzaga.edu/faculty/campbell/howells/norris.htm.
More-than-adequate page that contains authoritative criticism and resources contributed by major Norris scholars. Features a select bibliography of *McTeague* and of recent books and articles on Norris; biographical essay, "Frank Norris," by Don Graham (of the Western Literature Association's *Literary History of the American West*), with a short annotated bibliography; historical essay, "Frank Norris," by William Dean Howells; links to texts of Norris's articles in journals like *Atlantic Monthly* and *Century Magazine* as well as his novels; and Norris's "Fantaisie Printanière," by Joseph R. McElrath, Jr., of Florida State U., that identifies major themes and classroom teaching strategies for one short story, complete with ready-made questions.

The Octopus. 14 Mar. 2000, http://www.worldwideschool.org/library/books/lit/
socialcommentary/TheOctopus/toc.html.

Biographies and Criticism

"(Benjamin) Frank(lin) Norris (Jr.)." Bryfonski, *Twentieth-Century Literary Criticism* 24:414-53.
Excerpts of comments and criticism on Norris from 1899-1979, with an annotated bibliography.

"Frank Norris." Harris and Fitzgerald, *Short Story Criticism* 28:194-219.
Excerpts of criticism on Norris from 1896-1993, with an annotated bibliography.

McElrath, Joseph R., Jr. "Frank Norris." Gale, *Nineteenth-Century American Western Writers* (*Dictionary of Literary Biography* 186) 260-72.

———. "Frank Norris." Pizer and Harbert, *American Realists and Naturalists* (*Dictionary of Literary Biography* 12) 379-97.

———. "Frank Norris." Rathbun and Grecu, *American Literary Critics and Scholars,
1880-1900* (*Dictionary of Literary Biography* 71) 168-79.

———. *Frank Norris Revisited*. New York: Twayne, 1992.

Journals

Frank Norris Studies. Tallahassee: Frank Norris Soc., 1986- .
Features "Current Publications Update," a checklist of Norris scholarship.

Bibliographies

Crisler, Jesse S., and Joseph R. McElrath, Jr. *Frank Norris: A Reference Guide*. Boston: G. K. Hall, 1974.
Describes about 700 works on Norris.

Dillingham, William B. "Frank Norris." Harbert and Rees, *Fifteen American Authors
before 1900* 402-38.
Survey of research.

Etulain, Richard W., and N. Jill Howard. "Frank Norris." *Bibliographical Guide to
the Study of Western American Literature* 324-29.

French, Warren. "Frank Norris." Erisman and Etulain, *Fifty Western Writers* 347-57.

Glitsch, Catherine. "Norris, Frank." *American Novel Explication, 1991-1995* 194-95.

McElrath, Joseph R., Jr. "Frank Norris." Nagel, Nagel, and Baughman, *Bibliography
of American Fiction, 1866-1918* 294-97.

———. *Frank Norris: A Descriptive Bibliography*. Pittsburgh: U of Pittsburgh P,
1992.
Standard listing of Norris's works, with complete descriptions.

Stephen Crane, 1871-1900

Web Sites

Crane Texts Online. 14 Mar. 2000, http://www.anova.org/stephen-crane-links.html.

"Stephen Crane." *Pegasos.* 14 Mar. 2000, http://www.kirjasto.sci.fi/scrane.htm.

"Stephen Crane (1871-1900)." *American Authors.* 14 Mar. 2000, http://www.gonzaga.edu/faculty/campbell/enl311/crane.htm.

Stephen Crane: Man, Myth, & Legend. 14 Mar. 2000, http://www.cwrl.utexas.edu/~mmaynard/Crane/crane.html.

Stephen Crane Society. Ed. Stanley Wertheim. 19 Oct. 1998. Earthlink. 14 Mar. 2000, http://home.earthlink.net/~warburg/.
Disappointing site despite Wertheim's prestigious academic credentials and links to the texts of Crane's most important novels, poems, and short stories. Site needs better editing, more development, and more regular updating as well as information about the Society.

Biographies and Criticism

Colvert, James B. "Stephen Crane." Pizer and Harbert, *American Realists and Naturalists* (*Dictionary of Literary Biography* 12) 100-124.

Gibson, Donald B. *The Red Badge of Courage: Redefining the Hero.* Boston: Twayne, 1988.

Johnson, Glen M. "Stephen Crane." Kimbel and Grant, *American Short-Story Writers, 1880-1910* (*Dictionary of Literary Biography* 78) 117-35.

Quartermain, Peter. "Stephen Crane." Quartermain, *American Poets, 1880-1945, Third Series* (*Dictionary of Literary Biography* 54) 48-57.

"Stephen Crane." Bryfonski, *Twentieth-Century Literary Criticism* 11:119-69.
Excerpts of comments and criticism on Crane from 1893-1980, with an annotated bibliography.

———. Bryfonski, *Twentieth-Century Literary Criticism* 17:63-83.
Excerpts of comments and criticism on Crane from 1978-1984, with an annotated bibliography.

———. Bryfonski, *Twentieth-Century Literary Criticism* 32:132-90.
Excerpts of comments and criticism on *Red Badge of Courage* from 1895-1985, with an annotated bibliography.

"Stephen Crane." Harris and Fitzgerald, *Short Story Criticism* 7:97-158.
Excerpts of criticism on Crane from 1900-1988, with an annotated bibliography.

Wolford, Chester L. *Stephen Crane: A Study of the Short Fiction.* Boston: Twayne, 1989.

Dictionaries, Encyclopedias, and Handbooks

Schaefer, Michael W. *Reader's Guide to the Short Stories of Stephen Crane*. New York: G. K. Hall, 1996.

Wertheim, Stanley. *Stephen Crane Encyclopedia*. Westport: Greenwood, 1997.

Indexes and Concordances

Baron, Herman. *Concordance to the Poems of Stephen Crane*. Boston: G. K. Hall, 1974.
Indexes *Poems of Stephen Crane: A Critical Edition*, ed. Joseph Katz (New York: Cooper Square, 1972).

Crosland, Andrew T. *Concordance to the Complete Poetry of Stephen Crane*. Detroit: Gale, 1975.
Based on *Poems and Literary Remains*, ed. Fredson Bowers (Charlottesville: U of Virginia P, 1975), vol. 10 of *Works of Stephen Crane*.

Journals

Stephen Crane Studies. Blacksburg: Dept. of English, Virginia Polytechnic Institute and SU, 1992- .

Bibliographies

Colvert, James B. "Stephen Crane." Nagel, Nagel, and Baughman, *Bibliography of American Fiction, 1866-1918* 135-40.

Dooley, Patrick K. *Stephen Crane: An Annotated Bibliography of Secondary Scholarship*. New York: G. K. Hall, 1992.
Awkwardly organized but comprehensive guide to works about Crane since 1901; updates Stallman, below.

Etulain, Richard W., and N. Jill Howard. "Stephen Crane." *Bibliographical Guide to the Study of Western American Literature* 206-08.

Evans, Robert C. "Stephen Crane: 'The Open Boat'." Evans, Little, and Wiedemann, *Short Fiction* 22-26.
Describes nine studies.

Glitsch, Catherine. "Crane, Stephen." *American Novel Explication, 1991-1995* 54-55.

Pizer, Donald. "Stephen Crane." Harbert and Rees, *Fifteen American Authors before 1900* 97-184.
Survey of research.

Ruppert, James. "Crane, Stephen." *Guide to American Poetry Explication* 12-16.

Stallman, R. W. *Stephen Crane: A Critical Bibliography*. Ames: Iowa State UP, 1972.
Complete descriptions of works by Crane and extensively annotated entries for works about him since 1888.

Theodore (Herman Albert) Dreiser, 1871-1945

Web Sites

International Theodore Dreiser Society. Ed. Keith Newlin. 17 June 1999. U of North
   Carolina at Wilmington. 14 Mar. 2000, http://www2.uncwil.edu/dreiser/.
   Provides tables of contents of recent issues of *Dreiser Studies* and links to collections containing Dreiser archives and fulltexts of his novels (including two of *Sister Carrie*). Membership link gives society's constitution and bylaws, application,
and link for subscribing to a listserv.

"Theodore Dreiser." *Pegasos*. 14 Mar. 2000, http://www.kirjasto.sci.fi/dreiser.htm.

Theodore Dreiser. 14 Mar. 2000, http://www.wwnorton.com/naal/explore/dreiser.htm.

Theodore Dreiser: The Naturalist. 14 Mar. 2000, http://www2.cwrl.utexas.edu/
   VANDER/316S97/MTRICE/story/..%5Cproject%5Cindex.htm.

Biographies and Criticism

"*An American Tragedy*: Theodore Dreiser." Bryfonski, *Twentieth-Century Literary
   Criticism* 83:1-124.
   Excerpts of comments and criticism on Dreiser's work from 1926-1997, with an
annotated bibliography.

Applegate, Edd. "Theodore Dreiser." Riley, *American Magazine Journalists,
   1900-1960* (*Dictionary of Literary Biography* 137) 85-95.

Gerber, Philip L. "Theodore Dreiser." Martine, *American Novelists, 1910-1945* (*Dictionary of Literary Biography* 9) 236-57.

———. *Theodore Dreiser Revisited*. New York: Twayne, 1992.

Orlov, Paul A. "Theodore Dreiser." Kimbel, *American Short-Story Writers,
   1910-1945, Second Series* (*Dictionary of Literary Biography* 102) 48-69.

Pizer, Donald. "Theodore Dreiser." Pizer and Harbert, *American Realists and Naturalists* (*Dictionary of Literary Biography* 12) 145-65.

Sloane, David E. E. *Sister Carrie: Theodore Dreiser's Sociological Tragedy*. New
   York: Twayne, 1992.

"Theodore Dreiser." Harris and Fitzgerald, *Short Story Criticism* 30:106-60.
   Excerpts of criticism on Dreiser from 1918-1985, with an annotated bibliography.

"Theodore (Herman Albert) Dreiser." Bryfonski, *Twentieth-Century Literary Criticism* 10:161-203.
   Excerpts of comments and criticism on Dreiser from 1901-1981, with an annotated bibliography.

———. Bryfonski, *Twentieth-Century Literary Criticism* 18:49-76.
   Excerpts of comments and criticism on Dreiser from 1959-1984, with an annotated bibliography.

————. Bryfonski, *Twentieth-Century Literary Criticism* 35:30-86.
Excerpts of comments and criticism on Dreiser from 1927-1988, with an annotated bibliography.

Dictionaries, Encyclopedias, and Handbooks

Gerber, Philip L. *Plots and Characters in the Fiction of Theodore Dreiser.* Hamden: Archon, 1977.

Journals

Dreiser Studies. Terre Haute: International Dreiser Soc., 1970- .
Formerly *Dreiser Newsletter* (1970-87); includes annual "Dreiser Checklist."

Bibliographies

Boswell, Jeanetta. *Theodore Dreiser and the Critics, 1911-1982: A Bibliography with Selective Annotations.* Metuchen: Scarecrow, 1986.
Valuable descriptions of 1,708 comments and criticisms.

Carpenter, Charles A. "Dreiser, Theodore." *Modern Drama Scholarship and Criticism, 1981-1990* 54.

Elias, Robert W. "Theodore Dreiser." Bryer, *Sixteen Modern American Authors* 123-79.
Survey of research; supplemented by James L. W. West III in Bryer, *Sixteen Modern American Authors: Volume 2* 120-53.

Glitsch, Catherine. "Dreiser, Theodore." *American Novel Explication, 1991-1995* 66-68.

Kellman, Steven G. "Theodore Dreiser." *Modern American Novel* 35-46.
Describes about 70 critical works.

Orlov, Paul A., and Miriam Gogol. "Prospects for the Study of Theodore Dreiser." *Resources for American Literary Study* 24.1 (1998): [1]-21.
Survey of research.

Pizer, Donald. "Theodore Dreiser." Nagel, Nagel, and Baughman, *Bibliography of American Fiction, 1866-1918* 158-62.

————, Richard W. Dowell, and Frederic E. Rusch. *Theodore Dreiser: A Primary Bibliography and Reference Guide.* 2nd ed. Boston: G. K. Hall, 1991.
Comprehensive listings of works by Dreiser and more than 4,300 works about him; updated by Shigeo Mizuguchi's "Addenda and Corrigenda to Theodore Dreiser: A Primary Bibliography and Reference Guide: English Language Instruction Texts Published in Japan," *Dreiser Studies* 25.1 (Spring 1994): 51-52.

James Weldon Johnson, 1871-1938

Web Sites

"James Weldon Johnson." *Academy of American Poets.* 8 Mar. 2000, http://www.poets.org/lit/poet/jwjohfst.htm.

James Weldon Johnson. 14 Mar. 2000, http://www.afn.org/~sigma1/jwjohn.html.

James Weldon Johnson. 14 Mar. 2000, http://www.nku.edu/~diesmanj/johnson.html.

The Making of Harlem. 14 Mar. 2000, http://etext.lib.virginia.edu/harlem/JohMakiF. html.

Biographies and Criticism

Fleming, Robert E. *James Weldon Johnson.* Boston: Twayne, 1987.

"James Weldon Johnson." Bryfonski, *Twentieth-Century Literary Criticism* 3:239-50.
Excerpts of comments and criticism on Johnson from 1917-1974, with an annotated bibliography.

———. Bryfonski, *Twentieth-Century Literary Criticism* 19:203-58.
Excerpts of comments and criticism on Johnson from 1917-1983, with an annotated bibliography.

"James Weldon Johnson." Young, *Poetry Criticism* 24:126-71.
Excerpts of comments and criticism on Johnson from 1918-1993, with an annotated bibliography.

Kinnamon, Keneth. "James Weldon Johnson." Harris, *Afro-American Writers from the Harlem Renaissance to 1940 (Dictionary of Literary Biography* 51) 168-82.

Bibliographies

Fleming, Robert E. *James Weldon Johnson and Arna Wendell Bontemps: A Reference Guide.* Boston: G. K. Hall, 1978.
Critical descriptions for about 350 works on Johnson since 1905.

Glitsch, Catherine. "Johnson, James Weldon." *American Novel Explication, 1991-1995* 138.

Kinnamon, Keneth. "James Weldon Johnson." Nagel, Nagel, and Baughman, *Bibliography of American Fiction, 1866-1918* 253-54.

Mason, Julian. "James Weldon Johnson." Flora and Bain, *Fifty Southern Writers after 1900* 280-89.

Miller, Ruth, and Peter J. Katopes. "The Harlem Renaissance: Arna W. Bontemps, Countee Cullen, James Weldon Johnson, Claude McKay, and Jean Toomer." Inge, Duke, and Bryer, *Black American Writers* I, 161-86.
Survey of research.

Perry, Margaret. "Johnson, James Weldon." *Harlem Renaissance* 108-16.

Pratt, Louis Hill. "James Weldon Johnson." Nelson, *African American Authors, 1745-1945* 297-305.
Survey of research.

Ruppert, James. "Johnson, James Weldon." *Guide to American Poetry Explication* 128.

Paul Laurence Dunbar, 1872-1906

Web Sites

"Chapter 6: Late Nineteenth Century: Paul Laurence Dunbar." *PAL: Perspectives in American Literature*. 14 Mar. 2000, http://www.csustan.edu/english/reuben/pal/chap6/dunbar.html.

Paul Laurence Dunbar Digital Text Collection. 14 Mar. 2000, http://www.libraries.wright.edu/dunbar/#Biblio.

"Selected Poetry of Paul Laurence Dunbar." *Representative Poetry On-line*. 19 Mar. 2000, http://www.library.utoronto.ca/utel/rp/authors/dunbarp.html.

Welcome to the Poetry of Paul Laurence Dunbar. Ed. Thomas M. Columbus. 1 Jan. 1998. U of Dayton. 14 Mar. 2000, http://www.udayton.edu/~dunbar/.
Offers a good introduction to Dunbar's life and poetry, with links to his biography and texts of his poems.

Biographies and Criticism

Giles, James R. "Paul Laurence Dunbar." Kimbel and Grant, *American Short-Story Writers, 1880-1910* (*Dictionary of Literary Biography* 78) 154-59.

Laryea, Doris Lucas. "Paul Laurence Dunbar." Harris, *Afro-American Writers before the Harlem Renaissance* (*Dictionary of Literary Biography* 50) 106-22.

"Paul Laurence Dunbar." Bryfonski, *Twentieth-Century Literary Criticism* 2:127-34.
Excerpts of comments and criticism on Dunbar from 1896-1975.

———. Bryfonski, *Twentieth-Century Literary Criticism* 12:101-31.
Excerpts of comments and criticism on Dunbar from 1896-1981, with an annotated bibliography.

"Paul Laurence Dunbar." Harris and Fitzgerald, *Short Story Criticism* 8:116-51.
Excerpts of criticism on Dunbar from 1898-1979, with an annotated bibliography.

"Paul Laurence Dunbar." Young, *Poetry Criticism* 5:113-49.
Excerpts of comments and criticism on Dunbar from 1896-1980, with an annotated bibliography.

Revell, Peter. "Paul Laurence Dunbar." Quartermain, *American Poets, 1880-1945, Third Series* (*Dictionary of Literary Biography* 54) 69-82.

Bibliographies

Glitsch, Catherine. "Dunbar, Paul Laurence." *American Novel Explication, 1991-1995* 69.

Jason, Philip K. "Paul Laurence Dunbar." *Nineteenth Century American Poetry* 244-48.
Describes 20 studies.

Metcalf, E. W., Jr. *Paul Laurence Dunbar: A Bibliography*. Metuchen: Scarecrow, 1975.
Brief descriptive listings for works by and about Dunbar.

Miller, Ruth, and Peter J. Katopes. "The Polemicists: David Walker, Frederick Douglass, Booker T. Washington, and W. E. B. Du Bois." Inge, Duke, and Bryer, *Black American Writers* I, 133-60.
Survey of research.

Mvuyekure, Pierre-Damian. "Paul Laurence Dunbar." Nelson, *African American Authors, 1745-1945* 132-38.
Survey of research.

Ruppert, James. "Dunbar, Paul Laurence." *Guide to American Poetry Explication* 109-10.

Willa (Sibert) Cather, 1873-1947

Web Sites

"Willa Cather." *Access Indiana: Teaching & Learning Center*. 15 Mar. 2000, http://tlc.ai.org/cather.htm.

"Willa Cather." *American Women in Literature Database*. 24 Aug. 1997. Ed. Bette Reagan. 15 Mar. 2000, http://www.kutztown.edu/~reagan/cather.html.
Biographical essay containing a brief bibliography.

"Willa Cather." *Great Books Index*. 3 Mar. 2000, http://books.mirror.org/gb.cather.html.

Willa Cather Memorial Web Site. 15 Mar. 2000, http://willacather.org/.

Willa Cather Site. 15 Mar. 2000, http://fp.image.dk/fpemarxlind/.

Willa Sibert Cather. Ed. and update unknown. Harvard U. 15 Mar. 2000, http://icg.fas.harvard.edu/~cather/.
Onsite links include "Events," "Publications," "Locations," "Quotations," "Biography," "Other," and "Papers." Several offsite links are also included. Site contains many layers. For instance, an offsite link to Project Gutenberg is found at the third layer, after "Publications" and after "Books."

Biographies and Criticism

Gerber, Philip L. *Willa Cather*. Rev. ed. New York: Twayne, 1995.

Hewitt, Rosalie. "Willa Cather." Kimbel and Grant, *American Short-Story Writers, 1880-1910* (*Dictionary of Literary Biography* 78) 54-63.

Lathrop, JoAnna. "Willa Cather." Quartermain, *American Poets, 1880-1945, Third Series* (*Dictionary of Literary Biography* 54) 21-28.

Murphy, John J. *My Antonia: The Road Home*. Boston: Twayne, 1989.

Wasserman, Loretta. *Willa Cather: A Study of the Short Fiction*. Boston: Twayne, 1991.

"Willa Cather." Bryfonski, *Twentieth-Century Literary Criticism* 1:150-67.
　　Excerpts of criticism on Cather from 1922-1974.

————. Bryfonski, *Twentieth-Century Literary Criticism* 11:90-118.
　　Excerpts of comments and criticism on Cather from 1905-1982, with an annotated bibliography.

————. Bryfonski, *Twentieth-Century Literary Criticism* 31:23-70.
　　Excerpts of comments and criticism on *My Antonia* from 1918-1987, with an
annotated bibliography.

"Willa (Sibert) Cather." Harris and Fitzgerald, *Short Story Criticism* 2:88-123.
　　Excerpts of criticism on Cather from 1905-1987, with an annotated bibliography.

Woodress, James. "Willa Cather." Martine, *American Novelists, 1910-1945* (*Dictionary of Literary Biography* 9) 140-54.

Dictionaries, Encyclopedias, and Handbooks

March, John, Marilyn Arnold, and Debra Lynn Thornton. *Reader's Companion to the
Fiction of Willa Cather*. Westport: Greenwood, 1993.

Meyering, Sheryl L. *Reader's Guide to the Short Stories of Willa Cather*. New York:
G. K. Hall, 1994.

Journals

Cather Studies. Lincoln: U of Nebraska, and Willa Cather Pioneer Memorial & Educational Foundation, 1990- .

Willa Cather Pioneer Memorial Newsletter. Red Cloud: Willa Cather Pioneer Museum,
1957- .
　　Features list of "Works on Cather."

Bibliographies

Arnold, Marilyn. *Willa Cather: A Reference Guide*. Boston: G. K. Hall, 1986.
　　Describes about 1,800 writings on Cather since 1895.

Barstow, Jane Missner. "Willa Cather." *One Hundred Years of American Women
Writing, 1848-1948* 86-93.
　　Describes selected editions, biographies, and criticism.

Crane, Joan. *Willa Cather: A Bibliography*. Lincoln: U of Nebraska P, 1982.
　　Standard guide to Cather's writings, with complete descriptions.

Etulain, Richard W., and N. Jill Howard. "Willa Cather." *Bibliographical Guide to
the Study of Western American Literature* 170-83.

Evans, Robert C. "Willa Cather: 'Paul's Case'." Evans, Little, and Wiedemann, *Short
Fiction* 17-21.
　　Describes 13 studies.

Glitsch, Catherine. "Cather, Willa." *American Novel Explication, 1991-1995*
43-45.

Kellman, Steven G. "Willa Cather." *Modern American Novel* 14-27.
Describes about 80 critical works.

Murphy, John J. "Willa Cather." Erisman and Etulain, *Fifty Western Writers* 51-62.

Rosowski, Susan J. "Willa Cather." Kopley, *Prospects for the Study of American Literature* 219-40.
The most up-to-date survey of research.

Slote, Bernice. "Willa Cather." Bryer, *Sixteen Modern American Authors* 29-74.
Survey of research; supplemented by James Woodress in Bryer, *Sixteen Modern American Authors: Volume 2* 42-72.

Woodress, James. "Willa Cather." Nagel, Nagel, and Baughman, *Bibliography of American Fiction, 1866-1918* 102-09.

———. "Willa Cather." Bruccoli and Baughman, *Modern Women Writers* 1-14.

Ellen (Anderson Gholson) Glasgow, 1874-1945

Web Sites

"Ellen Anderson Gholson Glasgow, 1873-1945." *Documenting the American South.* 15 Mar. 2000, http://metalab.unc.edu/docsouth/authors.html#G.
Contains texts and illustrations of four of Glasgow's novels: *The Battle-Ground, The Deliverance, Virginia,* and *The Voice of the People*; contains biographical sketch from the *Encyclopedia of Southern Culture.*

"Ellen Glasgow." *American Women in Literature Database.* 15 Mar. 2000, http://www.kutztown.edu/faculty/reagan/glasgow.html.
Site contains plot synopses of Glasgow's works, critical commentary, an excellent chronology and life, a bibliography, and list of "other sites to search."

Ellen Glasgow (1873[?]-1945). Ed. and update unknown. U of Virginia. 15 Mar. 2000, http://www.virginia.edu/~history/courses/courses.old/hius323/glasgow.html.
Excellent, if brief, biography of Glasgow, with a very brief bibliography of works about her.

"Point in Morals" [by] Glasgow, Ellen. Ed. Judy Boss. Update unknown. U of Virginia. 15 Mar. 2000, http://www.people.virginia.edu/~tsawyer/DRBR/glasgow.html.
Text of Glasgow's "A Point of Morals," an allegorical short story originally featured in *Harper's New Monthly Magazine* (May 1899), pp. 976-82.

Biographies and Criticism

"Ellen (Anderson Gholson) Glasgow." Bryfonski, *Twentieth-Century Literary Criticism* 2:175-91.
Excerpts of criticism on Glasgow from 1909-1971.

———. Bryfonski, *Twentieth-Century Literary Criticism* 7:331-50.
Excerpts of criticism on Glasgow from 1897-1980, with an annotated bibliography.

McDowell, Frederick P. W. "Ellen Glasgow." Martine, *American Novelists, 1910-1945* (*Dictionary of Literary Biography* 9) 44-65.

Wagner, Linda W. "Ellen Glasgow." Pizer and Harbert, *American Realists and Naturalists* (*Dictionary of Literary Biography* 12) 213-26.

Journals

Ellen Glasgow Newsletter. Austin: Ellen Glasgow Soc., 1974- .

Bibliographies

Barstow, Jane Missner. "Ellen Glasgow." *One Hundred Years of American Women Writing, 1848-1948* 93-97.
Describes selected editions, biographies, and criticism.

Glitsch, Catherine. "Glasgow, Ellen." *American Novel Explication, 1991-1995* 97-99.

Kellman, Steven G. "Ellen Glasgow." *Modern American Novel* 80-86.
Describes about 40 critical works.

Kelly, William W. *Ellen Glasgow: A Bibliography.* Charlottesville: UP of Virginia, 1964.
Standard guide to works by Glasgow, with lists of works about her.

MacDonald, Edgar E. "Ellen Glasgow." Duke, Bryer, and Inge, *American Women Writers* 167-200.

———, and Tonette Bond Inge. *Ellen Glasgow: A Reference Guide.* Boston: G. K. Hall, 1986.
Describes about 1,500 works on Glasgow since 1897; updated by Margaret Bauer's "Secondary Sources on Ellen Glasgow, 1986-1990," *Ellen Glasgow Newsletter* 26 (Spring 1991): 10-19.

Matthews, Pamela R. "Ellen Glasgow." Nagel, Nagel, and Baughman, *Bibliography of American Fiction, 1866-1918* 191-94.

Wagner-Martin, Linda. "Ellen Glasgow." Flora and Bain, *Fifty Southern Writers after 1900* 206-14.

Robert (Lee) Frost, 1874-1963

Web Sites

"Robert Frost." *Academy of American Poets.* 15 Mar. 2000, http://www.poets.org/lit/poet/rfrosfst.htm.

"Robert Frost." *American Literature on the Web.* 15 Mar. 2000, http://www.nagasaki-gaigo.ac.jp/ishikawa/amlit/f/frost20.htm.

Robert Frost. 15 Mar. 2000, http://athena.louisville.edu/~bhwhit01/jccclass/eng101/frost.html.

Robert Frost: A Web Site Introducing Robert Frost to a New Generation. Ed. Sarah R. Jackson. Feb. 1998. Stephen F. Austin State U. 15 Mar. 2000, http://www.libarts.sfasu.edu/Frost/index.html.

Offers a very good introduction to the poetry and life of Frost although confusingly organized and less than fully linked to other Frost sites. Links to Frost's chronology, selected bibliography (including audiovisual selections), academic positions, and awards and honors; "new points of interest" of related sites; texts on Frost's reception and his attitudes toward theory; and texts and sound recordings of selected poems and public readings by Frost.

"Robert Frost: Four Volumes." *Project Bartleby Archive.* 15 Mar. 2000, http://www.bartleby.com/index.html.

Those who remember the old Columbia site will probably regret the new, commercial look. Site offers four volumes of Frost's poetry, listing each collection, and indexing poems by titles and first lines. Fully and completely identifies the source editions. The link has been placed at the author index.

Robert Frost on the Web. Ed. and update unknown. Amherstcommon.com. 15 Mar. 2000, http://www.amherstcommon.com/demo/walking_tour/frost.html.

Mainly valuable for links to good biographical materials, including Peter Davison's essay on the relationship between Frost and the editor Ellery Sedgwick as well as texts of interviews. Otherwise, the site suffers from an absence of editorial selection, organization, updating, and maintenance, linking to unauthoritative poetry archives as well as to many no longer extant sites while providing very poor bibliographic information.

Robert Frost Resources. 15 Mar. 2000, http://www.lib.virginia.edu/exhibits/frost/related.html.

The Robert Frost Web. 15 Mar. 2000, http://www.pro-net.co.uk/home/catalyst/RF/rfcover.html.

"Selected Poetry of Robert Frost." *Representative Poetry On-line.* 19 Mar. 2000, http://www.library.utoronto.ca/utel/rp/authors/frost.html.

Biographies and Criticism

Gerber, Philip L. *Robert Frost.* Rev. ed. Boston: Twayne, 1982.

Greiner, Donald J. "Robert Frost." Quartermain, *American Poets, 1880-1945, Third Series* (*Dictionary of Literary Biography* 54) 93-121.

———. *Robert Frost: The Poet and His Critics.* Chicago: American Library Association, 1974.

"Robert Frost." Young, *Poetry Criticism* 1:190-232.

Excerpts of comments and criticism on Frost from 1913-1984, with an annotated bibliography.

Dictionaries, Encyclopedias, and Handbooks

Cramer, Jeffrey S. *Robert Frost among His Poems: A Literary Companion to the Poet's Own Biographical Contexts and Associations.* Jefferson: McFarland, 1996.

Indexes and Concordances

Lathem, Edward Connery. *Concordance to the Poetry of Robert Frost*. New York: Holt Information Systems, 1971.
    Based on Lathem's edition of *Poetry of Robert Frost* (New York: Holt, Rinehart & Winston, 1969).

Journals

Robert Frost Review. Rock Hill: Robert Frost Soc., 1991- .
    Irregularly features "Current Frost Scholarship" and "Robert Frost: A Current Bibliography."

Bibliographies

Cook, Reginald L. "Robert Frost." Bryer, *Sixteen Modern American Authors* 323-66.
    Survey of research; supplemented by Cook and John McWilliams in Bryer, *Sixteen Modern American Authors: Volume 2* 360-403.

Crane, Joan St. C. *Robert Frost: A Descriptive Catalog of Books and Manuscripts in the Clifton Waller Barrett Library, University of Virginia*. Charlottesville: UP of Virginia, 1974.
    Comprehensive guide to Frost's writings, with complete descriptions.

Lentricchia, Frank, and Melissa Christensen Lentricchia. *Robert Frost: A Bibliography, 1913-1974*. Metuchen: Scarecrow, 1976.
    Describes works by and about Frost.

Leo, John R. "Frost, Robert." *Guide to American Poetry Explication* 157-91.

Van Egmond, Peter. *Critical Reception of Robert Frost: An Annotated Bibliography of Secondary Comment*. Boston: G. K. Hall, 1974.
    Brief and selective descriptions of about 3,000 works on Frost.

————. *Robert Frost: A Reference Guide, 1974-1990*. Boston: G. K. Hall, 1991.
    Describes about 800 items on Frost to update Van Egmond, above.

Amy (Lawrence) Lowell, 1874-1925

Web Sites

"Amy Lowell." *Heath Anthology*. 13 Mar. 2000, http://www.georgetown.edu/bassr/heath/syllabuild/iguide/lowella.html.

"Amy Lowell, 1874-1925." *Historical Lesbian Poetry*. 16 Mar. 2000, http://www.sappho.com/poetry/historical/a_lowell.html.
    Brief biography of Lowell, fulltexts of selected works, and a list of further readings, some linked to fulltexts.

Biographies and Criticism

"Amy Lowell." Bryfonski, *Twentieth-Century Literary Criticism* 1:370-80.
    Excerpts of criticism on Lowell from 1915-1969.

———. Bryfonski, *Twentieth-Century Literary Criticism* 8:222-38.
Excerpts of comments and criticism on Lowell from 1914-1980, with an annotated bibliography.

"Amy Lowell." Young, *Poetry Criticism* 13:58-101.
Excerpts of comments and criticism on Lowell from 1924-1985, with an annotated bibliography.

Benvenuto, Richard. *Amy Lowell.* Boston: Twayne, 1985.

Healey, E. Claire, and Laura Ingram. "Amy Lowell." Quartermain, *American Poets, 1880-1945, Third Series* (*Dictionary of Literary Biography* 54) 251-60.

Mackall, Leonard L. "Amy Lowell." Rosenblum, *American Book-Collectors and Bibliographers* (*Dictionary of Literary Biography* 140) 141-46.

Dictionaries, Encyclopedias, and Handbooks

Damon, S. Foster. *Amy Lowell: A Chronicle with Extracts from Her Correspondence.* 1935. Hamden: Archon, 1966.

Bibliographies

Barstow, Jane Missner. "Amy Lowell." *One Hundred Years of American Women Writing, 1848-1948* 165-67.
Describes selected editions, biographies, and criticism.

Hurff, Carmen Russell. *Descriptive Catalogue of the Amy Lowell Collection.* Gainesville: UP of Florida, 1992.

Leo, John R. "Lowell, Amy." *Guide to American Poetry Explication* 244-45.

John M. Oskison, 1874-1947

Web Sites

"John Milton Oskison." *Internet Public Library: Native American Authors Project.* 16 Mar. 2000, http://www.ipl.org/cgi/ref/native/browse.pl/A84.

Biographies and Criticism

"John M(ilton) Oskison." Bryfonski, *Twentieth-Century Literary Criticism* 35:274-81.
Excerpts of comments and criticism on Oskison from 1925-1982, with an annotated bibliography.

Ronnow, Gretchen. "John Milton Oskison." Roemer, *Native American Writers of the United States* (*Dictionary of Literary Biography* 175) 222-32.

Bibliographies

Etulain, Richard W., and N. Jill Howard. "John Milton Oskison." *Bibliographical Guide to the Study of Western American Literature* 331.

Gertrude Stein, 1874-1946

Web Sites

"Chapter 7: Early Twentieth Century: Gertrude Stein." *PAL: Perspectives in American Literature*. 16 Mar. 2000, http://www.csustan.edu/english/reuben/pal/chap7/stein.html.
Up-to-date selected bibliography of works by and about Stein.

Critical Bibliography: Gertrude Stein Online. Ed. Sonja Streuber. Update unknown. Tenderbuttons.com. 16 Mar. 2000, http://www.tenderbuttons.com/critbib.html.
Well-conceived and well-executed content-rich site features internal links for biographical material, bibliographies, literary criticism, interdisciplinary criticism, and dissertations; links for theoretical criticism, creative works about Stein, and creative works about her in various media do not work. Editor Streuber does not give her academic background or affiliation.

"Gertrude Stein." *Knitting Circle*. 18 Mar. 2000, http://www.sbu.ac.uk/stafflag/gertrudestein.html.

"Poetry of Gertrude Stein." *Historical Lesbian Poetry*. 16 Mar. 2000, http://www.sappho.com/poetry/historical/g_stein.html.

Stein, Gertrude. 16 Mar. 2000, http://www.english.upenn.edu/~afilreis/88/stein-bio.html.
Biographical sketch.

The World of Gertrude Stein. 16 Mar. 2000, http://www.ionet.net/~jellenc/gstein1.html.

Biographies and Criticism

"Gertrude Stein." Bryfonski, *Twentieth-Century Literary Criticism* 1:425-42.
Excerpts of criticism on Stein from 1923-1976.

———. Bryfonski, *Twentieth-Century Literary Criticism* 6:402-17.
Excerpts of criticism on Stein from 1923-1981, with an annotated bibliography.

———. Bryfonski, *Twentieth-Century Literary Criticism* 28:303-43.
Excerpts of criticism on Stein from 1914-1986, with an annotated bibliography.

———. Bryfonski, *Twentieth-Century Literary Criticism* 48:206-65.
Excerpts of criticism on Stein from 1934-1990, with an annotated bibliography.

"Gertrude Stein." Young, *Poetry Criticism* 18:306-56.
Excerpts of comments and criticism on Stein from 1956-1995, with an annotated bibliography.

Kimbel, Bobby Ellen. "Gertrude Stein." Kimbel, *American Short-Story Writers, 1910-1945, First Series* (*Dictionary of Literary Biography* 86) 272-97.

Mellow, James R. "Gertrude Stein." Rood, *American Writers in Paris, 1920-1939* (*Dictionary of Literary Biography* 4) 361-73.

Yearsley, Meredith. "Gertrude Stein." Quartermain, *American Poets, 1880-1945, Third Series* (*Dictionary of Literary Biography* 54) 428-63.

Dictionaries, Encyclopedias, and Handbooks

Kellner, Bruce. *Gertrude Stein Companion: Content with the Example.* New York: Greenwood, 1988.

Bibliographies

Barstow, Jane Missner. "Gertrude Stein." *One Hundred Years of American Women Writing, 1848-1948* 176-80.
Describes selected editions, biographies, and criticism.

Carpenter, Charles A. "Stein, Gertrude." *Modern Drama Scholarship and Criticism, 1981-1990* 87.

Fearnow, Mark. "Gertrude Stein." Demastes, *American Playwrights, 1880-1945* [408]-16.

Kostelanetz, Richard. "Gertrude Stein." Shatzky and Taub, *Contemporary Jewish-American Novelists* 409-13.

Leo, John R. "Stein, Gertrude S." *Guide to American Poetry Explication* 384-85.

Liston, Maureen R., and Gina D. Peterman. "Gertrude Stein." Bruccoli and Baughman, *Bibliography of American Fiction, 1919-1988* 470-76.

———. "Gertrude Stein." Bruccoli and Baughman, *Modern Women Writers* 50-61.
Revises and updates Liston and Peterman, above.

Wagner-Martin, Linda. "Gertrude Stein." Shapiro, *Jewish American Women Writers* 431-39.

Walker, Jayne L. "Gertrude Stein." Duke, Bryer, and Inge, *American Women Writers* 109-33.
Survey of research.

White, Ray Lewis. *Gertrude Stein and Alice B. Toklas: A Reference Guide.* Boston: G. K. Hall, 1984.
Describes 1,920 works about Stein and Toklas since 1909.

Wilson, Robert A. *Gertrude Stein: A Bibliography.* New York: Phoenix Bookshop, 1974.
Complete descriptions of Stein's writings, with a list of Alice B. Toklas's works and a selected list of works about them.

Sherwood Anderson, 1876-1941

Web Sites

"Sherwood Anderson." *American Literature on the Web.* 16 Mar. 2000, http://www.nagasaki-gaigo.ac.jp/ishikawa/amlit/20/f_authors20.htm.
Excellent classified list of links for Anderson.

"Sherwood Anderson." *Pegasos.* 16 Mar. 2000, http://www.kirjasto.sci.fi/shanders.htm.

Sherwood Anderson Foundation Home Page. Ed. and update unknown. U of Richmond. 16 Mar. 2000, http://www.urich.edu/~journalm/sahome.html.
Brief biography, chronology of Anderson's books, and information about *Sherwood Anderson Review*, as well as a history of the foundation and information about U of Richmond's journalism program and awards.

The Sherwood Anderson Page. Ed. Robert L. Liebold. Update unknown. Arrel Diversified Technologies. 16 Mar. 2000, http://www.nwohio.com/clydeoh/sherwood.htm.
Mainly useful for links for editions of Anderson's works and works about him that may be purchased, although many links are broken.

Sherwood Anderson Review (formerly *The Winesburg Eagle*). Ed. and update unknown. U of Richmond. 16 Mar. 2000, http://www.urich.edu/~journalm/eagle.html.
Contents of issues (1997-) and subscription information.

The Storyteller. 16 Mar. 2000, http://netva.com/SMYTHCOC/sherwood.htm.

Winesburg, Ohio. Ed. Judith Boss. Feb. 1996. Project Gutenberg. 16 Mar. 2000, ftp://uiarchive.cso.uiuc.edu/pub/etext/gutenberg/etext96/wnbrg11.txt.
Text of *Winesburg, Ohio.*

Biographies and Criticism

Anderson, David D. "Sherwood Anderson." Kimbel, *American Short-Story Writers, 1910-1945, First Series* (*Dictionary of Literary Biography* 86) 3-30.

Cox, Leland H., Jr. "Sherwood Anderson." Rood, *American Writers in Paris, 1920-1939* (*Dictionary of Literary Biography* 4) 10-13.

Papinchak, Robert Allen. *Sherwood Anderson: A Study of the Short Fiction.* New York: Twayne, 1992.

Rideout, Walter B. "Sherwood Anderson." Martine, *American Novelists, 1910-1945* (*Dictionary of Literary Biography* 9) 19-35.

"Sherwood Anderson." Bryfonski, *Twentieth-Century Literary Criticism* 1:34-65.
Excerpts of criticism on Anderson from 1922-1972.

———. Bryfonski, *Twentieth-Century Literary Criticism* 10:29-57.
Excerpts of comments and criticism on Anderson from 1916-1981, with an annotated bibliography.

"Sherwood (Burton) Anderson." Bryfonski, *Twentieth-Century Literary Criticism* 24:15-61.
Excerpts of comments and criticism on *Winesburg, Ohio* from 1919-1986, with an annotated bibliography.

"Sherwood (Burton) Anderson." Harris and Fitzgerald, *Short Story Criticism* 1: 15-65.
Excerpts of criticism on Anderson from 1919-1986, with an annotated bibliography.

White, Ray Lewis. *Winesburg, Ohio: An Exploration.* Boston: Twayne, 1990.

Dictionaries, Encyclopedias, and Handbooks

Small, Judy Jo. *Reader's Guide to the Short Stories of Sherwood Anderson.* New York: G. K. Hall, 1994.

Journals

Winesburg Eagle: The Official Publication of the Sherwood Anderson Society. Blacksburg: Sherwood Anderson Soc., 1975- .
Annually publishes "A Sherwood Anderson Checklist."

Bibliographies

Rideout, Walter B. "Sherwood Anderson." Bryer, *Sixteen Modern American Authors* 3-28.
Survey of research; supplemented by Rideout in Bryer's *Sixteen Modern American Authors: Volume 2* 1-41.

Sheehy, Eugene P., and Kenneth A. Lohf. *Sherwood Anderson: A Bibliography.* Los Gatos: Talisman, 1960.
Comprehensive guide to Anderson's works, with a list of about 1,000 works on Anderson.

White, Ray Lewis. "Sherwood Anderson." Nagel, Nagel, and Baughman, *Bibliography of American Fiction, 1866-1918* 50-54.

———. *Sherwood Anderson: A Reference Guide.* Boston: G. K. Hall, 1977.
Describes 2,550 works about Anderson.

Gertrude Simmons Bonnin (Zitkala-Ša), 1876-1938

Web Sites

Gertrude Bonnin. 16 Mar. 2000, http://indy4.fdl.cc.mn.us/~isk/stories/authors/bonnin. html.

"Gertrude Bonnin." *Heath Anthology.* 13 Mar. 2000, http://www.georgetown.edu/ bassr/heath/syllabuild/iguide/bonnin.html.

Native American Authors—Teacher Resources. 19 Mar. 2000, http://falcon.jmu.edu/ ~ramseyil/natauth.htm#D.

Biographies and Criticism

Lukens, Margo. "Zitkala-Ša (Gertrude Bonnin)." Roemer, *Native American Writers of the United States* (*Dictionary of Literary Biography* 175) 331-36.

Bibliographies

Barstow, Jane Missner. "Native American Writers." *One Hundred Years of American Women Writing, 1848-1948* 307-11.
Describes criticism of Zitkala-Ša, E. Pauline Johnson, and Humishma.

Jack London (John Griffith London), 1876-1916

Web Sites

American Literature Online: Jack London. 16 Mar. 2000, http://faculty.millikin.edu/
~moconner.hum.faculty.mu/e232/londonbio.html.

Digital Jack. Ed. and update unknown. Centenary C. 16 Mar. 2000, http://london.
centenary.edu/.
Mainly useful for searchable classified bibliography of works about London
(covers criticism, biography, compilations and anthologies, periodicals and journals,
London on film and stage, and foreign translations and criticism).

"Jack London." *American Literature on the Web.* 16 Mar. 2000, http://www.nagasaki-
gaigo.ac.jp/ishikawa/amlit/l/london19re.htm.
Particularly useful list of fulltexts of London's works.

Jack London—His Life and Books. 16 Mar. 2000, http://parks.sonoma.net/JLStory.
html.

The Jack London Collection. Ed. unknown. 11 Nov. 1999. U of California at Berkeley. 16 Mar. 2000, http://sunsite.berkeley.edu/London/.
Excellent multimedia site includes fulltexts of 30 selected novels, short stories,
plays, nonfiction (including journal articles, like London's eyewitness account of the
great earthquake and fire in San Francisco, published in *Collier's* in 1906), and letters. Also offers biographies, concordances, literary chronologies, and criticism of
London (signed by contributing scholars) and links to organizations, publications,
announcements, listservs, and other sites (for events and symposia).

Jack London Main Page. 16 Mar. 2000, http://www.jacklondon.com.

Biographies and Criticism

Beauchamp, Gorman. "Jack London." Cowart and Wymer, *Twentieth-Century
American Science-Fiction Writers* (*Dictionary of Literary Biography* 8)
297-303.

Hogge, Robert M. "Jack London." Cracroft, *Twentieth-Century American Western
Writers, Second Series* (*Dictionary of Literary Biography* 212) 172-84.

"Jack London." Bryfonski, *Twentieth-Century Literary Criticism* 15:253-82.
Excerpts of comments and criticism on London from 1970-1983, with an annotated bibliography.

———. Bryfonski, *Twentieth-Century Literary Criticism* 39:259-91.
Excerpts of comments and criticism on *Call of the Wild* from 1903-1987, with
an annotated bibliography.

"Jack London." Harris and Fitzgerald, *Short Story Criticism* 4:248-97.
Excerpts of criticism on London from 1900-1983, with an annotated bibliography.

Labor, Earle. "Jack London." Kimbel and Grant, *American Short-Story Writers,
1880-1910* (*Dictionary of Literary Biography* 78) 245-71.

———. "Jack London." Pizer and Harbert, *American Realists and Naturalists* (*Dictionary of Literary Biography* 12) 350-73.

———, and Jeanne Campbell Reesman. *Jack London*. Rev. ed. New York: Twayne, 1994.

Reesman, Jeanne Campbell. *Jack London: A Study of the Short Fiction*. New York: Twayne, 1999.

Tavernier-Courbin, Jacqueline. *The Call of the Wild: A Naturalistic Romance*. New York: Twayne, 1994.

Journals

Call: The Official Newsletter of the Jack London Society. San Antonio: Jack London Soc., 1991- .

Jack London Newsletter. Carbondale: Southern Illinois U, 1967-1988.

Bibliographies

Carpenter, Charles A. "London, Jack." *Modern Drama Scholarship and Criticism, 1981-1990* 64.

Etulain, Richard W., and N. Jill Howard. "Jack London." *Bibliographical Guide to the Study of Western American Literature* 292-99.

Evans, Robert C. "Jack London: 'To Build a Fire'." Evans, Little, and Wiedemann, *Short Fiction* 158-64.
Describes 11 studies.

Glitsch, Catherine. "London, Jack." *American Novel Explication, 1991-1995* 158-59.

Hamilton, David Mike. *"The Tools of My Trade": The Annotated Books in Jack London's Library*. Seattle: U of Washington P, 1986.

Kellman, Steven G. "Jack London." *Modern American Novel* 115-20.
Describes about 30 critical works.

Korb, Scott Matthew. "To Understand the 'London Myth': The Life and Writings of Jack London." *Bulletin of Bibliography* 55.1 (1998): 3-10.

Labor, Earle. "Jack London." Nagel, Nagel, and Baughman, *Bibliography of American Fiction, 1866-1918* 271-76.

———. "Jack London." Erisman and Etulain, *Fifty Western Writers* 268-79.

Sherman, Joan R. *Jack London: A Reference Guide*. Boston: G. K. Hall, 1977.
Describes about 1,500 works on London.

Woodbridge, Hensley C., John London, and George H. Tweney. *Jack London: A Bibliography*. Enlarged ed. Millwood: Kraus Reprint, 1973.
Comprehensive guide to works by and about London, with complete descriptions.

Carl (August) Sandburg, 1878-1967

Web Sites

"Carl Sandburg." *Academy of American Poets*. 9 Mar. 2000, http://www.poets.org/lit/
   poet/csandfst.htm.

"Carl Sandburg." *Pegasos*. 16 Mar. 2000, http://www.kirjasto.sci.fi/sandburg.htm.

"Carl Sandburg: Two Volumes." *Project Bartleby Archive*. 16 Mar. 2000, http://www.
   bartleby.com/.
   Fulltexts of two collections: *Chicago Poems* and *Cornhuskers*.

Sandburg, Carl. 16 Mar. 2000, http://www.inform.umd.edu/EdRes/ReadingRoom/Poetry/
   Sandburg/.
   Good list of fulltext poems. No bibliography.

"Selected Poetry of Carl Sandburg." *Representative Poetry On-line*. 19 Mar. 2000,
   http://www.library.utoronto.ca/utel/rp/authors/sandburg.html.

Biographies and Criticism

"Carl Sandburg." Young, *Poetry Criticism* 2:298-342.
   Excerpts of comments and criticism on Sandburg from 1916-1979, with an annotated bibliography.

Neely, Mark E., Jr. "Carl Sandburg." Wilson, *Twentieth-Century American Historians* (*Dictionary of Literary Biography* 17) 378-82.

Niven, Penelope. "Carl Sandburg." Quartermain, *American Poets, 1880-1945, Third
   Series* (*Dictionary of Literary Biography* 54) 388-406.

Bibliographies

Leo, John R. "Sandburg, Carl S." *Guide to American Poetry Explication* 359-61.

Salwak, Dale. *Carl Sandburg: A Reference Guide*. Boston: G. K. Hall, 1988.
   Brief descriptions of works about Sandburg since 1904.

Upton (Beall) Sinclair, 1878-1968

Web Sites

"Etexts by Upton Sinclair." *Project Gutenberg*. 16 Mar. 2000, http://promo.net/
   cgi-promo/pg/t9.cgi.
   Text of *Damaged Goods*.

Merriam-Sinclair Battle Outstanding in National Political Scene. 16 Mar. 2000,
   http://www.best.com/~sfmuseum/hist1/sinclair2.html.
   Informative links.

"Upton Beall Sinclair." *Pegasos*. 16 Mar. 2000, http://www.kirjasto.sci.fi/sinclair.
   htm.

"Upton Sinclair." *Heath Anthology.* 13 Mar. 2000, http://www.georgetown.edu/bassr/heath/syllabuild/iguide/sinclair.html.

Upton Sinclair. 16 Mar. 2000, http://www.ssa.gov/history/sinclair.html.

Biographies and Criticism

Bloodworth, William A. "Upton Sinclair." Martine, *American Novelists, 1910-1945* (*Dictionary of Literary Biography* 9) 25-32.

"Upton Sinclair." Riley, *Contemporary Literary Criticism* 63:342-77.
    Excerpts of criticism on Sinclair from 1933-1988, with an annotated bibliography.

Bibliographies

Ahouse, John B. *Upton Sinclair: A Descriptive, Annotated Bibliography.* Los Angeles: Mercer & Aitchison, 1994.
    Complete descriptions of Sinclair's books; supplements Gottesman, below.

——, and Cheryl Z. Oreovicz. "Upton Sinclair." Nagel, Nagel, and Baughman, *Bibliography of American Fiction 1866-1918* 322-27.

Etulain, Richard W., and N. Jill Howard. "Upton Sinclair." *Bibliographical Guide to the Study of Western American Literature* 371-72.

Gottesman, Ronald. *Upton Sinclair: An Annotated Checklist.* Kent: Kent State UP, 1973.
    Brief descriptions of Sinclair's works and listings for works about him.

Wallace Stevens, 1879-1955

Web Sites

Hartford Friends of Wallace Stevens. 16 Mar. 2000, http://www.wesleyan.edu/wstevens/stevens.html.

"Wallace Stevens." *Academy of American Poets.* 9 Mar. 2000, http://www.poets.org/lit/poet/wstevfst.htm.
    Fulltexts of eight poems by Stevens, with audio ("Anecdote of the Jar," "The Emperor of Ice-Cream," "The Snow Man," "Thirteen Ways of Looking at a Blackbird," "Bantams in Pine-Woods," "Metaphors of a Magnifico," "The Idea of Order at Key West," and "The High-Toned Old Christian Woman"); a bibliography of works by Stevens; a good biographical sketch; and offsite links.

"Wallace Stevens." *Connecticut Writers.* (U of Connecticut Libraries). 16 Mar. 2000, http://spirit.lib.uconn.edu/CTWriters/stevens.html.

"Wallace Stevens." *Literature Online.* 16 Mar. 2000, http://longman.awl.com/kennedy/stevens/biography.html.
    Biography, critical overview, unannotated bibliography of works by and about Stevens, and links to Addison-Wesley's *Literature Online.*

"Wallace Stevens." *Twentieth-Century Poetry in English.* 16 Mar. 2000, http://www.lit.kobe-u.ac.jp/~hishika/stevens.htm.
Mainly useful for bibliography of literary criticism of Stevens's poetry and good set of links to other sites.

Wallace Stevens. 16 Mar. 2000, http://www.cwru.edu/artsci/engl/VSALM/mod/socha/links.htm.

Wallace Stevens (1879-1955). Ed. Alan Filreis. 17 Jun. 1999. U of Pennsylvania. 16 Mar. 2000, http://www.english.upenn.edu/~afilreis/88/stevens-poems.html.
Because two levels are required to find it, this course site is easily missed. Includes links to six poems ("Gray Room," "Thirteen Ways of Looking at a Blackbird," "Anecdote of the Jar," "The Snow Man," "Of Modern Poetry," and "Not Ideas about the Thing But the Thing Itself"), a 1948 photograph of Stevens, quotations from Stevens in the *Oxford English Dictionary* (with restricted access, though unmarked), and "a good deal more." Also includes links to texts about Stevens's deathbed conversion, *New York Times* obituary, correspondence with Jose Rodriguez Feo, and other Stevens sites.

"Wallace Stevens (1879-1955)." *Pegasos.* 16 Mar. 2000, http://www.kirjasto.sci.fi/wsteven.htm.
Includes a very good biography, bibliography of literary criticism of Stevens's poetry, and good set of links to other sites.

Wallace Stevens: Biography. Ed. and update unknown. U of Connecticut. 16 Mar. 2000, http://www.ucc.uconn.edu/~klh95001/bio.html.
Biographical sketch of Stevens that discusses his literary tastes and friendships. Unsigned.

Wallace Stevens: Essays, Poems, Pictures, and More. Ed. Alan Filreis. 17 Dec. 1999. English Dept., U of Pennsylvania. 5 Mar. 2000, http://www.english.upenn.edu/~afilreis/Stevens/home.html.
Links to selected texts, listservs, and major Stevens sites; includes topical essays and reviews by Filreis as well as links to selected critical texts about Stevens.

Wallace Stevens Walking Tour. 16 Mar. 2000, http://www.wesleyan.edu/wstevens/Wallywalk.html.

Biographies and Criticism

McCann, Janet. *Wallace Stevens Revisited: "The Celestial Possible."* New York: Twayne, 1995.

Miller, Joseph. "Wallace Stevens." Quartermain, *American Poets, 1880-1945, Third Series (Dictionary of Literary Biography* 54) 471-505.

Richardson, Joan. *Wallace Stevens: A Biography: The Early Years, 1879-1923.* New York: Beech Tree, 1986.

———. *Wallace Stevens: A Biography: The Later Years,1923-1955.* New York: Beech Tree, 1988.

Sukenick, Ronald. *Wallace Stevens: Musing the Obscure: Readings, Interpretation, and a Guide to the Collected Poetry.* New York: New York UP, 1967.
Brief "paraphrases" of Stevens's poems in *Collected Poems* (New York: Knopf, 1954) and *Opus Posthumous*, ed. Samuel French Morse (New York: Knopf, 1957).

"Wallace Stevens." Bryfonski, *Twentieth-Century Literary Criticism* 3:444-79.
Excerpts of comments and criticism on Stevens from 1924-1979, with an annotated bibliography.

———. Bryfonski, *Twentieth-Century Literary Criticism* 12:354-88.
Excerpts of comments and criticism on Stevens from 1931-1982, with an annotated bibliography.

———. Bryfonski, *Twentieth-Century Literary Criticism* 45:266-357.
Excerpts of comments and criticism on Stevens from 1935-1988, with an annotated bibliography.

"Wallace Stevens." Young, *Poetry Criticism* 6:290-344.
Excerpts of comments and criticism on Stevens from 1924-1990, with an annotated bibliography.

Indexes and Concordances

Walsh, Thomas F. *Concordance to the Poetry of Wallace Stevens.* University Park: Pennsylvania State UP, 1963.
References *Collected Poems of Wallace Stevens* (New York: Knopf, 1954), *Necessary Angel* (New York: Knopf, 1951), and *Opus Posthumous*, ed. Samuel French Morse (New York: Knopf, 1957).

Journals

Wallace Stevens Journal. Potsdam: Wallace Stevens Soc., 1977- .
Features "Current Bibliography." Web site at http://www.clarkson.edu/~wsj/ index.html, indexes contents to all volumes.

Bibliographies

Carpenter, Charles A. "Stevens, Wallace." *Modern Drama Scholarship and Criticism, 1981-1990* 87.

Edelstein, J. M. *Wallace Stevens: A Descriptive Bibliography.* Pittsburgh: U of Pittsburgh P, 1973.
Comprehensive guide to Stevens's works, with complete descriptions, and references to about 700 works on Stevens.

Leo, John R. "Stevens, Wallace." *Guide to American Poetry Explication* 386-428.

Riddell, Joseph N. "Wallace Stevens." Bryer, *Sixteen Modern American Authors* 529-71.
Survey of research; supplemented by Riddell in Bryer, *Sixteen Modern American Authors: Volume 2* 623-74.

Serio, John N. *Wallace Stevens: An Annotated Secondary Bibliography*. Pittsburgh: U of Pittsburgh P, 1994.
Detailed descriptions of 1,875 works on Stevens since 1916.

Willard, Abbie F. *Wallace Stevens: The Poet and His Critics*. Chicago: American Library Association, 1978.
Surveys research.

Georgia Douglas Johnson, 1880-1966

Web Sites

"Georgia Douglas Johnson." *Women of Color, Women of Words*. Ed. Angela Weaver. 13 May 1999. State U of New Jersey (Rutgers). 16 Mar. 2000, http://www.scils. rutgers.edu/~cybers/john.html.
Best available page, with a very brief biography and links to a few works by Johnson.

Biographies and Criticism

Fletcher, Winona. "Georgia Douglas Johnson." Harris, *Afro-American Writers from the Harlem Renaissance to 1940* (*Dictionary of Literary Biography* 51) 153-64.

Bibliographies

Anderson, Addell Austin. "Georgia Douglas Johnson." Demastes, *American Playwrights, 1880-1945* [224]-29.

Carpenter, Charles A. "Johnson, Georgia Douglas." *Modern Drama Scholarship and Criticism, 1981-1990* 62.

Jones, Gwendoyn S. "Georgia Douglas Johnson." Nelson, *African American Authors, 1745-1945* 284-89.
Survey of research.

H(enry) L(ouis) Mencken, 1880-1956

Web Sites

"H. L. Mencken." *Pegasos*. 16 Mar. 2000, http://www.kirjasto.sci.fi/mencken.htm.

H. L. Mencken (1880-1956). Ed. "*Monkey* John." Update and sponsor unknown. 16 Mar. 2000, http://w3.one.net/~muir/hlm/.
Good place to start research on Mencken with a useful introduction, well-conceived and sober analyses of Mencken and his views, including Walter Lippman's famous appraisal of Mencken published in *Saturday Review of Literature*; selected quotations from Mencken; and an extensive unannotated bibliography of Mencken's works. Linked sound files did not load and the site needs to be updated.

H. L. Mencken: Writer, Editor, and Social Critic. 16 Mar. 2000, http://www.msu.edu/ course/mc/112/1920s/Mencken/index.html.

H. L. Mencken Society Home Page: Official Web Page of the H. L. Mencken Society.
Ed. unknown. 15 Mar. 2000. H. L. Mencken Soc. 16 Mar. 2000, http://www.
mencken.org.
Brief biography; texts of selected works and quotes by Mencken and reviews of
his works; a good set of FAQs and advice for researchers; "Where do I start?" advice
and an extensive classified "Recommended Reading" list that provides broad subject
access to much of Mencken's work; and links to other Mencken web sites.

Biographies and Criticism

Fitzpatrick, Vincent. "H. L. Mencken." Riley, *American Magazine Journalists,
1900-1960 (Dictionary of Literary Biography* 137) 179-204.

"H(enry) L(ouis) Mencken." Bryfonski, *Twentieth-Century Literary Criticism*
13:355-98.
Excerpts of comments and criticism on Mencken from 1906-1981, with an annotated bibliography.

McElveen, J. James. "H. L. Mencken." Ashley, *American Newspaper Journalists,
1926-1950 (Dictionary of Literary Biography* 29) 223-40.

Miles, Elton. "H. L. Mencken." Trachtenberg, *American Humorists, 1800-1950 (Dictionary of Literary Biography* 11) 323-31.

Nolte, William H. "H. L. Mencken." Jay, *Modern American Critics, 1920-1955 (Dictionary of Literary Biography* 63) 149-62.

Williams, W. H. A. *H. L. Mencken Revisited.* New York: Twayne, 1998.

Indexes and Concordances

DuBasky, Mayo. *Gist of Mencken: Quotations from America's Critic: Gleaned from
Newspapers, Magazines, Books, Letters, and Manuscripts.* Metuchen: Scarecrow, 1990.

Journals

Menckeniana: A Quarterly Review. Baltimore: Enoch Pratt Free Library, 1962- .
Features occasional "Books on HLM" and regular "Bibliographic Check List."

Bibliographies

Adler, Betty. *H. L. M.: The Mencken Bibliography.* Baltimore: Johns Hopkins UP,
1961.
With supplements of Adler and Fitzpatrick, below, comprehensive listings of
works by and about Mencken.

———. *H. L. M.: The Mencken Bibliography: A Ten-Year Supplement, 1962-1971.*
Baltimore: Enoch Pratt Free Library, 1971.

Blusterbaum, Allison. *H. L. Mencken: A Research Guide.* New York: Garland, 1988.
Describes a selection of about 800 works on Mencken.

Etulain, Richard W., and N. Jill Howard. "H. L. Mencken." *Bibliographical Guide to
the Study of Western American Literature* 310.

Fitzpatrick, Vincent. *H. L. M.: The Mencken Bibliography: A Second Ten-Year Supplement, 1972-1981.* Baltimore: Enoch Pratt Free Library, 1981.

Hobson, Fred. "H. L. Mencken." Flora and Bain, *Fifty Southern Writers after 1900* 313-23.

Schrader, Richard J. *H. L. Mencken: A Descriptive Bibliography.* Pittsburgh: U of Pittsburgh P, 1998.
Complete descriptions of Mencken's works. Updated by Schrader at http://www2.bc.edu/~schrader/mencken.html.

Anzia Yezierska, 1885-1970

Web Sites

"Anzia Yezierska." *American Literature on the Web.* 16 Mar. 2000, http://www.nagasaki-gaigo.ac.jp/ishikawa/amlit/20/f_authors20.htm.

"Anzia Yezierska." *Heath Anthology.* 13 Mar. 2000, http://www.georgetown.edu/bassr/heath/syllabuild/iguide/yeziersk.html.

Biographies and Criticism

Goodman, Charlotte. "Anzia Yezierska." Walden, *Twentieth-Century American-Jewish Fiction Writers* (*Dictionary of Literary Biography* 28) 332-35.

Schoen, Carol B. *Anzia Yezierska.* Boston: Twayne, 1982.

Bibliographies

Barstow, Jane Missner. "Anzia Yezierska." *One Hundred Years of American Women Writing, 1848-1948* 126-29.
Describes selected editions, biographies, and criticism.

Glitsch, Catherine. "Yezierska, Anzia." *American Novel Explication, 1991-1995* 276.

John G(neisenau) Neihardt, 1881-1973

Web Site

John G. Neihardt: Poet of the American West. 12 Mar. 2000, http://www.system.missouri.edu/whmc/neihardt/intro.htm.
An excellent site, including biography, papers, and letters.

Biographies and Criticism

Aly, Lucile F. "John G. Neihardt." Martine, *American Novelists, 1910-1945* (*Dictionary of Literary Biography* 9) 238-41.

Globe, Alexander. "John G. Neihardt." Quartermain, *American Poets, 1880-1945, Third Series* (*Dictionary of Literary Biography* 54) 333-44.

Bibliographies

Aly, Lucile F. "John G. Neihardt." Erisman and Etulain, *Fifty Western Writers* 336-46.

Etulain, Richard W., and N. Jill Howard. "John G. Neihardt." *Bibliographical Guide to the Study of Western American Literature* 322-23.

Richards, John Thomas. *Rawhide Laureate, John G. Neihardt: A Selected, Annotated Bibliography*. Metuchen: Scarecrow, 1983.
    Detailed contents and lists of Neihardt's works and annotated entries for works about him.

Susan Glaspell, 1882-1948

Web Sites

"Chapter 8: American Drama: Susan Glaspell." *PAL: Perspectives in American Literature*. 16 Mar. 2000, http://www.csustan.edu/english/reuben/pal/chap8/glaspell.html.
    List of works by Glaspell, selected bibliography of works about her, and study questions.

"Susan Glaspell." *American Literature on the Web*. 16 Mar. 2000, http://www.nagasaki-gaigo.ac.jp/ishikawa/amlit/20/f_authors20.htm.
    Good list of links for Glaspell.

Susan Glaspell. 16 Mar. 2000, http://www.tcnj.edu/~verasteg/glaspell.htm.

Biographies and Criticism

France, Rachel. "Susan Glaspell." MacNicholas, *Twentieth-Century American Dramatists* (*Dictionary of Literary Biography* 7) 215-23.

Noe, Marcia. "Susan Glaspell." Martine, *American Novelists, 1910-1945* (*Dictionary of Literary Biography* 9) 66-72.

"Susan Glaspell." Bryfonski, *Twentieth-Century Literary Criticism* 55:232-77.
    Excerpts of comments and criticism on Glaspell from 1922-1990, with an annotated bibliography.

"Susan Glaspell." Trudeau, *Drama Criticism* 10:143-211.
    Excerpts of criticism on Glaspell and *Trifles* from 1966-1997, with an annotated bibliography.

Waterman, Arthur. "Susan Glaspell." Kimbel and Grant, *American Short-Story Writers, 1880-1910* (*Dictionary of Literary Biography* 78) 198-204.

Bibliographies

Barstow, Jane Missner. "Susan Glaspell." *One Hundred Years of American Women Writing, 1848-1948* 153-55.
    Describes selected editions, biographies, and criticism.

Carpenter, Charles A. "Glaspell, Susan." *Modern Drama Scholarship and Criticism, 1981-1990* 57.

Gainor, J. Ellen. "Susan Keating Glaspell." Demastes, *American Playwrights, 1880-1945* [109]-120.

Papke, Mary E. *Susan Glaspell: A Research and Production Sourcebook*. Westport: Greenwood, 1993.
Plot summaries, production details, and overviews of critical receptions for Glaspell's 14 plays, with cross-references to criticism since 1916 and lists of her other works.

Shuman, R. Baird. "Susan Glaspell." *American Drama, 1918-1960* 76-77.
Describes eight works on Glaspell.

Williams, Lori J. "Susan Glaspell." Nagel, Nagel, and Baughman, *Bibliography of American Fiction 1866-1918* 194-95.

William Carlos Williams, 1883-1963

Web Sites

Amy Munno's William Carlos Williams Page. 16 Mar. 2000, http://www.webspan.net/~amunno/wcw.html.

"William Carlos Williams." *Academy of American Poets*. 9 Mar. 2000, http://www.poets.org/lit/poet/wcwilfst.htm.

"William Carlos Williams." *Literary Kicks*. 16 Mar. 2000, http://www.charm.net/~brooklyn/People/WilliamCarlosWilliams.html.

William Carlos Williams. 16 Mar. 2000, http://www.cwrl.utexas.edu/~slatin/20c_poetry/projects/relatproject/WCW.html.

Biographies and Criticism

Christensen, Paul. "William Carlos Williams." Charters, *The Beats: Literary Bohemians in Postwar America* (*Dictionary of Literary Biography* 16) 583-90.

Cooper, John Xiros. "William Carlos Williams." Quartermain, *American Poets, 1880-1945, Third Series* (*Dictionary of Literary Biography* 54) 533-75.

Flachmann, Kim. "William Carlos Williams." Kimbel, *American Short-Story Writers, 1910-1945, First Series* (*Dictionary of Literary Biography* 86) 306-15.

Gish, Robert. *William Carlos Williams: A Study of the Short Fiction*. Boston: Twayne, 1989.

Tashjian, Dickran L. "William Carlos Williams." Rood, *American Writers in Paris, 1920-1939* (*Dictionary of Literary Biography* 4) 415-18.

Whitaker, Thomas R. *William Carlos Williams*. Rev. ed. Boston: Twayne, 1989.

"William Carlos Williams." Harris and Fitzgerald, *Short Story Criticism* 31:298-365.
Excerpts of criticism on Williams from 1938-1989, with an annotated bibliography.

"William Carlos Williams." Riley, *Contemporary Literary Criticism* 67:393-428.
Excerpts of criticism on Williams's epic poem *Patterson* from 1946-1988, with an annotated bibliography.

"William Carlos Williams." Young, *Poetry Criticism* 7:343-413.
Excerpts of comments and criticism on Williams from 1922-1989, with an annotated bibliography.

Journals

William Carlos Williams Review. Austin: U of Texas, 1975- .
Formerly *William Carlos Williams Newsletter*; publishes a current bibliography (including media and research in progress). The journal's web site, http://www.en. utexas.edu/wcw/index2.html, contains complete texts of selected current and back issues and a message forum, with extensive "William Carlos Williams Bibliography, 1986-1998" of works by and about Williams.

Bibliographies

Brogunier, Joseph. "An Annotated Bibliography of Works about William Carlos Williams: 1974-1982." *William Carlos Williams: Man and Poet.* Ed. Carroll F. Terrell. Orono: National Poetry Foundation, U of Maine, 1983. [453]-585.
Supplements Wagner's 1978 guide, below.

Carpenter, Charles A. "Williams, William Carlos." *Modern Drama Scholarship and Criticism, 1981-1990* 94.

Lawlor, William. "William Carlos Williams (1983-1963)." *Beat Generation: A Bibliographical Teaching Guide* 319-20.
Very brief up-to-date survey of criticism in relation to Beats.

Leo, John R. "Williams, William Carlos." *Guide to American Poetry Explication* 470-87.

Wagner, Linda W. *William Carlos Williams: A Reference Guide.* Boston: G. K. Hall, 1978.
Describes about 1,200 works on Williams.

———. "William Carlos Williams." Bryer, *Sixteen Modern American Authors* 573-85.
Survey of research; supplemented by Wagner-Martin (formerly Wagner) in Bryer, *Sixteen Modern American Authors: Volume 2* 675-715.

Wallace, Emily Mitchell. *A Bibliography of William Carlos Williams.* Middletown: Wesleyan UP, 1968.
Complete descriptions of Williams's writings.

Ring(gold) W(ilmer) Lardner,
1885-1933

Web Sites

"The Ring W. Lardner Page." *SAC LitWeb*. 16 Mar. 2000, http://www.accd.edu/
sac/english/bailey/lardner.htm.

Biographies and Criticism

Evans, Elizabeth. "Ring Lardner." Trachtenberg, *American Humorists, 1800-1950*
(*Dictionary of Literary Biography* 11) 242-56.

"Ring(gold Wilmer) Lardner." Bryfonski, *Twentieth-Century Literary Criticism*
2:325-41.
Excerpts of criticism on Lardner from 1924-1972.

———. Bryfonski, *Twentieth-Century Literary Criticism* 14:288-321.
Excerpts of criticism on Lardner from 1918-1981, with an annotated bibliography.

Bibliographies

Bruccoli, Matthew J., and Richard Layman. *Ring W. Lardner: A Descriptive Bibliog-*
raphy. Pittsburgh: U of Pittsburgh P, 1976.
Complete descriptions of Lardner's works with a list of selected works about
him.

Carpenter, Charles A. "Lardner, Ring." *Modern Drama Scholarship and Criticism,*
1981-1990 64.

Layman, Richard. "Ring Lardner." Bruccoli and Baughman, *Bibliography of Ameri-*
can Fiction, 1919-1988 285-86.

(Harry) Sinclair Lewis, 1885-1951

Web Sites

"Sinclair Lewis." *Nobel Prize Internet Archive*. 16 Mar. 2000, http://nobelprizes.com/
nobel/literature/1930a.html.

Sinclair Lewis. 16 Mar. 2000, http://www.robinsonresearch.com/LITERATE/AUTHORS/
Lewis.htm.

The Sinclair Lewis Home Page. 16 Mar. 2000, http://www.ilstu.edu/~separry/lewis.
html.
All in all, a very respectable site for Lewis. Contains biography, bibliography,
timeline, and offsite links.

Biographies and Criticism

Bucco, Martin. *Main Street: The Revolt of Carol Kennicott*. New York: Twayne,
1993.

"(Harry) Sinclair Lewis." Bryfonski, *Twentieth-Century Literary Criticism* 4:245-63.
Excerpts of comments and criticism on Lewis from 1914-1973, with an annotated bibliography.

———. Bryfonski, *Twentieth-Century Literary Criticism* 13:323-54.
Excerpts of comments and criticism on Lewis from 1914-1981, with an annotated bibliography.

———. Bryfonski, *Twentieth-Century Literary Criticism* 23:125-54.
Excerpts of comments and criticism on *Main Street* from 1920-1985, with an annotated bibliography.

Lasseter, Victor. "Sinclair Lewis." Kimbel, *American Short-Story Writers, 1910-1945, Second Series* (*Dictionary of Literary Biography* 102) 188-95.

Light, Martin. "Sinclair Lewis." Martine, *American Novelists, 1910-1945* (*Dictionary of Literary Biography* 9) 169-85.

Love, Glen A. *Babbitt: An American Life*. New York: Twayne, 1993.

"Sinclair Lewis." Bryfonski, *Twentieth-Century Literary Criticism* 39:199-258.
Excerpts of comments and criticism on *Babbitt* from 1921-1987, with an annotated bibliography.

Bibliographies

Etulain, Richard W., and N. Jill Howard. "Sinclair Lewis." *Bibliographical Guide to the Study of Western American Literature* 288-91.

Fleming, Robert E. *Sinclair Lewis: A Reference Guide*. Boston: G. K. Hall, 1980.
Describes about 1,400 works on Lewis since 1914; updated by Fleming's "Recent Research on Sinclair Lewis," *Modern Fiction Studies* 31 (1985): 609-16.

Glitsch, Catherine. "Lewis, Sinclair." *American Novel Explication, 1991-1995* 157.

Kasinec, Denise, and James S. Measell. "Sinclair Lewis." Bruccoli and Baughman, *Bibliography of American Fiction, 1919-1988* 295-99.

Kellman, Steven G. "Sinclair Lewis." *Modern American Novel* 105-14.
Describes about 50 critical works.

Ezra (Weston Loomis) Pound, 1885-1972

Web Sites

"Ezra Pound." *Academy of American Poets*. 9 Mar. 2000, http://www.poets.org/lit/poet/epounfst.htm.

"Ezra Pound." *Twentieth-Century Poetry in English*. 16 Mar. 2000, http://miyamizu.lit.kobe-u.ac.jp/~hishika/pound.htm.

"Ezra Pound." *Electronic Poetry Center*. 16 Mar. 2000, http://wings.buffalo.edu/epc/authors/pound/.

"Selected Poetry of Ezra Loomis Pound." *Representative Poetry On-line*. 19 Mar. 2000, http://www.library.utoronto.ca/utel/rp/authors/pound.html.

Biographies and Criticism

"Ezra Pound." Riley, *Contemporary Literary Criticism* 112:298-359.
Excerpts of criticism on Pound from 1989-1995, with an annotated bibliography.

"Ezra Pound." Young, *Poetry Criticism* 4:314-68.
Excerpts of comments and criticism on Pound from 1919-1991, with an annotated bibliography.

Flory, Wendy Stallard. "Ezra Pound." Quartermain, *American Poets, 1880-1945, First Series* (*Dictionary of Literary Biography* 45) 305-43.

Levenson, Michael. "Ezra Pound." Jay, *Modern American Critics, 1920-1955* (*Dictionary of Literary Biography* 63) 221-37.

Sieburth, Richard. "Ezra Pound." Rood, *American Writers in Paris, 1920-1939* (*Dictionary of Literary Biography* 4) 315-33.

Dictionaries, Encyclopedias, and Handbooks

Kearns, George. *Guide to Ezra Pound's Selected Cantos*. New Brunswick: Rutgers UP, 1980.

Nadel, Ira B. *Cambridge Companion to Ezra Pound*. New York: Cambridge UP, 1999.

Ruthven, K. K. *Guide to Ezra Pound's Personae: 1926*. Berkeley: U of California P, 1969.

Terrell, Carroll Franklin. *Companion to the Cantos of Ezra Pound*. Berkeley: U of California P, 1980-1985.
Canto-by-canto, allusion-by-allusion glosses and readings, with lists of additional background and critical studies.

Indexes and Concordances

Dilligan, Robert J., James W. Parins, and Todd K. Bender. *Concordance to Ezra Pound's Cantos*. New York: Garland, 1981.
Indexes *Cantos of Ezra Pound* (New York: New Directions, 1975).

Edwards, John Hamilton, and William W. Varse. *Annotated Index to the Cantos of Ezra Pound: Cantos 1-84*. Berkeley: U of California P, 1957.
References (New York: New Directions, 1948) edition.

Lane, Gary. *Concordance to Personae: The Shorter Poems of Ezra Pound*. New York: Haskell House, 1972.
Based on texts in *Personae: The Collected Poems of Ezra Pound* (New York: Boni and Liveright, 1926).

Journals

Paideuma: A Journal Devoted to Ezra Pound Scholarship. Orono: National Poetry
   Foundation, U of Maine, 1972- .
   "The Bibliographer" features lists of new works and survey reviews.

Bibliographies

Bischoff, Volker. *Ezra Pound Criticism, 1905-1985: A Chronological Listing of Publications in English.* Marburg: Universitatsbibliothek Marburg, 1991.
   Unannotated list of 5,390 works about Pound.

Carpenter, Charles A. "Pound, Ezra." *Modern Drama Scholarship and Criticism,
   1981-1990* 80.

Espey, John J. "Ezra Pound." Bryer, *Sixteen Modern American Authors* 445-71.
   Survey of research; supplemented by Espey in Bryer, *Sixteen Modern American
   Authors: Volume 2* 519-57.

Gallup, Donald. *Ezra Pound: A Bibliography.* Charlottesville: U of Virginia P, 1983.
   The best guide to Pound's works, with complete descriptions; supplemented by
   Elizabeth J. Bell and Mary Barnard's "Bibliographic Record of Periodical and Book
   Publication," *Paideuma* 23.1 (Spring 1994): 187-98.

Gildersleeve, D. Briton. "The Poet as Cartographer: A Survey of Scholarship on Ezra
   Pound's Chinese Cultural/Poetic Translations." *Bulletin of Bibliography* 55.4
   (1998): 223-41.

Leo, John R. "Pound, Ezra." *Guide to American Poetry Explication* 313-27.

Ricks, Beatrice. *Ezra Pound: A Bibliography of Secondary Works.* Metuchen: Scarecrow, 1986.
   Unannotated subject-arranged listings of 3,696 works about Pound.

Elinor (Hoyt) Wylie, 1885-1928

Web Sites

"The Elinor Wylie Page." *SAC LitWeb.* 12 Mar. 2000, http://www.accd.edu/sac/
   english/bailey/wylielin.htm.

Biographies and Criticism

"Elinor (Morton Hoyt) Wylie (Benét)." Bryfonski, *Twentieth-Century Literary Criticism* 8:520-39.
   Excerpts of comments and criticism on Wylie from 1922-1979, with an annotated bibliography.

"Elinor Wylie." Young, *Poetry Criticism* 23:299-336.
   Excerpts of comments and criticism on Wylie from 1922-1984, with an annotated bibliography.

Kelly, Edward. "Elinor Wylie." Martine, *American Novelists, 1910-1945 (Dictionary
   of Literary Biography* 9) 194-96.

Stein, Karen F. "Elinor Wylie." Quartermain, *American Poets, 1880-1945, First Series* (*Dictionary of Literary Biography* 45) 441-47.

Bibliographies

Leo, John R. "Wylie, Elinor." *Guide to American Poetry Explication* 491-92.

H(ilda) D(oolittle) (Aldington), 1886-1961

Web Sites

H. D. (Hilda Doolittle). 16 Mar. 2000, http://www.well.com/user/heddy/.

"Hilda Doolittle." *Academy of American Poets*. 8 Mar. 2000, http://www.poets.org/lit/poet/hdoolfst.htm.

Hilda Doolittle. 16 Mar. 2000, http://www.wwnorton.com/naal/explore/doolittle.htm.

The Pink Moth. 14 Feb. 1999. Ed. Louise Bialik. 17 Mar. 2000, http://www.idiom.com/~didogart/hilda/hdindex.html.
   A very complete Doolittle web site. Offers biography, bibliography, fulltext of poetry, and more.

Biographies and Criticism

Friedman, Susan Stanford. "Hilda Doolittle (H. D.)." Quartermain, *American Poets, 1880-1945, First Series* (*Dictionary of Literary Biography* 45) 115-49.

"H. D." Riley, *Contemporary Literary Criticism* 73:101-46.
   Excerpts of criticism on Doolittle from 1915-1983, with an annotated bibliography.

"H.D." Young, *Poetry Criticism* 5:264-318.
   Excerpts of comments and criticism on H.D. from 1917-1990, with an annotated bibliography.

Zajdel, Melody M. "Hilda Doolittle (H. D)." Rood, *American Writers in Paris, 1920-1939* (*Dictionary of Literary Biography* 4) 112-20.

Journals

H. D. Newsletter. Dallas: Dallas Institute of the Humanities, 1987-1991.

Bibliographies

Barstow, Jane Missner. "Hilda Doolittle (H. D.)." *One Hundred Years of American Women Writing, 1848-1948* 155-60.
   Describes selected editions, biographies, and criticism.

Boughn, Michael. *H. D.: A Bibliography, 1905-1990*. Charlottesville: UP of Virginia, 1993.
   Complete descriptions of works by H.D. and lists of about 1,200 works on her.

Carpenter, Charles A. "Doolittle, Hilda (H. D.)." *Modern Drama Scholarship and Criticism, 1981-1990* 54.

Leo, John R. "H. D. (Hilda Doolittle)." *Guide to American Poetry Explication* 102-05.

(John) Robinson Jeffers, 1887-1962

Web Sites

Jeffers Studies. Ed. Peter Quigley. 31 Mar. 1999. Robinson Jeffers Assoc. and Embry-Riddle U. 17 Mar. 2000, http://www.jeffers.org/.
Well-organized site containing the texts of current and retrospective issues of *Jeffers Studies*; an annotated bibliography of works about Jeffers; Jeffers chronology; and FAQs for Jeffers (under "Forum"). "Teaching Jeffers" includes contributed notes on Jeffer's works. "Book Reviews" link under construction.

"Robinson Jeffers." *Academy of American Poets.* 8 Mar. 2000, http://www.poets.org/lit/poet/rjefffst.htm.

Robinson Jeffers. 16 Mar. 2000, http://www.torhouse.org/thfrobin.htm.

Biographies and Criticism

Brophy, Robert. "Robinson Jeffers." Cracroft, *Twentieth-Century American Western Writers, Second Series (Dictionary of Literary Biography* 212) 143-52.

"Robinson Jeffers." Young, *Poetry Criticism* 17:104-49.
Excerpts of comments and criticism on Jeffers from 1926-1994, with an annotated bibliography.

Scott, Robert Ian. "Robinson Jeffers." Quartermain, *American Poets, 1880-1945, First Series (Dictionary of Literary Biography* 45) 196-213.

Journals

Robinson Jeffers Newsletter. Los Angeles: Robinson Jeffers Committee, Occidental C, 1962- .

Bibliographies

Albert, Sydney S. *Bibliography of the Works of Robinson Jeffers.* 1933. New York: Burt Franklin, 1968.
Complete descriptions of works by Jeffers.

Boswell, Jeanetta. *Robinson Jeffers and the Critics, 1912-1983: A Bibliography of Secondary Sources with Selective Annotations.* Metuchen: Scarecrow, 1986.
Describes 829 comments and critical studies on Jeffers.

Brophy, Robert. "Robinson Jeffers." Erisman and Etulain, *Fifty Western Writers.* 215-27.

Carpenter, Charles A. "Jeffers, Robinson." *Modern Drama Scholarship and Criticism, 1981-1990* 62.

Etulain, Richard W., and N. Jill Howard. "Robinson Jeffers." *Bibliographical Guide to the Study of Western American Literature* 266-71.

Leo, John R. "Jeffers, Robinson." *Guide to American Poetry Explication* 217-21.

Vardamis, Alex A. *The Critical Reputation of Robinson Jeffers: A Bibliographical Study*. Hamden: Archon, 1972.
Describes more than 1,000 works about Jeffers.

Marianne (Craig) Moore, 1887-1972

Web Sites

"Marianne (Craig) Moore (1887-1972)." *Pegasos*. 17 Mar. 2000, http://www.kirjasto. sci.fi/mmoor.htm.
Includes a good biographical sketch, a bibliography (listed all in capital letters and without full imprints), and a list of works for further reading. Generally, a very good site, only slightly marred by the editor's occasional misspellings (Ezea for Ezra, etc.), general penchant for trivia and even historical gossip, and reluctance to be more forthcoming about his or her academic credentials.

"Marianne Moore." *Academy of American Poets*. 8 Mar. 2000, http://www.poets.org/ lit/poet/mmoorfst.htm.
Good site that gives texts of selected poems and sketches ("Poetry," "The Paper Nautilus," He "Digesteth Harde Yron," "Spenser's Ireland," "Baseball and Writing," and "On Muhammad Ali"); a brief biographical sketch; a selected unannotated bibliography of works (poetry, prose, and translations) by Moore; and links to selected letters to Ezra Pound, William Carlos Williams, e. e. cummings, John Warner Moore, and the AAP pages for friends of Moore's who were themselves poets.

"Marianne Moore." *Twentieth-Century Poetry in English*. 17 Mar. 2000, http://www.lit. kobe-u.ac.jp/~hishika/moore.htm.

Marianne Moore. 17 Mar. 2000, http://www.cwrl.utexas.edu/~slatin/20c_poetry/projects/ lives/mm.html.

"Selected Poetry of Marianne Moore (1887-1972)." *Representative Poetry On-line*. 18 Mar. 2000, http://www.library.utoronto.ca/utel/rp/authors/moorem.html.
Essentially a site for finding the texts and notes for five representative poems by Moore ("Marriage," "Peter," "Poetry," "Silence," and "To an Intra-mural Rat"), with a brief biographical sketch giving her honors and prizes and a list of important Moore collections.

Biographies and Criticism

Engel, Bernard F. *Marianne Moore*. Rev. ed. Boston: Twayne, 1989.

"Marianne Moore." Young, *Poetry Criticism* 4:227-72.
Excerpts of comments and criticism on Moore from 1923-1989, with an annotated bibliography.

Phillips, Elizabeth. "Marianne Moore." Quartermain, *American Poets, 1880-1945, First Series* (*Dictionary of Literary Biography* 45) 277-300.

Indexes and Concordances

Lane, Gary. *Concordance to the Poems of Marianne Moore*. New York: Haskell House, 1972.
References *Complete Poems* (New York: Viking, 1967).

Bibliographies

Abbott, Craig S. *Marianne Moore: A Descriptive Bibliography*. Pittsburgh: U of Pittsburgh P, 1977.
Complete descriptions of Moore's writings.

———. *Marianne Moore: A Reference Guide*. Boston: G. K. Hall, 1978.
Describes works about Moore since 1916; updated by Honigsblum, below.

Barstow, Jane Missner. "Marianne Moore." *One Hundred Years of American Women Writing, 1848-1948* 170-74.
Describes selected editions, biographies, and criticism.

Carpenter, Charles A. "Moore, Marianne." *Modern Drama Scholarship and Criticism, 1981-1990* 69.

Hoffman, Cindy, Carol Duane, Katharen Soule, and Linda Wagner. "Three Contemporary Women Poets: Marianne Moore, Anne Sexton, and Sylvia Plath." Duke, Bryer, and Inge, *American Women Writers* 379-402.
Survey of research.

Honigsblum, Bonnie. "An Annotated Bibliography of Works about Marianne Moore, 1977-1990." *Marianne Moore, Woman and Poet*. Patricia C. Willis, ed. Orono: National Poetry Foundation, U of Maine, 1990. [443]-620.

Leo, John R. "Moore, Marianne." *Guide to American Poetry Explication* 275-82.

T(homas) S(tearns) Eliot, 1888-1965

Web Sites

TSE: The Web Site. Ed. Greg Foster. Update unknown. U of Missouri. 17 Mar. 2000, http://web.missouri.edu/~tselist/tse.html.
Essentially a webliography, or tool for finding what is available about Eliot on the web, the uncluttered and easy-to-use site (described as the official home of the T. S. Eliot discussion group) includes links to the listserv, online publications, a concordance, archives, and a well-annotated set of links to authoritative online sites for texts (Bartleby, Gutenberg, UTEL, and the Electronic Text Center at the U of Virginia).

"T. S. Eliot." *Academy of American Poets*. 9 Mar. 2000, http://www.poets.org/lit/poet/tselifst.htm.
Somewhat disappointing site given Eliot's prominence in American poetry and the sponsoring *Academy of American Poets*'s authority. Currently, includes the text of only one poem by Eliot ("La Figlia Che Piange"); earlier, there were six poems available. A brief biographical sketch; a bibliography of works by Eliot (collections of poetry, prose, and plays); and a dated list of links to only six other Eliot sites.

"T. S. Eliot." *Twentieth-Century Poetry in English.* 17 Mar. 2000, http://www.lit.kobe-u.ac. jp:80/~hishika/eliot.htm.

"T. S. Eliot." *Voices and Visions.* 17 Mar. 2000, http://www.learner.org/collections/ multimedia/literature/vvseries/vvspot/Eliot.html.
   A multimedia site of limited academic value. Mainly useful for links to HarperAudio, which includes Eliot reading "The Waste Land," and a video clip from "The Love Song of J. Alfred Prufrock." Links to only two of the most important sites (Columbia U's Bartleby and the U of Virginia's Electronic Texts Center) and not all of the links to other sites are particularly well chosen. Site lacks a traditional bibliography.

T. S. Eliot 1888-1965. Ed. Arwin van Arum. Update and sponsor unknown. 17 Mar. 2000, http://people.a2000.nl/avanarum/index.html.
   Searchable site that contains a biographical chronology for Eliot, annotated bibliographies of works by and about him, and an impressive list of 18 links to other Eliot sites. Annotations are clear and thoughtful and the "works by" section seems to link to everything available online (that is, pre-1924, which includes "Prufrock and Other Observations," "The Sacred Wood," and "The Waste Land," as well as two other collections from 1919 and 1920). Van Arum, a graduate student in the Netherlands, should be congratulated for having produced a major Eliot site.

"T. S. Eliot: Four Volumes." *Project Bartleby Archive.* 17 Mar. 2000, http://www.bartleby. com/index.html.
   Again, link has been placed at index.

"Selected Poetry of Thomas Stearns Eliot." *Representative Poetry On-line.* 19 Mar. 2000, http://www.library.utoronto.ca/utel/rp/authors/eliot.html.

Biographies and Criticism

Beehler, Michael. "T. S. Eliot." Jay, *Modern American Critics, 1920-1955 (Dictionary of Literary Biography* 63) 98-122.

Brooker, Jewel Spears. "T. S. Eliot." Quartermain, *American Poets, 1880-1945, First Series (Dictionary of Literary Biography* 45) 150-81.

Crawford, Fred D. "T. S. Eliot." Stanley Weintraub, ed. *Modern British Dramatists, 1900-1945 (Dictionary of Literary Biography* 10). Detroit: Gale, 1982. 163-85.

Gish, Nancy K. *The Waste Land: A Poem of Memory and Desire.* Boston: Twayne, 1988.

Hargrove, Nancy Duvall. "T. S. Eliot." MacNicholas, *Twentieth-Century American Dramatists (Dictionary of Literary Biography* 7) 151-72.

Headings, Philip Ray. *T. S. Eliot.* Rev. ed. Boston: Twayne, 1982.

" 'The Love Song of J. Alfred Prufrock': T. S. Eliot." Riley, *Contemporary Literary Criticism* 113:181-227.
   Excerpts of criticism on Eliot's poem from 1967-1994, with an annotated bibliography.

"T(homas) S(tearns) Eliot." Riley, *Contemporary Literary Criticism* 57:165-213.
Excerpts of criticism on Eliot's *The Waste Land* from 1922-1987.

"T. S. Eliot." Young, *Poetry Criticism* 5:150-220.
Excerpts of comments and criticism on Eliot from 1917-1989, with an annotated bibliography.

Dictionaries, Encyclopedias, and Handbooks

Behr, Caroline. *T. S. Eliot: A Chronology of His Life and Works*. London: Macmillan, 1983.

Kyle, Lorraine Marie. *Guide to the Major Criticism of T. S. Eliot*. Nashville: Vanderbilt U, 1979.

Southam, B. C. *Student's Guide to the Selected Poems of T. S. Eliot*. 6th ed. 1994. San Diego: Harcourt Brace, 1996.

Williamson, George. *Reader's Guide to T. S. Eliot: A Poem-by-Poem Analysis*. 2nd ed. 1966. New York: Octagon, 1974.

Indexes and Concordances

Dawson, J. L., P. D. Holland, and D. J. McKitterick. *Concordance to the Complete Poems and Plays of T. S. Eliot*. Ithaca: Cornell UP, 1995.
Based on *Complete Poems and Plays of T. S. Eliot* (London: Faber and Faber, 1969).

Journals

Journal of the T. S. Eliot Society of Korea. Seoul: T. S. Eliot Soc. of Korea, 1993- .

Yeats Eliot Review: A Quarterly Journal of Scholarship, Criticism, and Opinion in Cooperation with the National Poetry Foundation. Little Rock: Yeats Eliot Review, 1974- .
Formerly *T. S. Eliot Newsletter* (1974-1975) and *T. S. Eliot Review* (1975-1977); features "Bibliographical Update" that reviews new publications.

Bibliographies

Gallup, Donald C. *T. S. Eliot: A Bibliography*. Rev. and expanded ed. New York: Harcourt, Brace & World, 1969.
Standard guide to Eliot's works, with complete descriptions.

Knowles, Sebastian D. G., and Scott A. Leonard. *T. S. Eliot: Man and Poet, Volume 2: An Annotated Bibliography of a Decade of T. S. Eliot Criticism, 1977-1986*. Orono: National Poetry Foundation, U of Maine, 1992.
Selectively describes 1,423 works to update Ricks, below.

Leo, John R. "Eliot, T. S." *Guide to American Poetry Explication* 114-51.

Ludwig, Richard M. "T. S. Eliot." Bryer, *Sixteen Modern American Authors* 181-222.
Survey of research; supplemented by Stuart Y. McDougal in Bryer, *Sixteen Modern American Authors: Volume 2* 154-209.

Malamud, Randy. "T. S. Eliot." William W. Demastes and Katherine E. Kelly, eds. *British Playwrights, 1880-1956: A Research and Production Sourcebook.* Westport: Greenwood, 1995. [105]-16.

———. *T. S. Eliot's Drama: A Research and Production Sourcebook.* New York: Greenwood, 1992.
Companion for Eliot's seven plays and comments on drama with a bibliography of more than 200 reviews and 400 studies.

Ricks, Beatrice. *T. S. Eliot: A Bibliography of Secondary Works.* Metuchen: Scarecrow, 1980.
Selective descriptions of 4,319 items.

Schwartz, Sanford. "T. S. Eliot." Kopley, *Prospects for the Study of American Literature* 241-65.
The most up-to-date survey of research.

Shuman, R. Baird. "T. S. Eliot." *American Drama, 1918-1960* 63-74.
Describes about 50 works on Eliot's plays.

Eugene (Gladstone) O'Neill, 1888-1953

Web Sites

eOneill.com: An Electronic Archive. Ed. unknown. 1999. eOneill.com. 17 Mar. 2000, http://www.eoneill.com/.
Mainly useful for "eOneill.com Forum," with topically arranged texts of works about O'Neill (news, notes and comments; performance news and reviews; conference news and reports; and publication news and reviews). Also contains texts of contributed essays about O'Neill. Descriptions of first editions and manuscripts of O'Neill in collections of Harley J. Hammerman and the Eugene O'Neill Foundation, Tao House, are mainly useful to advanced scholars and O'Neill collectors.

"Eugene Gladstone O'Neill." *Nobel Prize Internet Archive.* 17 Mar. 2000, http://nobelprizes.com/nobel/literature/1936a.html.
Best list of links for O'Neill.

Eugene Gladstone O'Neill. 17 Mar. 2000, http://www.connect.net/ron/oneill.html.

"Eugene O'Neill." Ed. and update unknown. BBC. 17 Mar. 2000, http://www.bbc.co.uk/education/centurions/oneill/onelbiog.shtml.
The most informative page available for O'Neill, with a brief biography. "Further Information" is a bibliography of his works with links to texts of *Beyond the Horizon* and selected reviews of O'Neill's works and of works about him.

"Eugene O'Neill (1888-1953)." *PAL: Perspectives in American Literature.* 17 Mar. 2000, http://www.csustan.edu/english/reuben/pal/chap8/oneill.html.
The most complete lists of works by and about O'Neill.

Eugene O'Neill, American Playwright, 1888-1953. Ed. Robin Chew. October 1995. Lucid Interactive. 17 Mar. 2000, http://www2.lucidcafe.com/lucidcafe/library/95oct/egoneill.html.

"Eugene O'Neill: Beyond the Horizon." *Project Bartleby Archive*. 17 Mar. 2000, http://www.bartleby.com/index.html.
Fulltext to *Beyond the Horizon*. Link has been placed at the author index.

Biographies and Criticism

"Eugene (Gladstone) O'Neill." Bryfonski, *Twentieth-Century Literary Criticism* 6:323-38.
Excerpts of criticism on O'Neill from 1922-1981, with an annotated bibliography.

———. Bryfonski, *Twentieth-Century Literary Criticism* 27:156-95.
Excerpts of criticism on *Long Day's Journey into Night* from 1956-1979, with an annotated bibliography.

"Eugene O'Neill." Bryfonski, *Twentieth-Century Literary Criticism* 1:381-407.
Excerpts of criticism on O'Neill from 1920-1976.

"Eugene O'Neill: *Desire under the Elms*." Bryfonski, *Twentieth-Century Literary Criticism* 49:237-99.
Excerpts of criticism on the play from 1924-1987, with an annotated bibliography.

Hinden, Michael. *Long Day's Journey into Night: Native Eloquence*. Boston: Twayne, 1990.

Jensen, George H. "Eugene O'Neill." MacNicholas, *Twentieth-Century American Dramatists* (*Dictionary of Literary Biography* 7) 139-65.

Dictionaries, Encyclopedias, and Handbooks

Manheim, Michael. *Cambridge Companion to Eugene O'Neill*. New York: Cambridge UP, 1998.

Ranald, Margaret Loftus. *Eugene O'Neill Companion*. Westport: Greenwood, 1984.
Extensive summaries and information for O'Neill's writings and productions, with a "Bibliographic Essay" (pp. 765-89).

Indexes and Concordances

Bryan, George B., and Wolfgang Mieder. *Proverbial Eugene O'Neill: An Index to Proverbs in the Works of Eugene Gladstone O'Neill*. Westport: Greenwood, 1995.
Keyed to *Complete Plays of Eugene O'Neill* (New York: Library of America, 1988) and other standard editions (listed on pp. 79-84).

Reaver, J. Russell. *O'Neill Concordance*. Detroit: Gale, 1969.
Indexes 28 selected plays published after 1924 in *Plays of Eugene O'Neill* (New York: Random House, 1951), *Moon for the Misbegotten* (New York: Random House, 1952), *Long Day's Journey into Night* (New Haven: Yale UP, 1956), *Touch of the Poet* (New Haven: Yale UP, 1957), *Hughie* (New Haven: Yale UP, 1959), and *More Stately Mansions* (New Haven: Yale UP, 1964).

Journals

Eugene O'Neill Review. Boston: Eugene O'Neill Soc., Suffolk U, 1977- .
Formerly *Eugene O'Neill Newsletter* (1977-88).

Bibliographies

Atkinson, Jennifer McCabe. *Eugene O'Neill: A Descriptive Bibliography*. Pittsburgh: U of Pittsburgh P, 1974.
Complete descriptions of O'Neill's writings, with a brief appendix of film, radio, and musical adaptations.

Carpenter, Charles A. "O'Neill, Eugene [Gladstone]." *Modern Drama Scholarship and Criticism, 1981-1990* 71-79.

Miller, Jordan Y. *Eugene O'Neill and the American Critic: A Bibliographical Checklist*. 2nd ed. Hamden: Archon Books, 1973.
Evaluative descriptions of criticism of O'Neill and information on major productions.

Raleigh, John H. "Eugene O'Neill." Bryer, *Sixteen Modern American Authors* 417-43.
Survey of research; supplemented by Raleigh in Bryer, *Sixteen Modern American Authors: Volume 2* 480-518.

Ranald, Margaret Loftus. "Eugene O'Neill." Demastes, *American Playwrights, 1880-1945* [323]-47.

Shuman, R. Baird. "Eugene O'Neill." *American Drama, 1918-1960* 126-44.
Describes about 100 critical works.

Smith, Madeline. *Eugene O'Neill: An Annotated Bibliography*. New York: Garland, 1988.
Describes criticism and gives information about productions to update Miller, above.

John Crowe Ransom, 1888-1974

Web Sites

"John Crowe Ransom." *Academy of American Poets*. 9 Mar. 2000, http://www.poets. org/lit/poet/jcranfst.htm.
Brief biography of Ransom and a selected bibliography of his works and offsite links. Offers audio of Ransom reading his poem "Blue Girls," and a link to downloadable text of "Blue Girls."

Special Collections: Ransom. 17 Mar. 2000, http://www.library.vanderbilt.edu/speccol/ ransom.html.

Biographies and Criticism

Young, Thomas Daniel. "John Crowe Ransom." Jay, *Modern American Critics, 1920-1955* (*Dictionary of Literary Biography* 63) 237-47.

———. "John Crowe Ransom." Quartermain, *American Poets, 1880-1945, First Series* (*Dictionary of Literary Biography* 45) 344-58.

Bibliographies

Abbott, Craig S. *John Crowe Ransom: A Descriptive Bibliography*. Troy: Whitston, 1999.

Hindle, John J. "John Crowe Ransom." Flora and Bain, *Fifty Southern Writers after 1900* 391-400.

Leo, John R. "Ransom, John Crowe." *Guide to American Poetry Explication* 329-37.

Young, Thomas Daniel. *John Crowe Ransom: An Annotated Bibliography*. New York: Garland, 1982.
Describes about 900 works by and about Ransom.

Conrad (Potter) Aiken, 1889-1973

Web Sites

"Aiken, Conrad." *Modern English Collection*. Ed. and update unknown. U of Virginia E-text Library. 17 Mar. 2000, http://etext.lib.virginia.edu/modeng.browse.html.
Includes (enhanced format) texts of Aiken's "An Old Man Sees Himself," as originally published in *Dial* (1921), and *The House of Dust: A Symphony* (dated 1916-1917), a significant collection of 39 poems.

"Aiken, Conrad Potter." *Project Gutenberg*. 17 Mar. 2000, http://promo.net/pg/. (Use search engine to find author.)
Text of poems collected in *The House of Dust: A Symphony* (dated 1916-1917), some without titles. No pagination and no prefatory material.

Conrad Aiken. 17 Mar. 2000, http://www.access.victoria.bc.ca/~joannee/poetry/aiken.htm.

"Conrad Aiken (1889-1973)." *Pegasos*. 17 Mar. 2000, http://www.kirjasto.sci.fi/caiken.htm.

Conrad Aiken Chronology. 17 Mar. 2000, http://uhura.cc.rochester.edu/~mh001h/aiken/index.html.

Mississippi Quarterly: The Journal of Southern Culture: Conrad Aiken Links. 17 Mar. 2000, http://www.msstate.edu/Archives/MQ/links/aiken.html.

Biographies and Criticism

"Conrad Aiken." Harris and Fitzgerald, *Short Story Criticism* 9:1-47
Excerpts of criticism on Aiken from 1925-1989, with an annotated bibliography.

Cummings, Stephen. "Conrad Aiken." Quartermain, *American Poets, 1880-1945, First Series* (*Dictionary of Literary Biography* 45) 3-22.

Killorin, Joseph. "Conrad Aiken." Kimbel, *American Short-Story Writers, 1910-1945, Second Series* (*Dictionary of Literary Biography* 102) 3-11.

MacMillan, Duane J. "Conrad Aiken." Martine, *American Novelists, 1910-1945* (*Dictionary of Literary Biography* 9) 7-10.

Journals

Conrad Aiken Studies Journal. 17 Mar. 2000, http://members.pgonline.com/~iankluge/aiktitle.htm.

Bibliographies

Bonnell, F. W., and F. C. Bonnell. *Conrad Aiken: A Bibliography (1902-1978).* San Marino: Huntington Library, 1982.
Complete descriptions of Aiken's works.

Harris, Catherine Kirk. *Conrad Aiken: Critical Recognition, 1914-1981: A Bibliographic Guide.* New York: Garland, 1983.
Selective descriptions.

Leo, John R. "Aiken, Conrad." *Guide to American Poetry Explication* 2-3.

Claude McKay, 1890-1948

Web Sites

Claude McKay. 17 Mar. 2000, http://www.siu.edu/~carib/McKay.html.
Biographical sketch.

Claude McKay. 17 Mar. 2000, http://www.unc.edu/courses/eng81br1/claude2.html.
Biographical sketch, with photographs.

The Poetry of Claude McKay. 17 Mar. 2000, http://dana.ucc.nau.edu/~ld/Claude.html.
Five poems, a timeline, and a few links.

"Selected Poetry of Claude McKay." *Representative Poetry On-line.* 19 Mar. 2000, http://www.library.utoronto.ca/utel/rp/authors/mckay.html.

Biographies and Criticism

Ali, Schavi Mali. "Claude McKay." Harris, *Afro-American Writers from the Harlem Renaissance to 1940* (*Dictionary of Literary Biography* 51) 201-12.

Cagan, Penni. "Claude McKay." Quartermain, *American Poets, 1880-1945, First Series* (*Dictionary of Literary Biography* 45) 261-63.

"Claude McKay." Bryfonski, *Twentieth-Century Literary Criticism* 7:454-71.
Excerpts of comments and criticism on McKay from 1919-1976, with an annotated bibliography.

———. Bryfonski, *Twentieth-Century Literary Criticism* 41:315-46.
Excerpts of comments and criticism on McKay from 1922-1989, with an annotated bibliography.

"Claude McKay." Young, *Poetry Criticism* 2:203-30.
Excerpts of comments and criticism on McKay from 1922-1989, with an annotated bibliography.

Grant, William E. "Claude McKay." Rood, *American Writers in Paris, 1920-1939* (*Dictionary of Literary Biography* 4) 281-82.

McLeod, Alan L. "Claude McKay." Lindfors and Sander, *Twentieth-Century Caribbean and Black African Writers* (*Dictionary of Literary Biography* 117) 227-35.

Bibliographies

Glitsch, Catherine. "McKay, Claude." *American Novel Explication, 1991-1995* 163.

Krishnamurthy, Sarala. "Claude McKay." Nelson, *African American Authors, 1745-1945* 338-48.
Survey of research.

Leo, John R. "McKay, Claude." *Guide to American Poetry Explication* 258.

Miller, Ruth, and Peter J. Katopes. "The Harlem Renaissance: Arna W. Bontemps, Countee Cullen, James Weldon Johnson, Claude McKay, and Jean Toomer." Inge, Duke, and Bryer, *Black American Writers* I, 161-86.
Survey of research.

Perry, Margaret. "McKay, Claude." *Harlem Renaissance* 118-30.

Katherine Anne Porter, 1890-1980

Web Sites

"Chapter 7: Early Twentieth Century—Katherine Anne Porter." *PAL: Perspectives in American Literature.* 17 Mar. 2000, http://www.csustan.edu/english/reuben/ pal/chap7/porter.html.
The most respectable site found for Porter.

Guide to the Papers of Katherine Anne Porter. University of Maryland Libraries, Archives and Manuscripts Department. 17 Mar. 2000, http://www.lib.umd.edu/ UMCP/ARCV/kap/kaptofc.html.
Multiple pages, most valuable for advanced research on Porter. Also includes solid biography of Porter, bibliography of works about her (through May 1996); and information about the Katherine Anne Porter Soc., with text of its newsletters.

"The Katherine Anne Porter Page." *SAC LitWeb.* 19 Mar. 2000, http://www.accd.edu/ sac/english/bailey/porterka.htm.

Biographies and Criticism

" 'Flowering Judas': Katherine Anne Porter." Harris and Fitzgerald, *Short Story Criticism* 31:123-81.
Excerpts of criticism on Porter's short story from 1947-1991, with an annotated bibliography.

Givner, Joan. "Katherine Anne Porter." Kimbel, *American Short-Story Writers, 1910-1945, Second Series* (*Dictionary of Literary Biography* 102) 223-47.

———. "Katherine Anne Porter." Rood, *American Writers in Paris, 1920-1939* (*Dictionary of Literary Biography* 4) 311-14.

Hendrick, Willene, and George Hendrick. *Katherine Anne Porter*. Rev. ed. Boston: Twayne, 1988.

"Katherine Anne Porter." Harris and Fitzgerald, *Short Story Criticism* 4:324-66.
Excerpts of criticism on Porter from 1930-1980, with an annotated bibliography.

"Katherine Anne Porter." Riley, *Contemporary Literary Criticism* 101:207-59.
Excerpts of criticism on Porter from 1930-1995, with an annotated bibliography.

Kiernan, Robert F. "Katherine Anne Porter." Martine, *American Novelists, 1910-1945* (*Dictionary of Literary Biography* 9) 296-301.

Bibliographies

Barstow, Jane Missner. "Katherine Anne Porter." *One Hundred Years of American Women Writing, 1848-1948* 101-06.
Describes selected editions, biographies, and criticism.

Etulain, Richard W., and N. Jill Howard. "Katherine Anne Porter." *Bibliographical Guide to the Study of Western American Literature* 336-38.

Givner, Joan. "Katherine Anne Porter." Flora and Bain, *Fifty Southern Writers after 1900* 356-67.

———, Jane DeMouy, and Ruth M. Alvarez. "Katherine Anne Porter." Duke, Bryer, and Inge, *American Women Writers* 201-31.
Survey of research.

Hilt, Kathryn, and Ruth M. Alvarez. *Katherine Anne Porter: An Annotated Bibliography*. New York: Garland, 1990.
Brief information for Porter's works and descriptions of about 600 works on Porter.

Kiernan, Robert F. *Katherine Anne Porter and Carson McCullers: A Reference Guide*. Boston: G. K. Hall, 1976.
Describes about 500 works on Porter since 1924.

Unrue, Darlene Harbour. "Katherine Anne Porter." Bruccoli and Baughman, *Bibliography of American Fiction, 1919-1988* 406-08.

———. "Katherine Anne Porter." Bruccoli and Baughman, *Modern Women Writers* 44-49.

Waldrip, Louise, and Shirley Ann Bauer. *A Bibliography of the Works of Katherine Anne Porter, and a Bibliography of the Criticism of the Works of Katherine Anne Porter*. Metuchen: Scarecrow, 1969.
Most valuable for complete descriptions of Porter's works.

Wiedemann, Barbara. "Katherine Anne Porter: 'Flowering Judas'." Evans, Little, and Wiedemann, *Short Fiction* 228-35.
Describes 11 studies.

———. "Katherine Anne Porter: 'The Jilting of Granny Weatherall'." Evans, Little, and Wiedemann, *Short Fiction* 236-40.
Describes nine studies.

Henry Miller, 1891-1980

Web Sites

"Henry Miller." *Bohemian Ink*. 17 Mar. 2000, http://www.levity.com/corduroy/millerh.
htm.
   Offers an informative, if less than polished, biographical sketch of Miller (with
references) and acceptable set of offsite links, including a worthwhile unannotated
bibliography.

Henry Miller, American Author. 17 Mar. 2000, http://www.geocities.com/SoHo/Cafe/
1538/henry.htm.

A Henry Miller Bibliography. Ed., update, and sponsor unknown. 17 Mar. 2000,
http://www.maui.net/~coast/Miller_Bibliography.HTML.
   Unannotated listings of works by and about Miller (the latter covering criticism,
biographical studies, and bibliographies).

Henry Valentine Miller. Ed., update, and sponsor unknown. 17 Mar. 2000,
http://www.henrymiller.org/.
   A very disappointing site, especially from an organization representing an
author of Miller's stature. The links are poorly chosen, and many broken links were
found.

Home of the Henry Miller Bibliography. Ed. William Ashley. Update and sponsor unknown. 17 Mar. 2000, http://www.hmbiblio.com/.
   Valuable for complete bibliographic information for works by Miller, describing fully, for example, over sixty editions of *Tropic of Cancer*. Intended for scholars
and book collectors, the site should be used in conjunction with Lawrence J. Shifreen
and Roger Jackson's *Henry Miller*, below. Also includes a list of links for Miller and
literature.

Biographies and Criticism

Brown, J. D. "Henry Miller." Rood, *American Writers in Paris, 1920-1939 (Dictionary of Literary Biography* 4) 282-94.

Fowlie, Wallace. "Henry Miller." Martine, *American Novelists, 1910-1945 (Dictionary of Literary Biography* 9) 211-24.

"*Tropic of Cancer*: Henry Miller." Riley, *Contemporary Literary Criticism*.
   Excerpts of criticism on Miller's novel from 1934-1991, with an annotated
bibliography.

Widmer, Kingsley. *Henry Miller*. Rev. ed. Boston: Twayne, 1990.

Indexes and Concordances

Fielding, Blair. *Nothing but the Marvelous: Wisdoms of Henry Miller*. Santa Barbara:
Capra, 1991.
   Selected topically arranged quotations.

Bibliographies

Dearborn, Mary, and Margaret Donovan DuPriest. "Henry Miller." Bruccoli and Baughman, *Bibliography of American Fiction, 1919-1988* 348-51.

Shifreen, Lawrence J. *Henry Miller: A Bibliography of Secondary Sources*. Metuchen: Scarecrow, 1979.
International and comprehensive coverage extends from 1925.

————, and Roger Jackson. *Henry Miller: A Bibliography of Primary Sources, with an Original Preface by Henry Miller*. Chelsea: The Authors, 1993.
Complete descriptions.

Archibald MacLeish, 1892-1982

Web Sites

"Archibald MacLeish." *Academy of American Poets*. 8 Mar. 2000, http://www.poets.org/lit/poet/amaclfst.htm.
Includes fulltext of the poems "Ars Poetica" and "You, Andrew Marvell."

Roth Publishing—Archibald MacLeish. 17 Mar. 2000, http://www.rothpoem.com/duk_am.html.

Biographies and Criticism

"Archibald MacLeish." Riley, *Contemporary Literary Criticism* 68:268-94.
Excerpts of criticism on MacLeish from 1926-1973, with an annotated bibliography.

French, Warren. "Archibald MacLeish." Rood, *American Writers in Paris, 1920-1939* (*Dictionary of Literary Biography* 4) 261-65.

Jones, Victor H. "Archibald MacLeish." Quartermain, *American Poets, 1880-1945, First Series* (*Dictionary of Literary Biography* 45) 237-56.

McWilliams, James L., III. "Archibald MacLeish." MacNicholas, *Twentieth-Century American Dramatists* (*Dictionary of Literary Biography* 7) 53-63.

Bibliographies

Carpenter, Charles A. "MacLeish, Archibald." *Modern Drama Scholarship and Criticism, 1981-1990* 65.

Ellis, Helen E., Bernard A. Drabeck, and Margaret E. C. Howland. *Archibald MacLeish: A Selectively Annotated Bibliography*. Lanham: Scarecrow, 1995.
Covers works by and about MacLeish.

Leo, John R. "MacLeish, Archibald." *Guide to American Poetry Explication* 259-61.

Edna St. Vincent Millay, 1892-1950

Web Sites

"Edna St. Vincent Millay." *Historical Lesbian Poetry*. 17 Mar. 2000, http://www.
sappho.com/poetry/historical/e_millay.html.

Edna St. Vincent Millay. 17 Mar. 2000, http://members.aol.com/MillayGirl/millay.htm.

"Selected Poetry of Edna St. Vincent Millay (1892-1950)." *Representative Poetry
On-line*. 17 Mar. 2000, http://www.library.utoronto.ca/utel/rp/authors/millay.html.
Links to texts of 18 of Millay's poems, including "Ashes of Life," "The Be-
trothal," "Departure," "Dirge," "Ebb," "Feast," "First Fig," "[Four Sonnets (1922)],"
"Grown-up," "Humoresque," "Lament," "The Penitent," "Recuerdo," "Second Fig,"
"Sonnets (1923)," "Sonnets from an Ungrafted Tree," "Sorrow," and "Spring"; a very
brief biographical sketch; a list of major works by Millay; and a bibliography of
works about her. Most notably, this site does not include "Renascence," arguably
Millay's most famous poem.

Biographies and Criticism

Brittin, Norman A. *Edna St. Vincent Millay*. Rev. ed. Boston: Twayne, 1982.

"Edna St. Vincent Millay." Bryfonski, *Twentieth-Century Literary Criticism*
4:305-23.
Excerpts of comments and criticism on Millay from 1918-1977, with an annotated bibliography.

———. Bryfonski, *Twentieth-Century Literary Criticism* 49:199-236.
Excerpts of comments and criticism on Millay from 1918-1986, with an annotated bibliography.

"Edna St. Vincent Millay." Young, *Poetry Criticism* 6:203-47.
Excerpts of comments and criticism on Millay from 1918-1986, with an annotated bibliography.

Hart, Paula L. "Edna St. Vincent Millay." Quartermain, *American Poets, 1880-1945,
First Series* (*Dictionary of Literary Biography* 45) 264-76.

Journals

Tamarack: Journal of the Edna St. Vincent Millay Society. Cambridge: Edna St. Vincent Millay Soc., 1981-86.

Bibliographies

Barstow, Jane Missner. "Edna St. Vincent Millay." *One Hundred Years of American
Women Writing, 1848-1948* 167-70.
Describes selected editions, biographies, and criticism.

Carpenter, Charles A. "Millay, Edna St. Vincent." *Modern Drama Scholarship and
Criticism, 1981-1990* 66.

Leo, John R. "Millay, Edna St. Vincent." *Guide to American Poetry Explication* 271-73.

Nierman, Judith. *Edna St. Vincent Millay: A Reference Guide.* Boston: G. K. Hall, 1977.
Describes about 1,000 works on Millay since 1918.

Yost, Karl. *A Bibliography of the Works of Edna St. Vincent Millay.* 1937. New York: Burt Franklin, 1968.
Complete descriptions; also lists about 70 works on Millay.

Dorothy (Rothschild) Parker, 1893-1967

Web Sites

"Dorothy Parker." *Bohemian Ink* 17 Mar. 2000, http://www.levity.com/corduroy/parker. htm.

Dorothy Parker. 17 Mar. 2000, http://www.users.interport.net/~lynda/sections.html.

"The Dorothy Parker Page." *SAC LitWeb.* 17 Mar. 2000, http://www.accd.edu/sac/ english/bailey/parker.htm.
Lists major works by Parker, including poems, short stories, plays, articles, and reviews, and works about her. Most of the links to sites about Parker are not working.

The Dorothy Parker Bibliography. Ed. Rahne Alexander. May 1999. Sponsor unknown. 17 Mar. 2000, http://www.xantippe.com/dorothy/bibliography.html.
Useful and comprehensive classified unannotated list of works by and about Parker, covering both printed works and media, with a Parker chronology.

Biographies and Criticism

Bloom, Lynn Z. "Dorothy Parker." Quartermain, *American Poets, 1880-1945, First Series (Dictionary of Literary Biography* 45) 300-305.

"Dorothy Parker." Riley, *Contemporary Literary Criticism* 68:321-41.
Excerpts of criticism on Parker from 1928-1990, with an annotated bibliography.

"Dorothy (Rothschild) Parker." Harris and Fitzgerald, *Short Story Criticism* 2:271-87.
Excerpts of criticism on Parker from 1930-1984, with an annotated bibliography.

Freibert, Lucy M. "Dorothy (Rothschild) Parker." *American Short-Story Writers, 1910-1945, First Series (Dictionary of Literary Biography* 86) 223-33.

Grant, Thomas. "Dorothy Parker." Trachtenberg, *American Humorists, 1800-1950 (Dictionary of Literary Biography* 11) 369-82.

Kinney, Arthur F. *Dorothy Parker, Revised.* New York: Twayne, 1998.

Indexes and Concordances

Brownlow, S. T., ed. *Sayings of Dorothy Parker.* London: Duckworth, 1996.

Bibliographies

Barstow, Jane Missner. "Dorothy Parker." *One Hundred Years of American Women Writing, 1848-1948* 174-76.
Describes selected editions, biographies, and criticism.

Calhoun, Randall. *Dorothy Parker: A Bio-Bibliography.* Westport: Greenwood, 1993.
Brief descriptions of works by Parker and annotated entries for 196 criticisms of Parker since 1922.

Kinney, Arthur F. "Dorothy Parker." Bruccoli and Baughman, *Bibliography of American Fiction 1919-1988* 397-98.

E(dward) E(stlin) Cummings, 1894-1962

Web Sites

Edward Estlin Cummings. 17 Mar. 2000, http://www.island-of-freedom.com/CUMMINGS.HTM.

"e. e. [Edward Estlin] cummings." *American Literature on the Web.* 18 Mar. 2000, http://www.nagasaki-gaigo.ac.jp/ishikawa/amlit/20/f_authors20.htm.
Excellent classified list of links for Cummings, particularly for fulltext sources of his works.

"E. E. Cummings." *Academy of American Poets.* 18 Mar. 2000, http://www.poets.org/lit/poet/eecumfst.htm.
Includes texts of 11 poems by Cummings and links to other Cummings sites.

e. e. cummings. 17 Mar. 2000, http://www.imsa.edu/~junkee/cummings.html.

E. E. Cummings Society. Ed. Mike Webster. Update unknown. Grand Valley SU. 18 Mar. 2000, http://www.gvsu.edu/english/Cummings/Society.htm.
Contains excellent bibliography of works by and about Cummings; contents of issues of the journal *Spring*; contributed notes (by Webster and others) on aspects of Cummings's works; and links to other Cummings sites.

An Unofficial EE Cummings Starting Point. 17 Mar. 2000, http://members.tripod.com/~DWipf/cummings.html.

Biographies and Criticism

"E. E. Cummings." Riley, *Contemporary Literary Criticism* 68:23-52.
Excerpts of criticism on Cummings from 1931-1982, with an annotated bibliography.

"E. E. Cummings." Young, *Poetry Criticism* 5:68-112.
Excerpts of comments and criticism on Cummings from 1927-1984, with an annotated bibliography.

Kennedy, Richard S. *E. E. Cummings Revisited.* New York: Twayne, 1994.

Martin, Robert K. "E. E. Cummings." Rood, *American Writers in Paris, 1920-1939* (*Dictionary of Literary Biography* 4) 105-11.

Penberthy, Jenny. "E. E. Cummings." Quartermain, *American Poets, 1880-1945, Second Series* (*Dictionary of Literary Biography* 48) 117-37.

Indexes and Concordances

McBride, Katharine Winters. *Concordance to the Complete Poems of E. E. Cummings*. Ithaca: Cornell UP, 1989.
    Based on *E. E. Cummings: Complete Poems, 1913-1962* (New York: Harcourt, Brace, Jovanovich, 1972).

Journals

Spring: The Journal of the E. E. Cummings Society. Flushing: E. E. Cummings Soc., 1980-90; new ser., 1992- .

Bibliographies

Carpenter, Charles A. "Cummings, E[dward] E[stlin]." *Modern Drama Scholarship and Criticism, 1981-1990* 54.

Firmage, George J. *E. E. Cummings: A Bibliography*. Middletown: Wesleyan UP, 1960.
    Complete descriptions of Cummings's works.

Leo, John R. "Cummings, E. E." *Guide to American Poetry Explication* 82-95.

Rotella, Guy L. *E. E. Cummings: A Reference Guide*. Boston: G. K. Hall, 1979.
    Describes about 1,200 works on Cummings since 1927; continued by Rotella's "E. E. Cummings: A Reference Guide (Again) Updated: Part One (to 1986)," *Spring* new ser., 1.1 (1992): 127-43.

James (Grover) Thurber, 1894-1961

Web Sites

A James Thurber Page. 18 Mar. 2000, http://home.earthlink.net/~ritter/thurber/index.html.

Pathfinder: James Grover Thurber (1894-1961). 8 Feb. 2000. Ed. Heather Chapman. 18 Mar. 2000, http://budgetweb.com/heather/thurber/Thurber.html.
    Brief descriptions of Thurber's works, biographies, autobiographical materials and collections, bibliographies, and interviews.

Thurberelia. Ed. Andrew Boyer. 19 Dec. 1999. Sponsor unknown. 18 Mar. 2000, http://users.erols.com/aboyer/thurber.html.
    Useful links to texts of several short works by Thurber and other pages.

Biographies and Criticism

Baughman, Judith S. "James Thurber." Rood, *American Writers in Paris, 1920-1939* (*Dictionary of Literary Biography* 4) 385-88.

Gale, Steven H. "James Thurber." Kimbel, *American Short-Story Writers, 1910-1945, Second Series* (*Dictionary of Literary Biography* 102) 319-34.

"James Thurber." Harris and Fitzgerald, *Short Story Criticism* 1:411-36.
Excerpts of criticism on Thurber from 1933-1985, with an annotated bibliography.

Scholl, Peter A. "James Thurber." Trachtenberg, *American Humorists, 1800-1950* (*Dictionary of Literary Biography* 11) 505-26.

Vousden, E. Charles. "James Thurber." Cech, *American Writers for Children, 1900-1960* (*Dictionary of Literary Biography* 22) 315-20.

Bibliographies

Bowden, Edwin T. *James Thurber: A Bibliography*. Columbus: Ohio State UP, 1968.
Complete descriptions of Thurber's works.

Toombs, Sarah Eleanora. "James Thurber." Bruccoli and Baughman, *Bibliography of American Fiction, 1919-1988* 500-503.

———. *James Thurber: An Annotated Bibliography of Criticism*. New York: Garland, 1987.
Selectively describes 1,150 works in English with lists of non-English-language studies.

Jean Toomer, 1894-1967

Web Sites

"Chapter 9: Harlem Renaissance: Jean Toomer." *PAL: Perspectives in American Literature*. 18 Mar. 2000, http://www.csustan.edu/english/reuben/pal/chap9/toomer.html.

"Jean Toomer." *Academy of American Poets*. 18 Mar. 2000, http://www.poets.org/lit/poet/jtoomfst.htm.

Jean Toomer. 18 Mar. 2000, http://www.unc.edu/courses/eng81br1/toomer.html.

"The Jean Toomer Page." *SAC LitWeb*. 18 Mar. 2000, http://www.accd.edu/sac/english/bailey/toomer.htm.

Biographies and Criticism

Deakin, Motley. "Jean Toomer." Quartermain, *American Poets, 1880-1945, First Series* (*Dictionary of Literary Biography* 45) 405-09.

"Jean Toomer." Harris and Fitzgerald, *Short Story Criticism* 1:437-63.
Excerpts of criticism on Toomer from 1923-1975, with an annotated bibliography.

"Jean Toomer." Young, *Poetry Criticism* 7:307-42.
Excerpts of comments and criticism on Toomer from 1962-1989, with an annotated bibliography.

McKay, Nellie. "Jean Toomer." Harris, *Afro-American Writers from the Harlem Renaissance to 1940* (*Dictionary of Literary Biography* 51) 274-88.

Bibliographies

Carpenter, Charles A. "Toomer, Jean." *Modern Drama Scholarship and Criticism, 1981-1990* 88.

Dawson, Emma Waters. "Eugene (Jean) Pinchback Toomer." Nelson, *African American Authors, 1745-1945* 408-17.
Survey of research.

Etulain, Richard W., and N. Jill Howard. "Jean Toomer." *Bibliographical Guide to the Study of Western American Literature* 402.

Jones, Robert B. "Jean Toomer: An Annotated Checklist of Criticism, 1923-1993." *Resources for American Literary Study* 21.1 (1995): [68]-121.

Leo, John R. "Toomer, Jean." *Guide to American Poetry Explication* 441-46.

Miller, Ruth, and Peter J. Katopes. "The Harlem Renaissance: Arna W. Bontemps, Countee Cullen, James Weldon Johnson, Claude McKay, and Jean Toomer." Inge, Duke, and Bryer, *Black American Writers* I, 161-86.
Survey of research.

Perry, Margaret. "Toomer, Jean." *Harlem Renaissance* 138-58.

Reilly, John M. "Jean Toomer." Flora and Bain, *Fifty Southern Writers after 1900* 479-90.

Rusch, Frederik L. "Jean Toomer." Bruccoli and Baughman, *Bibliography of American Fiction, 1919-1988* 504-06.

———. "Jean Toomer." Bruccoli and Baughman, *Modern African American Writers* 51-55.

John (Roderigo) Dos Passos, 1896-1970

Web Sites

"Chapter Fifteen: The Adventures of John Dos Passos." *Literature & Culture of the American 1950s*. 18 Mar. 2000, http://www.english.upenn.edu/~afilreis/50s/aaron-chap15.html.

"Chapter 7: Early Twentieth Century: John Dos Passos." *PAL: Perspectives in American Literature*. 18 Mar. 2000, http://www.csustan.edu/english/reuben/pal/chap7/dospassos.html.
Good selective list of works by and about Dos Passos.

"John Dos Passos." *Heath Anthology*. 18 Mar. 2000, http://www.georgetown.edu/bassr/heath/syllabuild/iguide/dospasso.html.
No bibliography.

John Dos Passos: An Amateur Appreciation Page. Ed. Chris Thomas. 18 Mar. 2000, http://grimace.ucsd.edu/~cthomas/Authors/passos.html.
Brief biography of Dos Passos with a list of his works and links to other pages.

Biographies and Criticism

Knowles, A. S., Jr. "John Dos Passos." Martine, *American Novelists, 1910-1945* (*Dictionary of Literary Biography* 9) 217-36.

Nanney, Lisa. *John Dos Passos*. New York: Twayne, 1998.

Strickland, Ruth L. "John Dos Passos." Rood, *American Writers in Paris, 1920-1939* (*Dictionary of Literary Biography* 4) 120-25.

"*U. S. A.*: John Dos Passos." Riley, *Contemporary Literary Criticism* 82:59-114.
Excerpts of criticism on Dos Passos's work from 1930-1988, with an annotated bibliography.

Bibliographies

Carpenter, Charles A. "Dos Passos, John." *Modern Drama Scholarship and Criticism, 1981-1990* 54.

Glitsch, Catherine. "Dos Passos, John." *American Novel Explication, 1991-1995* 65-66.

Kellman, Steven G. "John Dos Passos." *Modern American Novel* 28-34.
Describes about 40 critical works.

Layman, Richard. "John Dos Passos." Bruccoli and Baughman, *Bibliography of American Fiction, 1919-1988* 155-58.

Rohrkemper, John. *John Dos Passos: A Reference Guide*. Boston: G. K. Hall, 1980.
Describes about 1,700 works on Dos Passos since 1921.

Sanders, David. *John Dos Passos: A Comprehensive Bibliography*. New York: Garland, 1987.
Complete descriptions of works by Dos Passos and annotated entries for works about him.

F(rancis) Scott (Key) Fitzgerald, 1896-1940

Web Sites

"Chapter 7: Early Twentieth Century: F. Scott Fitzgerald." *PAL: Perspectives in American Literature*. 18 Mar. 2000, http://www.csustan.edu/english/reuben/pal/chap7/fitzgerald.html.

"F. Scott Fitzgerald." *American Literature on the Web*. 18 Mar. 2000, http://www.nagasaki-gaigo.ac.jp/ishikawa/amlit/f/fitzgerald20.htm.
Excellent classified list of general resources and fulltexts for Fitzgerald.

F. Scott Fitzgerald. 18 Mar. 2000, http://www.pioneerplanet.com/archive/fitzgerald/.
Site emphasizes Fitzgerald's St. Paul (Minnesota) background.

F. Scott Fitzgerald Centennial Homepage. Ed. unknown. 17 Dec. 1999. U of South
Carolina. 18 Mar. 2000, http://www.sc.edu/fitzgerald/.
Comprehensive and authoritative web site with links to selected texts (including
"Winter Dreams," "The Diamond as Big as the Ritz," and others); classified list of
works by Fitzgerald (facsimile collection, critical edition, stories and plays, articles
and essays, prose parody and humor, verse, book reviews, public letters and statements, interviews, unlocated interviews, movie-writing assignments); classified list
of works about Fitzgerald (bibliographies, biographies and memoirs, critical studies,
collections of essays, journals, and articles); a brief biography and chronology; and
texts of articles about Fitzgerald (including contributions by Matthew J. Bruccoli and
other major scholars). "Facts on Fitzgerald" amounts to notes on a wide variety of
topics, like "H. L. Mencken and 'The Smart Set'," "Ridiculed by Hemingway," and
"Fitzgerald in Asheville, North Carolina." Page also contains information about the
1996 Fitzgerald centenary, selected quotes from Fitzgerald, Fitzgerald voice and
video clips, and information on Scribner's. Some of the material is reprinted from
various volumes of the *Dictionary of Literary Biography*.

"The F. Scott Fitzgerald Page." *SAC LitWeb* 18 Mar. 2000, http://www.accd.edu/
sac/english/bailey/fitzgera.htm.

The Great Great Gatsby Guide. Ed. Ross David Kulberg. Michigan State U. 18 Mar.
2000, http://www.msu.edu/~kulbergr/gatsbyguide.htm.
The best of several *Great Gatsby* pages, with plot summaries, character identifications, and links.

Biographies and Criticism

Anderson, W. R. "F. Scott Fitzgerald." Rood, *American Writers in Paris, 1920-1939*
(*Dictionary of Literary Biography* 4) 132-50.

" 'Babylon Revisited': F. Scott Fitzgerald." Harris and Fitzgerald, *Short Story Criticism* 31:1-38.
Excerpts of criticism on Fitzgerald's short story from 1958-1995, with an annotated bibliography.

Donaldson, Scott. "F. Scott Fitzgerald." Martine, *American Novelists, 1910-1945*
(*Dictionary of Literary Biography* 9) 3-18.

"F(rancis) Scott (Key) Fitzgerald." Bryfonski, *Twentieth-Century Literary Criticism*
1:233-74.
Excerpts of criticism on Fitzgerald from 1922-1976.

———. Bryfonski, *Twentieth-Century Literary Criticism* 6:158-74.
Excerpts of criticism on Fitzgerald from 1920-1981, with an annotated
bibliography.

———. Bryfonski, *Twentieth-Century Literary Criticism* 14:146-90.
Excerpts of criticism on *The Great Gatsby* from 1925-1983, with an annotated
bibliography.

———. Bryfonski, *Twentieth-Century Literary Criticism* 28:84-128.
Excerpts of criticism on *Tender Is the Night* from 1932-1985, with an annotated
bibliography.

"F(rancis) Scott (Key) Fitzgerald." Harris and Fitzgerald, *Short Story Criticism* 6:43-106.
Excerpts of criticism on Fitzgerald from 1920-1989, with an annotated bibliography.

Gross, Dalton, and MaryJean Gross. *Understanding The Great Gatsby: A Student Casebook to Issues, Sources, and Historical Documents*. Westport: Greenwood, 1998.

Kuehl, John Richard. *F. Scott Fitzgerald: A Study of the Short Fiction*. Boston: Twayne, 1991.

"*The Last Tycoon*: F. Scott Fitzgerald." Bryfonski, *Twentieth-Century Literary Criticism* 55:190-231.
Excerpts of criticism on *The Last Tycoon* from 1941-1981, with an annotated bibliography.

Lehan, Richard. *The Great Gatsby: The Limits of Wonder*. Boston: Twayne, 1990.

Prigozy, Ruth. "F. Scott Fitzgerald." Kimbel, *American Short-Story Writers, 1910-1945, First Series* (*Dictionary of Literary Biography* 86) 99-123.

Stern, Milton R. *Tender Is the Night: The Broken Universe*. New York: Twayne, 1994.

Tredell, Nicolas *F. Scott Fitzgerald: The Great Gatsby*. New York: Columbia UP, 1999.

Dictionaries, Encyclopedias, and Handbooks

Gale, Robert L. *F. Scott Fitzgerald Encyclopedia*. Westport: Greenwood, 1998.

Tate, Mary Jo. *F. Scott Fitzgerald A to Z: The Essential Reference to His Life and Work*. New York: Facts on File, 1998.

Indexes and Concordances

Crosland, Andrew T. *Concordance to F. Scott Fitzgerald's The Great Gatsby*. Detroit: Gale, 1975.
References *The Great Gatsby* (New York: Scribner's, 1925), with emendations from Matthew J. Bruccoli's *Apparatus for a Definitive Edition of The Great Gatsby* (Columbia: U of South Carolina P, 1974).

Journals

F. Scott Fitzgerald Society Newsletter. Hempstead: The F. Scott Fitzgerald Soc., 1991- .
Features "F. Scott Fitzgerald—Current Bibliography."

Bibliographies

Bruccoli, Matthew J. "F. Scott Fitzgerald." Bruccoli and Baughman, *Bibliography of American Fiction, 1919-1988* 196-201.

———. "F. Scott Fitzgerald." Bruccoli and Baughman, *Modern Classic Writers* 21-32.

Bruccoli, Matthew J. *F. Scott Fitzgerald: A Descriptive Bibliography*. Rev. ed. Pittsburgh: U of Pittsburgh P, 1987.

Bryer, Jackson R. *Critical Reputation of F. Scott Fitzgerald: A Bibliographical Study*. Hamden: Archon, 1967.
Describes about 2,000 works since 1912.

———. *Critical Reputation of F. Scott Fitzgerald: A Bibliographical Study: Supplement One through 1981*. Hamden: Archon, 1984.
Updates Bryer, above, with about 2,500 items.

———. "F. Scott Fitzgerald." Bryer, *Sixteen Modern American Authors* 277-321.
Survey of research; supplemented by Bryer in Bryer, *Sixteen Modern American Authors: Volume 2* 301-59.

Etulain, Richard W., and N. Jill Howard. "F. Scott Fitzgerald." *Bibliographical Guide to the Study of Western American Literature* 233.

Glitsch, Catherine. "Fitzgerald, F. Scott." *American Novel Explication, 1991-1995* 85-88.

Kellman, Steven G. "F. Scott Fitzgerald." *Modern American Novel* 70-79.
Describes about 60 critical works.

Little, Anne C. "F. Scott Fitzgerald: 'Absolution'." Evans, Little, and Wiedemann, *Short Fiction* 49-56.
Describes 14 studies.

———. "F. Scott Fitzgerald: 'Babylon Revisited'." Evans, Little, and Wiedemann, *Short Fiction* 57-63.
Describes 12 studies.

Stanley, Linda C. *Non-English Critical Reputation of F. Scott Fitzgerald: An Analysis and Annotated Bibliography*. Westport: Greenwood, 1980.

West, James L., III. "Prospects for the Study of F. Scott Fitzgerald." *Resources for American Literary Study* 23.2 (1997): [147]-58.
Survey of research.

Louise Bogan, 1897-1970

Web Sites

"Louise Bogan." *Academy of American Poets*. 18 Mar. 2000, http://www.poets.org/lit/poet/lbogafst.htm.

Louise Bogan Resource Site. Ed. Chantal Linquist. DePaul U. 18 Mar. 2000, http://shrike.depaul.edu/~cfosterl/lb.html.
Texts of selected poems by Bogan with a brief biography and a list of works about her. Inoperable links to texts of works about Bogan.

Biographies and Criticism

"Louise Bogan." Riley, *Contemporary Literary Criticism* 93:59-107.
    Excerpts of criticism on Bogan from 1937-1987, with an annotated bibliography.

"Louise Bogan." Young, *Poetry Criticism* 12:84-132.
    Excerpts of comments and criticism on Bogan from 1923-1993, with an annotated bibliography.

Millier, Brett C. "Louise Bogan." Conte, *American Poets since World War II, Fifth Series* (*Dictionary of Literary Biography* 169) 54-62.

Ridgeway, Jacqueline. *Louise Bogan*. Boston: Twayne, 1984.

Shloss, Carol. "Louise Bogan." Quartermain, *American Poets, 1880-1945, First Series* (*Dictionary of Literary Biography* 45) 52-59.

Bibliographies

Barstow, Jane Missner. "Louise Bogan." *One Hundred Years of American Women Writing, 1848-1948* 142-44.
    Describes selected editions, biographies, and criticism.

Knox, Claire E. *Louise Bogan: A Reference Source*. Metuchen: Scarecrow, 1990.
    Gives brief information for works by Bogan and describes about 200 works on her since 1922.

Leo, John R. "Bogan, Louise." *Guide to American Poetry Explication* 39-41.

William (Cuthbert) Faulkner, 1897-1962

Web Sites

Center For Faulkner Studies. Southeast Missouri SU. 18 Mar. 2000, http://www2. semo.edu/cfs/homepage.html.

"William Faulkner." *Mississippi Writers Page*. 18 Mar. 2000, http://cedar.olemiss.edu/ depts/english/ms-writers/dir/faulkner_william/.
    Comprehensive, well-organized, and carefully constructed site that is a fitting tribute to the author: "Biographical Sketch" contains sections for early years, failed poet, Nobel laureate, and statesman to the world and well-chosen photographs; "Publications by Faulkner" lists drama (plays and screenplays), fiction (novels and short stories), nonfiction, poetry, and scholarly editions of Faulkner's work; "Selected Bibliography" includes scholarly and popular biographies and general critical works on Faulkner; "Media Adaptations" lists screenplays (credited and uncredited) and television screenplays, film adaptations of Faulkner's work, plays by Faulkner, and stage adaptations of Faulkner; and "Internet Resources" focuses on scholarly web sites but also identifies other major web sites; papers, conferences, and publications; manuscripts, libraries, and special collections; 1997 centennial celebration sites; and listservs.

"William Faulkner." *Nobel Prize Internet Archive*. 18 Mar. 2000, http://nobelprizes.com/ nobel/literature/1949a.html.

William Faulkner. 18 Mar. 2000, http://www.virginia.edu/~history/courses/courses.old/
hius323/faulkner.html.
Biographical sketch and short bibliography.

William Faulkner: Nobel Prize Acceptance Speech. 18 Mar. 2000, http://www.rjgeib.com/
thoughts/faulkner/faulkner.html.

William Faulkner on the Web. 18 Mar. 2000, http://cypress.mcsr.olemiss.edu/~egjbp/
faulkner/faulkner.html.

The William Faulkner Society. Ed. Gail Mortimer. 7 Mar. 2000. U of Texas at El Paso.
18 Mar. 2000, http://www.utep.edu/mortimer/faulkner/mainfaulkner.htm.
Affiliated with *The Faulkner Journal.*

Biographies and Criticism

Berland, Alwyn. *Light in August: A Study in Black and White.* New York: Twayne,
1992.

Hinkle, James C., and Robert McCoy. *Reading Faulkner: The Unvanquished: Glossary and Commentary.* Jackson: UP of Mississippi, 1995.

Inge, M. Thomas. "William Faulkner." Trachtenberg, *American Humorists,
1800-1950 (Dictionary of Literary Biography* 11) 134-46.

Kawin, Bruce. "William Faulkner." Clark, Morsberger, and Lesser, *American
Screenwriters (Dictionary of Literary Biography* 44) 123-31.

Kinney, Arthur F. *Go Down, Moses: The Miscegenation of Time.* New York:
Twayne, 1996.

Matthews, John T. *The Sound and the Fury: Faulkner and the Lost Cause.* Boston:
Twayne, 1991.

Parker, Robert Dale. *Absalom, Absalom!: The Questioning of Fictions.* Boston:
Twayne, 1991.

Ross, Stephen M., and Noel Polk. *Reading Faulkner: The Sound and the Fury: Glossary and Commentary.* Jackson: UP of Mississippi, 1996.

Skei, Hans H. "William Faulkner." Kimbel, *American Short-Story Writers,
1910-1945, Second Series (Dictionary of Literary Biography* 102) 75-102.

Wagner, Linda W. "William Faulkner." Martine, *American Novelists, 1910-1945
(Dictionary of Literary Biography* 9) 282-302.

"William (Cuthbert) Faulkner." Harris and Fitzgerald, *Short Story Criticism* 1:
145-88.
Excerpts of criticism on Faulkner from 1931-1985, with an annotated bibliography.

"William (Cuthbert) Faulkner." Riley, *Contemporary Literary Criticism* 52:104-47.
Excerpts of criticism on Faulkner's novel *Absalom, Absalom!* from 1936-1980.

"William Faulkner." Riley, *Contemporary Literary Criticism* 68:104-36.
Excerpts of criticism on Faulkner's *The Sound and the Fury* from 1929-1980,
with an annotated bibliography.

Dictionaries, Encyclopedias, and Handbooks

Brown, Calvin S. *Glossary of Faulkner's South*. New Haven: Yale UP, 1976.

Connolly, Thomas E. *Faulkner's World: A Directory of His People and Synopses of Actions in His Published Works*. Lanham: UP of America, 1988.

Dasher, Thomas E. *William Faulkner's Characters: An Index to the Published and Unpublished Fiction*. New York: Garland, 1981.

Gresset, Michel, and Arthur B. Scharff. *Faulkner Chronology*. Jackson: UP of Mississippi, 1985.
Translation of Gresset's *Faulkner: Oeuvres Romanesques* (Paris: Editions Gallimard, 1977).

Hamblin, Robert W., and Charles A. Peek. *William Faulkner Encyclopedia*. Westport: Greenwood, 1999.

Jones, Diane Brown. *Reader's Guide to the Short Stories of William Faulkner*. New York: G. K. Hall, 1994.

Indexes and Concordances

Capps, Jack L. *As I Lay Dying: A Concordance to the Novel*. West Point: Faulkner Concordance Advisory Board, 1977.
Based on 1967 Modern Library edition.

———. *Go Down, Moses: A Concordance to the Novel*. West Point: Faulkner Concordance Advisory Board, 1977.
Keyed to 1955 Modern Library issue of New York: Random House, 1942 edition.

———. *Light in August: A Concordance to the Novel*. West Point: Faulkner Concordance Advisory Board, 1979.
Indexes 1968 Modern Library reprint of New York: Smith & Haas, 1932 first printing.

Polk, Noel. *Intruder in the Dust: A Concordance to the Novel*. West Point: Faulkner Concordance Advisory Board, 1983.
Keyed to New York: Random House, 1948 first printing.

———. *Requiem for a Nun: A Concordance to the Novel*. West Point: Faulkner Concordance Advisory Board, 1979.
Based on New York: Random House, 1951 "fourth printing."

———, and John D. Hart. *Absalom, Absalom!: A Concordance to the Novel*. West Point: Faulkner Concordance Advisory Board, 1989.
Based on corrected New York: Random House, 1986 edition and variants.

———. *Collected Stories of William Faulkner: A Concordance to the Forty-Two Short Stories: With Statistical Summaries and Vocabulary Listings for Collected Stories, These 13, and Dr. Martino and Other Stories*. West Point: Faulkner Concordance Advisory Board, 1990.

———. *Hamlet: A Concordance to the Novel.* West Point: Faulkner Concordance Advisory Board, 1990.
Indexes text in Faulkner's *Novels, 1936-1940* (New York: Library of America, 1990) 731-1075.

———. *Mansion: A Concordance to the Novel.* West Point: Faulkner Concordance Advisory Board, 1988.
Indexes New York: Random House, 1959 first printing and variants.

———. *Pylon: A Concordance to the Novel.* West Point: Faulkner Concordance Advisory Board, 1989.
Based on text in Faulkner's *Novels, 1930-1935* (New York: Library of America, 1985) 779-992, and variants.

———. *Reivers: A Concordance to the Novel.* West Point: Faulkner Concordance Advisory Board, 1990.
Based on New York: Random House, 1962 first printing and variants.

———. *Sanctuary: Corrected First Edition Text, 1985: A Concordance to the Novel.* West Point: Faulkner Concordance Advisory Board, 1990.
Based on first printing in Faulkner's *Novels, 1930-1935* (New York: Library of America, 1985) 181-398.

———. *Sanctuary: The Original Text, 1981: A Concordance to the Novel.* West Point: Faulkner Concordance Advisory Board, 1990.
Indexes New York: Random House, 1981 first printing.

———. *Uncollected Stories of William Faulkner: Concordance of the Forty-Five Short Stories.* West Point: Faulkner Concordance Advisory Board, 1990.
Indexes texts of New York: Random House, 1959 edition and 20 stories revised for later books.

———. *Unvanquished: A Concordance to the Novel.* West Point: Faulkner Concordance Advisory Board, 1989.
Keyed to Faulkner's *Novels, 1936-1940* (New York: Library of America, 1990) 321-492.

Polk, Noel, and Kenneth L. Privratsky. *A Fable: A Concordance to the Novel.* West Point: Faulkner Concordance Advisory Board, 1981.
Keyed to New York: Random House, 1954 first printing and corrections.

———. *The Sound and the Fury: A Concordance to the Novel.* West Point: Faulkner Concordance Advisory Board, 1980.
Based on 1963 Vintage Books reprint of New York: Jonathan Cape and Harrison Smith, 1929 first printing.

Polk, Noel, and Lawrence Z. Pizzi. *Town: A Concordance to the Novel.* West Point: Faulkner Concordance Advisory Board, 1985.
References New York: Random House, 1957 edition and variants.

Privratsky, Kenneth L. *Wild Palms: A Concordance to the Novel.* West Point: Faulkner Concordance Advisory Board, 1983.
Indexes New York: Random House, 1939 first printing and variants.

Journals

The Faulkner Journal. Akron: U of Akron, 1985- .

Faulkner Studies. Kyoto: Yamaguchi Publishing House, 1992- .

Bibliographies

Bassett, John Earl. *Faulkner: An Annotated Checklist of Criticism.* New York: David Lewis, 1972.
Describes about 5,000 works

——. *Faulkner: An Annotated Checklist of Recent Criticism.* Kent: Kent State UP, 1983.
Updates Bassett's 1972 guide with 1,950 items.

——. *Faulkner in the Eighties: An Annotated Critical Bibliography.* Metuchen: Scarecrow, 1991.
Describes 1,816 items on Faulkner.

Brodsky, Louis Daniel, and Robert W. Hamblin. *Faulkner: A Comprehensive Guide to the Brodsky Collection.* Jackson: UP of Mississippi, 1982-1985.
The major descriptive listing of Faulkner's works.

Carpenter, Charles A. "Faulkner, William." *Modern Drama Scholarship and Criticism, 1981-1990* 55.

Dasher, Thomas E. "William Faulkner." Flora and Bain, *Fifty Southern Writers after 1900* 158-76.

Evans, Robert C. "William Faulkner: 'Barn Burning'." Evans, Little, and Wiedemann, *Short Fiction* 27-39.
Describes 24 studies.

——. "William Faulkner: A Rose for Emily." Evans, Little, and Wiedemann, *Short Fiction* 40-48.
Describes 14 studies.

Glitsch, Catherine. "Faulkner, William." *American Novel Explication, 1991-1995* 76-82.

Kellman, Steven G. "William Faulkner." *Modern American Novel* 47-69.
Describes about 130 critical works.

McHaney, Thomas L. "William Faulkner." Bruccoli and Baughman, *Bibliography of American Fiction, 1919-1988* 173-85.

——. "William Faulkner." Bruccoli and Baughman, *Modern Classic Writers* 1-20.

——. "William Faulkner." Kopley, *Prospects for the Study of American Literature* 297-314.
The most up-to-date survey of research.

Meriwether, James B. "William Faulkner." Bryer, *Sixteen Modern American Authors*
223-75.
Survey of research; supplemented by Philip G. Cohen in Bryer, *Sixteen Modern
American Authors: Volume 2* 210-300.

Ricks, Beatrice. *William Faulkner: A Bibliography of Secondary Works*. Metuchen:
Scarecrow, 1981.
8,712 very briefly and selectively annotated entries.

Sensibar, Judith L., and Nancy L. Stegall. *Faulkner's Poetry: A Bibliographical
Guide to Texts and Criticism*. Ann Arbor: UMI Research, 1988.
Complete descriptions of all of Faulkner's "known extant poems" (p. [xiii]).

Sweeney, Patricia E. *William Faulkner's Women Characters: An Annotated Bibliography of Criticism, 1930-1983*. Santa Barbara: ABC-Clio, 1985.

Thornton (Niven) Wilder, 1897-1975

Web Sites

"Thornton Wilder." *Bohemian Ink*. 18 Mar. 2000, http://www.levity.com/corduroy/
wilder.htm.

Thornton Wilder. 18 Mar. 2000, http://danenet.wicip.org/hmi/wilder.htm.

The Thornton Wilder Page. Ed. Emily Parris. Update and sponsor unknown. 18 Mar.
2000, http://www.sky.net/~emily/thornton.html.
Collection of links for information, listservs, and other Wilder pages.

Biographies and Criticism

French, Warren. "Thornton Wilder." Rood, *American Writers in Paris, 1920-1939*
(*Dictionary of Literary Biography* 4) 414-15.

Goldstone, Richard H. "Thornton Wilder." Martine, *American Novelists, 1910-1945*
(*Dictionary of Literary Biography* 9) 146-53.

Haberman, Donald. *Our Town: An American Play*. Boston: Twayne, 1989.

Johns, Sally. "Thornton Wilder." MacNicholas, *Twentieth-Century American
Dramatists* (*Dictionary of Literary Biography* 7) 304-19.

"Thornton Wilder." Riley, *Contemporary Literary Criticism* 82:336-93.
Excerpts of criticism on Wilder from 1927-1989, with an annotated bibliography.

"Thornton Wilder." Trudeau, *Drama Criticism* 1:472-519.
Excerpts of criticism on Wilder in general and on *Our Town* and *The Skin of Our
Teeth* from 1938-1986, with an annotated bibliography.

Bibliographies

Carpenter, Charles A. "Wilder, Thornton [Niven]." *Modern Drama Scholarship and
Criticism, 1981-1990* 89-90.

Edelstein, J. M. *Bibliographical Checklist of the Writings of Thornton Wilder*. New Haven: Yale UP, 1959.
Complete descriptions.

Goldstone, Richard. "Thornton Wilder." Bruccoli and Baughman, *Bibliography of American Fiction, 1919-1988* 542-44.

———, and Gary Anderson. *Thornton Wilder: An Annotated Bibliography of Works by and about Thornton Wilder*. New York: AMS, 1982.
Brief descriptive entries (largely summaries of contents) for Wilder's works and 500 works on him.

Kellman, Steven G. "Thornton Wilder." *Modern American Novel* 145-48.
Describes about 20 critical works.

Shuman, R. Baird. "Thornton Wilder." *American Drama, 1918-1960* 155-60.
Describes about 25 critical works.

Walsh, Claudette. *Thornton Wilder: A Reference Guide, 1926-1990*. New York: G. K. Hall, 1993.
Describes about 2,500 works on Wilder.

Wheatley, Christopher J. "Thornton Wilder." Demastes, *American Playwrights, 1880-1945* [437]-52.

(Harold) Hart Crane, 1899-1932

Web Sites

"Chapter 7: Early Twentieth Century: Hart Crane." *PAL: Perspectives in American Literature*. 18 Mar. 2000, http://www.csustan.edu/english/reuben/pal/chap7/crane_hart.html.
Mainly useful for a list of works about Crane.

"Hart Crane." *Academy of American Poets*. 18 Mar. 2000, http://www.poets.org/lit/poet/hcranfst.htm.

"Hart Crane." *American Literature on the Web*. 18 Mar. 2000, http://www.nagasaki-gaigo.ac.jp/ishikawa/amlit/c/crane_h20.htm.
Excellent list of links for general resources and fulltexts for Crane.

"Hart Crane." *Twentieth-Century Poetry in English*. 18 Mar. 2000, http://www.lit.kobe-u.ac.jp/~hishika/crane.htm.
Brief biography and bibliography of works about Crane, with notes and interlinear readings for "The Bridge" and links.

Hart Crane Quotations. 18 Mar. 2000, http://webdesk.com/quotations/crane-hart.html.
Includes poetry and lengthy quotations from letters.

The Hart Crane WebBridge. 18 Mar. 2000, http://unr.edu/homepage/brad/hart/crane.html.

Biographies and Criticism

"*The Bridge*: Hart Crane." Bryfonski, *Twentieth-Century Literary Criticism* 80:76-217.
 Excerpts of comments and criticism on Crane's work from 1933-1992, with an annotated bibliography.

"(Harold) Hart Crane." Bryfonski, *Twentieth-Century Literary Criticism* 2:111-26.
 Excerpts of criticism on Crane from 1928-1978, with an annotated bibliography.

———. Bryfonski, *Twentieth-Century Literary Criticism* 5:183-96.
 Excerpts of criticism on Crane from 1926-1980.

"Hart Crane." Young, *Poetry Criticism* 3:78-113.
 Excerpts of comments and criticism on Crane from 1925-1989, with an annotated bibliography.

Lewis, Thomas S. W. "Hart Crane." Rood, *American Writers in Paris, 1920-1939* (*Dictionary of Literary Biography* 4) 82-84.

Miller, Joseph. "Hart Crane." Quartermain, *American Poets, 1880-1945, Second Series* (*Dictionary of Literary Biography* 48) 78-97.

Indexes and Concordances

Lane, Gary. *Concordance to the Poems of Hart Crane.* New York: Haskell House, 1972.
 Based on *Complete Poems and Selected Letters and Prose of Hart Crane*, ed. Brom Weber (New York: Liveright, 1966).

Landry, Hilton, Elaine Landry, and Robert DeMott. *Concordance to the Poems of Hart Crane.* Metuchen: Scarecrow, 1973.
 Also based on Weber's 1966 edition, above.

Bibliographies

Leo, John R. "Crane, Hart." *Guide to American Poetry Explication* 59-74.

Schwartz, Joseph. *Hart Crane: A Reference Guide.* Boston: G. K. Hall, 1983.
 Thorough descriptions of works on Crane since 1919.

———, and Robert C. Schweik. *Hart Crane: A Descriptive Bibliography.* Pittsburgh: U of Pittsburgh P, 1972.
 Complete descriptions of Crane's works.

Weber, Brom. "Hart Crane." Bryer, *Sixteen Modern American Authors* 75-122.
 Survey of research; supplemented in Bryer, *Sixteen Modern American Authors: Volume 2* 73-119.

Ernest (Miller) Hemingway, 1899-1961

Web Sites

Ernest Hemingway. 18 Mar. 2000, http://www.ernest.hemingway.com/page9.htm.

Ernest Hemingway. 18 Mar. 2000, http://www.geocities.com/SoHo/Cafe/2310/.

Ernest Hemingway in Oak Park, Illinois. Ed. unknown. 28 Jan. 1999. Hemingway Foundation of Oak Park. 18 Mar. 2000, http://www.hemingway.org/.
   Aimed at those interested in Hemingway's life in Oak Park, Illinois. Apart from organization links, the best major links are for information on Hemingway's life and works (including offsite photo galleries, a very good onsite chronology, and a fair bibliography, but lacking balance in several topics, like "Library" and "Wives") and other web resources. Misspellings and mistakes in grammar mar the site.

Hemingway Resource Center. Ed. unknown. 18 Mar. 2000. The Lost Generation Bookstore. 18 Mar. 2000, http://www.lostgeneration.com/hrc.htm.
   The site provides an informative and pleasingly illustrated (unsigned) biographical sketch; an up-to-date classified unannotated bibliography mainly limited to books by and about Hemingway; and FAQs that ably explain "lost generation" but fall flat in attempting to explain Hemingway's suicide by cataloging his physical ailments.

Life and Works of Ernest Hemingway. 18 Mar. 2000, http://www.empirezine.com/spotlight/hemmingway/hem1.htm.
   Note misspelling "hemmingway" in URL.

Biographies and Criticism

Beegel, Susan F. "Ernest Hemingway." Kimbel, *American Short-Story Writers, 1910-1945, Second Series* (*Dictionary of Literary Biography* 102) 127-65.

Benson, Jackson J. *New Critical Approaches to the Short Stories of Ernest Hemingway*. Durham: Duke UP, 1990.
   Includes "A Comprehensive Checklist of Hemingway Short Fiction Criticism, Explication, and Commentary, 1975-1990" (393-458).

Brenner, Gerry. *The Old Man and the Sea: Story of a Common Man*. Boston: Twayne, 1991.

"Ernest Hemingway." Harris and Fitzgerald, *Short Story Criticism* 1:204-53.
   Excerpts of criticism on Hemingway from 1924-1986, with an annotated bibliography.

"Ernest Hemingway." Riley, *Contemporary Literary Criticism* 61:188-234.
   Excerpts of criticism on Hemingway's novel *The Sun Also Rises* from 1926-1988, with an annotated bibliography.

Flora, Joseph M. *Ernest Hemingway: A Study of the Short Fiction*. Boston: Twayne, 1989.

"*For Whom the Bell Tolls*: Ernest Hemingway." Riley, *Contemporary Literary Criticism* 80:100-60.
   Excerpts of criticism on Hemingway's novel from 1940-1991, with an annotated bibliography.

Gerogiannis, Nicholas. "Ernest Hemingway." Rood, *American Writers in Paris, 1920-1939* (*Dictionary of Literary Biography* 4) 187-211.

Josephs, Allen. *For Whom the Bell Tolls: Ernest Hemingway's Undiscovered Country*. New York: Twayne, 1994.

Lewis, Robert W. *A Farewell to Arms: The War of the Words*. New York: Twayne, 1992.

Mandel, Miriam B. *Reading Hemingway: The Facts in the Fictions*. Metuchen: Scarecrow, 1995.
Useful guide to characters and named elements in Hemingway's novels.

Nagel, James. "Ernest Hemingway." Martine, *American Novelists, 1910-1945* (*Dictionary of Literary Biography* 9) 100-120.

Reynolds, Michael S. *The Sun Also Rises: A Novel of the Twenties*. Boston: Twayne, 1988.

Rovit, Earl H., and Gerry Brenner. *Ernest Hemingway*. Rev. ed. Boston: Twayne, 1986.

" 'The Snows of Kilimanjaro': Ernest Hemingway." Harris and Fitzgerald, *Short Story Criticism* 25:78-128.
Excerpts of criticism on Hemingway's short story from 1952-1988, with an annotated bibliography.

Dictionaries, Encyclopedias, and Handbooks

Reynolds, Michael S. *Hemingway: An Annotated Chronology: An Outline of the Author's Life and Career Detailing Significant Events, Friendships, Travels, and Achievements*. Detroit: Omnigraphics, 1991.

Smith, Paul. *Reader's Guide to the Short Stories of Ernest Hemingway*. Boston: G. K. Hall, 1989.

Indexes and Concordances

Hays, Peter L. *Concordance to Hemingway's In Our Time*. Boston: G. K. Hall, 1990.
Based on New York: Boni & Liveright, 1925 edition.

Journals

Hemingway Review. Moscow: Hemingway Soc., 1979- .
Formerly *Hemingway Notes* (1971-81); includes a current "Hemingway Bibliography."

Bibliographies

Brasch, James D., and Joseph Sigman. *Hemingway's Library: A Complete Record*. New York: Garland, 1981.

Carpenter, Charles A. "Hemingway, Ernest." *Modern Drama Scholarship and Criticism, 1981-1990* 60.

DeFazio, Albert J., III. "Ernest Hemingway." Bruccoli and Baughman, *Bibliography of American Fiction, 1919-1988* 240-46.

————. "Ernest Hemingway." Bruccoli and Baughman, *Modern Classic Writers* 33-47.

Etulain, Richard W., and N. Jill Howard. "Ernest Hemingway." *Bibliographical Guide to the Study of Western American Literature* 253-54.

Glitsch, Catherine. "Hemingway, Ernest." *American Novel Explication, 1991-1995* 112-17.

Hanneman, Audrey. *Ernest Hemingway: A Comprehensive Bibliography*. Princeton: Princeton UP, 1967.
Complete descriptions of Hemingway's works and descriptively annotated entries for about 2,000 critical studies.

————. *Supplement to Ernest Hemingway: A Comprehensive Bibliography*. Princeton: Princeton UP, 1975.
Updates Hanneman, above, with entries for editions and about 1,500 criticisms.

Hoffman, Frederick J., and Melvin J. Friedman. "Ernest Hemingway" Bryer, *Sixteen Modern American Authors* 367-416.
Survey of research; supplemented by Bruce Stark in Bryer, *Sixteen Modern American Authors: Volume 2* 404-79.

Kellman, Steven G. "Ernest Hemingway." *Modern American Novel* 87-99.
Describes about 70 critical works.

Larson, Kelli A. *Ernest Hemingway: A Reference Guide, 1974-1989*. Boston: G. K. Hall, 1991.
Updates Wagner, below, describing more than 1,700 items about Hemingway.

Little, Anne C. "Ernest Hemingway: 'The Short Happy Life of Francis Macomber'." Evans, Little, and Wiedemann, *Short Fiction* 92-103.
Describes 16 studies.

————. "Ernest Hemingway: 'The Snows of Kilimanjaro'." Evans, Little, and Wiedemann, *Short Fiction* 104-11.
Describes 12 studies.

Monteiro, George. "Ernest Hemingway's *A Farewell to Arms*—The First Sixty-Five Years: A Checklist of Criticism, Scholarship, and Commentary." *Bulletin of Bibliography* 53.4 (1996): 273-92.

Reynolds, Michael S. "Ernest Hemingway." Kopley, *Prospects for the Study of American Literature* 266-82.
The most up-to-date survey of research.

Wagner, Linda Welshimer. *Ernest Hemingway: A Reference Guide*. Boston: G. K. Hall, 1977.
Describes about 2,400 English-language criticisms since 1923.

Vladimir Nabokov, 1899-1977

Web Sites

International Vladimir Nabokov Society. Eds. John Burt Foster, Jr., D. Barton Johnson, Dieter E. Zimmer, and Jeff Edmunds. Aug. 1999. Nabokov Soc.; Pennsylvania SU. 18 Mar. 2000, http://www.libraries.psu.edu/iasweb/nabokov/nabsoc.htm.
Nominal homepage for a collection of pages that represent comprehensive resources for Nabokov. Major links to the Society's page include a searchable classified unannotated bibliography of works about Nabokov (compiled by Zimmer and Edmunds) that claims to be "the most extensive listing of Nabokov criticism currently available"; selected texts about Nabokov in English and Russian (linked under "Criticism"); contents, indexes, and information for quarterly *Nabokovian* and annual *Nabokov Studies* journals; NABOKV-L listserv; and a guide to Nabokov special collections (under "ZEMBLARCHIVE"). Without any doubt, "Vladimir Nabokov: A Bibliography of Criticism" is among the most thorough bibliographies of literary criticism on the web: there are 174 citations for *Lolita* alone.

"Vladimir Nabokov." *American Literature on the Web*. 18 Mar. 2000, http://www.nagasaki-gaigo.ac.jp/ishikawa/amlit/n/nabokov21.htm.

"Vladimir Nabokov." *Pegasos*. 18 Mar. 2000, http://www.kirjasto.sci.fi/nabokov.htm.
Bibliography of works by Nabokov, a list of books for further reading, and a good biographical sketch.

The Vladimir Nabokov Appreciation Site. Ed. J. Martinez. 3 Mar. 2000. Sponsor unknown. 18 Mar. 2000, http://members.tripod.com/~pigbodine/waxwing/nabokov.html.

The World of Vladimir Nabokov. 18 Mar. 2000, http://www.geocities.com/Hollywood/Screen/2578/index.html.
Contains excellent links page.

Biographies and Criticism

Hagopian, John V. "Vladimir Nabokov." Helterman and Layman, *American Novelists since World War II, First Series* (*Dictionary of Literary Biography* 2) 350-64.

Olsen, Lance. *Lolita: A Janus Text*. New York: Twayne, 1995.

"Vladimir Nabokov." Harris and Fitzgerald, *Short Story Criticism* 11:106-61.
Excerpts of criticism on Nabokov from 1958-1988, with an annotated bibliography.

"Vladimir Nabokov." Riley, *Contemporary Literary Criticism* 64:330-69.
Excerpts of criticism on Nabokov's novel *Lolita* from 1958-1988, with an annotated bibliography.

Dictionaries, Encyclopedias, and Handbooks

Alexandrov, Vladimir E. *Garland Companion to Vladimir Nabokov*. New York: Garland, 1995.
Detailed and thorough critical overviews, but no plot summaries.

Appel, Alfred, Jr. *The Annotated Lolita*. 1970. Rev. ed. New York: Vintage, 1991.

Barabtarlo, Gennady. *Phantom of Fact: A Guide to Nabokov's Pnin*. Ann Arbor: Ardis, 1989.

Connolly, Julian W., ed. *Nabokov's Invitation to a Beheading: A Critical Companion*. Evanston: Northwestern UP, American Association of Teachers of Slavic and East European Languages, 1997.

Mason, Bobbie Ann. *Nabokov's Garden: A Guide to Ada*. Ann Arbor: Ardis, 1974.

Nakhimovsky, Alexander D., and S. Paperno. *English-Russian Dictionary of Nabokov's Lolita*. Ann Arbor: Ardis, 1982.
Keyed to the Russian-language edition of Lolita (1967; Ann Arbor: Ardis, 1976).

Proffer, Carl. *Keys to Lolita*. Bloomington: Indiana UP, 1968.

Journals

Nabokovian. Lawrence: Vladimir Nabokov Soc., 1978- .
Formerly *Vladimir Nabokov Research Newsletter* (1978-1984).

Bibliographies

Carpenter, Charles A. "Nabokov, Vladimir." *Modern Drama Scholarship and Criticism, 1981-1990* 70.

Glitsch, Catherine. "Nabokov, Vladimir." *American Novel Explication, 1991-1995* 189-90.

Jones, Nancy C. "Vladimir Nabokov's Lolita: A Survey of Scholarship and Criticism in English, 1977-1995." *Bulletin of Bibliography* 54.2 (1997): 129-47.

Juliar, Michael. "Vladimir Nabokov." Bruccoli and Baughman, *Bibliography of American Fiction, 1919-1988* 366-76.

———. *Vladimir Nabokov: A Descriptive Bibliography*. New York: Garland, 1986.
Complete descriptions of Nabokov's works.

Schuman, Samuel. *Vladimir Nabokov: A Reference Guide*. Boston: G. K. Hall, 1979.
Describes about 800 works on Nabokov since 1931.

(John Orley) Allen Tate, 1899-1979

Web Sites

"Allen Tate." *Academy of American Poets*. 9 Mar. 2000, http://www.poets.org/lit/
poet/atatefst.htm.
Useful for a brief biography and fulltexts of two poems by Tate; only one offsite
link provided.

Biographies and Criticism

Hart, James A. "Allen Tate." Quartermain, *American Poets, 1880-1945, First Series*
(*Dictionary of Literary Biography* 45) 381-95.

Jones, James T. "Allen Tate." Jay, *Modern American Critics, 1920-1955* (*Dictionary
of Literary Biography* 63) 257-66.

Wilkie, Everett C., Jr. "Allen Tate." Rood, *American Writers in Paris, 1920-1939*
(*Dictionary of Literary Biography* 4) 378-82.

Bibliographies

Fallwell, Marshall, Jr. *Allen Tate: A Bibliography*. New York: D. Lewis, 1969.
Briefly describes Tate's writings and about 200 works on Tate.

Leo, John R. "Tate, Allen." *Guide to American Poetry Explication* 431-37.

Young, Thomas Daniel. "Allen Tate." Flora and Bain, *Fifty Southern Writers after
1900* 457-68.

Thomas (Clayton) Wolfe, 1900-1938

Web Sites

"Thomas Wolfe." *Literary Kicks*. 18 Mar. 2000, http://www.charm.net/~brooklyn/
People/ThomasWolfe.html.
Brief biographical sketch.

Thomas Wolfe Collection. Ed. unknown. 13 May 1998. U of North Carolina. 18 Mar.
2000, http://www.lib.unc.edu/ncc/wolfe/index.html.
Guide to U of North Carolina Library's collection of correspondence, manuscripts, legal documents, family memorabilia, printed material by and about Wolfe,
photographs, clippings, and recorded materials with a comprehensive index.

Thomas Wolfe Web Site. Ed. Sharon Connelly. 13 Apr. 1999. U of North Carolina
(Wilmington). 18 Mar. 2000, http://library.uncwil.edu/wolfe/wolfe.html.
Most useful Wolfe site, containing bibliographies of works by and about Wolfe;
information on *Thomas Wolfe Review* and tables of contents (1978-); a brief Wolfe
biography; a photo tour of the Thomas Wolfe Memorial North Carolina Historic Site;
and news related to Wolfe.

Biographies and Criticism

Field, Leslie. "Thomas Wolfe." Martine, *American Novelists, 1910-1945* (*Dictionary of Literary Biography* 9) 172-88.

"*Of Time and the River*: Thomas Wolfe." Bryfonski, *Twentieth-Century Literary Criticism* 61:279-320.
    Excerpts of comments and criticism on *Of Time and the River* from 1935-1987, with an annotated bibliography.

Payne, Ladell. "Thomas Wolfe." Kimbel, *American Short-Story Writers, 1910-1945, Second Series* (*Dictionary of Literary Biography* 102) 366-78.

"Thomas (Clayton) Wolfe." Bryfonski, *Twentieth-Century Literary Criticism* 4:505-40.
    Excerpts of comments and criticism on Wolfe from 1929-1979, with an annotated bibliography.

———. Bryfonski, *Twentieth-Century Literary Criticism* 13:465-97.
    Excerpts of comments and criticism on Wolfe from 1929-1983, with an annotated bibliography.

———. Bryfonski, *Twentieth-Century Literary Criticism* 29:394-434.
    Excerpts of comments and criticism on *Look Homeward, Angel* from 1929-1985, with an annotated bibliography.

Dictionaries, Encyclopedias, and Handbooks

Idol, John Lane, Jr. *Thomas Wolfe Companion*. Westport: Greenwood, 1987.
    Plot and character summaries.

Journals

Thomas Wolfe Review. Akron: Thomas Wolfe Soc., 1977-.
    Formerly *Thomas Wolfe Newsletter*; features "The Wolfe Pack: Bibliography."

Bibliographies

Bassett, John E. *Thomas Wolfe: An Annotated Critical Bibliography*. Lanham: Scarecrow, 1996.
    2,876 selectively annotated entries.

Carpenter, Charles A. "Wolfe, Thomas." *Modern Drama Scholarship and Criticism, 1981-1990* 95.

Etulain, Richard W., and N. Jill Howard. "Thomas Wolfe." *Bibliographical Guide to the Study of Western American Literature* 428.

Glitsch, Catherine. "Wolfe, Thomas." *American Novel Explication, 1991-1995* 272-73.

Holman, C. Hugh. "Thomas Wolfe." Bryer, *Sixteen Modern American Authors* 587-624.
    Survey of research; supplemented by Richard S. Kennedy in Bryer, *Sixteen Modern American Authors: Volume 2* 716-55.

Johnston, Carol. "Thomas Wolfe." Bruccoli and Baughman, *Bibliography of American Fiction, 1919-1988* 549-52.

———. "Thomas Wolfe." Bruccoli and Baughman, *Modern Classic Writers* 73-81.
Revises and updates Johnston, above.

———. *Thomas Wolfe: A Descriptive Bibliography*. Pittsburgh: U of Pittsburgh P, 1987.
Complete descriptions of Wolfe's works.

Kellman, Steven G. "Thomas Wolfe." *Modern American Novel* 149-55.
Describes about 30 critical works.

Kennedy, Richard S. "Thomas Wolfe." Flora and Bain, *Fifty Southern Writers after 1900* 535-44.

Phillipson, John S. *Thomas Wolfe: A Reference Guide*. Boston: G. K. Hall, 1977.
Describes about 800 works on Wolfe since 1929; updated by Phillipson's "Thomas Wolfe: A Reference Guide Updated," *Resources for American Literary Study* 11 (Spring 1981): 37-80.

Sterling A(llan) Brown, 1901-1989

Web Sites

Literary Tribute to Sterling A. Brown. Ed. Andre Kareem Mekkawi and Imogene Zachery. Feb. 1998. Howard U. 18 Mar. 2000, http://www.founders.howard.edu/sterlingbrown.htm.
Very commendable site that combines biography with a bibliography (including literary criticism and even harder-to-find items like obituaries) and guidance for further study. The site would benefit, overall, from better updating and, specifically, from increasing the objectivity of its biographical sketch. Zachery provided the research and Mekkawi the web production.

"Sterling A. Brown." *Academy of American Poets*. 18 Mar. 2000, http://www.poets.org/lit/poet/sbrown.htm.
Includes texts of three of Brown's poems: "Slim Greer in Hell" (also available in audio), "Riverbank Blues," and "Southern Road"; a very brief biographical sketch; and an even briefer "selected bibliography" of Brown's works that fails to list any books written by Brown between the years 1937 and 1975.

"The Sterling A. Brown Page." *SAC LitWeb*. 18 Mar. 2000, http://www.accd.edu/sac/english/bailey/brownsa.htm.

Biographies and Criticism

Burnette, R. V. "Sterling A. Brown." Jay, *Modern American Critics, 1920-1955 (Dictionary of Literary Biography* 63) 60-67.

Gabbin, Joanne V. "Sterling A. Brown." Harris, *Afro-American Writers from the Harlem Renaissance to 1940 (Dictionary of Literary Biography* 51) 22-34.

Wood, Don. "Sterling Brown." Quartermain, *American Poets, 1880-1945, Second Series (Dictionary of Literary Biography* 48) 57-63.

Bibliographies

Kapai, Leela. "Sterling A. Brown." Nelson, *African American Authors, 1745-1945*
   57-63.
   Survey of research.

Perry, Margaret. "Brown, Sterling A." *Harlem Renaissance* 62-64.

Zora Neale Hurston, 1901?-1960

Web Sites

"Zora Neale Hurston." *Voices from the Gaps: Women Writers of Color.* 18 Mar.
   2000, http://voices.cla.umn.edu/authors/zoranealehurston.html.
   A good place for beginning research on Hurston.

Zora Neale Hurston. 18 Mar. 2000, http://www.geocities.com/SoHo/3035/bio.html.

Zora Neale Hurston. 18 Mar. 2000, http://pages.prodigy.com/zora/.

Zora Neale Hurston. 18 Mar. 2000, http://www.uky.edu/StudentOrgs/AWARE/archives/
   zora.html.

"Zora Neale Hurston: Teacher Resource File" *African American Writers.* Ed. Inez
   Ramsey. 18 Mar. 2000, http://falcon.jmu.edu/~ramseyil/hurston.htm.
   Contains links to the texts of Hurston's works and an excellent partially annotated bibliography covering works by and about her, including plays, fiction, nonfiction, biography and autobiography, study guides, nonprint media, and criticism and
interpretation.

Biographies and Criticism

Howard, Lillie P. "Zora Neale Hurston." Harris, *Afro-American Writers from the
   Harlem Renaissance to 1940 (Dictionary of Literary Biography* 51) 133-45.

Zaidman, Laura M. "Zora Neale Hurston." Kimbel, *American Short-Story Writers,
   1910-1945, First Series (Dictionary of Literary Biography* 86) 159-71.

"Zora Neale Hurston." Harris and Fitzgerald, *Short Story Criticism* 4:132-61.
   Excerpts of criticism on Hurston from 1934-1987, with an annotated bibliography.

"Zora Neale Hurston." Riley, *Contemporary Literary Criticism* 61:235-76.
   Excerpts of criticism on Hurston's novel *Their Eyes Were Watching God* from
1937-1988, with an annotated bibliography.

Journals

Zora Neale Hurston Forum. Baltimore: Zora Neale Hurston Soc., 1986-1991.

Bibliographies

Awkward, Michael, and Michelle Johnson. "Zora Neale Hurston." Kopley, *Prospects
   for the Study of American Literature* 283-96.
   The most up-to-date survey of research.

Barstow, Jane Missner. "Zora Neale Hurston." *One Hundred Years of American Women Writing, 1848-1948* 268-75.
Describes selected editions, biographies, and criticism.

Carpenter, Charles A. "Hurston, Zora Neale." *Modern Drama Scholarship and Criticism, 1981-1990* 61.

Champion, Laurie, and Bruce A. Glasrud. "Zora Neale Hurston." Nelson, *African American Authors, 1745-1945* 259-69.
Survey of research.

Dance, Daryl C. "Zora Neale Hurston." Duke, Bryer, and Inge, *American Women Writers* 321-51.

Davis, Rose Parkman. *Zora Neale Hurston: An Annotated Bibliography and Reference Guide.* Westport: Greenwood, 1997.

Glitsch, Catherine. "Hurston, Zora Neale." *American Novel Explication, 1991-1995* 126-29.

Holt, Elvin. "Zora Neale Hurston." Flora and Bain, *Fifty Southern Writers after 1900* 259-69.

Kellman, Steven G. "Zora Neale Hurston." *Modern American Novel* 100-104.
Describes about 20 critical works.

Lowe, John. "Zora Neale Hurston." Demastes, *American Playwrights, 1880-1945* [206]-13.

Millsaps, Ellen M. "Zora Neale Hurston." Bruccoli and Baughman, *Bibliography of American Fiction, 1919-1988* 262-64.

———. "Zora Neale Hurston." Bruccoli and Baughman, *Modern African American Writers* 32-38.

Newson, Adele S. *Zora Neale Hurston: A Reference Guide.* Boston: G. K. Hall, 1987.
Describes about 300 works on Hurston since 1931; supplemented by Bonnie Crarey Ryan's "Zora Neale Hurston—A Checklist of Secondary Sources," *Bulletin of Bibliography* 45 (1988): 33-39.

Perry, Margaret. "Hurston, Zora Neale." *Harlem Renaissance* 100-107.

Arna (Wendell) Bontemps, 1902-1973

Web Sites

"Arna Bontemps." *Heath Anthology.* 13 Mar. 2000, http://www.georgetown.edu/bassr/heath/syllabuild/iguide/bontemps.html.
This page contains no bibliography.

"Arna Wendell Bontemps: Teacher Resource File." *African American Writers.* Ed. Inez Ramsey. 18 Mar. 2000, http://falcon.jmu.edu/~ramseyil/bontemps.htm.

Biographies and Criticism

Gwin, Minrose C. "Arna Bontemps." Quartermain, *American Poets, 1880-1945, Second Series* (*Dictionary of Literary Biography* 48) 38-45.

Jones, Kirkland C. "Arna Bontemps." Harris, *Afro-American Writers from the Harlem Renaissance to 1940* (*Dictionary of Literary Biography* 51) 10-21.

Bibliographies

Fleming, Robert E. "Arna Bontemps." Bruccoli and Baughman, *Bibliography of American Fiction, 1919-1988* 93-94.

———. *James Weldon Johnson and Arna Wendell Bontemps: A Reference Guide.* Boston: G. K. Hall, 1978.
Critical descriptions for about 350 works on Bontemps since 1926.

Jones, Jacqueline C. "Arna Bontemps." Nelson, *African American Authors, 1745-1945* 36-43.
Survey of research.

Miller, Ruth, and Peter J. Katopes. "The Harlem Renaissance: Arna W. Bontemps, Countee Cullen, James Weldon Johnson, Claude McKay, and Jean Toomer." Inge, Duke, and Bryer, *Black American Writers* I, 161-86.
Survey of research.

Perry, Margaret. "Bontemps, Arna." *Harlem Renaissance* 59-62.

(James) Langston Hughes, 1902-1967

Web Sites

"Langston Hughes." *Academy of American Poets.* 8 Mar. 2000, http://www.poets.org/lit/poet/lhughfst.htm.

"Langston Hughes." *Pegasos.* 18 Mar. 2000, http://www.kirjasto.sci.fi/lhughes.htm.

"Langston Hughes." *Voices and Visions.* 17 Mar. 2000, http://www.learner.org/collections/multimedia/literature/vvseries/vvspot/Hughes.html.

Langston Hughes Biography. 18 Mar. 2000, http://www.cwrl.utexas.edu/~nick/e309k/texts/hughes/hughes-bio.html.
Biographical sketch taken from Volume 2 of the *Heath Anthology of American Literature*, 1990.

Langston Hughes: Biography. Ed. Andrew P. Jackson. 4 Aug. 1997. Queens Borough Public Library. 18 Mar. 2000, http://mickey.queens.lib.ny.us/special/langston.bio.html.

Biographies and Criticism

Bevilacqua, Winifred Farrant. "Langston Hughes." Kimbel, *American Short-Story Writers, 1910-1945, First Series* (*Dictionary of Literary Biography* 86) 139-50.

Grant, William E. "Langston Hughes." Rood, *American Writers in Paris, 1920-1939* (*Dictionary of Literary Biography* 4) 213-14.

Hurst, Catherine Daniels. "Langston Hughes." MacNicholas, *Twentieth-Century American Dramatists* (*Dictionary of Literary Biography* 7) 314-24.

"(James) Langston Hughes." Harris and Fitzgerald, *Short Story Criticism* 6:107-47. Excerpts of criticism on Hughes from 1934-1984, with an annotated bibliography.

"Langston Hughes." Riley, *Contemporary Literary Criticism* 108:280-337. Excerpts of criticism on Hughes from 1963-1994, with an annotated bibliography.

"Langston Hughes." Trudeau, *Drama Criticism* 3:265-92.
Excerpts of criticism on Hughes in general and on *Mule Bone, Mulatto, Soul Gone Home, Black Nativity*, and *Tambourines to Glory* from 1935-1991, with an annotated bibliography.

"Langston Hughes." Young, *Poetry Criticism* 1:233-72.
Excerpts of comments and criticism on Hughes from 1925-1986, with an annotated bibliography.

Miller, R. Baxter. "Langston Hughes." Harris, *Afro-American Writers from the Harlem Renaissance to 1940* (*Dictionary of Literary Biography* 51) 112-33.

———. "Langston Hughes." Quartermain, *American Poets, 1880-1945, Second Series* (*Dictionary of Literary Biography* 48) 218-35.

Ostrom, Hans A. *Langston Hughes: A Study of the Short Fiction.* New York: Twayne, 1993.

Indexes and Concordances

Mandelik, Peter, and Stanley Schatt. *Concordance to the Poetry of Langston Hughes.* Detroit: Gale, 1975.
Indexes poems in *Langston Hughes Reader* (New York: Braziller, 1958), *Selected Poems of Langston Hughes* (New York: Knopf, 1959), and other editions.

Journals

Langston Hughes Review. Athens: Langston Hughes Soc., U of Georgia, 1982- .

Bibliographies

Babcock, Granger. "Langston Hughes." Demastes, *American Playwrights, 1880-1945* [196]-205.

Carpenter, Charles A. "Hughes, Langston." *Modern Drama Scholarship and Criticism, 1981-1990* 61.

Dickinson, Donald C. *A Bio-Bibliography of Langston Hughes, 1902-1967.* 2nd rev. ed. Hamden: Shoe String, 1972.
Describes Hughes's works and about 250 works about him.

Jackson, Blyden. "Langston Hughes." Inge, Duke, and Bryer, *Black American Writers* I, 187-206.
Survey of research.

Leo, John R. "Hughes, Langston." *Guide to American Poetry Explication* 207-08.

Mikolyzk, Thomas A. *Langston Hughes: A Bio-Bibliography*. New York: Greenwood, 1990.
Plot summaries and contents for Hughes's works and descriptive entries for about 700 critical works; updated by Sharynn Owens Etheridge's "Langston Hughes: An Annotated Bibliography (1977-1986)," *Langston Hughes Review* 11.1 (Spring 1992): 41-57.

Miller, R. Baxter. *Langston Hughes and Gwendolyn Brooks: A Reference Guide*. Boston: G. K. Hall, 1978.
Describes about 350 comments and criticism on Hughes since 1924.

Nelson, Emmanuel S. "Langston Hughes." Nelson, *African American Authors, 1745-1945* 249-58.
Survey of research.

Perry, Margaret. "Hughes, Langston." *Harlem Renaissance* 87-100.

Shuman, R. Baird. "Langston Hughes." *American Drama, 1918-1960* 94-97.
Describes about 15 critical works.

John (Ernst) Steinbeck, 1902-1968

Web Sites

"John Steinbeck." *Access Indiana: Teaching & Learning Center*. 18 Mar. 2000, http://tlc.ai.org/steinbec.htm.
Excellent classified list of links for Steinbeck's works, works about him, and background materials.

John Steinbeck Bibliography Pages. Ed., update, and sponsor unknown. 18 Mar. 2000, http://www.hit.net/~mhenry/Steinbeck/Home.html.
Mainly useful for a list of Stenbeck biographies, bibliographies, and web pages.

John Steinbeck Page. Ed. Scott Simkins. Update unknown. U of Southern Mississippi. 18 Mar. 2000, http://ocean.st.usm.edu/~wsimkins/steinb.html.
Valuable access to texts of selected works by Steinbeck, like his 1962 Nobel Prize acceptance speech, as well as to texts of selected works about him, including Alfred Kazin's essay on Steinbeck's primitivism and Malcolm Bradbury's "Emersonian Steinbeck." Also includes a selectively annotated bibliography of works about Steinbeck and links to other information pages and texts.

John Steinbeck: The California Novels. Ed. Edward Stephan. Update and sponsor unknown. 18 Mar. 2000, http://www.ac.wwu.edu/~stephan/Steinbeck/index.html.
Most useful page for plot summaries, character identifications, and notes for Steinbeck's selected works, including *The Red Pony, Tortilla Flat, Of Mice and Men, The Grapes of Wrath, Cannery Row*, and *East of Eden*, with links to texts and other background materials on the dust bowl, California, and other topics related to Steinbeck.

San Jose State University: Martha Heasley Cox Center For Steinbeck Studies. Ed.
   various. Nov. 1999. San Jose S U. 18 Mar. 2000, http://www.sjsu.edu/depts/
   steinbec/srchome.html.
       Most useful features are lists of Steinbeck's fiction and nonfiction works (cov-
   ering both books and contributions to periodicals), with selected works about him;
   and *Steinbeck Newsletter*, with sample articles and a cumulative index (1987-1995).
   "About Steinbeck and His Times" contains a chronology and directories of places in
   Steinbeck's life and works.

Biographies and Criticism

Astro, Richard. "John Steinbeck." Martine, *American Novelists, 1910-1945* (*Dictionary
   of Literary Biography* 9) 43-68.

French, Warren G. *John Steinbeck's Fiction Revisted.* New York: Twayne, 1994.

———. *John Steinbeck's Nonfiction Revisited.* New York: Twayne, 1996.

Hadella, Charlotte Cook. *Of Mice and Men: A Kinship of Powerlessness.* New York:
   Twayne, 1995.

Hearle, Kevin. "John Steinbeck." Cracroft, *Twentieth-Century American Western
   Writers, Second Series* (*Dictionary of Literary Biography* 212) 278-94.

Hughes, R. S. *John Steinbeck: A Study of the Short Fiction.* Boston: Twayne, 1989.

"John Steinbeck." Harris and Fitzgerald, *Short Story Criticism* 11:201-60.
       Excerpts of criticism on Steinbeck from 1958-1990, with an annotated
   bibliography.

"John (Ernest) Steinbeck." Riley, *Contemporary Literary Criticism* 45:368-85.
       Excerpts of criticism on Steinbeck's novel *East of Eden* from 1952-1986.

"John Steinbeck: *Of Mice and Men.*" Riley, *Contemporary Literary Criticism*
   75:334-66.
       Excerpts of criticism on Steinbeck's novel from 1937-1982, with an annotated
   bibliography.

Owens, Louis. *The Grapes of Wrath: Trouble in the Promised Land.* Boston:
   Twayne, 1989.

Thesing, William B. "John Steinbeck." MacNicholas, *Twentieth-Century American
   Dramatists* (*Dictionary of Literary Biography* 7) 271-76.

Dictionaries, Encyclopedias, and Handbooks

French, Warren G. *Companion to the Grapes of Wrath.* 1963. New York: Penguin,
   1989.

Hayashi, Tetsumaro. *John Steinbeck: A Dictionary of His Fictional Characters.*
   Metuchen: Scarecrow, 1976.

———. *Study Guide to Steinbeck: A Handbook to His Major Works.* 1974. Metuchen:
   Scarecrow, 1979.

Hughes, R. S. *Beyond the Red Pony: A Reader's Companion to Steinbeck's Complete Short Stories*. Metuchen: Scarecrow, 1987.

Journals

Steinbeck Quarterly. Muncie: International John Steinbeck Soc., 1968- . Formerly *Steinbeck Newsletter* (1968).

Bibliographies

Astro, Richard. "John Steinbeck." Erisman and Etulain, *Fifty Western Writers* 477-87.

Carpenter, Charles A. "Steinbeck, John." *Modern Drama Scholarship and Criticism, 1981-1990* 87.

DeMott, Robert J. *Steinbeck's Reading: A Catalogue of Books Owned and Borrowed*. New York: Garland, 1984.

Etulain, Richard W., and N. Jill Howard. "John Steinbeck." *Bibliographical Guide to the Study of Western American Literature* 384-95.

Evans, Robert C. "John Steinbeck: 'The Chrysanthemums'." Evans, Little, and Wiedemann, *Short Fiction* 241-45.
Describes 10 studies.

French, Warren. "John Steinbeck." Bryer, *Sixteen Modern American Authors* 499-527.
Survey of research; supplemented by French in Bryer, *Sixteen Modern American Authors: Volume 2* 582-622.

Glitsch, Catherine. "Steinbeck, John." *American Novel Explication, 1991-1995* 231-33.

Goldstone, Adrian H., and John R. Payne. *John Steinbeck: A Bibliographical Catalogue of the Adrian H. Goldstone Collection*. Austin: Humanities Research Center, U of Texas, 1974.
The best listing of Steinbeck's works, with complete descriptions.

Harmon, Robert B. *Steinbeck Bibliographies: An Annotated Guide*. Metuchen: Scarecrow, 1987.
A bibliography of bibliographies, not a listing of criticism.

———, and John F. Early. *The Grapes of Wrath: A Fifty Year Bibliographic Survey*. San Jose: Steinbeck Research Center, San Jose State U, 1990.

Hayashi, Tetsumaro. *A New Steinbeck Bibliography: 1929-1971*. Metuchen: Scarecrow, 1973.
Brief entries for Steinbeck's works and about 1,800 works on him.

———. *A New Steinbeck Bibliography: 1971-1981*. Metuchen: Scarecrow, 1983.
Continues Hayashi, above, with brief entries for 282 editions and about 700 critical works.

Kellman, Steven G. "John Steinbeck." *Modern American Novel* 123-32.
Describes about 50 critical works.

Meyer, Michael J. *Hayashi Steinbeck Bibliography, 1982-1996*. Lanham: Scarecrow, 1998.

Shillinglaw, Susan. "John Steinbeck." Bruccoli and Baughman, *Bibliography of American Fiction, 1919-1988* 476-81.

——. "John Steinbeck." Bruccoli and Baughman, *Modern Classic Writers* 48-60.

Countee Cullen, 1903-1946

Web Sites

"Countee Cullen." *Academy of American Poets*. 8 Mar. 2000, http://www.poets.org/lit/poet/ccullfst.htm.
Texts of three poems with a bibliography and links.

"Countee Cullen." *Pegasos*. 18 Mar. 2000, http://www.kirjasto.sci.fi/ccullen.htm.

Countee Cullen. Ed. Jill Diesman. 18 Mar. 2000, http://www.nku.edu/~diesmanj/cullen.html.
Site consists of fulltexts of 13 Cullen poems.

Poetry Today Online: Countee Cullen. 18 Mar. 2000, http://www.poetrytodayonline.com/NOVcp.html.
Biographical sketch, four poems, bibliography.

Biographies and Criticism

"Countee Cullen." Bryfonski, *Twentieth-Century Literary Criticism* 4:39-54.
Excerpts of comments and criticism on Cullen from 1925-1976, with an annotated bibliography.

——. Bryfonski, *Twentieth-Century Literary Criticism* 37:134-72.
Excerpts of comments and criticism on Cullen from 1926-1987, with an annotated bibliography.

"Countee Cullen." Young, *Poetry Criticism* 20:50-88.
Excerpts of comments and criticism on Cullen from 1925-1989, with an annotated bibliography.

Grant, William E. "Countee Cullen." Rood, *American Writers in Paris, 1920-1939* (*Dictionary of Literary Biography* 4) 103-04.

Lumpkin, Shirley. "Countee Cullen." Quartermain, *American Poets, 1880-1945, Second Series* (*Dictionary of Literary Biography* 48) 109-16.

Shucard, Alan. "Countee Cullen." Harris, *Afro-American Writers from the Harlem Renaissance to 1940* (*Dictionary of Literary Biography* 51) 35-46.

Bibliographies

Leo, John R. "Cullen, Countee." *Guide to American Poetry Explication* 81-82.

Miller, Ruth, and Peter J. Katopes. "The Harlem Renaissance: Arna W. Bontemps, Countee Cullen, James Weldon Johnson, Claude McKay, and Jean Toomer." Inge, Duke, and Bryer, *Black American Writers* I, 161-86.
Survey of research.

Morris, Gilbert N. M. O. "Countee Cullen." Nelson, *African American Authors, 1745-1945* 88-97.
Survey of research.

Perry, Margaret. *A Bio-Bibliography of Countee P. Cullen, 1903-1946.* Westport: Greenwood, 1971.
Brief information for Cullen's major writings and about 300 biographical and critical studies.

―――. "Cullen, Countee." *Harlem Renaissance* 64-75.

Lorine Niedecker, 1903-1970

Web Sites

Lorine Niedecker. Ed. M. Michele Arms. 18 Mar. 2000, http://www.fort.lib.wi.us/lorine. html.
Brief biography, with complete citations from major biographical sources.

Biographies and Criticism

Faranda, Lisa Pater. "Lorine Niedecker." Quartermain, *American Poets, 1880-1945, Second Series* (*Dictionary of Literary Biography* 48) 304-19.

Bibliographies

Leo, John R. "Niedecker, Lorine." *Guide to American Poetry Explication* 287.

Anaïs Nin, 1903-1977

Web Sites

Anaïs Nin. Ed. Anja Beckmann. 30 Dec. 1999. U of Leipzig. 18 Mar. 2000, http://stinfwww.informatik.uni-leipzig.de/~beckmann/nin.html.

Biographies and Criticism

"Anaïs Nin." Harris and Fitzgerald, *Short Story Criticism* 10:298-328.
Excerpts of criticism on Nin from 1944-1982, with an annotated bibliography.

"Anaïs Nin." Riley, *Contemporary Literary Criticism* 60:264-81.
Excerpts of criticism on Nin from 1942-1989, with an annotated bibliography.

Franklin, Benjamin, V. "Anaïs Nin." Helterman and Layman, *American Novelists since World War II, First Series* (*Dictionary of Literary Biography* 2) 364-71.

―――. "Anaïs Nin." Rood, *American Writers in Paris, 1920-1939* (*Dictionary of Literary Biography* 4) 299-303.

Jason, Philip K. "Anaïs Nin." Giles and Giles, *American Novelists since World War II, Fourth Series* (*Dictionary of Literary Biography* 152) 128-39.

Scholar, Nancy. *Anaïs Nin.* Boston: Twayne, 1984.

Journals

Anaïs: An International Journal. Los Angeles: Anaïs Nin Foundation, 1983- . "Readings" lists new publications.

Bibliographies

Cutting, Rose Marie. *Anaïs Nin: A Reference Guide.* Boston: G. K. Hall, 1978. Describes about 800 works on Nin from 1937 through 1977.

Franklin, Benjamin, V. "Anaïs Nin." Bruccoli and Baughman, *Bibliography of American Fiction, 1919-1988* 379-81.

———. *Anaïs Nin: A Bibliography.* Kent: Kent State UP, 1973. Complete descriptions of Nin's works.

Griffin, Barbara J. "Two Experimental Writers: Djuna Barnes and Anaïs Nin." Duke, Bryer, and Inge, *American Women Writers* 135-66. Survey of research.

Nathanael West, 1903-1940

Web Sites

"Nathanael West." *Pegasos.* 12 Mar. 2000, http://www.kirjasto.sci.fi/nwest.htm.

Biographies and Criticism

Martin, Jay. "Nathanael West." Rood, *American Writers in Paris, 1920-1939* (*Dictionary of Literary Biography* 4) 405-07.

"Nathanael West." Bryfonski, *Twentieth-Century Literary Criticism* 1:478-93. Excerpts of criticism on West from 1957-1974.

———. Bryfonski, *Twentieth-Century Literary Criticism* 14:466-95. Excerpts of criticism on West from 1931-1981, with an annotated bibliography.

"Nathanael West: *Miss Lonelyhearts.*" Bryfonski, *Twentieth-Century Literary Criticism* 44:365-419. Excerpts of criticism on *Miss Lonelyhearts* from 1933-1985, with an annotated bibliography.

"Nathanael West." Harris and Fitzgerald, *Short Story Criticism* 16:341-420. Excerpts of criticism on West from 1948-1986, with an annotated bibliography.

Walden, Daniel. "Nathanael West." Martine, *American Novelists, 1910-1945* (*Dictionary of Literary Biography* 9) 116-26.

———. "Nathanael West." Walden, *Twentieth-Century American-Jewish Fiction Writers* (*Dictionary of Literary Biography* 28) 323-31.

Widmer, Kingsley. *Nathanael West*. Boston: Twayne, 1982.

Bibliographies

Etulain, Richard W., and N. Jill Howard. "Nathan Wallenstein Weinstein (Nathanael West)." *Bibliographical Guide to the Study of Western American Literature* 413-15.

Kellman, Steven G. "Nathanael West." *Modern American Novel* 133-35.
Describes 14 critical works.

Kelly, James R. "Nathanael West." Bruccoli and Baughman, *Bibliography of American Fiction, 1919-1988* 535-37.

Vannatta, Dennis P. *Nathanael West: An Annotated Bibliography of the Scholarship and Works*. New York: Garland, 1976.
Describes about 500 items.

White, William. *Nathanael West: A Comprehensive Bibliography*. Kent: Kent State UP, 1975.
Descriptions of West's works and works about him.

Christopher Isherwood, 1904-1986

Web Sites

"Christopher Isherwood." *Pegasos*. 18 Mar. 2000, http://www.kirjasto.sci.fi/isherwoo. htm.

"Christopher William Bradshaw Isherwood." *Knitting Circle*. 18 Mar. 2000, http://www.sbu.ac.uk/stafflag/isherwood.html.

Biographies and Criticism

Dukes, Thomas. "Christopher Isherwood." Barbara Brothers and Julia Gergits, eds. *British Travel Writers, 1910-1939* (*Dictionary of Literary Biography* 195). Detroit: Gale, 1998. 168-76.

Summers, Claude J. "Christopher Isherwood." Bernard Oldsey, ed. *British Novelists, 1930-1959* (*Dictionary of Literary Biography* 15). Detroit: Gale, 1983. 206-19.

Bibliographies

Funk, Robert W. *Christopher Isherwood: A Reference Guide*. Boston: G. K. Hall, 1979.
Describes about 1,100 works on Isherwood since 1928.

Westby, Selmer, and Clayton M. Brown. *Christopher Isherwood: A Bibliography, 1923-1967*. Los Angeles: California State College at Los Angeles Foundation, 1968.
Brief information for Isherwood's works.

Isaac Bashevis Singer, 1904-1991

Web Sites

"Isaac Bashevis Singer." *Nobel Prize Internet Archive*. 18 Mar. 2000, http://nobelprizes.
  com/nobel/literature/1978a.html.
  Brief Singer biography and texts of his obituary and other critical responses
with lists of works by and about Singer and links to other papers. No comprehensive
page for Singer now exists.

"Isaac Bashevis Singer." *Pegasos*. 18 Mar. 2000, http://www.kirjasto.sci.fi/ibsinger.
  htm.

"Nobel Prize in Literature 1978." *Electronic Nobel Museum Project*. 18 Mar. 2000,
  http://nobel.sdsc.edu/laureates/literature-1978.html.

Biographies and Criticism

Alexander, Edward. *Isaac Bashevis Singer: A Study of the Short Fiction*. Boston:
  Twayne, 1990.

Allison, Alida. *Isaac Bashevis Singer: Children's Stories and Childhood Memoirs*.
  New York: Twayne, 1996.

Gittleman, Edwin. "Isaac Bashevis Singer." Kibler, *American Novelists since World
  War II, Second Series* (*Dictionary of Literary Biography* 6) 296-313.

"Isaac Beshevis Singer." Harris and Fitzgerald, *Short Story Criticism* 3:351-90.
  Excerpts of criticism on Singer from 1958-1988, with an annotated bibliography.

"Isaac Bashevis Singer." Riley, *Contemporary Literary Criticism* 69:300-322.
  Excerpts of criticism on Singer from 1982-1991, with an annotated bibliography.

————. Riley, *Contemporary Literary Criticism* 111:289-348.
  Excerpts of criticism on Singer from 1966-1994, with an annotated bibliography.

Iskander, Sylvia W. "Isaac Bashevis Singer." Estes, *American Writers for Children
  since 1960: Fiction* (*Dictionary of Literary Biography* 52) 334-52.

Waxman, Barbara Frey. "Isaac Bashevis Singer." Walden, *Twentieth-Century
  American-Jewish Fiction Writers* (*Dictionary of Literary Biography* 28)
  297-305.

Bibliographies

Friedman, Lawrence S. "Isaac Bashevis Singer." Bruccoli and Baughman, *Bibliography of American Fiction, 1919-1988* 459-61.

Miller, David Neal. *Bibliography of Isaac Bashevis Singer, 1924-1949*. New York:
  Peter Lang, 1983.
  Complete descriptions of Singer's works.

Lillian Hellman, 1905-1984

Web Sites

"Chapter 8: American Drama: Lillian Hellman." *PAL: Perspectives in American Literature.* 18 Mar. 2000, http://www.csustan.edu/english/reuben/pal/chap8/hellman. html.

ISU Play Concordances. Ed. Rosanne G. Potter. Update unknown. Iowa SU. 18 Mar. 2000, http://www1.iastate.edu/~spires/concord.html.
Includes searchable concordances of *The Children's Hour* and *The Little Foxes.*

"Lillian Hellman." *Literature & Culture of the American 1950s.* 18 Mar. 2000, http://dept.english.upenn.edu/~afilreis/50s/hellman-refs.html.
Includes links to several essays and book chapters relating to Hellman.

"Lillian Hellman." *Pegasos.* 18 Mar. 2000, http://www.kirjasto.sci.fi/lhellman.htm.

Biographies and Criticism

"Lillian Hellman." Trudeau, *Drama Criticism* 1:177-210.
Excerpts of criticism on Hellman in general and on *The Children's Hour* and *The Little Foxes* from 1934-1989, with an annotated bibliography.

MacNicholas, Carol. "Lillian Hellman." MacNicholas, *Twentieth-Century American Dramatists* (*Dictionary of Literary Biography* 7) 275-95.

Bibliographies

Adler, Jacob H. "Lillian Hellman." Flora and Bain, *Fifty Southern Writers after 1900* 247-58.

Barstow, Jane Missner. "Lillian Hellman." *One Hundred Years of American Women Writing, 1848-1948* 160-62.
Describes selected editions, biographies, and criticism.

Bills, Steven. *Lillian Hellman: An Annotated Bibliography.* New York: Garland, 1979.
Describes works on Hellman.

Carpenter, Charles A. "Hellman, Lillian." *Modern Drama Scholarship and Criticism, 1981-1990* 59-60.

Estrin, Mark. *Lillian Hellman—Plays, Films, Memoirs: A Reference Guide.* Boston: G. K. Hall, 1980.
Lists Hellman's works and describes about 2,000 works on Hellman since 1934.

Haedicke, Janet V. "Lillian Hellman." Demastes, *American Playwrights, 1880-1945* [132]-44.

Henderson, Bruce. "Lillian Hellman." Shapiro, *Jewish American Women Writers* 101-10.

Riordan, Mary Marguerite. *Lillian Hellman: A Bibliography, 1926-1978*. Metuchen: Scarecrow, 1980.
Brief bibliographic descriptions of Hellman's works.

Shuman, R. Baird. "Lillian Hellman." *American Drama, 1918-1960* 86-91.
Describes about 25 critical works.

Robert Penn Warren, 1905-1989

Web Sites

"Robert Penn Warren." *Academy of American Poets*. 9 Mar. 2000, http://www.poets.org/lit/poet/rpwarfst.htm.
Brief biography of Warren with a selective bibliography of his works and links to the texts of "A Way to Love God," "Evening Hawk," "True Love," "Mortal Limit," and "Tell Me a Story." Poems are available onsite, with edition fully credited. All selections are from *New and Selected Poems 1923-1985* (New York: Random House, 1985).

"Robert Penn Warren." *KYLit: A Site Devoted to Kentucky Writers*. Ed. Joe Pellegrino. 5 Oct. 1997. English Dept., Eastern Kentucky U. 18 Mar. 2000, http://www.english.eku.edu/services/kylit/warren.htm.
Solid biocritical essay by George Brosi, with selectively annotated bibliography of Warren's writings.

Biographies and Criticism

Bohner, Charles H. *Robert Penn Warren*. Rev. ed. Boston: Twayne, 1981.

Millichap, Joseph R. *Robert Penn Warren: A Study of the Short Fiction*. New York: Twayne, 1992.

"Robert Penn Warren." Harris and Fitzgerald, *Short Story Criticism* 4:386-405.
Excerpts of criticism on Warren from 1948-1972, with an annotated bibliography.

Runyon, Randolph Paul. "Robert Penn Warren." Giles and Giles, *American Novelists since World War II, Fourth Series* (*Dictionary of Literary Biography* 152) 282-98.

Strandberg, Victor. "Robert Penn Warren." Quartermain, *American Poets, 1880-1945, Second Series* (*Dictionary of Literary Biography* 48) 425-44.

Wilkie, Everett, and Josephine Helterman. "Robert Penn Warren." Helterman and Layman, *American Novelists since World War II, First Series* (*Dictionary of Literary Biography* 2) 513-24.

Bibliographies

Carpenter, Charles A. "Warren, Robert Penn." *Modern Drama Scholarship and Criticism, 1981-1990* 88-89.

Glitsch, Catherine. "Warren, Robert Penn." *American Novel Explication, 1991-1995* 259-60.

Grimshaw, James A., Jr. "Robert Penn Warren." Bruccoli and Baughman, *Bibliography of American Fiction, 1919-1988* 522-26.

———. "Robert Penn Warren." Bruccoli and Baughman, *Modern Classic Writers* 61-72.

———. *Robert Penn Warren: A Descriptive Bibliography, 1922-79*. Charlottesville: UP of Virginia, 1982.
Complete descriptions of Warren's works and lists of works about him.

Justus, James H. "Robert Penn Warren." Flora and Bain, *Fifty Southern Writers after 1900* 505-15.

Leo, John R. "Warren, Robert Penn." *Guide to American Poetry Explication* 455-61.

Nakadate, Neil. *Robert Penn Warren: A Reference Guide*. Boston: G. K. Hall, 1977.
Describes criticism since 1925.

Clifford Odets, 1906-1963

Web Sites

"Chapter 8: American Drama: Clifford Odets."*PAL: Perspectives in American Literature*. 18 Mar. 2000, http://www.csustan.edu/english/reuben/pal/chap8/odets. html.

"Clifford Odets: Anguish in Many Colours." *Literature & Culture of the American 1950s*. 3 Mar. 2000, http://www.english.upenn.edu/~afilreis/50s/odets.html.
Contains text of a *New York Times* review of an exhibition of Odets's paintings.

Biographies and Criticism

"Clifford Odets." Riley, *Contemporary Literary Criticism* 98:188-254.
Excerpts of criticism on Odets from 1946-1994, with an annotated bibliography.

"Clifford Odets." Trudeau, *Drama Criticism* 6:203-39.
Excerpts of criticism on Odets in general and on *Awake and Sing!*, *Waiting for Lefty*, and *Golden Boy* from 1935-1991, with an annotated bibliography.

Fleischman, Beth. "Clifford Odets." MacNicholas, *Twentieth-Century American Dramatists* (*Dictionary of Literary Biography* 7) 126-39.

Goodwin, James. "Clifford Odets." Morsberger, Lesser, and Clark, *American Screenwriters* (*Dictionary of Literary Biography* 26) 235-39.

Bibliographies

Carpenter, Charles A. "Odets, Clifford." *Modern Drama Scholarship and Criticism, 1981-1990* 70-71.

Cooperman, Robert. *Clifford Odets: An Annotated Bibliography, 1935-1989*. Westport: Meckler, 1990.
Brief descriptions of works by and about Odets.

Demastes, William W. "Clifford Odets." Demastes, *American Playwrights, 1880-1945* [310]-22.

———. *Clifford Odets: A Research and Production Sourcebook*. Westport: Greenwood, 1991.
Plot and production information for Odets's works and descriptions of 608 works on Odets since 1935.

Shuman, R. Baird. "Clifford Odets." *American Drama, 1918-1960* 119-25.
Describes about 30 critical works.

George Oppen, 1908-1984

Web Sites

Books by George Oppen. Ed. Alan Filreis. Update unknown. U of Pennsylvania. 18 Mar. 2000, http://www.english.upenn.edu/~afilreis/88/oppen-bib.html.

"Psalm." 18 Mar. 2000, http://www.wmich.edu/english/tchg/lit/pms/oppen.poem.html.

Biographies and Criticism

Adams, Michael. "George Oppen." Greiner, *American Poets since World War II, First Series* (*Dictionary of Literary Biography* 5) 129-33.

Peterson, Jeffrey. "George Oppen." Conte, *American Poets since World War II, Fourth Series* (*Dictionary of Literary Biography* 165) 188-206.

Bibliographies

Leo, John R. "Oppen, George." *Guide to American Poetry Explication* 296-98.

Theodore Roethke, 1908-1963

Web Sites

Theodore Huebner Roethke. Ed. Ted Tapia. 20 July 1997. Sponsor unknown. 18 Mar. 2000, http://www.thebrothers.com/eraaz/roethke1.html.

Theodore Roethke. Ed., update, and sponsor unknown. 18 Mar. 2000, http://pw2.netcom.com/~iluvbeer/roethke.html.
Texts of four poems ("Highway: Michigan," "Once More, The Round," "I Knew a Woman," and "My Papa's Waltz") and a very brief biographical introduction.

Theodore Roethke. Ed. Ken Hope. Update and sponsor unknown. 18 Mar. 2000, http://www.northshore.net/homepages/hope/engRoethke.html.
Texts of three poems ("I Knew a Woman," "Elegy for Jane," and "The Waking"); no links.

Theodore Roethke. Ed. and update unknown. U of Georgia. 18 Mar. 2000, http://www.arches.uga.edu/~squirt33/theodore.htm.
Mostly a chronology of events in the life of Roethke; includes some links and text of one poem ("My Papa's Waltz").

Biographies and Criticism

Butterworth, Keen. "Theodore Roethke." Greiner, *American Poets since World War II, First Series* (*Dictionary of Literary Biography* 5) 196-207.

McFarland, Ron. "Theodore Roethke." Cracroft, *Twentieth-Century American Western Writers, First Series* (*Dictionary of Literary Biography* 206) 261-71.

"Theodore Roethke." Riley, *Contemporary Literary Criticism* 101:260-343.
    Excerpts of criticism on Roethke from 1959-1991, with an annotated bibliography.

"Theodore Roethke." Young, *Poetry Criticism* 15:243-321.
    Excerpts of comments and criticism on Roethke from 1941-1989, with an annotated bibliography.

Wolff, George. *Theodore Roethke*. Boston: Twayne, 1981.

Indexes and Concordances

Lane, Gary. *Concordance to the Poems of Theodore Roethke*. Metuchen: Scarecrow, 1972.
    Keyed to *Collected Poems of Theodore Roethke* (1966; London: Faber and Faber, 1968).

Bibliographies

Etulain, Richard W., and N. Jill Howard. "Theodore Roethke." *Bibliographical Guide to the Study of Western American Literature* 350-53.

Leo, John R. "Roethke, Theodore R." *Guide to American Poetry Explication* 343-58.

McLeod, James Richard. *Theodore Roethke: A Bibliography*. Kent: Kent State UP, 1973.
    Complete descriptions of Roethke's works.

———, and Judith A. Sylte. "Theodore Roethke." Baughman, *Contemporary Authors: Bibliographical Series: American Poets* 269-305.

Moul, Keith R. *Theodore Roethke's Career: An Annotated Bibliography*. Boston: G. K. Hall, 1977.
    Critical descriptions of about 1,500 works on Roethke since 1922.

Sullivan, Rosemary. "Theodore Roethke." Erisman and Etulain, *Fifty Western Writers* 389-401.

William Saroyan, 1908-1981

Web Sites

Kalinian: Saroyan Homepage. 18 Mar. 2000, http://members.aol.com/kalinian/saroyan. html.

"William Saroyan." *Pegasos*. 18 Mar. 2000, http://www.kirjasto.sci.fi/saroyan.htm.

William Saroyan. Ed. Raffi Kojian. Update and sponsor unknown. 18 Mar. 2000, http://www.cilicia.com/armo22_william_saroyan.html.
Selected texts of works by and about Saroyan.

Biographies and Criticism

Bufithis, Philip. "William Saroyan." Martine, *American Novelists, 1910-1945* (*Dictionary of Literary Biography* 9) 8-14.

Foster, Edward Halsey. *William Saroyan: A Study of the Short Fiction*. Boston: Twayne, 1991.

Keeler, Greg. "William Saroyan." Kimbel, *American Short-Story Writers, 1910-1945, First Series* (*Dictionary of Literary Biography* 86) 252-63.

Matalene, H. W. "William Saroyan." MacNicholas, *Twentieth-Century American Dramatists* (*Dictionary of Literary Biography* 7) 204-27.

"William Saroyan." Harris and Fitzgerald, *Short Story Criticism* 21:129-77.
Excerpts of criticism on Saroyan from 1934-1987, with an annotated bibliography.

"William Saroyan." Riley, *Contemporary Literary Criticism* 56:366-88.
Excerpts of criticism on Saroyan's play *The Time of Your Life* from 1939-1985.

Bibliographies

Carpenter, Charles A. "Saroyan, William." *Modern Drama Scholarship and Criticism, 1981-1990* 82.

Etulain, Richard W., and N. Jill Howard. "William Saroyan." *Bibliographical Guide to the Study of Western American Literature* 362-63.

Foard, Elizabeth C. *William Saroyan: A Reference Guide*. Boston: G. K. Hall, 1989.
Describes works about Saroyan since 1934.

Hamalian, Leo. "William Saroyan." Bruccoli and Baughman, *Bibliography of American Fiction, 1919-1988* 439-42.

Kherdian, David. *Bibliography of William Saroyan, 1934-1964*. San Francisco: Roger Beacham, 1965.
Complete descriptions of Saroyan's works.

Monaco, Pamela Jean. "William Saroyan." Demastes, *American Playwrights, 1880-1945* [362]-73.

Shuman, R. Baird. "William Saroyan." *American Drama, 1918-1960* 149-52.
Describes about 17 critical works.

Whitmore, Jon. *William Saroyan: A Research and Production Sourcebook*. Westport: Greenwood, 1994.
Plot and production information, critical overviews, and brief descriptions of Saroyan's writings, with annotated entries for about 800 works on Saroyan since 1935.

Richard (Nathaniel) Wright, 1908-1960

Web Sites

"Richard Wright." *Mississippi Writers Page.* 18 Mar. 2000, http://www.olemiss.edu/depts/
english/ms-writers/dir/wright_richard/.
An excellent site for Wright. Lists works by Wright (including the original productions of two plays, one of which he co-authored, and media adaptations), works
about Wright, and links to a few other Wright sites. Disappointing list of links may
simply reflect the paucity of material available on the web, but the editors should be
admonished to update the list of links and to include all known editions of works in
their bibliography.

"Richard Wright." *Writing and Resistance.* 18 Mar. 2000, http://www.public.asu.edu/~metro/
aflit/wright/index.html.

Richard Wright: Black Boy. 18 Mar. 2000, http://www.pbs.org/rwbb/rwtoc.html.

Richard Wright—His Life Revealed. 18 Mar. 2000, http://www.geocities.com/Athens/
Agora/9700/.
Chronology of Wright's life. No bibliography.

Biographies and Criticism

Butler, Robert. *Native Son: The Emergence of a New Black Hero.* Boston: Twayne,
1991.

Clark, Edward D. "Richard Wright." Harris, *Afro-American Writers, 1940-1955*
(*Dictionary of Literary Biography* 76) 199-221.

Fabre, Michel. *Richard Wright: Books and Writers.* Jackson: UP of Mississippi,
1990.
Identifies books owned or read by Wright.

Hakutani, Yoshinobu. "Richard Wright." Kimbel, *American Short-Story Writers,
1910-1945, Second Series* (*Dictionary of Literary Biography* 102) 378-86.

"Richard (Nathaniel) Wright." Riley, *Contemporary Literary Criticism* 48:415-40.
Excerpts of criticism on Wright's novel *Native Son* from 1940-1986.

"Richard Wright." Harris and Fitzgerald, *Short Story Criticism* 2:358-94.
Excerpts of criticism on Wright from 1938-1987, with an annotated bibliography.

"Richard Wright: *Black Boy.*" Riley, *Contemporary Literary Criticism* 74:354-97.
Excerpts of criticism on Wright's autobiography from 1945-1985, with an
annotated bibliography.

Bibliographies

Alsen, Eberhard. "Richard Wright." Nelson, *African American Authors, 1745-1945*
488-507.
Survey of research.

Carpenter, Charles A. "Wright, Richard." *Modern Drama Scholarship and Criticism,
1981-1990* 96.

Davis, Charles T., and Michel Fabre. *Richard Wright: A Primary Bibliography*. Boston: G. K. Hall, 1982.
Detailed descriptions of contents of Wright's works.

Davis, Thadious M. "Richard Wright." Flora and Bain, *Fifty Southern Writers after 1900* 545-59.

Glitsch, Catherine. "Wright, Richard." *American Novel Explication, 1991-1995* 274-76.

Kinnamon, Keneth. "Richard Wright." Bruccoli and Baughman, *Bibliography of American Fiction, 1919-1988* 556-61.

———. "Richard Wright." Bruccoli and Baughman, *Modern African American Writers* 63-73.

———. "Richard Wright." Kopley, *Prospects for the Study of American Literature* 315-30.
The most up-to-date survey of research.

———. *Richard Wright Bibliography: Fifty Years of Criticism, 1933-1982*. New York: Greenwood, 1988.
13,117 briefly annotated entries.

Leo, John R. "Wright, Richard." *Guide to American Poetry Explication* 491.

Reilly, John M. "Richard Wright." Inge, Duke, and Bryer, *Black American Writers* II, 1-46.
Survey of research.

Chester (Bomar) Himes, 1909-1984

Web Sites

"Chester Himes." *Pegasos*. 18 Mar. 2000, http://www.kirjasto.sci.fi/chimes.htm.
An interesting site that places Himes in the tradition of the detective story. Contains a brief bibliography (citations are incomplete). Marred by occasional bad grammar and spelling.

"The Chester Himes Page." *SAC LitWeb*. 3 Mar. 2000, http://www.accd.edu/sac/english/bailey/himes.htm.
Lists major works by and about Himes, but does not include biographical information nor links to other sites.

Biographies and Criticism

Butler, Robert J. "Chester Himes." Giles and Giles, *American Novelists since World War II, Third Series* (*Dictionary of Literary Biography* 143) 33-50.

Campenni, Frank. "Chester Himes." Helterman and Layman, *American Novelists since World War II, First Series* (*Dictionary of Literary Biography* 2) 240-44.

"Chester Himes." Riley, *Contemporary Literary Criticism* 108:218-79.
Excerpts of criticism on Himes from 1977-1996, with an annotated bibliography.

Muller, Gilbert H. *Chester Himes*. Boston: Twayne, 1989.

Reckley, Ralph. "Chester Himes." Harris, *Afro-American Writers, 1940-1955* (*Dictionary of Literary Biography* 76) 89-103.

Bibliographies

Ellery, Chris. "Chester Himes." Bruccoli and Baughman, *Bibliography of American Fiction, 1919-1988* 254-55.

Fabre, Michel, Robert E. Skinner, and Lester Sullivan. *Chester Himes: An Annotated Primary and Secondary Bibliography*. Westport: Greenwood, 1992.
Describes the contents of Himes's works and about 680 works on Himes since 1945.

Glitsch, Catherine. "Himes, Chester." *American Novel Explication, 1991-1995* 120.

Eudora Welty, 1909-

Web Sites

"Eudora Welty." *Mississippi Writers Page*. 18 Mar. 2000, http://www.olemiss.edu/depts/english/ms-writers/dir/welty_eudora/.
Useful biocritical article by Carol Ann Johnston, with bibliographies of works by and about Welty, including media adaptations.

Eudora Welty: Biography. 18 Mar. 2000, http://www.anova.org/welty.html.

Eudora Welty Newsletter. Ed. Thomas McHaney. Update unknown. Georgia SU. 18 Mar. 2000, http://www.gsu.edu/~wwwewn/.
Brief biography and bibliographies of works by and about Welty with sample issues of the newsletter.

Featured Author: Eudora Welty. Ed. and update unknown. New York Times. 18 Mar. 2000, http://channel.nytimes.com/books/98/11/22/specials/welty.html.
Texts of selected *New York Times* features by and about Welty.

Biographies and Criticism

"Eudora Welty." Harris and Fitzgerald, *Short Story Criticism* 1:464-99.
Excerpts of criticism on Welty from 1941-1985, with an annotated bibliography.

"Eudora Welty." Riley, *Contemporary Literary Criticism* 105:290-385.
Excerpts of criticism on Welty from 1980-1993, with an annotated bibliography.

Johnston, Carol Ann. *Eudora Welty: A Study of the Short Fiction*. New York: Twayne, 1997.

Kreyling, Michael. "Eudora Welty." Kimbel, *American Short-Story Writers, 1910-1945, Second Series* (*Dictionary of Literary Biography* 102) 335-50.

Vande Kieft, Ruth. "Eudora Welty." Helterman and Layman, *American Novelists since World War II, First Series* (*Dictionary of Literary Biography* 2) 524-37.

———. *Eudora Welty*. Rev. ed. Boston: Twayne, 1987.

Weston, Ruth D. "Eudora Welty." Giles and Giles, *American Novelists since World War II, Third Series* (*Dictionary of Literary Biography* 143) 303-20.

" 'A Worn Path': Eudora Welty." Harris and Fitzgerald, *Short Story Criticism* 27:331-67.
Excerpts of criticism on Welty's short story from 1957-1994, with an annotated bibliography.

Dictionaries, Encyclopedias, and Handbooks

Pingatore, Diana R. *Reader's Guide to the Short Stories of Eudora Welty*. Thorndike: G. K. Hall, 1996.

Journals

Eudora Welty Newsletter. Atlanta: Georgia SU, 1977- . 2/yr.
Includes an annual "Checklist of Welty Scholarship." See web site, above.

Bibliographies

Bryant, James A., Jr. "Eudora Welty." Flora and Bain, *Fifty Southern Writers after 1900* 516-25.

Glitsch, Catherine. "Welty, Eudora." *American Novel Explication, 1991-1995* 262-63.

McDonald, William U. "Eudora Welty." Martine, *Contemporary Authors: Bibliographical Series: American Novelists* 383-421.
Survey of research.

Polk, Noel. *Eudora Welty: A Bibliography of Her Work*. Jackson: UP of Mississippi, 1994.
Complete descriptions of Welty's works with an extensive chronology (pp. 433-81).

Prenshaw, Peggy W. "Eudora Welty." Duke, Bryer, and Inge, *American Women Writers* 233-67.
Survey of research.

Swearingen, Bethany C. *Eudora Welty: A Critical Bibliography, 1936-1958*. Jackson: UP of Mississippi, 1984.

Thompson, Victor H. "Eudora Welty." Bruccoli and Baughman, *Bibliography of American Fiction, 1919-1988* 529-32.

———. "Eudora Welty." Bruccoli and Baughman, *Modern Women Writers* 67-75.
Revises and updates Thompson, above.

———. *Eudora Welty: A Reference Guide*. Boston: G. K. Hall, 1976.
Describes criticism since 1936.

Wiedemann, Barbara. "Eudora Welty: 'A Worn Path'." Evans, Little, and Wiedemann, *Short Fiction* 265-70.
Describes 11 studies.

Charles Olson, 1910-1970

Web Sites

"Charles Olson." *Electronic Poetry Center.* 18 Mar. 2000, http://wings.buffalo.edu/epc/authors/olson/.
A kind of academic fan site that fails to provide much of real substance. Disappointing biographical and bibliographical material and links for Olson.

Biographies and Criticism

Bollobas, Eniko. *Charles Olson.* New York: Twayne, 1992.

Butterick, George F. "Charles Olson." Greiner, *American Poets since World War II, First Series* (*Dictionary of Literary Biography* 5) 115-28.

———, and Robert J. Bertholf "Charles Olson." Conte, *American Poets since World War II* (*Dictionary of Literary Biography* 193) 234-51.

"Charles Olson." Young, *Poetry Criticism* 19:265-323.
Excerpts of comments and criticism on Olson from 1970-1991, with an annotated bibliography.

Christensen, Paul. "Charles Olson." Charters, *The Beats: Literary Bohemians in Postwar America* (*Dictionary of Literary Biography* 16) 427-33.

Indexes and Concordances

Butterick, George F. *Guide to the Maximus Poems of Charles Olson.* Berkeley: U of California P, 1978.
Glosses and explications keyed to *Maximus Poems* (New York: Jargon/Corinth, 1960), *Maximus Poems IV, V, VI* (London: Cape, Goliard, 1968), and *Maximus Poems: Volume Three* (New York: Grossman, 1975).

Bibliographies

Butterick, George F., and Albert Glover. *Bibliography of Works by Charles Olson.* New York: Phoenix Book Shop, 1967.
Full bibliographic details for Olson's works.

Golding, Alan. "Charles Olson." Baughman, *Contemporary Authors: Bibliographical Series: American Poets* 233-68.
Survey of research.

Lawlor, William. "Charles Olson (1910-1970)." *Beat Generation: A Bibliographical Teaching Guide* 297-98.
Very brief up-to-date critical survey.

Leo, John R. "Olson, Charles." *Guide to American Poetry Explication* 292-95.

McPheron, William. *Charles Olson: The Critical Reception, 1941-1983: A Bibliographic Guide.* New York: Garland, 1986.
Annotated entries for 1,630 works about Olson since 1938.

Elizabeth Bishop, 1911-1979

Web Sites

"Elizabeth Bishop." *Heath Anthology.* 13 Mar. 2000, http://www.georgetown.edu/bassr/heath/syllabuild/iguide/bishop.html.

Elizabeth Bishop. Ed. Sebastian Damman. 18 Mar. 2000, http://ikarus.pclab-phil.uni-kiel.de/daten/anglist/PoetryProject/Bishop.htm.

Elizabeth Bishop. Ed. Barbara Page. 13 Dec. 1999. Vassar C. 18 Mar. 2000, http://iberia.vassar.edu/bishop/.
Includes texts of papers from the 1994 Bishop Symposium at Vassar, brief biography of Bishop, bibliographies of works by and about her (including recordings), detailed descriptions of her papers at Vassar and elsewhere, information on the Elizabeth Bishop Soc. and *Elizabeth Bishop Bulletin,* and links to other sites.

Biographies and Criticism

Brown, Ashley. "Elizabeth Bishop." Greiner, *American Poets since World War II, First Series* (*Dictionary of Literary Biography* 5) 66-76.

"Elizabeth Bishop." Young, *Poetry Criticism* 3:34-77.
Excerpts of comments and criticism on Bishop from 1935-1988, with an annotated bibliography.

Millier, Brett C. "Elizabeth Bishop." Conte, *American Poets since World War II, Fifth Series* (*Dictionary of Literary Biography* 169) 35-53.

Indexes and Concordances

Greenhalgh, Anne Merrill. *Concordance to Elizabeth Bishop's Poetry.* New York: Garland, 1985.
Keyed to *Complete Poems, 1927-1979* (New York: Farrar, Straus & Giroux, 1979).

Bibliographies

Leo, John R. "Bishop, Elizabeth." *Guide to American Poetry Explication* 26-33.

MacMahon, Candace W. *Elizabeth Bishop: A Bibliography, 1927-1979.* Charlottesville: UP of Virginia, 1980.
Complete descriptions of Bishop's works.

Page, Barbara. "Elizabeth Bishop." Baughman, *Contemporary Authors: Bibliographical Series: American Poets* 35-69.
Survey of research.

Wyllie, Diana E. *Elizabeth Bishop and Howard Nemerov: A Reference Guide.* Boston: G. K. Hall, 1983.
Describes about 300 works on Bishop since 1935.

Tennessee (Thomas Lanier) Williams, 1911-1983

Web Sites

"Tennessee Williams." *Mississippi Writers Page*. 18 Mar. 2000, http://www.olemiss.edu/ depts/english/ms-writers/dir/williams_tennessee/.
An excellent site for bibliography and filmography. Offsite links also provided. However, given that the editors are less than candid about Williams's sexuality, the site is less useful for biography. (For a more balanced appraisal of Williams's life, consult the lambda.net site, below.)

Tennessee Williams. 18 Mar. 2000, http://www.eiu.edu/~eng1002/authors/williams3/.

The Tennessee Williams Page. Ed. Tom Sullivan. Update and sponsor unknown. 18 Mar. 2000, http://www.lambda.net/~maximum/williams.html.
Gives an open appraisal of Williams's life that complements the *Mississippi Writers Page*, above. Lacks a bibliography and links.

Biographies and Criticism

Adler, Thomas P. *A Streetcar Named Desire: The Moth and the Lantern*. Boston: Twayne, 1990.

Arnott, Catherine M. *Tennessee Williams on File*. New York: Methuen, 1985.

Falk, Signi. *Tennessee Williams*. 2nd ed. Boston: Twayne, 1978.

Johns, Sally. "Tennessee Williams." MacNicholas, *Twentieth-Century American Dramatists* (*Dictionary of Literary Biography* 7) 320-50.

Presley, Delma E. *The Glass Menagerie: An American Memory*. Boston: Twayne, 1990.

"Tennessee Williams." Riley, *Contemporary Literary Criticism* 111:374-425.
Excerpts of criticism on Williams from 1955-1995, with an annotated bibliography.

"Tennessee Williams." Trudeau, *Drama Criticism* 4:369-434.
Excerpts of criticism on Williams in general and on *The Glass Menagerie, A Streetcar Named Desire, Cat on a Hot Tin Roof*, and *The Night of the Iguana* from 1945-1987, with an annotated bibliography.

"Tennessee Williams: *The Glass Menagerie*." Riley, *Contemporary Literary Criticism* 71:354-407.
Excerpts of criticism on Williams's play from 1945-1991, with an annotated bibliography.

Vannatta, Dennis P. *Tennessee Williams: A Study of the Short Fiction*. Boston: Twayne, 1988.

Journals

Tennessee Williams Literary Journal. Metairie: W. Kenneth Holditch, 1989- .
   Continues *Tennessee Williams Newsletter* (1979-80) and *Tennessee Williams Review* (1980-83); irregularly features "A Checklist of Tennessee Williams Scholarship."

Bibliographies

Carpenter, Charles A. "Williams, Tennessee." *Modern Drama Scholarship and Criticism, 1981-1990* 90-94.

Crandell, George W. *Tennessee Williams: A Descriptive Bibliography*. Pittsburgh: U of Pittsburgh P, 1995.
   Complete descriptions of Williams's works

Gunn, Drewey Wayne. *Tennessee Williams: A Bibliography*. 2nd ed. Metuchen: Scarecrow, 1991.
   Comprehensive listing of works by and about Williams.

Kolin, Philip C. *Tennessee Williams: A Guide to Research and Performance*. Westport: Greenwood, 1998.

Londre, Felicia Hardison. "Tennessee Williams." Kolin, *American Playwrights since 1945* [488]-517.

McCann, John S. *Critical Reputation of Tennessee Williams: A Reference Guide*. Boston: G. K. Hall, 1983.
   Describes works on Williams since 1939.

McHaney, Amelia. "Tennessee Williams." Roudane, *Contemporary Authors: Bibliographical Series: American Dramatists* 385-429.
   Survey of research.

Shuman, R. Baird. "Tennessee Williams." *American Drama, 1918-1960* 161-71.
   Describes about 50 critical works.

Tischler, Nancy M. "Tennessee Williams." Flora and Bain, *Fifty Southern Writers after 1900* 526-34.

John Cheever, 1912-1982

Web Sites

"John Cheever." *Pegasos*. 18 Mar. 2000, http://www.kirjasto.sci.fi/cheever.htm.

John Cheever: Parody and The Suburban Aesthetic. 18 Mar. 2000, http://xroads. virginia.edu/~CLASS/MA95/dyer/cheever4.htm.
   Long critical essay.

Biographies and Criticism

"John Cheever." Harris and Fitzgerald, *Short Story Criticism* 1: 86-116.
   Excerpts of criticism on Cheever from 1943-1983, with an annotated bibliography.

"John Cheever." Riley, *Contemporary Literary Criticism* 64:42-71.
Excerpts of criticism on Cheever from 1982-1990, with an annotated bibliography.

Meanor, Patrick. *John Cheever Revisited.* New York: Twayne, 1994.

Morace, Robert A. "John Cheever." Helterman and Layman, *American Novelists since World War II, First Series* (*Dictionary of Literary Biography* 2) 88-100.

O'Hara, James. "John Cheever." Kimbel, *American Short-Story Writers, 1910-1945, Second Series* (*Dictionary of Literary Biography* 102) 26-42.

―――. *John Cheever: A Study of the Short Fiction.* Boston: Twayne, 1989.

Bibliographies

Bosha, Francis J. *John Cheever: A Reference Guide.* Boston: G. K. Hall, 1981.
Annotated entries for about 600 works in all languages about Cheever since 1943.

Chaney, Bev, Jr., and William Burton. "John Cheever: A Bibliographical Checklist." *American Book Collector* 7 (1986): 22-31.
Updates Bosha, above.

Coates, Dennis E. "John Cheever." Bruccoli and Baughman, *Bibliography of American Fiction 1919-1988* 128-30.

Glitsch, Catherine. "Cheever, John." *American Novel Explication, 1991-1995* 47.

Morace, Robert A. "John Cheever." Martine, *Contemporary Authors: Bibliographical Series: Volume 1: American Novelists* 157-92.
Survey of research.

(Eleanor) May Sarton, 1912-1995

Web Sites

"May A. Sarton: A Poet's Life." *Celebration of Women Writers.* 18 Mar. 2000, http://www.cs.cmu.edu/People/mmbt/women/sarton/blouin-biography.html.
Biographical essay.

May Eleanor Sarton. 18 Mar. 2000, http://ourworld.compuserve.com/homepages/Tielemans/hp87marc.htm.

Biographies and Criticism

Evans, Elizabeth. *May Sarton, Revisited.* Boston: Twayne, 1989.

Hunting, Constance. "May Sarton." Quartermain, *American Poets, 1880-1945, Second Series* (*Dictionary of Literary Biography* 48) 376-86.

Bibliographies

Blouin, Lenora P. *May Sarton: A Bibliography.* Metuchen: Scarecrow, 1978.
Brief descriptions of Sarton's works and about 400 works on her.

Glitsch, Catherine. "Sarton, May." *American Novel Explication, 1991-1995* 224.

Nelson, Ronald J. "May Sarton." Bruccoli and Baughman, *Bibliography of American Fiction, 1919-1988* 442-44.

Osborne, Nancy Seale. "May Sarton (1912-)." Pollack and Knight, *Contemporary Lesbian Writers of the United States* [507]-13.

Robert Hayden, 1913-1980

Web Sites

"Robert Hayden." *Academy of American Poets*. 18 Mar. 2000, http://www.poets.org/lit/poet/rhaydfst.htm.
   Includes the texts of seven poems ("Full Moon," "Middle Passage," "The Whipping," "Those Winter Sundays," "Soledad," "Frederick Douglass," and "Runagate Runagate"). Also links to Addison-Wesley Literature Online site.

Biographies and Criticism

Fetrow, Fred M. *Robert Hayden*. Boston: Twayne, 1984.

Jones, Norma R. "Robert Hayden." Harris, *Afro-American Writers, 1940-1955* (*Dictionary of Literary Biography* 76) 75-88.

Mann, James. "Robert Hayden." Greiner, *American Poets since World War II, First Series* (*Dictionary of Literary Biography* 5) 310-18.

"Robert Hayden." Young, *Poetry Criticism* 6:175-202.
   Excerpts of comments and criticism on Hayden from 1973-1989, with an annotated bibliography.

Bibliographies

Fetrow, Fred M. "Robert Hayden." Baughman, *Contemporary Authors: Bibliographical Series: American Poets* 107-28.
   Survey of research.

Leo, John R. "Hayden, Robert." *Guide to American Poetry Explication* 202-03.

Muriel Rukeyser, 1913-1980

Web Sites

"Muriel Rukeyser." *Academy of American Poets*. 9 Mar. 2000, http://www.poets.org/lit/poet/mrukefst.htm.

Muriel Rukeyser. Ed. Tova Stabin. 1997. Sponsor unknown. 18 Mar. 2000, http://www.waystation.com/~tova/publications/rukeyser.html.
   Contains a biography of Rukeyser with bibliographies of works by and about her.

Biographies and Criticism

"Muriel Rukeyser." Young, *Poetry Criticism* 12:201-37.
Excerpts of comments and criticism on Rukeyser from 1936-1994, with an annotated bibliography.

Turner, Alberta. "Muriel Rukeyser." Quartermain, *American Poets, 1880-1945, Second Series* (*Dictionary of Literary Biography* 48) 369-75.

Bibliographies

Healy, Eloise Klein. "Muriel Rukeyser (1913-1980)." Pollack and Knight, *Contemporary Lesbian Writers of the United States* [461]-67.
Survey of research.

Leo, John R. "Rukeyser, Muriel." *Guide to American Poetry Explication* 358-59.

Tillie Olsen, 1913-

Web Sites

"Tillie Lerner Olsen." *Women Writers in the West.* Ed. unknown. 18 Mar. 2000, http://www.aml.wsu.edu/womenswest/OlsenBio.html.
Useful biography of Olsen with lists of her writings, excerpts of selected reviews, and an essay on Olsen's "Cultural Context."

"Tillie Olsen." *Nebraska Center for Writers.* 18 Mar. 2000, http://mockingbird. creighton.edu/NCW/olsen.htm.
Well-conceived and informative page with a brief biography of Olsen, an excerpt from *Tell Me a Riddle* (New York: Delacorte, 1989); and excerpted critical comments (under "What the Critics Say") on *Mothers and Daughters, Silences, Tell Me a Riddle,* and *Yonnondio: From the Thirties.*

Biographies and Criticism

Barr, Marleen. "Tillie Olsen." Walden, *Twentieth-Century American-Jewish Fiction Writers* (*Dictionary of Literary Biography* 28) 196-203.

Dresdner, Lisa Fry. "Tillie Olsen." Cracroft, *Twentieth-Century American Western Writers, First Series* (*Dictionary of Literary Biography* 206) 234-42.

Frye, Joanne S. *Tillie Olsen: A Study of the Short Fiction.* New York: Twayne, 1995.

Pearlman, Mickey, and Abby H. P. Werlock. *Tillie Olsen.* Boston: Twayne, 1991.

"Tillie Olsen." Harris and Fitzgerald, *Short Story Criticism* 11:162-200.
Excerpts of criticism on Olsen from 1961-1989, with an annotated bibliography.

"Tillie Olsen." Riley, *Contemporary Literary Criticism* 114:190-250.
Excerpts of criticism on Olsen from 1963-1994, with an annotated bibliography.

Bibliographies

Etulain, Richard W., and N. Jill Howard. "Tillie Olsen." *Bibliographical Guide to the Study of Western American Literature* 330.

Glitsch, Catherine. "Olsen, Tillie." *American Novel Explication, 1991-1995* 198.

Polster, Karen L. "Tillie Olsen." Shatzky and Taub, *Contemporary Jewish-American Novelists* 242-51.

Wiedemann, Barbara. "Tillie Olsen: 'I Stand Here Ironing'." Evans, Little, and Wiedemann, *Short Fiction* 205-10.
Describes eight studies.

John Berryman, 1914-1972

Web Sites

"John Berryman." *Academy of American Poets.* 8 Mar. 2000, http://www.poets.org/lit/poet/jberrfst.htm.
Brief biography of Berryman with the texts of "The Ball Poem," "Sonnet 117," "Dream Song 1," "Dream Song 4," "Dream Song 13," "Dream Song 22," "Dream Song 29," "Dream Song 77," and "Dream Song 324: An Elegy for W. C. W., the Lovely Man" from *The Dream Songs* (New York: Farrar, Straus & Giroux, 1969) and others editions and a selected bibliography of his works.

"John Berryman." *Language of the Land Project.* Ed. Richard J. Kelly. 18 Mar. 2000, http://www.mnbooks.org/lol/umn-ber1.htm.
Exhibit site.

Biographies and Criticism

Haffenden, John. "John Berryman." Quartermain, *American Poets, 1880-1945, Second Series* (*Dictionary of Literary Biography* 48) 20-38.

Bibliographies

Arpin, Gary Q. *John Berryman: A Reference Guide.* Boston: G. K. Hall, 1976.
Describes about 600 works on Berryman since 1935.

Jones, Sonya. "John Berryman." Baughman, *Contemporary Authors: Bibliographical Series: American Poets* 3-33.
Survey of research.

Leo, John R. "Berryman, John." *Guide to American Poetry Explication* 24-26.

Stefanik, Ernest C., Jr. *John Berryman: A Descriptive Bibliography.* Pittsburgh: U of Pittsburgh P, 1974.
Complete descriptions of Berryman's writings.

William S(eward) Burroughs, 1914-1997

Web Sites

"William S. Burroughs." *Literary Kicks*. 18 Mar. 2000, http://www.charm.net/~brooklyn/People/WilliamSBurroughs.html.
Good site, with an honest appraisal of the life of Burroughs. Though crowded in its presentation, the site includes a bibliography, discography, and filmography of the works of Burroughs (novels, letters, collaborations, interviews, and recordings) and many good links. Better organized and easier to use than the Electronic Freedom Foundation site, below.

William S. Burroughs. Ed., update, and sponsor unknown. 18 Mar. 2000, http://www.bigtable.com/.
Site offers a wealth of biographical information. Important sections include "Burroughs Primer" and "Concordance to *The Naked Lunch*." Lack of full bibliographic citations and poor organization mar the site.

William S. Burroughs Archive. Ed. unknown. 26 May 1999. Electronic Freedom Foundation. 18 Mar. 2000, http://www.eff.org/pub/Publications/Misc/William_S_Burroughs/.
In spite of its gopher-like structure, this site offers the texts of selected works by Burroughs (three interviews, some short works, and at least one album review, with excerpts from longer works); the most complete bibliography, discography, and filmography of Burroughs found on the web (including productions of plays, sound recordings, movies and videos, and books); and a few offsite links. Overall, the lack of organization and the absence of descriptions of the various parts of the site make its use cumbersome. More offsite links would enhance the site's value.

William S. Burroughs Files. Ed. Malcolm Humes. 3 Aug. 1997. Hyperreal InterWeb-Zone. 18 Mar. 2000, http://www.hyperreal.org/wsb/index.html.
Links to selected texts of works by or about Burroughs provided by "wps.com William S. Burroughs gopher site" as well as links to other Beats. Briefly annotated bibliography of works by and about Burroughs through 1972 (including media and recordings) based on Joe Maynard and Barry Miles's *William S. Burroughs*, below. Some empty links.

Biographies and Criticism

Lewis, Leon. "William S. Burroughs." Giles and Giles, *American Novelists since World War II, Fourth Series* (*Dictionary of Literary Biography* 152) 14-34.

Palumbo, Donald. "William S. Burroughs." Cowart and Wymer, *Twentieth-Century American Science-Fiction Writers* (*Dictionary of Literary Biography* 8) 92-96.

Skerl, Jennie. *William S. Burroughs*. Boston: Twayne, 1985.

"William S. Burroughs: *Naked Lunch*." Riley, *Contemporary Literary Criticism* 75:83-111.
Excerpts of criticism on Burroughs's novel from 1962-1984, with an annotated bibliography.

Bibliographies

Etulain, Richard W., and N. Jill Howard. "William S. Burroughs." *Bibliographical Guide to the Study of Western American Literature* 166-67.

Goodman, Michael B. "William S. Burroughs." Bruccoli and Baughman, *Bibliography of American Fiction, 1919-1988* 111-14.

————, and Lemuel B. Coley. *William S. Burroughs: A Reference and Research Guide.* New York: Garland, 1990.
Summaries of contents of Burroughs's works and annotated entries for 196 criticisms.

Lawlor, William. "William S. Burroughs (1914-1997)." *Beat Generation: A Bibliographical Teaching Guide* 97-139.
Excellent starting point; critically describes works by and about Burroughs (including web sites and multimedia).

Maynard, Joe, and Barry Miles. *William S. Burroughs: A Bibliography, 1953-1973.* Charlottesville: UP of Virginia, 1978.
Complete descriptions of Burroughs's works.

Ralph (Waldo) Ellison, 1914-1994

Web Sites

"Chapter 10: Late Twentieth Century: 1945 to the Present: Ralph Ellison." *PAL: Perspectives in American Literature.* 18 Mar. 2000, http://www.csustan.edu/english/reuben/pal/chap10/ellison.html.
Fulltexts of two reviews of Wright's posthumous novel, *Juneteenth*, with selected bibliographies of works by and about Ellison.

"Ralph Ellison." *American Literature on the Web.* 19 Jan. 2000. 3 Mar. 2000, http://www.nagasaki-gaigo.ac.jp/ishikawa/amlit/e/ellison21.htm.

"Ralph Ellison." *Bohemian Ink.* 18 Mar. 2000, http://www.levity.com/corduroy/ellison.htm.
A good starting place with brief biographical and good links.

"Ralph Ellison." *Pegasos.* 18 Mar. 2000, http://www.kirjasto.sci.fi/rellison.htm.

"Ralph Ellison." *Writing and Resistance.* 18 Mar. 2000, http://www.public.asu.edu/~metro/aflit/ellison/index.html.

"The Ralph Ellison Page." *SAC LitWeb.* 18 Mar. 2000, http://www.accd.edu/sac/english/bailey/ellisonr.htm.
Includes study notes and summaries of chapters of novels like *Invisible Man.* Lists major works by Ellison, two books about Ellison, and some good links.

"Ralph Ellison's Invisible Man." *Literature & Culture of the American 1950s.* 18 Mar. 2000, http://www.english.upenn.edu/~afilreis/50s/ellison-main.html.
Includes summaries of the novel's chapters and fulltexts of classic critical works like Saul Bellow's and Irving Howe's reviews of *Invisible Man*, Howe's essay "Black Boys and Native Sons," Ernest Kaiser's "A Critical Look at Ellison's Fiction

& at Social & Literary Criticism by and about the Author," and John Corry's "Profile of an American Novelist: A White View of Ralph Ellison."

Biographies and Criticism

Busby, Mark. *Ralph Ellison*. Boston: Twayne, 1991.

Deutsch, Leonard J. "Ralph Ellison." Harris, *Afro-American Writers, 1940-1955* (*Dictionary of Literary Biography* 76) 37-56.

———. "Ralph Waldo Ellison." Helterman and Layman, *American Novelists since World War II, First Series* (*Dictionary of Literary Biography* 2) 136-41.

McSweeney, Kerry. *Invisible Man: Race and Identity*. Boston: Twayne, 1988.

"Ralph Ellison." Harris and Fitzgerald, *Short Story Criticism* 26:1-30.
    Excerpts of criticism on Ellison from 1972-1978, with an annotated bibliography.

"Ralph Ellison." Riley, *Contemporary Literary Criticism* 114:84-139.
    Excerpts of criticism on Ellison from 1955-1997, with an annotated bibliography.

"Ralph (Waldo) Ellison." Riley, *Contemporary Literary Criticism* 54:104-49.
    Excerpts of criticism on Ellison's *Invisible Man* from 1952-1988.

Bibliographies

Covo, Jacqueline. *Blinking Eye: Ralph Waldo Ellison and His American, French, German, and Italian Critics, 1952-1971: Bibliographic Essays and a Checklist*. Metuchen: Scarecrow, 1974.
    Critical and evaluative descriptions; updated by Joe Weixlmann and John O'Banion's "A Checklist of Ellison Criticism, 1972-1978," *Black American Literature Forum* 12 (Summer 1978): 51-55.

Deutsch, Leonard J. "Ralph Ellison." Bruccoli and Baughman, *Bibliography of American Fiction, 1919-1988* 161-66.

———. "Ralph Ellison." Bruccoli and Baughman, *Modern African American Writers* 19-31.

Giza, Joanne. "Ralph Ellison." Inge, Duke, and Bryer, *Black American Writers* II, 47-71.
    Survey of research.

Glitsch, Catherine. "Ellison, Ralph." *American Novel Explication, 1991-1995* 72-73.

Greene, J. Lee. "Ralph Ellison." Flora and Bain, *Fifty Southern Writers after 1900* 147-57.

Randall Jarrell, 1914-1965

Web Sites

"Faded Ink Spots: April 1998." *Sabine Magazine*. 18 Mar. 2000, http://www.sabine-mag.com/archive/ar05010.htm.
    Lengthy biographical essay.

"Randall Jarrell." *Academy of American Poets*. 8 Mar. 2000, http://www.poets.org/lit/poet/rjarrfst.htm.
Fulltexts of Jarrell's poems, "The Death of the Ball Turret Gunner," "The Woman at the Washington Zoo," "Well Water," "Bombers," and "Next Day," with a brief biography of Jarrell and selected bibliography of his works.

Randall Jarrell Collection at UNCG. Ed. Carolyn Shankle. 3 June 1999. U of North Carolina at Greensboro. 18 Mar. 2000, http://library.uncg.edu/depts/speccoll/jarrell/.
Contains an excellent illustrated Jarrell chronology, a biography, and description of the Jarrell manuscripts and books at UNCG.

Biographies and Criticism

Ferguson, Suzanne. "Randall Jarrell." Quartermain, *American Poets, 1880-1945, Second Series* (*Dictionary of Literary Biography* 48) 246-66.

Lovell, Barbara. "Randall Jarrell." Estes, *American Writers for Children since 1960: Fiction* (*Dictionary of Literary Biography* 52) 209-13.

Quinn, Mary Bernetta. *Randall Jarrell*. Boston: Twayne, 1981.

Bibliographies

Lensing, George S. "Randall Jarrell." Flora and Bain, *Fifty Southern Writers after 1900* 270-79.

Leo, John R. "Jarrell, Randall." *Guide to American Poetry Explication* 212-17.

Quinn, Sr. Bernetta. "Randall Jarrell." Baughman, *Contemporary Authors: Bibliographical Series: American Poets* 129-62.
Survey of research.

Wright, Stuart T. *Randall Jarrell: A Descriptive Bibliography, 1929-1983*. Charlottesville: UP of Virginia, 1986.
Complete descriptions of Jarrell's works.

Bernard Malamud, 1914-1986

Web Sites

"Bernard Malamud." *Outline of American Literature*. 18 Mar. 2000, http://odur.let.rug.nl/~usa/LIT/malamud.htm.

Bernard Malamud. 18 Mar. 2000, http://www2.dokkyo.ac.jp/~esemi006/malamud/.

Bernard Malamud. 18 Mar. 2000, http://www.emanuelnyc.org/bulletin/archive/35.html.

Bernard Malamud, Writer. 18 Mar. 2000, http://shell12.ba.best.com/~zzmaster/HF/malamud_bernard.html.

"Malamud, Bernard." *Literature, Arts, and Medicine Database*. Ed. Felice Aull. 36th Edition, Aug. 1999. New York U. 18 Mar. 2000, http://mchip00.med.nyu.edu/lit-med/lit-med-db/webdocs/webauthors/malamud176-au-.html.
Brief profile of Malamud and contributed signed summaries of *God's Grace*, *Idiots First*, and *The Silver Crown*.

Biographies and Criticism

Abramson, Edward A. *Bernard Malamud Revisited*. New York: Twayne, 1993.

"Bernard Malamud." Harris and Fitzgerald, *Short Story Criticism* 15:167-245.
Excerpts of criticism on Malamud from 1958-1993, with an annotated bibliography.

"Bernard Malamud: *The Assistant*." Riley, *Contemporary Literary Criticism* 78:247-86.
Excerpts of criticism on Malamud's novel from 1957-1985, with an annotated bibliography.

Field, Leslie. "Bernard Malamud." Walden, *Twentieth-Century American-Jewish Fiction Writers* (*Dictionary of Literary Biography* 28) 166-75.

Helterman, Jeffrey. "Bernard Malamud." Helterman and Layman, *American Novelists since World War II, First Series* (*Dictionary of Literary Biography* 2) 291-304.

———. *Understanding Bernard Malamud*. Columbia: U of South Carolina P, 1985.

" 'The Magic Barrel': Bernard Malamud." Riley, *Contemporary Literary Criticism* 85:189-221.
Excerpts of criticism on Malamud's work from 1964-1991, with an annotated bibliography.

Salzberg, Joel. "Bernard Malamud." Giles and Giles, *American Novelists since World War II, Fourth Series* (*Dictionary of Literary Biography* 152) 107-27.

Solotaroff, Robert. *Bernard Malamud: A Study of the Short Fiction*. Boston: Twayne, 1989.

Bibliographies

Etulain, Richard W., and N. Jill Howard. "Bernard Malamud." *Bibliographical Guide to the Study of Western American Literature* 308.

Glitsch, Catherine. "Malamud, Bernard." *American Novel Explication, 1991-1995* 168

Habich, Robert D. "Bernard Malamud." Martine, *Contemporary Authors: Bibliographical Series: American Novelists* 261-91.
Survey of research.

Kosofsky, Rita N. *Bernard Malamud: A Descriptive Bibliography*. New York: Greenwood, 1991.
Brief bibliographic information and contents for Malamud's works and annotated entries for about 1,000 works on him.

Pinsker, Sanford. "Bernard Malamud." Shatzky and Taub, *Contemporary Jewish-American Novelists* 204-14.

Salzberg, Joel. "Bernard Malamud." Bruccoli and Baughman, *Bibliography of American Fiction, 1919-1988* 311-14.

———. *Bernard Malamud: A Reference Guide*. Boston: G. K. Hall, 1985.
Describes about 900 works on Malamud published since 1952.

Saul Bellow, 1915-

Web Sites

"Saul Bellow." *Heath Anthology*. 13 Mar. 2000, http://www.georgetown.edu/bassr/heath/syllabuild/iguide/bellow.html.

"Saul Bellow." *Nobel Prize Internet Archive*. 18 Mar. 2000, http://nobelprizes.com/nobel/literature/1976a.html.
Selected texts of works by and about Bellow, brief biography and bibliographies of works by and about him, and links to other Bellow pages.

Biographies and Criticism

Dutton, Robert R. *Saul Bellow*. Rev. ed. Boston: Twayne, 1982.

Marin, Daniel B. "Saul Bellow." Helterman and Layman, *American Novelists since World War II, First Series* (*Dictionary of Literary Biography* 2) 39-50.

Opdahl, Keith M. "Saul Bellow." Walden, *Twentieth-Century American-Jewish Fiction Writers* (*Dictionary of Literary Biography* 28) 8-25.

"Saul Bellow." Harris and Fitzgerald, *Short Story Criticism* 14:1-63.
Excerpts of criticism on Bellow from 1957-1992, with an annotated bibliography.

"Saul Bellow." Riley, *Contemporary Literary Criticism* 63:25-45.
Excerpts of criticism on Bellow from 1987-1989, with an annotated bibliography.

"*Seize the Day*: Saul Bellow." Riley, *Contemporary Literary Criticism* 79:60-104.
Excerpts of criticism on Bellow's novel from 1956-1987, with an annotated bibliography.

Wilson, Jonathan. *Herzog: The Limits of Ideas*. Boston: Twayne, 1990.

Journals

Saul Bellow Journal. West Bloomfield: Liela Goldman, 1981- .
Features a current "Selected Annotated Critical Bibliography."

Bibliographies

Ahokas, Pirjo. "Saul Bellow." Shatzky and Taub, *Contemporary Jewish-American Novelists* 28-40.

Carpenter, Charles A. "Bellow, Saul." *Modern Drama Scholarship and Criticism, 1981-1990* 52.

Cronin, Gloria L., and Blaine H. Hall. *Saul Bellow: An Annotated Bibliography*. 2nd ed. New York: Garland, 1987.
Describes works by Bellow and 1,231 works about him.

——, and Liela H. Goldman. "Saul Bellow." Martine, *Contemporary Authors: Bibliographical Series: American Novelists* 83-155.
Survey of research.

Glitsch, Catherine. "Bellow, Saul." *American Novel Explication, 1991-1995* 27-28.

Nault, Marianne. *Saul Bellow: His Works and His Critics: An Annotated International Bibliography*. New York: Garland, 1977.
Most useful for descriptions of Bellow's works.

Opdahl, Keith. "Saul Bellow." Bruccoli and Baughman, *Bibliography of American Fiction 1919-1988* 82-86.

Arthur Miller, 1915-

Web Sites

"Arthur Miller." *Literature Online*. 18 Mar. 2000, http://www.longman.awl.com/kennedy/miller/biography.html.
Brief biography of Miller with a selected bibliography of works by and about him. "Critical Archive" suggests traditional critical approaches to Miller. Links to other resources inoperable.

"Arthur Miller." *Pegasos*. 18 Mar. 2000, http://www.kirjasto.sci.fi/amiller.htm.

Arthur Miller. 18 Mar. 2000, http://www.imagi-nation.com/moonstruck/clsc10.htm.

"Arthur Miller's The Crucible: Fact & Fiction." *17th C. Colonial New England*. Ed. Margo Burns. 18 Jan. 2000. Sponsor unknown. 18 Mar. 2000, http://www.ogram.org/17thc/crucible.shtml.

Biographies and Criticism

"Arthur Miller." Trudeau, *Drama Criticism* 1:289-346.
Excerpts of criticism on Miller in general and on *Death of a Salesman* and *The Crucible* from 1949-1985, with an annotated bibliography.

"Arthur Miller: *The Crucible*." Riley, *Contemporary Literary Criticism* 78:287-329.
Excerpts of criticism on Miller's play from 1953-1992, with an annotated bibliography.

Griffin, Alice. *Understanding Arthur Miller*. Columbia: U of South Carolina P, 1996.

Helterman, Jeffrey. "Arthur Miller." MacNicholas, *Twentieth-Century American Dramatists* (*Dictionary of Literary Biography* 7) 86-111.

Martine, James J. *The Crucible: Politics, Property, and Pretense*. New York: Twayne, 1993.

Dictionaries, Encyclopedias, and Handbooks

Bigsby, Christopher. *Cambridge Companion to Arthur Miller*. New York: Cambridge UP, 1997.

Bibliographies

Carpenter, Charles A. "Miller, Arthur." *Modern Drama Scholarship and Criticism, 1981-1990* 66-69.

Ferres, John H. *Arthur Miller: A Reference Guide*. Boston: G. K. Hall, 1979.
Describes about 1,200 works on Miller since 1944.

Goldfarb, Alvin. "Arthur Miller." Kolin, *American Playwrights since 1945* [309]-38.

Jensen, George H. *Arthur Miller: A Bibliographical Checklist*. Columbia: J. Faust, 1976.
Complete descriptions of Miller's works.

Schlueter, June. "Arthur Miller." Roudane, *Contemporary Authors: Bibliographical Series: American Dramatists* 189-270.
Survey of research.

Shuman, R. Baird. "Arthur Miller." *American Drama, 1918-1960* 110-18.
Describes about 50 critical works.

Gwendolyn Brooks, 1917-

Web Sites

"Brooks, Gwendolyn." *Literature, Arts, and Medicine Database*. 18 Mar. 2000, http://mchip00.med.nyu.edu/lit-med/lit-med-db/webdocs/webauthors/brooks66-au-. html.

"Gwendolyn Brooks." *Academy of American Poets*. 18 Mar. 2000, http://www.poets.org/ lit/poet/gbroofst.htm.
Brief biography of Brooks with the audiotext of Brooks reading "We Real Cool," a bibliography of her works, and links to other Brooks sites.

"Gwendolyn Brooks." *Heath Anthology*. 13 Mar. 2000, http://www.georgetown.edu/ bassr/heath/syllabuild/iguide/brooks.html.

Biographies and Criticism

Griffin, Farah Jasmine. "Gwendolyn Brooks." Conte, *American Poets since World War II, Fourth Series* (*Dictionary of Literary Biography* 165) 81-91.

"Gwendolyn Brooks." Young, *Poetry Criticism* 7:51-109.
Excerpts of comments and criticism on Brooks from 1945-1990, with an annotated bibliography.

Israel, Charles. "Gwendolyn Brooks." Greiner, *American Poets since World War II, First Series* (*Dictionary of Literary Biography* 5) 100-106.

Kent, George E. "Gwendolyn Brooks." Harris, *Afro-American Writers, 1940-1955* (*Dictionary of Literary Biography* 76) 11-24.

Bibliographies

Leo, John R. "Brooks, Gwendolyn." *Guide to American Poetry Explication* 46-48.

Miller, R. Baxter. *Langston Hughes and Gwendolyn Brooks: A Reference Guide.* Boston: G. K. Hall, 1978.
Describes about 300 works on Brooks since 1944.

Carson (Smith) McCullers, 1917-1967

Web Sites

"Carson McCullers." *American Women in Literature Database.* 18 Mar. 2000, http://www.kutztown.edu/faculty/reagan/McCullers.html.

"Carson McCullers." *EducETH*. 18 Mar. 2000, http://www.educeth.ch/english/readinglist/mccullersc/.

Carson McCullers Project. Ed. unknown. 4 Feb. 2000. Miller Group. 18 Mar. 2000, http://www.carson-mccullers.com/.
Mainly valuable for a bibliography of McCullers's works, including stories published in magazines; texts of a few works on McCullers (including a review by Richard Wright), with a very good list of critical sources and an extensive unannotated bibliography that includes articles, chapters, and dissertations; an excellent chronology with well-selected photographs; and links to other resources.

Biographies and Criticism

" 'The Ballad of the Sad Café': Carson McCullers." Harris and Fitzgerald, *Short Story Criticism* 24:230-87.
Excerpts of criticism on McCullers's short story from 1951-1990, with an annotated bibliography.

Carr, Virginia Spencer. *Understanding Carson McCullers*. Columbia: U of South Carolina P, 1990.

"Carson McCullers." Harris and Fitzgerald, *Short Story Criticism* 9:321-61.
Excerpts of criticism on McCullers from 1951-1990, with an annotated bibliography.

"Carson McCullers." Riley, *Contemporary Literary Criticism* 100:239-73.
Excerpts of criticism on McCullers from 1940-1994, with an annotated bibliography.

Everson, Judith L. "Carson McCullers." Giles and Giles, *American Novelists since World War II, Fifth Series* (*Dictionary of Literary Biography* 173) 148-69.

Kiernan, Robert F. "Carson McCullers." Helterman and Layman, *American Novelists since World War II, First Series* (*Dictionary of Literary Biography* 2) 317-25.

McDowell, Margaret B. *Carson McCullers*. New York: Twayne, 1980.

Nalley, Sara. "Carson McCullers." MacNicholas, *Twentieth-Century American Dramatists* (*Dictionary of Literary Biography* 7) 70-74.

Bibliographies

Carpenter, Charles A. "McCullers, Carson." *Modern Drama Scholarship and Criticism, 1981-1990* 64-65.

Carr, Virginia Spencer. "Carson McCullers." Flora and Bain, *Fifty Southern Writers after 1900* 301-12.

———. "Carson McCullers." Bruccoli and Baughman, *Modern Women Writers* 20-26.

———. "Carson McCullers." Martine, *Contemporary Authors: Bibliographical Series: Volume 1: American Novelists* 293-345.

———, and Joseph R. Millichap. "Carson McCullers." Duke, Bryer, and Inge, *American Women Writers* 297-319.

———, and Laurie A. Scott. "Carson McCullers." Bruccoli and Baughman, *Bibliography of American Fiction 1919-1988* 338-41.

McDowell, Margaret B. "Carson McCullers." Roudane, *Contemporary Authors: Bibliographical Series: American Dramatists* 171-88.

Shapiro, Adrian M., Jackson R. Bryer, and Kathleen Field. *Carson McCullers: A Descriptive Listing and Annotated Bibliography of Criticism.* New York: Garland, 1980.
   Complete descriptions of works by McCullers and annotated entries for about 900 works about her; updated by George Bixby's "Carson McCullers: A Bibliographical Checklist," *American Book Collector* 5 (1984): 38-43.

Shuman, R. Baird. "Carson McCullers." *American Drama, 1918-1960* 107-09.
   Describes about 15 critical works.

Wilson, Mary Ann. "Carson McCullers." Kolin, *American Playwrights since 1945* [289]-96.

Robert (Traill Spence) Lowell, (Jr.), 1917-1977

Web Sites

"Robert Lowell." *Academy of American Poets.* 8 Mar. 2000, http://www.poets.org/lit/poet/rlowefst.htm.

"Robert Lowell." *Pegasos.* 18 Mar. 2000, http://www.kirjasto.sci.fi/rlowell.htm.

"Robert Lowell." *Twentieth-Century Poetry in English.* 18 Mar. 2000, http://www.lit.kobe-u.ac.jp/~hishika/lowell.htm.
   Text of "Father's Bedroom," with brief biography and selected bibliography of works about Lowell.

Robert Lowell. 18 Mar. 2000, http://www.it.cc.mn.us/literature/lowell.htm.

Biographies and Criticism

Brown, Ashley. "Robert Lowell." Conte, *American Poets since World War II, Fifth Series* (*Dictionary of Literary Biography* 169) 165-78.

———. "Robert Lowell." Greiner, *American Poets since World War II, First Series* (*Dictionary of Literary Biography* 5) 24-33.

———. "Robert Lowell." Young, *Poetry Criticism* 3:197-246.
Excerpts of comments and criticism on Lowell from 1945-1986, with an annotated bibliography.

Dictionaries, Encyclopedias, and Handbooks

Hobsbaum, Philip. *Reader's Guide to Robert Lowell*. London: Thames and Hudson, 1988.

Indexes and Concordances

Rehor, Rosalind. *This Round Dome: An Analysis of Theme and Style in the Poetry of Robert Lowell*. Diss. Cleveland: Case Western Reserve U, 1972.
Concordance to 54 poems.

Bibliographies

Axelrod, Steven Gould. "Robert Lowell." Baughman, *Contemporary Authors: Bibliographical Series: American Poets* 163-202.
Survey of research.

———, and Helen Deese. *Robert Lowell: A Reference Guide*. Boston: G. K. Hall, 1982.
Describes 1,736 works about Lowell since 1943.

Carpenter, Charles A. "Lowell, Robert." *Modern Drama Scholarship and Criticism, 1981-1990* 64.

Leo, John R. "Lowell, Robert." *Guide to American Poetry Explication* 245-56.

Mazzaro, James. *Achievement of Robert Lowell, 1939-1959*. Detroit: U of Detroit P, 1960.
Describes Lowell's works.

Procopiow, Norma. *Robert Lowell: The Poet and His Critics*. Chicago: American Library Association, 1984.

Robert (Edward) Duncan, 1919-1988

Web Sites

"Robert Duncan." *Academy of American Poets*. 8 Mar. 2000, http://www.poets.org/lit/poet/rduncfst.htm.

Biographies and Criticism

Bertholf, Robert J. *Symposium of the Imagination: Robert Duncan in Word and Image*. Buffalo: Poetry/Rare Books Collection, U at Buffalo, State U of New York, 1993.

Butterick, George F. "Robert Duncan." Greiner, *American Poets since World War II, First Series* (*Dictionary of Literary Biography* 5) 217-29.

——, and Robert J. Bertholf. "Robert Duncan." Conte, *American Poets since World War II, Sixth Series* (*Dictionary of Literary Biography* 193) 95-113.

Davidson, Michael. "Robert Duncan." Charters, *The Beats: Literary Bohemians in Postwar America* (*Dictionary of Literary Biography* 16) 169-80.

Johnson, Mark Andrew. *Robert Duncan*. Boston: Twayne, 1988.

"Robert Duncan." Young, *Poetry Criticism* 2:99-129.
Excerpts of comments and criticism on Duncan from 1948-1988, with an annotated bibliography.

Bibliographies

Bertholf, Robert J. *Robert Duncan: A Descriptive Bibliography*. Santa Rosa: Black Sparrow, 1986.
Gives detailed descriptions of Duncan's works and lists 283 works about him.

Etulain, Richard W., and N. Jill Howard. "Robert Duncan." *Bibliographical Guide to the Study of Western American Literature* 219.

Fox, Willard. *Robert Creeley, Edward Dorn, and Robert Duncan: A Reference Guide*. Boston: G. K. Hall, 1989.
Includes annotated entries for about 1,000 works on Duncan since 1944.

Lawlor, William. "Robert Duncan (1919-1988)." *Beat Generation: A Bibliographical Teaching Guide* 262-63.
Very brief up-to-date critical survey.

Leo, John R. "Duncan, Robert." *Guide to American Poetry Explication* 107-11.

J(erome) D(avid) Salinger, 1919-

Web Sites

The Catcher in the Rye Homepage. 18 Mar. 2000, http://www.euronet.nl/users/los/tcitr.html.

"J. D. Salinger." *Bohemian Ink*. 18 Mar. 2000, http://www.levity.com/corduroy/salinger.htm.

"J. D. Salinger." *Subculture Pages*. Ed. Bonesy Jones. Update unknown. FringeWare, Inc. 18 Mar. 2000, http://www.fringeware.com/subcult/J_D_Salinger.html.
Biography of Salinger, bibliographies of selected works by and about him, and links to other pages.

"J[erome] D[avid] Salinger." *American Literature on the Web.* 18 Mar. 2000, http://www.nagasaki-gaigo.ac.jp/ishikawa/amlit/s/salinger21.htm.
Classified list of general resources for Salinger.

Salinger.org. 18 Mar. 2000, http://www.salinger.org/.

Biographies and Criticism

" 'Franny and Zooey': J. D. Salinger." Harris and Fitzgerald, *Short Story Criticism* 28:220-70.
Excerpts of criticism on Salinger's short story from 1958-1991, with an annotated bibliography.

French, Warren G. "J. D. Salinger." Giles and Giles, *American Novelists since World War II, Fifth Series* (*Dictionary of Literary Biography* 173) 235-48.

———. "J. D. Salinger." Helterman and Layman, *American Novelists since World War II, First Series* (*Dictionary of Literary Biography* 2) 434-44.

———. *J. D. Salinger, Revisited.* Boston: Twayne, 1988.

"J. D. Salinger." Harris and Fitzgerald, *Short Story Criticism* 2:288-320.
Excerpts of criticism on Salinger from 1953-1987, with an annotated bibliography.

"J. D. Salinger." Riley, *Contemporary Literary Criticism* 56:317-65.
Excerpts of criticism on Salinger's novel *The Catcher in the Rye* from 1957-1983.

Pinsker, Sanford. *The Catcher in the Rye: Innocence under Pressure.* New York: Twayne, 1993.

Stevick, Philip. "J. D. Salinger." Kimbel, *American Short-Story Writers, 1910-1945, Second Series* (*Dictionary of Literary Biography* 102) 258-65.

Wenke, John Paul. *J. D. Salinger: A Study of the Short Fiction.* Boston: Twayne, 1991.

Bibliographies

French, Warren. "J. D. Salinger." Bruccoli and Baughman, *Bibliography of American Fiction, 1919-1988* 435-37.

Glitsch, Catherine. "Salinger, J. D." *American Novel Explication, 1991-1995* 223.

Sublette, Jack R. *J. D. Salinger: An Annotated Bibliography, 1938-1981.* New York: Garland, 1984.
Describes works by Salinger and 1,462 works about him.

Isaac Asimov, 1920-1992

Web Sites

Isaac Asimov. 18 Mar. 2000, http://info.rutgers.edu/Library/Reference/Etext/Impact.of.Science.On.Society.hd/3/.

Isaac Asimov Home Page. Ed. Edward Seiler. Update and sponsor unknown. 18 Mar. 2000, http://www.clark.net/pub/edseiler/WWW/asimov_home_page.html.
Contains lists of Asimov's works with publication information; unannotated lists of selected books about Asimov; a hodgepodge of excerpted texts of some of Asimov's works, texts of his speeches and interviews, and texts of works about Asimov (encyclopedia articles, obituaries, interviews of others about him); and links to other Asimov and science fiction pages.

Isaac Asimov's Foundation Universe. 18 Mar. 2000, http://home.interstat.net/~slawcio/foundation/cover2.html.

Biographies and Criticism

Goldman, Stephen H. "Isaac Asimov." Cowart and Wymer, *Twentieth-Century American Science-Fiction Writers* (*Dictionary of Literary Biography* 8) 15-29.

"*I, Robot*: Isaac Asimov." Riley, *Contemporary Literary Criticism* 92:1-23.
Excerpts of criticism on Asimov's novel from 1951-1988, with an annotated bibliography.

Touponce, William F. *Isaac Asimov.* Boston: Twayne, 1991.

Bibliographies

Glitsch, Catherine. "Asimov, Isaac." *American Novel Explication, 1991-1995* 16-17.

Goldman, Stephen H. "Isaac Asimov." Bruccoli and Baughman, *Bibliography of American Fiction 1919-1988* 59-68.

Green, Scott E. *Isaac Asimov: An Annotated Bibliography of the Asimov Collection at Boston University.* Westport: Greenwood, 1995.
"Covers Asimov's personal book collection," with descriptions of nearly 400 editions of Asimov's different works ([xi]).

Ray (Douglas) Bradbury, 1920-

Web Sites

Ray Bradbury. Ed. unknown. 18 Mar. 2000, http://www.dragoncon.org/people/bradbur.html

Ray Bradbury Page. Eds. Richard Johnston and Chris Jepsen. 2 Nov. 1998. Sponsor unknown. 18 Mar. 2000, http://www.brookingsbook.com/bradbury/.
Contains bibliographies of works by and about Bradbury (including screen- and teleplays), news features about him and information on new publications, and links to other pages.

Biographies and Criticism

"*Fahrenheit 451*: Ray Bradbury." Riley, *Contemporary Literary Criticism* 98:101-49.
Excerpts of criticism on Bradbury's novel from 1961-1992, with an annotated bibliography.

Mogen, David. *Ray Bradbury*. Boston: Twayne, 1986.

"Ray Bradbury." Harris and Fitzgerald, *Short Story Criticism* 29:36-93.
Excerpts of criticism on Bradbury from 1950-1989, with an annotated bibliography.

Slusser, George Edgar. "Ray Bradbury." Helterman and Layman, *American Novelists since World War II, First Series* (*Dictionary of Literary Biography* 2) 60-65.

Wolfe, Gary K. "Ray Bradbury." Cowart and Wymer, *Twentieth-Century American Science-Fiction Writers* (*Dictionary of Literary Biography* 8) 61-76.

Bibliographies

Carpenter, Charles A. "Bradbury, Ray." *Modern Drama Scholarship and Criticism, 1981-1990* 52.

Nolan, William F. *Ray Bradbury Companion: A Life and Career History, Photolog, and Comprehensive Checklist of Writings with Facsimiles from Ray Bradbury's Unpublished and Uncollected Work in All Media*. Detroit: Gale, 1975.
Describes works by Bradbury and selectively annotates entries for about 200 works on him.

Welsh, James L. "Ray Bradbury." Bruccoli and Baughman, *Bibliography of American Fiction, 1919-1988* 101-03.

Lawrence Ferlinghetti, 1920-

Web Sites

Lawrence Ferlinghetti. 18 Mar. 2000, http://www.geocities.com/~beatgeneration/ferlinghetti.htm.

Lawrence Ferlinghetti. 18 Mar. 2000, http://www.cwrl.utexas.edu/~slatin/20c_poetry/projects/gh/bioferlin.html.

Biographies and Criticism

"Lawrence Ferlinghetti." Riley, *Contemporary Literary Criticism* 111:48-73.
Excerpts of criticism on Ferlinghetti from 1965-1995, with an annotated bibliography.

"Lawrence Ferlinghetti." Young, *Poetry Criticism* 1:163-89.
Excerpts of comments and criticism on Ferlinghetti from 1958-1989, with an annotated bibliography.

McClanahan, Thomas. "Lawrence Ferlinghetti." Greiner, *American Poets since World War II, First Series* (*Dictionary of Literary Biography* 5) 248-55.

Smith, Larry. "Lawrence Ferlinghetti." Charters, *The Beats: Literary Bohemians in Postwar America* (*Dictionary of Literary Biography* 16) 199-214.

Bibliographies

Etulain, Richard W., and N. Jill Howard. "Lawrence Ferlinghetti." *Bibliographical Guide to the Study of Western American Literature* 229.

Lawlor, William. "Lawrence Ferlinghetti (1919-)." *Beat Generation: A Bibliographical Teaching Guide* 268-71.
Very brief up-to-date critical survey.

Leo, John R. "Ferlinghetti, Lawrence." *Guide to American Poetry Explication* 153-55.

Morgan, Bill. *Lawrence Ferlinghetti: A Comprehensive Bibliography to 1980.* New York: Garland, 1982.
Complete bibliographic descriptions for Ferlinghetti's works and unannotated entries for about 600 works on him; updated by Morgan's "Lawrence Ferlinghetti: An Updated Bibliography, 1980-1993." *Bulletin of Bibliography* 51.2 (1994): 111-59.

Richard (Purdy) Wilbur, 1921-

Web Sites

"Richard Wilbur." *Academy of American Poets.* 9 Mar. 2000, http://www.poets.org/lit/poet/rwilbfst.htm.
Texts of "Advice to a Prophet," "The Prisoner of Zenda," and "The Writer." Texts of poems are all on the site, and the editions are fully credited. Includes a brief biography, but no bibliography. One offsite link is offered.

Web Resources for Richard Wilbur. 18 Mar. 2000, http://www2.centenary.edu/home/jhendric/102/wilbur_webres.html.

Biographies and Criticism

Calhoun, Richard J. "Richard Wilbur." Conte, *American Poets since World War II, Fifth Series* (*Dictionary of Literary Biography* 169) 297-311.

———. "Richard Wilbur." Greiner, *American Poets since World War II, First Series* (*Dictionary of Literary Biography* 5) 378-90.

"Richard Wilbur." Riley, *Contemporary Literary Criticism* 110:346-89.
Excerpts of criticism on Wilbur from 1956-1997, with an annotated bibliography.

Bibliographies

Bixler, Frances. *Richard Wilbur: A Reference Guide.* Boston: G. K. Hall, 1991.
Annotated entries for about 700 works on Wilbur since 1935.

———, and Jane Hoogestraat. "Richard Purdy Wilbur: A Review of the Research and Criticism." *Resources for American Literary Study* 20.1 (1994): [54]-88.
Survey of research.

Field, John P. *Richard Wilbur: A Bibliographical Checklist.* Kent: Kent State UP, 1971.
Describes Wilbur's works.

Leo, John R. "Wilbur, Richard." *Guide to American Poetry Explication* 464-68.

Michelson, Bruce. "Richard Wilbur." Baughman, *Contemporary Authors: Bibliographical Series: American Poets* 335-68.
Survey of research.

Jack Kerouac, 1922-1969

Web Sites

"Jack Kerouac." *Knitting Circle*. 18 Mar. 2000, http://www.sbu.ac.uk/stafflag/jackkerouac.html.

"Jack Kerouac." *Literary Kicks*. 18 Mar. 2000, http://www.charm.net:80/~brooklyn/People/JackKerouac.html.

Jack Kerouac. 18 Mar. 2000, http://www.empirezine.com/spotlight/jack/jack1.htm.

Biographies and Criticism

Charters, Ann. "Jack Kerouac." Helterman and Layman, *American Novelists since World War II, First Series* (*Dictionary of Literary Biography* 2) 255-61.

Dardess, George. "Jack Kerouac." Charters, *The Beats: Literary Bohemians in Postwar America* (*Dictionary of Literary Biography* 16) 278-303.

French, Warren G. *Jack Kerouac*. Boston: Twayne, 1986.

Holton, Robert. *On the Road: Kerouac's Ragged American Journey*. New York: Twayne, 1999.

"Jack Kerouac." Riley, *Contemporary Literary Criticism* 61:277-316.
Excerpts of criticism on Kerouac's *On the Road* from 1957-1989, with an annotated bibliography.

Journals

Moody Street Irregulars: A Jack Kerouac Newsletter. Clarence Center: Moody Street Irregulars, 1978- .

Bibliographies

Charters, Ann. *A Bibliography of Works by Jack Kerouac (Jean Louis Lebris De Kerouac) 1939-1975*. Rev. ed. New York: Phoenix Bookshop, 1975.
Complete bibliographic descriptions for Kerouac's works.

Etulain, Richard W., and N. Jill Howard. "Jack Kerouac." *Bibliographical Guide to the Study of Western American Literature* 273-75.

Gargan, William M. "Jack Kerouac." Bruccoli and Baughman, *Bibliography of American Fiction, 1919-1988* 274-77.

Glitsch, Catherine. "Kerouac, Jack." *American Novel Explication, 1991-1995* 142.

Lawlor, William. "Jack Kerouac (1922-1969)." *Beat Generation: A Bibliographical Teaching Guide* 193-40.
　　Excellent starting point; critically describes works by and about Kerouac (including web sites and multimedia).

Leo, John R. "Kerouac, Jack." *Guide to American Poetry Explication* 225-26.

Milewski, Robert J. *Jack Kerouac: An Annotated Bibliography of Secondary Sources, 1944-1979*. Metuchen: Scarecrow, 1981.
　　Describes about 800 works on Kerouac.

Grace Paley, 1922-

Web Sites

"Grace Paley." *New York State Writers Institute*. 18 Mar. 2000, http://www.albany.edu/writers-inst/paley.html.
　　Biography of Paley and bibliography of works by and about her.

Salon Departments: Lit Chat: Grace Paley. 18 Mar. 2000, http://www.salon.com/11/departments/litchat1.html.

Biographies and Criticism

Arcana, Judith. *Grace Paley's Life Stories: A Literary Biography*. Urbana: U of Illinois P, 1993.

"Grace Paley." Harris and Fitzgerald, *Short Story Criticism* 8:386-422.
　　Excerpts of criticism on Paley from 1959-1988, with an annotated bibliography.

Isaacs, Neil D. *Grace Paley: A Study of the Short Fiction*. Boston: Twayne, 1990.

Bibliographies

Aarons, Victoria. "Grace Paley." Shapiro, *Jewish American Women Writers* 278-87.

Frank, Thomas. "Grace Paley." Shatzky and Taub, *Contemporary Jewish-American Novelists* 264-74.

Sorkin, Adam J. "Grace Paley." Walden, *Twentieth-Century American-Jewish Fiction Writers* (*Dictionary of Literary Biography* 28) 225-31.

Kurt Vonnegut, Jr., 1922-

Web Sites

"Kurt Vonnegut." *American Literature on the Web*. 3 Mar. 2000, http://www.nagasaki-gaigo.ac.jp/ishikawa/amlit/v/vonnegut21.htm.
　　Excellent linked list of general resources for Vonnegut.

Kurt Vonnegut—Home Page. 18 Mar. 2000, http://www.vonnegut.com/.
　　Vonnegut's own proprietary site.

VonnegutWeb. Ed. Chris Huber. 1 Aug. 1999. Duke U. 18 Mar. 2000, http://www.duke.edu/
~crh4/vonnegut/.
A very complex site that rewards trial-and-error digging. Linked pages contain
excerpts for each of Vonnegut's works as well as works about them. "Critical Bibliography" is a selected list of books about Vonnegut. Other useful features include
FAQs, a chatroom, and links to other sources.

Biographies and Criticism

Group, Robert. "Kurt Vonnegut, Jr." Cowart and Wymer, *Twentieth-Century American Science-Fiction Writers* (*Dictionary of Literary Biography* 8) 184-90.

Klinkowitz, Jerome. *Slaughterhouse-Five: Reforming the Novel and the World.* Boston: Twayne, 1990.

"Kurt Vonnegut." Riley, *Contemporary Literary Criticism* 111:349-73.
Excerpts of criticism on Vonnegut from 1990-1997, with an annotated
bibliography.

"Kurt Vonnegut, Jr." Harris and Fitzgerald, *Short Story Criticism* 8:423-39.
Excerpts of criticism on Vonnegut from 1968-82, with an annotated
bibliography.

"Kurt Vonnegut, Jr." Riley, *Contemporary Literary Criticism* 60:404-41.
Excerpts of criticism on Vonnegut's novel *Slaughterhouse-Five* from
1971-1988, with an annotated bibliography.

Reed, Peter J. "Kurt Vonnegut." Giles and Giles, *American Novelists since World
War II, Fourth Series* (*Dictionary of Literary Biography* 152) 248-72.

———. "Kurt Vonnegut, Jr." Helterman and Layman, *American Novelists since
World War II, First Series* (*Dictionary of Literary Biography* 2) 493-508.

Dictionaries, Encyclopedias, and Handbooks

Leeds, Marc. *Vonnegut Encyclopedia: An Authorized Compendium.* Westport:
Greenwood, 1995.

Bibliographies

Glitsch, Catherine. "Vonnegut, Kurt." *American Novel Explication, 1991-1995* 255.

Pieratt, Asa B., Julie Huffman Klinkowitz, and Jerome Klinkowitz. *Kurt Vonnegut: A
Comprehensive Bibliography.* Hamden: Archon/Shoe String, 1987.
Complete descriptions of Vonnegut's works with lists of selected criticism.

Reed, Peter. "Kurt Vonnegut." Bruccoli and Baughman, *Bibliography of American
Fiction, 1919-1988* 516-18.

———. "Vonnegut, Kurt." McCaffery, *Postmodern Fiction: A Bio-Bibliographical
Guide* 533-35.

James (Lafayette) Dickey,
1923-1997

Web Sites

"James Dickey." *Pegasos*. 18 Mar. 2000, http://www.kirjasto.sci.fi/dickey.htm.

Biographies and Criticism

Baughman, Ronald. "James Dickey." Conte, *American Poets since World War II* (*Dictionary of Literary Biography* 193) 76-94.

———. *Understanding James Dickey*. Columbia: U of South Carolina, P, 1985.

Calhoun, Richard James, and Robert W. Hill. *James Dickey*. Boston: Twayne, 1983.

Hill, Robert W. "James Dickey." Greiner, *American Poets since World War II, First Series* (*Dictionary of Literary Biography* 5) 174-91.

Journals

James Dickey Newsletter. Atlanta: James Dickey Soc., 1984- .
    Includes annual "Continuing Bibliography."

Bibliographies

Baughman, Ronald. "James Dickey." Baughman, *Contemporary Authors: Bibliographical Series: American Poets* 71-105.
    Survey of research.

Bruccoli, Matthew J., and Judith S. Baughman. *James Dickey: A Descriptive Bibliography*. Pittsburgh: U of Pittsburgh P, 1990.
    Complete bibliographic descriptions for Dickey's works.

Calhoun, Richard J. "James Dickey." Bain and Flora, *Fifty Southern Writers after 1900* 136-46.
    Supplemented by Robert Bain and Joseph M. Flora, "James Dickey," in Bain and Flora, *Contemporary Poets, Dramatists, Essayists, and Novelists of the South* [564]-65.

Elledge, Jim. *James Dickey: A Bibliography, 1947-1974*. Metuchen: Scarecrow, 1979.
    1,242 entries for works by and about Dickey.

Glitsch, Catherine. "Dickey, James." *American Novel Explication, 1991-1995* 62-63.

Leo, John R. "Dickey, James." *Guide to American Poetry Explication* 99-101.

Reisman, Rosemary M. Canfield, and Suzanne Booker-Canfield. "James Dickey." *Contemporary Southern Men Fiction Writers* [140]-52.
    Describes about 50 critical works.

Joseph Heller, 1923-1999

Web Sites

Internet Resources: Joseph Heller & Catch-22. 18 Mar. 2000, http://www.websteruniv. edu/~barrettb/heller.htm.

"Joseph Heller." *Bohemian Ink*. 18 Mar. 2000, http://www.levity.com/corduroy/heller. htm.

"Joseph Heller (1923-)." *American Literature on the Web*. 3 Mar. 2000, http://www.nagasaki-gaigo.ac.jp/ishikawa/amlit/h/heller21.htm. List of links for Heller.

Biographies and Criticism

"Joseph Heller." Riley, *Contemporary Literary Criticism* 63:171-210. Excerpts of criticism on Heller's novel *Catch-22* from 1961-1986, with an annotated bibliography.

Kutt, Inge. "Joseph Heller." Helterman and Layman, *American Novelists since World War II, First Series* (*Dictionary of Literary Biography* 2) 231-36.

Merrill, Robert. *Joseph Heller*. Boston: Twayne, 1987.

Potts, Stephen W. *Catch-22: Antiheroic Antinovel*. Boston: Twayne, 1989.

Searles, George J. "Joseph Heller." Walden, *Twentieth-Century American-Jewish Fiction Writers* (*Dictionary of Literary Biography* 28) 101-07.

Bibliographies

Buehrer, David. "Joseph Heller." Shatzky and Taub, *Contemporary Jewish-American Novelists* 145-53.

Carpenter, Charles A. "Heller, Joseph." *Modern Drama Scholarship and Criticism, 1981-1990* 59.

Glitsch, Catherine. "Heller, Joseph." *American Novel Explication, 1991-1995* 112.

Keegan, Brenda M. *Joseph Heller: A Reference Guide*. Boston: G. K. Hall, 1978. Describes about 800 works on Heller since 1961.

Nagel, James. "Joseph Heller." Bruccoli and Baughman, *Bibliography of American Fiction, 1919-1988* 237-39.

———. "Joseph Heller." Martine, *Contemporary Authors: Bibliographical Series: American Novelists* 193-218. Survey of resources.

Denise Levertov, 1923-1997

Web Sites

"Denise Levertov." *Academy of American Poets*. 8 Mar. 2000, http://www.poets.org/lit/poet/dlevefst.htm.

"Denise Levertov." *Heath Anthology*. 13 Mar. 2000, http://www.georgetown.edu/bassr/heath/syllabuild/iguide/levertov.html.

Biographies and Criticism

"Denise Levertov." Riley, *Contemporary Literary Criticism* 66:234-54.
Excerpts of criticism on Levertov from 1985-1988, with an annotated bibliography.

"Denise Levertov." Young, *Poetry Criticism* 11:156-215.
Excerpts of comments and criticism on Levertov from 1957-1992, with an annotated bibliography.

Dewey, Anne Day. "Denise Levertov." Conte, *American Poets since World War II, Fourth Series* (*Dictionary of Literary Biography* 165) 147-64.

Matalene, Carolyn. "Denise Levertov." Greiner, *American Poets since World War II, First Series* (*Dictionary of Literary Biography* 5) 3-9.

Bibliographies

Leo, John R. "Levertov, Denise." *Guide to American Poetry Explication* 235-39.

Sakelliou-Schultz, Liana. *Denise Levertov: An Annotated Primary and Secondary Bibliography*. New York: Garland, 1988.
Covers works on Levertov since 1940.

Norman Mailer, 1923-

Web Sites

KC's Norman Mailer Page. 18 Mar. 2000, http://www.iol.ie/~kic/.

"Norman Mailer." *Pegasos*. 18 Mar. 2000, http://www.kirjasto.sci.fi/nmailer.htm.

"Norman Mailer." *New York State Writers Institute*. 18 Mar. 2000, http://www.albany.edu/writers-inst/mailer.html.
Solid but brief biography of Mailer, with excerpts from his works; links to texts of selected articles about him from Albany *Times Union*; and a bibliography of works by and about him.

Biographies and Criticism

Birkhead, Douglas. "Norman Mailer." Kaul, *American Literary Journalists, 1945-1995, First Series* (*Dictionary of Literary Biography* 185) 157-74.

Bufithis, Philip H. "Norman Mailer." Helterman and Layman, *American Novelists since World War II, First Series* (*Dictionary of Literary Biography* 2) 278-90.

Gordon, Andrew. "Norman Mailer." Walden, *Twentieth-Century American-Jewish Fiction Writers* (*Dictionary of Literary Biography* 28) 154-66.

Merrill, Robert. *Norman Mailer Revisited.* New York: Twayne, 1992.

"Norman Mailer." Riley, *Contemporary Literary Criticism* 111:92-154.
Excerpts of criticism on Mailer from 1967-1997, with an annotated bibliography.

"Norman Mailer." Riley, *Contemporary Literary Criticism* 74:200-247.
Excerpts of criticism on Mailer from 1983-1992, with an annotated bibliography.

Wenke, Joseph. "Norman Mailer." Charters, *The Beats: Literary Bohemians in Post-war America* (*Dictionary of Literary Biography* 16) 361-71.

Bibliographies

Adams, Laura. *Norman Mailer: A Comprehensive Bibliography.* Metuchen: Scarecrow, 1974.
Lists works by and about Mailer.

Alsen, Eberhard. "Norman Mailer." Shatzky and Taub, *Contemporary Jewish-American Novelists* 192-203.

Etulain, Richard W., and N. Jill Howard. "Norman Mailer." *Bibliographical Guide to the Study of Western American Literature* 307.

Glitsch, Catherine. "Mailer, Norman." *American Novel Explication, 1991-1995* 165-66.

Jason, Philip K. "Norman Mailer." *Vietnam War in Literature* 121-29.
Describes about 30 studies of *Armies of the Night* and *Why Are We in Vietnam?*

Lawlor, William. "Norman Mailer (1923-)." *Beat Generation: A Bibliographical Teaching Guide* 291-92.
Very brief up-to-date critical survey.

Lennon, J. Michael. "Norman Mailer." Bruccoli and Baughman, *Bibliography of American Fiction, 1919-1988* 306-10.

———. "Norman Mailer." Martine, *Contemporary Authors: Bibliographical Series: American Novelists* 219-60.
Survey of research.

James Baldwin, 1924-1987

Web Sites

"James Arthur Baldwin: Teacher Resource File." *African American Writers.* 18 Mar. 2000, http://falcon.jmu.edu/~ramseyil/baldwin.htm.
Site offers excerpts and quotes from selected texts of Baldwin's works, texts of selected works about him, and links to a bibliography and biographical information (some unopenable).

"James Baldwin." *American Literature on the Web*. 18 Mar. 2000, http://www.nagasaki-gaigo.ac.jp/ishikawa/amlit/b/baldwin21.htm.
Good set of links to sites with selected fulltexts of works by and about Baldwin, biographies, and other resources.

"James Baldwin." *Pegasos*. 18 Mar. 2000, http://www.kirjasto.sci.fi/jbaldwin.htm.

"James Baldwin." *Writing and Resistance*. 18 Mar. 2000, http://www.public.asu.edu/~metro/aflit/baldwin/link.html.

James Baldwin. 18 Mar. 2000, http://www.bridgesweb.com/baldwin.html.

James Baldwin. 18 Mar. 2000, http://oceanrush.com/baldwin.html.

"James Baldwin: Annotated Index." *English Pages: Literature Workbook*. Longman. 18 Mar. 2000, http://longman.awl.com/englishpages/lit_wkbk_baldwin_index.htm.

Biographies and Criticism

"James Baldwin." Harris and Fitzgerald, *Short Story Criticism* 10:1-28.
Excerpts of criticism on Baldwin from 1965-1985, with an annotated bibliography.

"James Baldwin." Riley, *Contemporary Literary Criticism* 67:1-34.
Excerpts of criticism on Baldwin's novel *Go Tell It on the Mountain* from 1953-1981, with an annotated bibliography.

"James Baldwin." Trudeau, *Drama Criticism* 1:1-29.
Excerpts of criticism on Baldwin in general and on *Blues for Mr. Charlie* and *The Amen Corner* from 1964-1978, with an annotated bibliography.

Roberts, John W. "James Baldwin." Davis and Harris, *Afro-American Fiction Writers after 1955* (*Dictionary of Literary Biography* 33) 3-16.

" 'Sonny's Blues': James Baldwin." Riley, *Contemporary Literary Criticism* 90:1-41.
Excerpts of criticism on Baldwin's work from 1970-1992, with an annotated bibliography.

Standley, Fred L. "James Baldwin." Helterman and Layman, *American Novelists since World War II, First Series* (*Dictionary of Literary Biography* 2) 15-22.

———. "James Baldwin." MacNicholas, *Twentieth-Century American Dramatists* (*Dictionary of Literary Biography* 7) 45-49.

Bibliographies

Carpenter, Charles A. "Baldwin, James." *Modern Drama Scholarship and Criticism, 1981-1990* 50.

Dance, Daryl. "James Baldwin." Inge, Duke, and Bryer, *Black American Writers* II, 73-120.
Survey of research.

Glitsch, Catherine. "Baldwin, James." *American Novel Explication, 1991-1995* 22-24.

Roberts, David H. "James Baldwin." Kolin, *American Playwrights since 1945* [42]-50.

Shuman, R. Baird. "James Baldwin." *American Drama, 1918-1960* 52-54.
Describes 15 works about Baldwin.

Smith, James F. "James Baldwin." Martine, *Contemporary Authors: Bibliographical Series: American Novelists* 3-41.
Survey of research.

Standley, Fred L. "James Baldwin." Bruccoli and Baughman, *Bibliography of American Fiction 1919-1988* 71-75.

———. "James Baldwin." Bruccoli and Baughman, *Modern African American Writers* 1-11.

———, and Nancy V. Standley. *James Baldwin: A Reference Guide*. Boston: G. K. Hall, 1980.
Annotated entries for about 1,300 works on Baldwin since 1946.

Flannery O'Connor, 1925-1964

Web Sites

"Flannery O'Connor." *American Literature on the Web*. 19 Mar. 2000, http://www.nagasaki-gaigo.ac.jp/ishikawa/amlit/o/o'connor21.htm.
Excellent classified list of links for O'Connor.

Flannery O'Connor Childhood Home. Ed. Bill McGloughlin. 15 May 1997. U of North Carolina. 19 Mar. 2000, http://ils.unc.edu/flannery/.
List of O'Connor's works, with a biography, information and news about The Flannery O'Connor Society, and good list of O'Connor links.

"The Flannery O'Connor Collection." *Sojourners Magazine: December 1994/January 1995*. 19 Mar. 2000, http://www2.ari.net/home/bsabath/soj9412.html.

Flannery O'Connor Collection. Ed. unknown. 17 Mar. 2000. Georgia C & SU. 19 Mar. 2000, http://peacock.gac.peachnet.edu/~sc/foc.html.
Searchable page with FAQs and advice for starting research on O'Connor; bibliography of works about her; a brief biography; information about *Flannery O'Connor Bulletin*; and links to an O'Connor listserv (Flannery-L) and other O'Connor-related sites.

'*Tin Jesus': The Intellectual in Selected Short Fiction of Flannery O'Connor*. 19 Mar. 2000, http://sunset.backbone.olemiss.edu/~jmitchel/flannery.htm.

Biographies and Criticism

Butterworth, Nancy K. "Flannery O'Connor." Giles and Giles, *American Novelists since World War II, Fourth Series* (*Dictionary of Literary Biography* 152) 158-81.

"*Everything That Rises Must Converge*: Flannery O'Connor." Riley, *Contemporary Literary Criticism* 104:101-203.
Excerpts of criticism on O'Connor's novel from 1965-1993, with an annotated bibliography.

"Flannery O'Connor." Harris and Fitzgerald, *Short Story Criticism* 1:333-73.
Excerpts of criticism on O'Connor from 1955-1987, with an annotated bibliography.

"Flannery O'Connor." Riley, *Contemporary Literary Criticism* 66:297-331.
Excerpts of criticism on O'Connor's novel *Wise Blood* from 1952-1989, with an annotated bibliography.

" 'A Good Man Is Hard to Find': Flannery O'Connor." Harris and Fitzgerald, *Short Story Criticism* 23:178-241.
Excerpts of criticism on O'Connor's short story from 1963-1993, with an annotated bibliography.

May, John R. "Flannery O'Connor." Helterman and Layman, *American Novelists since World War II, First Series* (*Dictionary of Literary Biography* 2) 382-87.

Paulson, Suzanne Morrow. *Flannery O'Connor: A Study of the Short Fiction.* Boston: Twayne, 1988.

Dictionaries, Encyclopedias, and Handbooks

Grimshaw, James A., Jr. *Flannery O'Connor Companion.* Westport: Greenwood, 1981.

Journals

Flannery O'Connor Bulletin. Milledgeville: Georgia College, 1972- .

Bibliographies

Cook, Martha E. "Flannery O'Connor." Duke, Bryer, and Inge, *American Women Writers* 269-96.
Survey of research.

Evans, Robert C. "Flannery O'Connor: 'A Good Man Is Hard to Find'." Evans, Little, and Wiedemann, *Short Fiction* 181-91.
Describes 21 studies.

———. "Flannery O'Connor: 'Everything That Rises Must Converge'." Evans, Little, and Wiedemann, *Short Fiction* 192-98.
Describes 16 studies.

Farmer, David. *Flannery O'Connor: A Descriptive Bibliography.* New York: Garland, 1981.
Detailed descriptions of O'Connor's works.

Glitsch, Catherine. "O'Connor, Flannery." *American Novel Explication, 1991-1995* 197.

Golden, Robert E., and Mary C. Sullivan. *Flannery O'Connor and Caroline Gordon: A Reference Guide*. Boston: G. K. Hall, 1977.
Describes works on O'Connor since 1952.

Payne, David H. "Flannery O'Connor." Bruccoli and Baughman, *Bibliography of American Fiction, 1919-1988* 390-93.

———. "Flannery O'Connor." Bruccoli and Baughman, *Modern Women Writers* 36-43.

Stephens, Martha. "Flannery O'Connor." Flora and Bain, *Fifty Southern Writers after 1900* 334-44.

William (Clark) Styron, 1925-

Web Sites

American Masters: William Styron. 19 Mar. 2000, http://www.wnet.org/ammasters/styron.html.
PBS documentary site.

William Styron. 19 Mar. 2000, http://www.virginia.edu/~history/courses/courses.old/hius323/styron.html.

William Styron. Ed., update, and sponsor unknown. 19 Mar. 2000, http://www.sirius.com/~fillius/styron.htm.
Mainly valuable for texts of selected works by and about Styron (under "Articles"), topically arranged quotes from Styron's works, and links to other resources. Brief biography and bibliography of Styron's works to 1976 are of limited value.

Biographies and Criticism

Butterworth, Keen. "William Styron." Helterman and Layman, *American Novelists since World War II, First Series* (*Dictionary of Literary Biography* 2) 460-75.

Coale, Samuel. *William Styron Revisited*. Boston: Twayne, 1991.

Leon, Philip W. "William Styron." Giles and Giles, *American Novelists since World War II, Third Series* (*Dictionary of Literary Biography* 143) 217-31.

"William Styron." Harris and Fitzgerald, *Short Story Criticism* 25:282-326.
Excerpts of criticism on Styron from 1961-1995, with an annotated bibliography.

"William Styron." Riley, *Contemporary Literary Criticism* 60:391-403.
Excerpts of criticism on Styron from 1982-1985, with an annotated bibliography.

Bibliographies

Bryer, Jackson R. *William Styron: A Reference Guide*. Boston: G. K. Hall, 1978.
Describes about 1,200 works on Styron since 1946.

Butterworth, Keen. "William Styron." Bruccoli and Baughman, *Bibliography of American Fiction, 1919-1988* 494-96.

Friedman, Melvin J. "William Styron." Flora and Bain, *Fifty Southern Writers after 1900* 444-56.
    Supplemented by Joseph M. Flora and Robert Bain, "William Styron," in Flora and Bain, *Contemporary Fiction Writers of the South* [518].

Glitsch, Catherine. "Styron, William." *American Novel Explication, 1991-1995* 237-38.

Leon, Philip W. *William Styron: An Annotated Bibliography of Criticism*. Westport: Greenwood, 1978.

Reisman, Rosemary M. Canfield, and Suzanne Booker-Canfield. "William Styron." *Contemporary Southern Men Fiction Writers* [361]-82.
    Describes about 70 critical studies.

West, James L. W., III. *William Styron: A Descriptive Bibliography*. Boston: G. K. Hall, 1977.
    Complete descriptions of Styron's works.

Gore Vidal, 1925-

Web Sites

"Eugene Luther Gore Vidal Jr." *Knitting Circle*. 18 Mar. 2000, http://www.sbu.ac.uk/stafflag/gorevidal.html.

"Gore Vidal." *Bohemian Ink*. 19 Mar. 2000, http://www.levity.com/corduroy/vidal.htm.

Gore Vidal. 19 Mar. 2000, http://mfp.es.emory.edu/vidal.html.
    Collection of Vidal quotations.

Gore Vidal Collection. 19 Mar. 2000, http://www.pitt.edu/~kloman/vidalframe.html.
    Useful for summary reviews of Vidal's books, texts of his essays, interviews, and comments on various topics (like sex and politics), and texts of selected works about Vidal.

Biographies and Criticism

"Gore Vidal." Riley, *Contemporary Literary Criticism* 72:375-407.
    Excerpts of criticism on Vidal from 1982-1990, with an annotated bibliography.

Graalman, Robert. "Gore Vidal." Kibler, *American Novelists since World War II, Second Series* (*Dictionary of Literary Biography* 6) 345-50.

Kiernan, Robert F. "Gore Vidal." Giles and Giles, *American Novelists since World War II, Fourth Series* (*Dictionary of Literary Biography* 152) 232-47.

White, Ray Lewis. *Gore Vidal*. New York: Twayne, 1968.

Bibliographies

Stanton, Robert J. *Gore Vidal: A Primary and Secondary Bibliography*. Boston: G. K. Hall, 1978.
    Brief information for works and annotated entries for about 1,000 writings on Vidal since 1946.

A(rchie) R(andolph) Ammons, 1926-

Web Sites

"A. R. Ammons." *Academy of American Poets* 8 Mar. 2000, http://www.poets.org/lit/poet/arammfst.htm.

"A. R. Ammons Home Page." *Poets in Person.* Ed. unknown. 16 Jul 1998. Wilmington.org. 25 Mar 2000, http://www.wilmington.org/poets/ammons.html.
Contains selected texts of works by Ammons (some annotated) and works about him.

Poems. 19 Mar. 2000, http://www.uccs.edu/~cwetheri/Mtns/ARA/.

Biographies and Criticism

"A. R. Ammons." Riley, *Contemporary Literary Criticism* 108:1-62.
Excerpts of criticism on Ammons from 1964-1996, with an annotated bibliography.

"A. R. Ammons." Young, *Poetry Criticism* 16:1-66.
Excerpts of comments and criticism on Ammons from 1964-1994, with an annotated bibliography.

Gilbert, Roger. "A. R. Ammons." Conte, *American Poets since World War II, Fourth Series* (*Dictionary of Literary Biography* 165) 3-24.

Smith, Tyler. "A. R. Ammons." Greiner, *American Poets since World War II, First Series* (*Dictionary of Literary Biography* 5) 3-13.

Bibliographies

Harmon, William. "A. R. Ammons." Bain and Flora, *Fifty Southern Writers after 1900* 21-32.
Supplemented by Robert Bain and Joseph M. Flora, "A. R. Ammons" in Bain and Flora, *Contemporary Poets, Dramatists, Essayists, and Novelists of the South* [563]-64.

Leo, John R. "Ammons, A. R." *Guide to American Poetry Explication* 5-7.

Wright, Stuart. *A. R. Ammons: A Bibliography, 1954-1979.* Winston-Salem: Wake Forest UP, 1980.
Complete descriptions of Ammons's works.

Robert (Elwood) Bly, 1926-

Web Sites

"Robert Bly (1926-)." *American Literature on the Web.* 19 Mar. 2000, http://www.nagasaki-gaigo.ac.jp/ishikawa/amlit/b/bly21.htm.
Identifies two pages containing texts of selected poems by Bly from unspecified editions.

Robert Bly. 19 Mar. 2000, http://www.wnet.org/archive/lol/bly.html.

Biographies and Criticism

Smith, C. Michael. "Robert Bly." Greiner, *American Poets since World War II, First Series* (*Dictionary of Literary Biography* 5) 77-82.

Sugg, Richard P. *Robert Bly*. Boston: Twayne, 1986.

Bibliographies

Etulain, Richard W., and N. Jill Howard. "Robert Bly." *Bibliographical Guide to the Study of Western American Literature* 160-61.

Leo, John R. "Bly, Robert." *Guide to American Poetry Explication* 37-39.

Roberson, William H. *Robert Bly: A Primary and Secondary Bibliography*. Metuchen: Scarecrow, 1986.
Detailed descriptions of Bly's works and critically annotated entries for about 550 works on Bly.

Robert (White) Creeley, 1926-

Web Sites

"Robert Creeley." *American Literature on the Web*. 19 Mar. 2000, http://www.nagasaki-gaigo.ac.jp/ishikawa/amlit/c/creeley21.htm.
Good list of links for Creeley pages.

"Robert Creeley." *Electronic Poetry Center*. 19 Mar. 2000, http://wings.buffalo.edu/epc/authors/creeley/.

"Robert Creeley." *Bohemian Ink*. 19 Mar. 2000, http://www.levity.com/corduroy/creeley.htm.

Robert Creeley. 19 Mar. 2000, http://www.keele.ac.uk/depts/as/Portraits/creeley.html.

"Robert White Creeley." *New York State Writers Institute*. 19 Mar. 2000, http://www.albany.edu/writers-inst/creeley.html.
Good biography of Creeley, with excerpts from his works, links to texts of articles about him from *Courtland Review*, and a bibliography of works by and about him.

Biographies and Criticism

Day, Frank. "Robert Creeley." Greiner, *American Poets since World War II, First Series* (*Dictionary of Literary Biography* 5) 152-59.

Faas, Ekbert. "Robert Creeley." Charters, *The Beats: Literary Bohemians in Postwar America* (*Dictionary of Literary Biography* 16) 141-48.

Glazier, Loss Pequeño. "Robert Creeley." Conte, *American Poets since World War II, Fifth Series* (*Dictionary of Literary Biography* 169) 78-97.

"Robert Creeley." Riley, *Contemporary Literary Criticism* 78:118-63.
Excerpts of criticism on Creeley from 1978-1991, with an annotated bibliography.

Bibliographies

Fox, Willard. *Robert Creeley, Edward Dorn, and Robert Duncan: A Reference Guide*. Boston: G. K. Hall, 1989.
Includes annotated entries for about 1,200 works on Creeley since 1951.

Lawlor, William. "Robert Creeley (1926-)." *Beat Generation: A Bibliographical Teaching Guide* 258-60.
Very brief up-to-date critical survey.

Leo, John R. "Creeley, Robert." *Guide to American Poetry Explication* 76-81.

Novik, Mary. *Robert Creeley: An Inventory, 1945-1970*. Kent: Kent State UP, 1973.
Brief bibliographic information for works by Creeley.

Allen Ginsberg, 1926-1997

Web Sites

"Allen Ginsberg." *Academy of American Poets*. 8 Mar. 2000, http://www.poets.org/lit/poet/aginsfst.htm.

"Allen Ginsberg." *American Literature on the Web*. 3 Mar. 2000, http://www.nagasaki-gaigo.ac.jp/ishikawa/amlit/g/ginsberg21.htm.
Excellent classified list of links for Ginsberg pages.

"Allen Ginsberg." *Bohemian Ink*. 19 Mar. 2000, http://www.levity.com/corduroy/ginsberg.htm.

"Allen Ginsberg." *Literary Kicks*. 19 Mar. 2000, http://www.charm.net/~brooklyn/People/AllenGinsberg.html.
Mainly useful for bibliography of works by and about Ginsberg.

Allen Ginsberg. 19 Mar. 2000, http://www.naropa.edu/ginsberg.html.

Allen Ginsberg Memorial Site. 19 Mar. 2000, http://www.buffnet.net/~deadbeat/ginsberg/.

Biographies and Criticism

"Allen Ginsberg." Young, *Poetry Criticism* 4:42-96.
Excerpts of comments and criticism on Ginsberg from 1956-1989, with an annotated bibliography.

"Allen Ginsberg: 'Howl'." Riley, *Contemporary Literary Criticism* 69:209-29.
Excerpts of criticism on Ginsberg's *Howl and Other Poems* from 1957-1987, with an annotated bibliography.

Christensen, Paul. "Allen Ginsberg." Charters, *The Beats: Literary Bohemians in Postwar America* (*Dictionary of Literary Biography* 16) 214-41.

Géfin, Laszlo K. "Allen Ginsberg." Conte, *American Poets since World War II, Fifth Series* (*Dictionary of Literary Biography* 169) 116-36.

Merrill, Thomas F. *Allen Ginsberg*. Rev. ed. Boston: Twayne, 1988.

Ower, John. "Allen Ginsberg." Greiner, *American Poets since World War II, First Series* (*Dictionary of Literary Biography* 5) 269-86.

Bibliographies

Etulain, Richard W., and N. Jill Howard. "Allen Ginsberg." *Bibliographical Guide to the Study of Western American Literature* 240-41.

Kraus, Michelle P. *Allen Ginsberg: An Annotated Bibliography, 1969-1977*. Metuchen: Scarecrow, 1980.
Useful critical guidance to about 800 works on Ginsberg.

Lawlor, William. "Allen Ginsberg (1926-1997)." *Beat Generation: A Bibliographical Teaching Guide* 140-92.
Up-to-date excellent starting point; critically describes selected works by and about Ginsberg (including web sites and multimedia).

Leo, John R. "Ginsberg, Allen." *Guide to American Poetry Explication* 193-94.

Morgan, Bill. *Response to Allen Ginsberg, 1926-1994: A Bibliography of Secondary Sources*. Westport: Greenwood, 1996.
Identifies 5,830 works about Ginsberg.

———. *Works of Allen Ginsberg, 1941-1994: A Descriptive Bibliography*. Westport: Greenwood, 1995.
Complete bibliographic descriptions of Ginsberg's works.

James (Ingram) Merrill, 1926-1995

Web Sites

James Merrill Discussion Forum. 19 Mar. 2000, http://www.missouri.edu/~engtim/jm.html.

Biographies and Criticism

Spiegelman, Willard. "James Merrill." Conte, *American Poets since World War II, Fourth Series* (*Dictionary of Literary Biography* 165) 173-87.

———. "James Merrill." Greiner, *American Poets since World War II, First Series* (*Dictionary of Literary Biography* 5) 53-65.

Bibliographies

Copel, Laurence, and Jessy Randall. *J. I. M.'s Book: A Collection of Works by James Ingram Merrill: The Collection of Dennis M. Silverman*. New York: Glenn Horowitz Bookseller, 1995.
Describes works by Merrill.

Leo, John R. "Merrill, James." *Guide to American Poetry Explication* 265-67.

Frank O'Hara, 1926-1966

Web Sites

"Frank O'Hara." *Academy of American Poets*. 8 Mar. 2000, http://www.poets.org/lit/
poet/foharfst.htm.

"Frank O'Hara: Poet Among Painters." *Electronic Poetry Center*. 19 Mar. 2000,
http://wings.buffalo.edu/epc/authors/perloff/ohara.html.

Frank O'Hara. 19 Mar. 2000, http://www.it.cc.mn.us/literature/frank.htm.
Fulltexts of poems by O'Hara.

Frank O'Hara: A Short Biography. 19 Mar. 2000, http://www2.cwrl.utexas.edu/
slatin/ohw/ohbio.html.

Biographies and Criticism

Berkson, Bill. "Frank O'Hara." Charters, *The Beats: Literary Bohemians in Postwar
America* (*Dictionary of Literary Biography* 16) 423-27.

Butterick, George F. "Frank O'Hara." Greiner, *American Poets since World War II,
First Series* (*Dictionary of Literary Biography* 5) 102-12.

————, and Robert J. Bertholf. "Frank O'Hara." Conte, *American Poets since World
War II* (*Dictionary of Literary Biography* 193) 213-26.

"Frank O'Hara." Riley, *Contemporary Literary Criticism* 78:330-77.
Excerpts of criticism on O'Hara from 1959-1991, with an annotated bibliography.

Bibliographies

Lawlor, William. "Frank O'Hara (1926-1966)." *Beat Generation: A Bibliographical
Teaching Guide* 296-97.
Very brief up-to-date critical survey.

Leo, John R. "O'Hara, Frank." *Guide to American Poetry Explication* 289-92.

Smith, Alexander, Jr. *Frank O'Hara: A Comprehensive Bibliography*. New York:
Garland, 1979.
Complete descriptions of O'Hara's works and annotated entries for 232 writ-
ings about O'Hara since 1951.

W(illiam) D(eWitt) Snodgrass, 1926-

Web Sites

"W. D. Snodgrass." *Academy of American Poets*. 19 Mar. 2000, http://www.poets.org/lit/
POET/Wdsnofst.htm.

Biographies and Criticism

Helterman, Jeffrey. "W. D. Snodgrass." Greiner, *American Poets since World War II,
First Series* (*Dictionary of Literary Biography* 5) 266-74.

"W. D. Snodgrass." Riley, *Contemporary Literary Criticism* 68:380-99.
Excerpts of criticism on Snodgrass from 1971-1990, with an annotated bibliography.

Bibliographies

Leo, John R. "Snodgrass, W. D." *Guide to American Poetry Explication* 374-75.

White, William. *W. D. Snodgrass: A Bibliography*. Detroit: Wayne State U Library, 1960.
Full descriptions of Snodgrass's writings with a list of 20 studies and reviews.

John (Lawrence) Ashbery, 1927-

Web Sites

"John Ashbery." *Academy of American Poets*. 9 Mar. 2000, http://www.poets.org/lit/poet/jashbfst.htm.

"John Ashbery." *Electronic Poetry Center*. 19 Mar. 2000, http://wings.buffalo.edu/epc/authors/ashbery/.
Texts of "At North Farm" and selected works about Ashbery, with a brief bibliography of works by and about him.

Biographies and Criticism

Carney, Raymond. "John Ashbery." Greiner, *American Poets since World War II, First Series* (*Dictionary of Literary Biography* 5) 14-20.

Gardner, Thomas. "John Ashbery." Conte, *American Poets since World War II, Fourth Series* (*Dictionary of Literary Biography* 165) 25-56.

"John Ashbery." Riley, *Contemporary Literary Criticism* 77:39-80.
Excerpts of criticism on Ashbery from 1982-1993, with an annotated bibliography.

Bibliographies

Carpenter, Charles A. "Ashbery, John." *Modern Drama Scholarship and Criticism, 1981-1990* 50.

Kermani, David K. *John Ashbery: A Comprehensive Bibliography, Including His Art Criticism, and with Selected Notes from Unpublished Materials*. New York: Garland, 1976.
Complete bibliographic descriptions of Ashbery's works.

Leo, John R. "Ashbery, John." *Guide to American Poetry Explication* 10-15.

Galway Kinnell, 1927-

Web Sites

Amy Munno's Galway Kinnell Page. 19 Mar. 2000, http://www.webspan.net/~amunno/galway.html.
Brief biography and three fulltext poems; no bibliography. The graphics on this site make it difficult to read.

Biographies and Criticism

Calhoun, Richard James. *Galway Kinnell*. New York: Twayne, 1992.

Frazier, Charles. "Galway Kinnell." Greiner, *American Poets since World War II, First Series* (*Dictionary of Literary Biography* 5) 397-402.

Bibliographies

Leo, John R. "Kinnell, Galway." *Guide to American Poetry Explication* 226-28.

W(illiam) S(tanley) Merwin, 1927-

Web Sites

"W. S. Merwin." *Academy of American Poets*. 8 Mar. 2000, http://www.poets.org/lit/poet/wsmerfst.htm.

Biographies and Criticism

Davis, Cheri. *W. S. Merwin*. Boston: Twayne, 1981.

Hartley, Eric. "W. S. Merwin." Greiner, *American Poets since World War II, First Series* (*Dictionary of Literary Biography* 5) 65-74.

McCorkle, James. "W. S. Merwin." Conte, *American Poets since World War II, Fifth Series* (*Dictionary of Literary Biography* 169) 192-214.

"W. S. Merwin." Riley, *Contemporary Literary Criticism* 88:183-214.
Excerpts of criticism on Merwin from 1982-1994, with an annotated bibliography.

Bibliographies

Leo, John R. "Merwin, W. S." *Guide to American Poetry Explication* 267-71.

James (Arlington) Wright, 1927-1980

Web Sites

"James Wright." *Academy of American Poets*. 9 Mar. 2000, http://www.poets.org/lit/poet/jwrigfst.htm.

Biographies and Criticism

Dougherty, David C. *James Wright*. Boston: Twayne, 1987.

Elkins, Andrew. "James Wright." Conte, *American Poets since World War II, Fifth Series* (*Dictionary of Literary Biography* 169) 312-25.

Walters, Keith. "James Wright." Greiner, *American Poets since World War II, First Series* (*Dictionary of Literary Biography* 5) 409-18.

Indexes and Concordances

Colvin, Claude R. *Concordance of the Poetry of James Wright*. S. l.: s. n., 1988.

Bibliographies

Etulain, Richard W., and N. Jill Howard. "James Arlington Wright." *Bibliographical Guide to the Study of Western American Literature* 430.

Leo, John R. "Wright, James." *Guide to American Poetry Explication* 490.

Roberson, William H. *James Wright: An Annotated Bibliography*. Metuchen: Scarecrow, 1995.
Descriptions of Wright's writings and approximately 500 works about him.

Edward (Franklin) Albee, 1928-

Web Sites

"Chapter 8: American Drama: Edward Albee." *PAL: Perspectives in American Literature*. 19 Mar. 2000, http://www.csustan.edu/english/reuben/pal/chap8/albee.html. Good bibliography, no biography.

"Edward Albee." *EducETH*. 19 Mar. 2000, http://www.educeth.ch/english/readinglist/albeee/.

International Theatre Institute: Listen to Edward Albee. 19 Mar. 2000, http://iti-usa.org/audio.html.

Biographies and Criticism

Amacher, Richard E. *Edward Albee*. Rev. ed. Boston: Twayne, 1982.

"Edward Albee." Riley, *Contemporary Literary Criticism* 113:1-55.
Excerpts of criticism on Albee from 1961-1995, with an annotated bibliography.

MacNicholas, John. "Edward Albee." MacNicholas, *Twentieth-Century American Dramatists (Dictionary of Literary Biography* 7) 3-23.

Roudane, Matthew. *Understanding Edward Albee*. Columbia: U of South Carolina P, 1990.

Bibliographies

Carpenter, Charles A. "Albee, Edward." *Modern Drama Scholarship and Criticism, 1981-1990* 48-50.

Giantvalley, Scott. *Edward Albee: A Reference Guide*. Boston: G. K. Hall, 1987.
Lists 88 works by Albee and 2,800 works about him since 1959.

Paolucci, Anne, and Henry Paolucci. "Edward Albee." Roudane, *Contemporary Authors: Bibliographical Series: American Dramatists* 3-47.
Survey of research.

Roudane, Matthew C. "Edward Albee." Kolin, *American Playwrights since 1945* [1]-27.

Shuman, R. Baird. "Edward Albee." *American Drama, 1918-1960* 33-45.

Tyce, Richard. *Edward Albee: A Bibliography*. Metuchen: Scarecrow, 1986.
Lists 2,711 works by and about Albee.

Cynthia Ozick, 1928-

Web Sites

Cynthia Ozick. 19 Mar. 2000, http://www.ngc.peachnet.edu/Academic/Arts_Let/LangLit/
dproyal/ozick.htm.

Biographies and Criticism

Cole, Diane. "Cynthia Ozick." Walden, *Twentieth-Century American-Jewish Fiction
Writers* (*Dictionary of Literary Biography* 28) 213-25.

"Cynthia Ozick." Harris and Fitzgerald, *Short Story Criticism* 15:296-340.
Excerpts of criticism on Ozick from 1971-1991, with an annotated bibliography.

"Cynthia Ozick." Riley, *Contemporary Literary Criticism* 62:339-59.
Excerpts of criticism on Ozick from 1987-1989, with an annotated bibliography.

Lowin, Joseph. *Cynthia Ozick*. Boston: Twayne, 1988.

Rosenberg, Ruth. "Cynthia Ozick." Giles and Giles, *American Novelists since World
War II, Fourth Series* (*Dictionary of Literary Biography* 152) 182-93.

Bibliographies

Glitsch, Catherine. "Ozick, Cynthia." *American Novel Explication, 1991-1995* 200.

Klingenstein, Suzanne. "Cynthia Ozick." Shatzky and Taub, *Contemporary Jewish-
American Novelists* 252-63.

Kremer, S. Lillian. "Cynthia Ozick." Shapiro, *Jewish American Women Writers*
265-77.

Scrafford, Barbara L., and Elaine M. Kauvar. "Cynthia Ozick." Bruccoli and Baughman, *Bibliography of American Fiction, 1919-1988* 396-97.

Philip Levine, 1928-

Web Sites

"Philip Levine." *Academy of American Poets*. 8 Mar. 2000, http://www.poets.org/lit/
poet/plevifst.htm.

Biographies and Criticism

"Philip Levine." Riley, *Contemporary Literary Criticism* 118:265-324.
Excerpts of criticism on Levine from 1977-1997, with an annotated bibliography.

"Philip Levine." Young, *Poetry Criticism* 22:210-35.
Excerpts of comments and criticism on Levine from 1975-1995, with an annotated bibliography.

Taylor, Joan. "Philip Levine." Greiner, *American Poets since World War II, First Series* (*Dictionary of Literary Biography* 5) 9-18.

Bibliographies

Leo, John R. "Levine, Philip." *Guide to American Poetry Explication* 239-40.

Anne Sexton, 1928-1974

Web Sites

"Anne Sexton." *Academy of American Poets*. 9 Mar. 2000, http://www.poets.org/lit/poet/asextfst.htm.
Includes texts of "Her Kind," "The Truth the Dead Know," "Wanting to Die," and "Snow White and the Seven Dwarfs." ("Her Kind" is also available in audio.) Also includes selected bibliography and offsite links.

Anne Sexton. Ed. unknown. 27 Mar. 1999. Sponsor unknown. 19 Mar. 2000, http://pages.prodigy.net/stesha/annesexton.html.
A large selection of poems and photographs. Very well laid-out site.

Anne Sexton Papers. Ed. and update unknown. Harry Ransom Humanities Research Center, U of Texas at Austin. 19 Mar. 2000, http://www.lib.utexas.edu/hrc/fa/sexton.hp.html.
Includes a very good biographical sketch, which complements other Sexton sites.

The Complete Works of Anne Sexton. Ed., update, and sponsor unknown. 19 Mar. 2000, http://members.tripod.com/~toryn/.
Excellent site, including the fulltexts of all of the poetry of Sexton.

Biographies and Criticism

"Anne Sexton." Young, *Poetry Criticism* 2:343-75.
Excerpts of comments and criticism on Sexton from 1960-1988, with an annotated bibliography.

Cowart, David. "Anne Sexton." Greiner, *American Poets since World War II, First Series* (*Dictionary of Literary Biography* 5) 225-35.

Hall, Caroline King Barnard. *Anne Sexton*. Boston: Twayne, 1989.

Middlebrook, Diane Wood. "Anne Sexton." Conte, *American Poets since World War II, Fifth Series* (*Dictionary of Literary Biography* 169) 244-52.

Bibliographies

Carpenter, Charles A. "Sexton, Anne." *Modern Drama Scholarship and Criticism, 1981-1990* 82.

George, Diana Hume. "Anne Sexton." Baughman, *Contemporary Authors: Bibliographical Series: American Poets* 307-34.
Survey of research.

Hoffman, Cindy, Carol Duane, Katharen Soule, and Linda Wagner. "Three Contemporary Women Poets: Marianne Moore, Anne Sexton, and Sylvia Plath." Duke, Bryer, and Inge, *American Women Writers* 379-402.
Survey of research.

Leo, John R. "Sexton, Anne." *Guide to American Poetry Explication* 365-68.

Northouse, Cameron, and Thomas P. Walsh. *Sylvia Plath and Anne Sexton: A Reference Guide.* Boston: G. K. Hall, 1974.
Describes about 100 works on Sexton since 1960.

Ursula K. Le Guin, 1929-

Web Sites

Le Guin's World. Ed. Fredrik Petersson. 10 Jan. 1999. Sponsor unknown. 19 Mar. 2000, http://hem1.passagen.se/peson42/lgw/.

The Unofficial Ursula K. Le Guin Page. 19 Mar. 2000, http://www.wenet.net/~lquilter/femsf/authors/leguin/.
Page contains limited biographical information, an incomplete bibliography of works by Le Guin, and a list of works about her, some with links to their texts. Many inoperable links.

Biographies and Criticism

Attebery, Brian. "Ursula K. Le Guin." Cowart and Wymer, *Twentieth-Century American Science-Fiction Writers* (*Dictionary of Literary Biography* 8) 263-80.

Gordon, Andrew. "Ursula K. Le Guin." Estes, *American Writers for Children since 1960: Fiction* (*Dictionary of Literary Biography* 52) 233-41.

Reid, Suzanne Elizabeth. *Presenting Ursula K. Le Guin.* New York: Twayne, 1997.

"Ursula K. Le Guin." Harris and Fitzgerald, *Short Story Criticism* 12:205-52.
Excerpts of criticism on Le Guin from 1975-1990, with an annotated bibliography.

"Ursula K. Le Guin: The *Earthsea* Cycle." Riley, *Contemporary Literary Criticism* 71:177-205.
Excerpts of criticism on Le Guin's four-novel cycle from 1971-1990, with an annotated bibliography.

Bibliographies

Cogell, Elizabeth Cummins. *Ursula K. Le Guin: A Primary and Secondary Bibliography.* Boston: G. K. Hall, 1983.
Brief information for works by Le Guin and annotated entries for 761 works about her.

Etulain, Richard W., and N. Jill Howard. "Ursula K. Le Guin." *Bibliographical Guide to the Study of Western American Literature* 285.

Glitsch, Catherine. "Le Guin, Ursula K." *American Novel Explication, 1991-1995* 154.

Jean, Lorraine A. "Ursula K. Le Guin." Bruccoli and Baughman, *Bibliography of American Fiction, 1919-1988* 288-90.

Keller, Donald G. "Le Guin, Ursula." McCaffery, *Postmodern Fiction: A Bio-Bibliographical Guide* 449-53.

Paule Marshall, 1929-

Web Sites

"Paule Marshall." *UCL Webliography of Twentieth Century Writers of Color.* 19 Mar. 2000, http://ucl.broward.cc.fl.us/writers/marshall.htm.
List of links for bibliographies, biographies, and other resources for Marshall.

Biographies and Criticism

Christian, Barbara T. "Paule Marshall." Davis and Harris, *Afro-American Fiction Writers after 1955 (Dictionary of Literary Biography* 33) 161-70.

Davies, Carole Boyce. "Paule Marshall." Lindfors and Sander, *Twentieth-Century Caribbean and Black African Writers, Third Series (Dictionary of Literary Biography* 157) 192-202.

Denniston, Dorothy Hamer. *Fiction of Paule Marshall: Reconstructions of History, Culture, and Gender.* Knoxville: U of Tennessee P, 1995.

"Paule Marshall." Harris and Fitzgerald, *Short Story Criticism* 3:297-310.
Excerpts of criticism on Marshall from 1961-1985, with an annotated bibliography.

"Paule Marshall." Riley, *Contemporary Literary Criticism* 72:210-62.
Excerpts of criticism on Marshall from 1970-1992, with an annotated bibliography.

Bibliographies

Glitsch, Catherine. "Marshall, Paule." *American Novel Explication, 1991-1995* 169-70.

Adrienne (Cecile) Rich, 1929-

Web Sites

"Adrienne Rich." *Academy of American Poets.* 9 Mar. 2000, http://www.poets.org/lit/poet/arichfst.htm.

"Adrienne Rich." *American Literature on the Web.* 19 Mar. 2000, http://www.nagasaki-gaigo.ac.jp/ishikawa/amlit/r/rich21.htm.
Excellent classified list of links for Rich and her works.

"Adrienne Rich." *Heath Anthology.* 13 Mar. 2000, http://www.georgetown.edu/bassr/heath/syllabuild/iguide/rich.html.
Site lacks an adequate bibliography.

Adrienne Rich: Barclay Agency. 19 Mar. 2000, http://www.barclayagency.com/rich.html.
Public relations site.

Biographies and Criticism

"Adrienne Rich." Riley, *Contemporary Literary Criticism* 73:312-38.
Excerpts of criticism on Rich from 1986-1991, with an annotated bibliography.

"Adrienne Rich." Young, *Poetry Criticism* 5:348-403.
Excerpts of comments and criticism on Rich from 1956-1991, with an annotated
bibliography.

Cooper, Jane Roberta, ed. *Reading Adrienne Rich: Reviews and Re-visions, 1951-81.*
Ann Arbor: U of Michigan P, 1984.

Meese, Elizabeth. "Adrienne Rich." Jay, *Modern American Critics since 1955 (Dictionary of Literary Biography* 67) 232-40.

Newman, Anne. "Adrienne Rich." Greiner, *American Poets since World War II, First Series (Dictionary of Literary Biography* 5) 184-96.

Werner, Craig Hansen. *Adrienne Rich: The Poet and Her Critics.* Chicago: American
Library Association, 1988.

Bibliographies

Leo, John R. "Rich, Adrienne." *Guide to American Poetry Explication* 340-42.

McPherson, Diane. "Adrienne Rich (1929-)." Pollack and Knight, *Contemporary
Lesbian Writers of the United States* [433]-45.
Survey of research.

Lorraine Hansberry, 1930-1965

Web Sites

"Lorraine Hansberry." *American Literature on the Web.* 19 Mar. 2000, http://www.
nagasaki-gaigo.ac.jp/ishikawa/amlit/h/hansberry21.htm.
Good list of links for Hansberry.

"Lorriane Hansberry." *Malaspina Great Books Home Page.* 19 Mar. 2000, http://www.
mala.bc.ca/~mcneil/hansberr.htm.

"Lorraine Hansberry." *Voices from the Gaps: Women Writers of Color.* 19 Mar.
2000, http://voices.cla.umn.edu/authors/LorraineHansberry.html.

"The Lorraine Hansberry Page." *SAC LitWeb.* 19 Mar. 2000, http://www.accd.edu/sac/
english/bailey/hansberr.htm.
Largely focuses on *A Raisin in the Sun*, with a brief biography of Hansberry and
links.

Biographies and Criticism

Adams, Michael. "Lorraine Hansberry." MacNicholas, *Twentieth-Century American
Dramatists (Dictionary of Literary Biography* 7) 247-54.

Carter, Steven R. "Lorraine Hansberry." Davis and Harris, *Afro-American Writers after 1955: Dramatists and Prose Writers* (*Dictionary of Literary Biography* 38) 120-34.

Cheney, Anne. *Lorraine Hansberry*. Boston: Twayne, 1984.

"Lorraine Hansberry." Riley, *Contemporary Literary Criticism* 62:209-48.
Excerpts of criticism on Hansberry's play *A Raisin in the Sun* from 1959-1988, with an annotated bibliography.

"Lorraine Hansberry." Trudeau, *Drama Criticism* 2:239-65.
Excerpts of criticism on Hansberry in general and on *A Raisin in the Sun* from 1959-1991, with an annotated bibliography.

Bibliographies

Carpenter, Charles A. "Hansberry, Lorraine." *Modern Drama Scholarship and Criticism, 1981-1990* 58-59.

Dedmond, Francis. "Lorraine Hansberry." Kolin, *American Playwrights since 1945* [155]-68.

Friedman, Sharon. "Lorraine Hansberry." Roudane, *Contemporary Authors: Bibliographical Series: American Dramatists* 69-89.
Survey of research.

Leeson, Richard M. *Lorraine Hansberry: A Research and Production Sourcebook.* Westport: Greenwood, 1997.

Shuman, R. Baird. "Lorraine Hansberry." *American Drama, 1918-1960* 81-85.
Describes 17 critical works.

Williams, Dana A. "Lorraine Hansberry." *Contemporary African American Female Playwrights: An Annotated Bibliography* 45-57.
Lists about 100 studies.

Derek Walcott, 1930-

Web Sites

"Derek Walcott." *International Writers Series*. Sweet Briar C. 19 Mar. 2000, http://worldwriters.english.sbc.edu/walcott.html.

"Derek Walcott." *Nobel Prize Internet Archive*. 19 Mar. 2000, http://nobelprizes.com/nobel/literature/1992a.html.

"Derek Walcott: An Overview." *Postcolonial and Postimperial Literature: An Overview*. 19 Mar. 2000, http://www.stg.brown.edu/projects/hypertext/landow/post/caribbean/walcott/walcottov.html.
Mainly useful for excellent biography and the bibliography of the works of Walcott. The site seems to be under construction, and it does not seem to be regularly updated. Also, the site does not include links to other Walcott sites. Only the (Walcott) links "biography, works, themes, imagery, literary relations, and political and

social context" have materials linked to them. Strangely, the site lacks parallel construction; similar links refer to different things.

Biographies and Criticism

"Derek Walcott." Riley, *Contemporary Literary Criticism* 67:340-68.
    Excerpts of criticism on Walcott from 1986-1991, with an annotated bibliography.

"Derek Walcott." Trudeau, *Drama Criticism* 7:307-34.
    Excerpts of criticism on Walcott in general and on *Dream on Monkey Mountain* from 1971-1995, with an annotated bibliography.

Hamner, Robert D. "Derek Walcott." Lindfors and Sander, *Twentieth-Century Caribbean and Black African Writers, First Series* (*Dictionary of Literary Biography* 117) 290-312.

Gary (Sherman) Snyder, 1930-

Web Sites

"Gary Snyder." *Academy of American Poets*. 19 Mar. 2000, http://www.poets.org/lit/poet/gsnydfst.htm.

"Gary Snyder." *Literary Kicks*. 19 Mar. 2000, http://www.charm.net/~brooklyn/People/GarySnyder.html.
    Gives the text of Snyder's poem "Riprap," bibliography of Snyder's works through 1995, and links to pages for Gregory Corso, Jack Kerouac, and other Beat poets.

Biographies and Criticism

Batman, Alex. "Gary Snyder." Greiner, *American Poets since World War II, First Series* (*Dictionary of Literary Biography* 5) 274-78.

"Gary Snyder." Riley, *Contemporary Literary Criticism* 120:306-60.
    Excerpts of criticism on Snyder from 1970-1997, with an annotated bibliography.

"Gary Snyder." Young, *Poetry Criticism* 21:282-329.
    Excerpts of comments and criticism on Snyder from 1970-1995, with an annotated bibliography.

McGuirk, Kevin. "Gary Snyder." Conte, *American Poets since World War II, Fourth Series* (*Dictionary of Literary Biography* 165) 254-66.

McLeod, Dan. "Gary Snyder." Charters, *The Beats: Literary Bohemians in Postwar America* (*Dictionary of Literary Biography* 16) 486-500.

O'Grady, John P. "Gary Snyder." Cracroft, *Twentieth-Century American Western Writers, Second Series* (*Dictionary of Literary Biography* 212) 269-77.

Bibliographies

Almon, Bert. "Gary Snyder." Erisman and Etulain, *Fifty Western Writers* 444-53.

Etulain, Richard W., and N. Jill Howard. "Gary Snyder." *Bibliographical Guide to the Study of Western American Literature* 373-76.

Lawlor, William. "Gary Snyder (1930-)." *Beat Generation: A Bibliographical Teaching Guide* 306-10.
Very brief up-to-date critical survey.

Leo, John R. "Snyder, Gary." *Guide to American Poetry Explication* 375-79.

McNeill, Katherine. *Gary Snyder: A Bibliography.* New York: Phoenix Bookshop, 1983.
Complete descriptions of Snyder's works with an unannotated list of 173 works about Snyder.

Donald Barthelme, 1931-1989

Web Sites

Donald Barthelme. Ed. "Jessamyn." 7 May 1999. Sponsor unknown. 19 Mar. 2000, http://www.eskimo.com/~jessamyn/barth/.
Mainly valuable for texts of selected works by Barthelme, with links to selected texts by and about him. Biography copied directly from *Contemporary Authors*.

Biographies and Criticism

"Donald Barthelme." Harris and Fitzgerald, *Short Story Criticism* 2:24-58.
Excerpts of criticism on Barthelme from 1964-1987, with an annotated bibliography.

"Donald Barthelme." Riley, *Contemporary Literary Criticism* 115:52-100.
Excerpts of criticism on Barthelme from 1969-1997, with an annotated bibliography.

Gordon, Lois G. *Donald Barthelme.* Boston: Twayne, 1981.

Klinkowitz, Jerome. "Donald Barthelme." Helterman and Layman, *American Novelists since World War II, First Series* (*Dictionary of Literary Biography* 2) 34-39.

Roe, Barbara L. *Donald Barthelme: A Study of the Short Fiction.* New York: Twayne, 1992.

Bibliographies

Couturier, Maurice. "Barthelme, Donald." McCaffery, *Postmodern Fiction: A Bio-Bibliographical Guide* 260-63.

Klinkowitz, Jerome, Asa Pieratt, and Robert Murray Davis. *Donald Barthelme: A Comprehensive and Annotated Secondary Checklist.* Hamden: Archon, 1977.
Lists about 150 works on Barthelme.

Toni Morrison, 1931-

Web Sites

"Anniina's Toni Morrison Page." *Luminarium*. 19 Mar. 2000, http://www.luminarium. org/contemporary/tonimorrison/toni.htm.

"Toni Morrison." *American Literature on the Web*. 19 Mar. 2000, http://www.nagasaki-gaigo.ac.jp/ishikawa/amlit/m/morrison21.htm.
Good list of links for Morrison.

"Toni Morrison." *Nobel Prize Internet Archive*. 19 Mar. 2000, http://nobelprizes.com/ nobel/literature/1993a.html.

Toni Morrison. 19 Mar. 2000, http://www.cwrl.utexas.edu/~mmaynard/Morrison/home. html.

Toni Morrison References on the Internet. 19 Mar. 2000, http://www.viconet.com/ ~ejb/intro.htm.

Biographies and Criticism

"*Beloved*: Toni Morrison." Riley, *Contemporary Literary Criticism* 87:261-311.
Excerpts of criticism on Morrison's novel from 1987-1991, with an annotated bibliography.

Blake, Susan L. "Toni Morrison." Davis and Harris, *Afro-American Fiction Writers after 1955* (*Dictionary of Literary Biography* 33) 187-99.

Furman, Marva Jannett. *Toni Morrison's Fiction*. Columbia: U of South Carolina P, 1995.

Heinze, Denise. "Toni Morrison." Giles and Giles, *American Novelists since World War II, Third Series* (*Dictionary of Literary Biography* 143) 171-87.

Joyner, Nancy Carol. "Toni Morrison." Kibler, *American Novelists since World War II, Second Series* (*Dictionary of Literary Biography* 6) 243-47.

Plasa, Carl. *Toni Morrison: Beloved*. New York: Columbia UP, 1998.

Samuels, Wilfred D., and Clenora Hudson-Weems. *Toni Morrison*. Boston: Twayne, 1990.

Bibliographies

Carpenter, Charles A. "Morrison, Toni." *Modern Drama Scholarship and Criticism, 1981-1990* 69.

Glitsch, Catherine. "Morrison, Toni." *American Novel Explication, 1991-1995* 180-87.

Joyner, Nancy Carol. "Morrison, Toni." McCaffery, *Postmodern Fiction: A Bio-Bibliographical Guide* 473-75.

Middleton, David L. *Toni Morrison: An Annotated Bibliography*. New York: Garland, 1987.
Describes 170 works about Morrison.

Mobley, Marilyn Sanders. "Toni Morrison." Bruccoli and Baughman, *Bibliography of American Fiction, 1919-1988* 361-64.

———. "Toni Morrison." Bruccoli and Baughman, *Modern African American Writers* 39-46.
Revises and updates Mobley, above.

Robert (Lowell) Coover, 1932-

Web Sites

Robert Coover. 19 Mar. 2000, http://www.stg.brown.edu/projects/hypertext/landow/HTatBrown/CooverOV.html.

Biographies and Criticism

Andersen, Richard. *Robert Coover*. Boston: Twayne, 1981.

Kennedy, Thomas E. *Robert Coover: A Study of the Short Fiction*. New York: Twayne, 1992.

McCaffery, Larry. "Robert Coover." Helterman and Layman, *American Novelists since World War II, First Series* (*Dictionary of Literary Biography* 2) 106-21.

"Robert Coover." Harris and Fitzgerald, *Short Story Criticism* 15:29-67.
Excerpts of criticism on Coover from 1970-1993, with an annotated bibliography.

"Robert Coover." Riley, *Contemporary Literary Criticism* 87:22-67.
Excerpts of criticism on Coover from 1979-1991, with an annotated bibliography.

Bibliographies

Bruccoli, Matthew J. "Robert Coover." Bruccoli and Baughman, *Bibliography of American Fiction, 1919-1988* 135-36.

Glitsch, Catherine. "Coover, Robert." *American Novel Explication, 1991-1995* 53-54.

McCaffery, Larry. "Coover, Robert." McCaffery, *Postmodern Fiction: A Bio-Bibliographical Guide* 308-11.

Stuprich, Michael. "Robert Lowell." Kolin, *American Playwrights since 1945* [250]-58.

Sylvia Plath, 1932-1963

Web Sites

Complete List of Sylvia Plath Links. 19 Mar. 2000, http://www.geocities.com/SoHo/7773/PlathLinks.html.
    Classified list of links to sites (full, small, individual works by Plath and about her, and the like), some empty.

"Sylvia Plath." *Academy of American Poets.* 9 Mar. 2000, http://www.poets.org/lit/poet/splatfst.htm.

"Sylvia Plath." *EducETH.* 19 Mar. 2000, http://www.educeth.ch/english/readinglist/plaths/.

Sylvia Plath. Ed. Joan Welz. 10 June 1998. U of Alberta. 19 Mar. 2000, http://dte6.educ.ualberta.ca/nethowto_support/examples/j_welz/.
    Excellent student-produced site mainly useful for a bibliography of works by and about Plath; also contains a brief biography, selected quotations, and other features.

Sylvia Plath. Ed. Anja Beckmann. 23 Oct. 1998. U of Leipzig. 19 Mar. 2000, http://stinfwww.informatik.uni-leipzig.de/~beckmann/plath.html.
    A comprehensive site containing selected texts of Plath's works (based on standard editions) and works about her; a biography; and an extensive bibliography of works by and about Plath, including multimedia.

The Sylvia Plath Forum. 19 Mar. 2000, http://www.hebdenbridge.co.uk/plath/.

Biographies and Criticism

Hall, Caroline King Barnard. *Sylvia Plath, Revised.* New York: Twayne, 1998.

Hargrove, Nancy Duvall. "Sylvia Plath." Kibler, *American Novelists since World War II, Second Series* (*Dictionary of Literary Biography* 6) 259-64.

Materer, Timothy. "Sylvia Plath." Giles and Giles, *American Novelists since World War II, Fourth Series* (*Dictionary of Literary Biography* 152) 194-201.

McClanahan, Thomas. "Sylvia Plath." Greiner, *American Poets since World War II, First Series* (*Dictionary of Literary Biography* 5) 163-68.

"Sylvia Plath." Riley, *Contemporary Literary Criticism* 111:155-222.
    Excerpts of criticism on Plath from 1973-1996, with an annotated bibliography.

"Sylvia Plath." Riley, *Contemporary Literary Criticism* 62:383-429.
    Excerpts of criticism on Plath's novel *The Bell Jar* from 1963-1986, with an annotated bibliography.

"Sylvia Plath." Young, *Poetry Criticism* 1:378-416.
    Excerpts of comments and criticism on Plath from 1966-1988, with an annotated bibliography.

Wagner-Martin, Linda. *The Bell Jar: A Novel of the Fifties.* New York: Twayne, 1992.

Indexes and Concordances

Matovich, Richard M. *Concordance to the Collected Poems of Sylvia Plath*. New York: Garland, 1986.
  Based on *Collected Poems* (London: Faber & Faber, 1981).

Bibliographies

Glitsch, Catherine. "Plath, Sylvia." *American Novel Explication, 1991-1995* 207.

Hoffman, Cindy, Carol Duane, Katharen Soule, and Linda Wagner. "Three Contemporary Women Poets: Marianne Moore, Anne Sexton, and Sylvia Plath." Duke, Bryer, and Inge, *American Women Writers* 379-402.
  Survey of research.

Leo, John R. "Plath, Sylvia." *Guide to American Poetry Explication* 302-13.

Meyerling, Sheryll. *Sylvia Plath: A Reference Guide, 1973-1988*. Boston: G. K. Hall, 1990.
  Describes about 800 works on Plath.

Tabor, Stephen. *Sylvia Plath: An Analytical Bibliography*. Westport: Meckler, 1987.
  Detailed descriptions of Plath's works and briefly annotated entries for about 950 criticisms.

John (Hoyer) Updike, 1932-

Web Sites

Centaurian: A Home Page for John Updike. Ed. James Yerkes. 16 Aug. 1999. Sponsor unknown. 19 Mar. 2000, http://www.users.fast.net/~joyerkes/.
  Well-designed and up-to-date site with clearly identified major links for texts of selected criticism ("Chiron's Forum"); a classified briefly annotated selected bibliography of works about Updike; descriptions of new and forthcoming publications and other information resources ("What's New in Updikiana"); an excellently illustrated brief biographical and literary chronology and an up-to-date list of Updike's lectures and appearances; and FAQs and popular responses and discussions related to Updike ("Grazing Among the Centaurs").

"John Updike." *Pegasos*. 19 Mar. 2000, http://www.kirjasto.sci.fi/updike.htm.

Biographies and Criticism

" 'A & P': John (Hoyer) Updike." Harris and Fitzgerald, *Short Story Criticism* 27:319-30.
  Excerpts of criticism on Updike's short story from 1972-1993, with an annotated bibliography.

Greiner, Donald J. "John Updike." Giles and Giles, *American Novelists since World War II, Third Series* (*Dictionary of Literary Biography* 143) 250-76.

———. "John Updike." Greiner, *American Poets since World War II, First Series* (*Dictionary of Literary Biography* 5) 327-34.

"John Updike." Harris and Fitzgerald, *Short Story Criticism* 13:346-411.
Excerpts of criticism on Updike from 1972-1988, with an annotated bibliography.

Klinkowitz, Jerome. "John Updike." Helterman and Layman, *American Novelists since World War II, First Series* (*Dictionary of Literary Biography* 2) 484-92.

Schiff, James A. *John Updike Revisited.* New York: Twayne, 1998.

Bibliographies

De Bellis, Jack. *John Updike: A Bibliography, 1967-1993.* Westport: Greenwood, 1994.
Brief information for Updike's works with unannotated lists of 1,748 works about him.

Glitsch, Catherine. "Updike, John." *American Novel Explication, 1991-1995* 250-51.

Greiner, Donald J. "John Updike." Bruccoli and Baughman, *Bibliography of American Fiction, 1919-1988* 507-10.

———. "John Updike." Martine, *Contemporary Authors: Bibliographical Series: American Novelists* 347-82.
Survey of research.

Leo, John R. "Updike, John." *Guide to American Poetry Explication* 447-48.

Little, Anne C., and Robert C. Evans. "John Updike: 'A&P'." Evans, Little, and Wiedemann, *Short Fiction* 252-55.
Describes 11 studies.

Ernest J. Gaines, 1933-

Web Sites

"About the Author." *Vintage Books.* 19 Mar. 2000, http://www.randomhouse.com/vintage/gaines/bio.html.

Corrington Award: Ernest Gaines. 19 Mar. 2000, http://www2.centenary.edu/gaines.htm.

Biographies and Criticism

Babb, Valerie Melissa. *Ernest Gaines.* Boston: Twayne, 1991.

Byerman, Keith E. "Ernest J. Gaines." Davis and Harris, *Afro-American Fiction Writers after 1955* (*Dictionary of Literary Biography* 33) 84-96.

———. "Ernest J. Gaines." Giles and Giles, *American Novelists since World War II, Fourth Series* (*Dictionary of Literary Biography* 152) 51-64.

Grant, William E. "Ernest J. Gaines." Helterman and Layman, *American Novelists since World War II, First Series* (*Dictionary of Literary Biography* 2) 170-75.

Bibliographies

Cash, Jean W. "Ernest J. Gaines." Bruccoli and Baughman, *Bibliography of American Fiction, 1919-1988* 207-08.

Doyle, Mary Ellen. "Ernest J. Gaines: An Annotated Bibliography, 1956-1988." *Black American Literature Forum* 24 (Spring 1990): 125-50.
List works by and about Gaines.

Glitsch, Catherine. "Gaines, Ernest J." *American Novel Explication, 1991-1995* 92-94.

Reisman, Rosemary M. Canfield, and Suzanne Booker-Canfield. "Ernest J. Gaines." *Contemporary Southern Men Fiction Writers* [174]-90.
Describes about 70 critical studies.

Shelton, Frank W. "Ernest J. Gaines." Flora and Bain, *Fifty Southern Writers after 1900* 196-205.
Supplemented by Joseph M. Flora and Robert Bain, "Ernest J. Gaines," in Flora and Bain, *Contemporary Fiction Writers of the South* [515]-16.

Jerzy (Nikodem) Kosinski, 1933-1991

Web Sites

"Jerzy Kosinski." *American Literature on the Web.* 19 Mar. 2000, http://www.nagasaki-gaigo.ac.jp/ishikawa/amlit/k/kosinski21.htm.
Identifies several pages for Kosinski that offer selected fulltexts, selective bibliographies of works by and about him, and brief biographies.

Biographies and Criticism

Lavers, Norman. *Jerzy Kosinski.* Boston: Twayne, 1982.

Northouse, Cameron. "Jerzy N. Kosinski." Helterman and Layman, *American Novelists since World War II, First Series* (*Dictionary of Literary Biography* 2) 266-75.

Bibliographies

Cronin, Gloria L., and Blaine H. Hall. *Jerzy Kosinski: An Annotated Bibliography.* New York: Greenwood, 1991.
Includes selectively annotated entries for about 400 criticisms.

Everman, Welch D. "Kosinski, Jerzy." McCaffery, *Postmodern Fiction: A Bio-Bibliographical Guide* 434-37.

Glitsch, Catherine. "Kosinski, Jerzy." *American Novel Explication, 1991-1995* 148.

Walsh, Thomas P., and Cameron Northouse. *John Barth, Jerzy Kosinski, and Thomas Pynchon: A Reference Guide.* Boston: G. K. Hall, 1977.

Philip Roth, 1933-

Web Sites

Philip Roth. Ed. Derek Royal. Update and sponsor unknown. 19 Mar. 2000, http://www.ngc.peachnet.edu/Academic/Arts_Let/LangLit/dproyal/roth.htm. Contains a classified bibliography (unannotated) of works by and about Roth.

Philip Roth Page. Ed. and update unknown. George Mason U. 19 Mar. 2000, http://mason.gmu.edu/~reastlan/roth/. Contains summaries of selected works by Roth.

Biographies and Criticism

Halio, Jay L. *Philip Roth Revisited.* New York: Twayne, 1992.

Helterman, Jeffrey. "Philip Roth." Helterman and Layman, *American Novelists since World War II, First Series* (*Dictionary of Literary Biography* 2) 423-34.

Kremer, S. Lillian. "Philip Roth." Giles and Giles, *American Novelists since World War II, Fifth Series* (*Dictionary of Literary Biography* 173) 202-34.

"Philip Roth." Riley, *Contemporary Literary Criticism* 66:384-423.
Excerpts of criticism on Roth's novel *Portnoy's Complaint* from 1968-1989, with an annotated bibliography.

Pinsker, Sanford. "Philip Roth." Walden, *Twentieth-Century American-Jewish Fiction Writers* (*Dictionary of Literary Biography* 28) 264-75.

Bibliographies

Baumgarten, Murray, and Barbara Gottfried. "Philip Roth." Bruccoli and Baughman, *Bibliography of American Fiction, 1919-1988* 429-31.

Glitsch, Catherine. "Roth, Philip." *American Novel Explication, 1991-1995* 220.

Leavey, Ann. "Philip Roth: A Bibliographic Essay (1984-1988)." *Studies in American Jewish Literature* 8 (Fall 1989): 212-18.

"Philip (Milton) Roth." Harris and Fitzgerald, *Short Story Criticism* 26:226-71.
Excerpts of criticism on Roth from 1954-1992, with an annotated bibliography.

Rodgers, Bernard F., Jr. *Philip Roth: A Bibliography.* 2nd ed. Metuchen: Scarecrow, 1984.
Includes unannotated entries for about 820 works on Roth since 1954.

Shechner, Mark. "Philip Roth." Shatzky and Taub, *Contemporary Jewish-American Novelists* 335-54.

Joan Didion, 1934-

Web Sites

"Joan Didion." *American Literature on the Web*. 19 Mar. 2000, http://www.nagasaki-gaigo.ac.jp/ishikawa/amlit/d/didion21.htm.
List of links to fulltexts of selected works by Didion and works about her as well as to brief biographies.

Biographies and Criticism

Ashdown, Paul. "Joan Didion." Kaul, *American Literary Journalists, 1945-1995, First Series* (*Dictionary of Literary Biography* 185) 69-77.

Feldman, Paula R. "Joan Didion." Helterman and Layman, *American Novelists since World War II, First Series* (*Dictionary of Literary Biography* 2) 121-27.

Winchell, Mark Royden. "Joan Didion." Giles and Giles, *American Novelists since World War II, Fifth Series* (*Dictionary of Literary Biography* 173) 37-53.

———. *Joan Didion*. Rev. ed. Boston: Twayne, 1989.

Bibliographies

Cash, Jean W. "Joan Didion." Bruccoli and Baughman, *Bibliography of American Fiction, 1919-1988* 150-51.

Chabot, C. Barry. "Didion, Joan." McCaffery, *Postmodern Fiction: A Bio-Bibliographical Guide* 335-37.

Etulain, Richard W., and N. Jill Howard. "Joan Didion." *Bibliographical Guide to the Study of Western American Literature* 214-15.

Glitsch, Catherine. "Didion, Joan." *American Novel Explication, 1991-1995* 63

Henderson, Katherine Usher. "Bibliography of Writings by Joan Didion"; "Bibliography of Writings about Joan Didion." Pearlman, *American Women Writing Fiction* 86-93.

Jacobs, Fred Rue. *Joan Didion: Bibliography*. Keene: Loop, 1977.

Jason, Philip K. "Joan Didion." *Vietnam War in Literature* 89-90.
Describes six studies of *Democracy*.

Olendorf, Donna. "Joan Didion: A Checklist, 1955-1980." *Bulletin of Bibliography* 38 (Jan.-Mar. 1981): 32-44.

LeRoi Jones (Imamu Amiri Baraka), 1934-

Web Sites

Amiri Baraka. 19 Mar. 2000, http://www.math.buffalo.edu/~sww/poetry/baraka_jones.html.
Fulltexts of many poems of Baraka.

"Chapter 10: Late Twentieth Century: 1945 to the Present: Amiri Baraka / LeRoi Jones." *PAL: Perspectives in American Literature*. 19 Mar. 2000, http://www.csustan.edu/english/reuben/pal/chap10/baraka.html.

Biographies and Criticism

"Amiri Baraka." Riley, *Contemporary Literary Criticism* 115:1-51.
Excerpts of criticism on Baraka from 1963-1997, with an annotated bibliography.

"Amiri Baraka." Trudeau, *Drama Criticism* 6:1-38.
Excerpts of criticism on Baraka in general and on *Dutchman, The Toilet*, and *Slave Ship* from 1964-1994, with an annotated bibliography.

"Amiri Baraka." Young, *Poetry Criticism* 4:1-41.
Excerpts of comments and criticism on Baraka from 1960-1986, with an annotated bibliography.

Gaffney, Floyd. "Amiri Baraka (LeRoi Jones)." Davis and Harris, *Afro-American Writers after 1955: Dramatists and Prose Writers (Dictionary of Literary Biography* 38) 22-42.

Gardner, Stephen. "Amiri Baraka (LeRoi Jones)." Greiner, *American Poets since World War II, First Series (Dictionary of Literary Biography* 5) 21-27.

Hurst, Catherine Daniels. "Amiri Baraka (LeRoi Jones)." MacNicholas, *Twentieth-Century American Dramatists (Dictionary of Literary Biography* 7) 49-56.

Miller, James A. "Amiri Baraka (LeRoi Jones)." Charters, *The Beats: Literary Bohemians in Postwar America (Dictionary of Literary Biography* 16) 3-24.

Bibliographies

Bonner, Thomas, Jr. "Amiri Baraka (LeRoi Jones)." Kolin, *American Playwrights since 1945* [51]-65.

Carpenter, Charles A. "Baraka, [Imamu] Amiri (LeRoi Jones)." *Modern Drama Scholarship and Criticism, 1981-1990* 50-51.

Dace, Letitia. "Amiri Baraka (LeRoi Jones)." Inge, Duke, and Bryer, *Black American Writers* II, 121-78.
Survey of research.

———. *LeRoi Jones (Imamu Amiri Baraka): A Checklist of Works by and about Him*. London: Nether, 1971.
Complete bibliographic descriptions for Baraka's works and an unannotated list of about 1,000 works on him.

Jackson, Paul K., Jr. "Amiri Baraka (LeRoi Jones)." Roudane, *Contemporary Authors: Bibliographical Series: American Dramatists* 49-68.
Survey of research.

King, Kimball. " Amiri Baraka" King, *Ten Modern American Playwrights* 109-35.

Lawlor, William. "Amiri Baraka (1934-)." *Beat Generation: A Bibliographical Teaching Guide* 242-44.
Very brief up-to-date critical survey.

Leo, John R. "Baraka, Imamu Amiri (LeRoi Jones)." *Guide to American Poetry Explication* 19-21.

Audre Lorde, 1934-1992

Web Sites

"Audre Lorde." *New York State Writers Institute.* 19 Mar. 2000, http://www.albany.edu/writers-inst/lorde.html.

"Audre Lorde." *Heath Anthology.* 13 Mar. 2000, http://www.georgetown.edu/bassr/heath/syllabuild/iguide/lorde.html.
Page includes a good bibliography.

Audre Lorde. 19 Mar. 2000, http://www.lambda.net/~maximum/lorde.html.

Audre Lorde. 19 Mar. 2000, http://www.emory.edu/ENGLISH/Bahri/RYAN.HTML.

Biographies and Criticism

"Audre Lorde." Riley, *Contemporary Literary Criticism* 71:230-64.
Excerpts of criticism on Lorde from 1979-1989, with an annotated bibliography.

"Audre Lorde." Young, *Poetry Criticism* 12:133-61.
Excerpts of comments and criticism on Lorde from 1977-1993, with an annotated bibliography.

McClaurin-Allen, Irma. "Audre Lorde." Harris and Davis, *Afro-American Poets since 1955 (Dictionary of Literary Biography* 41) 217-22.

Bibliographies

Leo, John R. "Lorde, Audre." *Guide to American Poetry Explication* 243-44.

Upton, Elaine Maria. "Audre Lorde (1934-1992)." Pollack and Knight, *Contemporary Lesbian Writers of the United States* [316]-24.

N(avarre) Scott Momaday, 1934-

Web Sites

"N. Scott Momaday." *Heath Anthology.* 13 Mar. 2000, http://www.georgetown.edu/bassr/heath/syllabuild/iguide/momaday.html.

Biographies and Criticism

"*House Made of Dawn*: N. Scott Momaday." Riley, *Contemporary Literary Criticism* 95:213-81.
Excerpts of criticism on Momaday's novel from 1970-1987, with an annotated bibliography.

"N. Scott Momaday." Riley, *Contemporary Literary Criticism* 85:222-83.
Excerpts of criticism on Momaday from 1967-1993, with an annotated bibliography.

Schubnell, Matthias. "N. Scott Momaday." Roemer, *Native American Writers of the United States* (*Dictionary of Literary Biography* 175) 174-86.

Velie, Alan R. "N. Scott Momaday." Giles and Giles, *American Novelists since World War II, Third Series* (*Dictionary of Literary Biography* 143) 159-70.

Bibliographies

Etulain, Richard W., and N. Jill Howard. "N. Scott Momaday." *Bibliographical Guide to the Study of Western American Literature* 314-16.

Glitsch, Catherine. "Momaday, N. Scott." *American Novel Explication, 1991-1995* 176.

Gunter, Susan Elizabeth. "N. Scott Momaday." Bruccoli and Baughman, *Bibliography of American Fiction, 1919-1988* 354-55.

Leo, John R. "Momaday, N. Scott." *Guide to American Poetry Explication* 273-74.

"N. Scott Momaday." Young, *Poetry Criticism* 25:183-222.
Excerpts of comments and criticism on Momaday from 1967-1993, with an annotated bibliography.

Trimble, Martha Scott. "N. Scott Momaday." Erisman and Etulain, *Fifty Western Writers* 313-24.

Tomás Rivera, 1935-1984

Web Sites

"Tomás Rivera." *Heath Anthology.* 13 Mar. 2000, http://www.georgetown.edu/bassr/heath/syllabuild/iguide/rivera.html.

Biographies and Criticism

Leal, Luis. "Tomás Rivera." Lomelí and Shirley, *Chicano Writers, First Series* (*Dictionary of Literary Biography* 82) 206-13.

Bibliographies

Etulain, Richard W., and N. Jill Howard. "Tomás Rivera." *Bibliographical Guide to the Study of Western American Literature* 348-49.

Somoza, Oscar U. "Tomás Rivera." Bruccoli and Baughman, *Bibliography of American Fiction 1919-1988* 421-23.

Spence, Juliette L. "Bibliography of Writings about Tomás Rivera and His Works." Vernon E. Lattin, Rolando Hinojosa, and Gary D. Keller, eds. *Tomas Rivera 1935-1984: The Man and His Work.* Tempe: Bilingual Rev. P, 1988. 153-58.

Clarence Major, 1936-

Web Sites

Clarence Major. Ed. unknown. 9 Oct. 1997. Sponsor unknown. 19 Mar. 2000, http://wwwenglish.ucdavis.edu/faculty/cmajor/cmajor.htm.
Very dense bibliographical essay in paragraph form. Lists the major works of Major incompletely and only alludes to his contributions to periodicals. Site could be improved by completing bibliographic citations.

Biographies and Criticism

Weixlmann, Joe. "Clarence Major." Davis and Harris, *Afro-American Fiction Writers after 1955* (*Dictionary of Literary Biography* 33) 153-61.

Bibliographies

Burris, William. "Clarence Major." Nagel, Nagel, and Baughman, *Bibliography of American Fiction, 1866-1918* 279.

Glitsch, Catherine. "Major, Clarence." *American Novel Explication, 1991-1995* 167.

Weixlmann, Joe. "Toward a Primary Bibliography of Clarence Major." *Black American Literature Forum* 13 (1979): 70-72.

Thomas Pynchon, 1937-

Web Sites

Lots of Thomas Pynchon Links. 19 Mar. 2000, http://www.city-net.com/~argus/pynchon.html.

Pynchon Notes. Ed. John M. Krafft. 29 June 1999. Miami U (Hamilton, OH). 19 Mar. 2000, http://www.ham.muohio.edu/~krafftjm/pynchon.html.
Contents of current and forthcoming issues, cumulative index, subscription information, and links to other Pynchon pages.

"Thomas Pynchon." *American Literature on the Web*. 19 Mar. 2000, http://www.nagasaki-gaigo.ac.jp/ishikawa/amlit/p/pynchon21.htm.
Excellent classified list of links for works by and about Pynchon.

Biographies and Criticism

Chambers, Judith. *Thomas Pynchon*. New York: Twayne, 1992.

Duyfhuizen, Bernard, and John M. Krafft. "Thomas Pynchon." Giles and Giles, *American Novelists since World War II, Fifth Series* (*Dictionary of Literary Biography* 173) 177-201.

Stark, John. "Thomas Pynchon." Helterman and Layman, *American Novelists since World War II, First Series* (*Dictionary of Literary Biography* 2) 411-17.

"Thomas Pynchon." Harris and Fitzgerald, *Short Story Criticism* 14:307-50.
Excerpts of criticism on Pynchon from 1974-1986, with an annotated bibliography.

"Thomas Pynchon." Riley, *Contemporary Literary Criticism* 62:430-55.
 Excerpts of criticism on Pynchon from 1986-1990, with an annotated bibliography.

"Thomas Pynchon: *The Crying of Lot 49.*" Riley, *Contemporary Literary Criticism* 72:294-342.
 Excerpts of criticism on Pynchon's novel from 1966-1987, with an annotated bibliography.

Journals

Pynchon Notes. Eau Claire: U of Wisconsin, 1979- .
 Features a current bibliography of Pynchon scholarship.

Bibliographies

Etulain, Richard W., and N. Jill Howard. "Thomas Pynchon." *Bibliographical Guide to the Study of Western American Literature* 340-41.

Glitsch, Catherine. "Pynchon, Thomas." *American Novel Explication, 1991-1995* 208-10.

Mead, Clifford. *Thomas Pynchon: A Bibliography of Primary and Secondary Materials*. Elmwood Park: Dalkey Archive, 1989.
 Brief bibliographic information for Pynchon's works and unannotated listings of about 1,500 works on him since 1962.

Newman, Robert D. "Thomas Pynchon." Bruccoli and Baughman, *Bibliography of American Fiction, 1919-1988* 413-14.

Tololyan, Khachig. "Pynchon, Thomas." McCaffery, *Postmodern Fiction: A Bio-Bibliographical Guide* 488-91.

Michael S. Harper, 1938-

Web Sites

Celebrating Harper: An Exhibition in Honor of Michael S. Harper. Eds. Susan Ravdin and Rosemary L. Cullen. Update unknown. Brown U. 19 Mar. 2000, http://www.brown.edu/Facilities/University_Library/publications/Harper/Harper_home.html.
 Text of exhibitions at Bowdoin C and Brown U, with a bibliography of Harper's works located at Brown.

"Michael S. Harper." *Heath Anthology*. 13 Mar. 2000, http://www.georgetown.edu/bassr/heath/syllabuild/iguide/harperm.html.

Biographies and Criticism

Clark, Norris B. "Michael S. Harper." Harris and Davis, *Afro-American Poets since 1955 (Dictionary of Literary Biography* 41) 152-66.

Bibliographies

Leo, John R. "Harper, Michael." *Guide to American Poetry Explication* 199-200.

Joyce Carol Oates, 1938-

Web Sites

Celestial Timepiece: A Joyce Carol Oates Home Page. Ed. Randy Souther. 2 Apr. 1999. U of San Francisco. 19 Mar. 2000, http://storm.usfca.edu/~southerr/jco. html.
Well-organized site that offers selective bibliographic guidance as well as information about Oates's career. "Works" gives the fulltext of "Where Are You Going, Where Have You Been?" (from an unspecified edition) but otherwise only provides images of dust jackets with bibliographic information, excerpts from works, and citations for reviews; separate links connect to excerpts of Oates's comments on other writers, such as Plath, Updike, and Shakespeare. "Criticism and Bibliography" contains a list of studies of "Where Are You Going, Where Have You Been?" and selected general books and articles, with links to their title pages and excerpts, and also excerpts from biographies of Oates.

"Joyce Carol Oates." *Bohemian Ink.* 19 Mar. 2000, http://www.levity.com/corduroy/ oates.htm.

"Joyce Carol Oates." *New York State Writer's Institute.* 19 Mar. 2000, http://www.albany. edu/writers-inst/oates.html.

Salon Magazine: Joyce Carol Oates. 19 Mar. 2000, http://www.salon1999.com/06/ departments/litchat.html.
Interview transcript.

Biographies and Criticism

Batman, Alex. "Joyce Carol Oates." Greiner, *American Poets since World War II, First Series* (*Dictionary of Literary Biography* 5) 99-102.

Creighton, Joanne V. *Joyce Carol Oates: Novels of the Middle Years.* New York: Twayne, 1992.

Johnson, Greg. *Joyce Carol Oates: A Study of the Short Fiction.* New York: Twayne, 1994.

Joslin, Michael. "Joyce Carol Oates." Helterman and Layman, *American Novelists since World War II, First Series* (*Dictionary of Literary Biography* 2) 371-81.

"Joyce Carol Oates." Harris and Fitzgerald, *Short Story Criticism* 6:222-56.
Excerpts of criticism on Oates from 1966-1988, with an annotated bibliography.

"Joyce Carol Oates." Riley, *Contemporary Literary Criticism* 108:338-97.
Excerpts of criticism on Oates from 1964-1995, with an annotated bibliography.

Wesley, Marilyn C. "Joyce Carol Oates." Meanor, *American Short-Story Writers since World War II* (*Dictionary of Literary Biography* 130) 241-52.

Bibliographies

Baughman, Judith S. "Joyce Carol Oates." Bruccoli and Baughman, *Bibliography of American Fiction, 1919-1988* 385-88.

———. "Joyce Carol Oates." Bruccoli and Baughman, *Modern Women Writers* 27-35.

Glitsch, Catherine. "Oates, Joyce Carol." *American Novel Explication, 1991-1995* 195-96.

Hiemstra, Anne. "Bibliography of Writings by Joyce Carol Oates"; "Bibliography of Writings about Joyce Carol Oates." Pearlman, *American Women Writing Fiction* 28-44.

Lercangee, Francine. *Joyce Carol Oates: An Annotated Bibliography*. New York: Garland, 1986.
Brief bibliographic descriptions of Oates's works and annotated entries for about 2,000 works on her.

Wiedemann, Barbara. "Joyce Carol Oates: 'Where Are You Going, Where Have You Been?' " Evans, Little, and Wiedemann, *Short Fiction* 173-80.
Describes 14 studies.

Ishmael (Scott) Reed, 1938-

Web Sites

"Ishmael Reed." *Heath Anthology*. 13 Mar. 2000, http://www.georgetown.edu/bassr/heath/syllabuild/iguide/reed.html.

Ishmael Reed by Spring. 19 Mar. 2000, http://www.math.buffalo.edu/~sww/reed/reed_ishmael0.html.

Biographies and Criticism

Bokinsky, Caroline G. "Ishmael Reed." Greiner, *American Poets since World War II, First Series* (*Dictionary of Literary Biography* 5) 180-84.

Duff, Gerald. "Ishmael Reed." Helterman and Layman, *American Novelists since World War II, First Series* (*Dictionary of Literary Biography* 2) 417-22.

Friedman, Robert S. "Ishmael Reed." Conte, *American Poets since World War II, Fifth Series* (*Dictionary of Literary Biography* 169) 224-34.

Gates, Henry Louis. "Ishmael Reed." Davis and Harris, *Afro-American Fiction Writers after 1955* (*Dictionary of Literary Biography* 33) 219-32.

"Ishmael Reed." Riley, *Contemporary Literary Criticism* 60:299-315.
Excerpts of criticism on Reed from 1974-1989, with an annotated bibliography.

Bibliographies

Duff, Gerld. "Reed, Ishmael." McCaffery, *Postmodern Fiction: A Bio-Bibliographical Guide* 493-96.

Etulain, Richard W., and N. Jill Howard. "Emmett Coleman (Ishmael Reed)." *Bibliographical Guide to the Study of Western American Literature* 198-99.

Glitsch, Catherine. "Reed, Ishmael." *American Novel Explication, 1991-1995* 212-13.

Martin, Reginald, and Margaret Donovan DuPriest. "Ishmael Reed." Bruccoli and Baughman, *Bibliography of American Fiction, 1919-1988* 418-19.

———. "Ishmael Reed." Bruccoli and Baughman, *Modern African American Writers* 47-50.
Revises and updates Martin and DuPriest, above.

Settle, Elizabeth A., and Thomas A. Settle. *Ishmael Reed: A Primary and Secondary Bibliography*. Boston: G. K. Hall, 1982.
Describe works by Reed and about 700 works on him.

Ward, Jerry W., Jr. "Ishmael Reed." Bain and Flora, *Contemporary Poets, Dramatists, Essayists, and Novelists of the South* [407]-17.

Charles Simic, 1938-

Web Sites

"Charles Simic." *Academy of American Poets*. 9 Mar. 2000, http://www.poets.org/lit/poet/csimifst.htm.

"Charles D. Simic." *Poetry Page*. Ed. Fred Muratori. 3 Nov. 1998. Cornell U. 19 Mar. 2000, http://oprf.com/Simic/index.html.
Text of "Against Winter" and selected interviews, list of works by and selected works about Simic, and brief biography.

Biographies and Criticism

"Charles Simic." Riley, *Contemporary Literary Criticism* 68:362-79.
Excerpts of criticism on Simic from 1972-1991.

Kirby, David. "Charles Simic." Gwynn, *American Poets since World War II, Second Series* (*Dictionary of Literary Biography* 105) 216-26.

Bibliographies

Avery, Brian C. "A Simic Bibliography." Bruce Weigl, ed. *Charles Simic: Essays on the Poetry*. Ann Arbor: U of Michigan P, 1996. 226-33.

Leo, John R. "Simic, Charles." *Guide to American Poetry Explication* 371.

Toni Cade Bambara, 1939-1995

Web Sites

In Praise of Toni Cade Bambara. 19 Mar. 2000, http://www.inmotionmagazine.com/bambara.html.

"Toni Cade Bambara." *Writing and Resistance*. 19 Mar. 2000, http://www.public.asu.edu/~metro/aflit/bambara/index.html.

Biographies and Criticism

Deck, Alice A. "Toni Cade Bambara." Davis and Harris, *Afro-American Writers after 1955: Dramatists and Prose Writers* (*Dictionary of Literary Biography* 38) 12-22.

"Toni Cade Bambara." Riley, *Contemporary Literary Criticism* 88:1-56.
Excerpts of criticism on Bambara from 1979-1992, with an annotated bibliography.

Bibliographies

Glitsch, Catherine. "Bambara, Toni Cade." *American Novel Explication, 1991-1995* 24.

Hargrove, Nancy D. "Toni Cade Bambara." Flora and Bain, *Contemporary Fiction Writers of the South* [32]-45.

Reisman, Rosemary M. Canfield, and Christopher J. Canfield. "Toni Cade Bambara." *Contemporary Southern Women Fiction Writers* [48]-56.
Describes 28 critical works.

Vertreace, Martha M. "Bibliography of Writings about Toni Cade Bambara," "Bibliography of Writings by Toni Cade Bambara." Pearlman, *American Women Writing Fiction* 166-71.

Raymond Carver, 1939-1989

Web Sites

GVB's Raymond Carver Page. Ed. Gregory Van Belle. 14 Oct. 1999. Edmonds Community C. 19 Mar. 2000, http://web.edcc.edu/gvb/carver.html.
Links to other Carver resources.

"Raymond Carver." *Pegasos*. 19 Mar. 2000, http://www.kirjasto.sci.fi/rcarver.htm.

Raymond Carver. Ed. unknown. 4 Jun. 1999. Sponsor unknown. 19 Mar. 2000, http://world.std.com/~ptc/.

Raymond Carver. Eds. Tom Luce and Brent Bryan. 20 Sept. 1997. Whitman C. 19 Mar. 2000, http://people.whitman.edu/~lucetb/carver/carver.cgi.
Authoritative site contains resources provided by Tess Gallagher, with a scholarly biography and chronology by William L. Stull, tables of contents of 14 major works by Carver, images of four working-draft copies of Carver's poem "Shooting," and photos of Carver's Port Angeles and Yakima haunts.

Biographies and Criticism

Campbell, Ewing. *Raymond Carver: A Study of the Short Fiction*. New York: Twayne, 1992.

Meyer, Adam. *Raymond Carver*. New York: Twayne, 1994.

Nordgen, Joe. "Raymond Carver." Meanor, *American Short-Story Writers since World War II* (*Dictionary of Literary Biography* 130) 65-74.

"Raymond Carver." Harris and Fitzgerald, *Short Story Criticism* 8:1-62.
Excerpts of criticism on Carver from 1976-1989, with an annotated bibliography.

Bibliographies

Etulain, Richard W., and N. Jill Howard. "Raymond Carver." *Bibliographical Guide to the Study of Western American Literature* 169.

Gunter, Susan. "Raymond Carver." Bruccoli and Baughman, *Bibliography of American Fiction 1919-1988* 124-25.

Mazza, Cris. "Carver, Raymond." McCaffery, *Postmodern Fiction: A Bio-Bibliographical Guide* 300-302.

Stull, William. "Raymond Carver: A Bibliographical Checklist." *American Book Collector* 8 (Jan. 1987): 17-30.

Maxine Hong Kingston, 1940-

Web Sites

"Maxine Hong Kingston." *American Literature on the Web*. 19 Mar. 2000, http://www.nagasaki-gaigo.ac.jp/ishikawa/amlit/k/kingston21.htm.

"Maxine Hong Kingston." *Voices from the Gaps: Women Writers of Color*. 19 Mar. 2000, http://voices.cla.umn.edu/authors/MaxineHongKingston.html.
Biography needs clearer focus and site needs better external links.

Maxine Hong Kingston: Warrior Woman. 19 Mar. 2000, http://www.cwrl.utexas.edu/~natasha/usauto_html/kingston/.

Biographies and Criticism

Feng, Pin-chia. "Maxine Hong Kingston." Giles and Giles, *American Novelists since World War II, Fifth Series* (*Dictionary of Literary Biography* 173) 84-97.

Lawrence, Keith, and John Dye. "Maxine Hong Kingston." Cracroft, *Twentieth-Century American Western Writers, Second Series* (*Dictionary of Literary Biography* 212) 153-63

Simmons, Diane. *Maxine Hong Kingston*. New York: Twayne, 1999.

"*The Warrior Woman*: Maxine Hong Kingston." Riley, *Contemporary Literary Criticism* 121:243-329.
Excerpts of criticism on Kingston's novel from 1979-1996, with an annotated bibliography.

Bibliographies

Currier, Susan. "Kingston, Maxine Hong." McCaffery, *Postmodern Fiction: A Bio-Bibliographical Guide* 427-29.

Etulain, Richard W., and N. Jill Howard. "Maxine Hong Kingston." *Bibliographical Guide to the Study of Western American Literature* 279-80.

Glitsch, Catherine. "Kingston, Maxine Hong." *American Novel Explication, 1991-1995* 146.

Bobbie Ann Mason, 1940-

Web Sites

Bobbie Ann Mason's Home Page. Eds. vary. 28 Apr. 1999. Eastern Illinios U. 19 Mar. 2000, http://www.eiu.edu/~eng1002/authors/mason2/.
Student-produced site with brief biography, list of works by Mason with summaries, links to other sites.

Biographies and Criticism

"Bobbie Ann Mason." Harris and Fitzgerald, *Short Story Criticism* 4:298-311.
Excerpts of criticism on Mason from 1982-1989, with an annotated bibliography.

"Bobbie Ann Mason." Riley, *Contemporary Literary Criticism* 82:232-61.
Excerpts of criticism on Mason from 1987-1993, with an annotated bibliography.

Kalb, John D. "Bobbie Ann Mason." Giles and Giles, *American Novelists since World War II, Fifth Series* (*Dictionary of Literary Biography* 173) 118-31.

Wilhelm, Albert. *Bobbie Ann Mason: A Study of the Short Fiction.* New York: Twayne, 1998.

Bibliographies

Flora, Joseph M. "Bobbie Ann Mason." Flora and Bain, *Contemporary Fiction Writers of the South* [275]-85.

Glitsch, Catherine. "Mason, Bobbie Ann." *American Novel Explication, 1991-1995* 171.

Jason, Philip K. "Bobbie Ann Mason." *Vietnam War in Literature* 130-34.
Describes 17 studies of *In Country*.

Reisman, Rosemary M. Canfield, and Christopher J. Canfield. "Bobbie Ann Mason." *Contemporary Southern Women Fiction Writers* [118]-25.
Describes 30 critical works.

Robert Pinsky, 1940-

Web Sites

America's Wordsmith. 19 Mar. 2000, http://www.pbs.org/newshour/bb/entertainment/april97/poet_4-2.html.
"In a discussion with Elizabeth Farnsworth, America's newest Poet Laureate, Robert Pinsky, discusses the state of poetry in America, his new job and poetry in cyberspace."

"Robert Pinsky."*Academy of American Poets*. 9 Mar. 2000, http://www.poets.org/lit/
poet/rpinsfst.htm.
Site includes texts of two poems ("Shirt" and "The Refinery") and a brief bio-
graphical sketch and a good list of external links; latest update has omitted to list
Pinsky's major works and awards, and the biographical sketch fails to emphasize
Pinsky's importance as a translator. Also at site: "Interview: Robert Pinsky."

Robert Pinsky. 19 Mar. 2000, http://www.barclayagency.com/pinsky.html.
Public relations site.

Biographies and Criticism

"Robert Pinsky." Riley, *Contemporary Literary Criticism* 94:297-323.
Excerpts of criticism on Pinsky from 1985-1995, with an annotated bibliography.

"Robert Pinsky." Riley, *Contemporary Literary Criticism* 121:422-55.
Excerpts of criticism on Pinsky from 1993-1997, with an annotated bibliography.

Bibliographies

Leo, John R. "Pinsky, Robert." *Guide to American Poetry Explication* 301.

David (William) Rabe, 1940-

Web Sites

Beyond Knowing. 19 Mar. 2000, http://www.citypaper.net/articles/032698/crtms.
rabe.shtml.

Biographies and Criticism

Patterson, James A. "David Rabe." MacNicholas, *Twentieth-Century American
Dramatists* (*Dictionary of Literary Biography* 7) 172-78.

Bibliographies

Carpenter, Charles A. "Rabe, David." *Modern Drama Scholarship and Criticism,
1981-1990* 80-81.

Jason, Philip K. "David Rabe." *Vietnam War in Literature* 146-53.
Describes 30 works on "Vietnam Trilogy."

Kolin, Philip C. "David Rabe." Kolin, *American Playwrights since 1945* [349]-68.

———. *David Rabe: A Stage History and a Primary and Secondary Bibliography*.
New York: Garland, 1988.
Brief information on works by Rabe and annotated entries for about 1,100
works on Rabe.

Simard, Rodney. "David Rabe." Roudane, *Contemporary Authors: Bibliographical
Series: American Dramatists* 289-303.
Survey of research.

Edmund White, 1940-

Web Sites

"Edmund Valentine White III." *Knitting Circle*. 19 Mar. 2000, http://www.sbu.ac.uk/
~stafflag/edmundwhite.html.
This site includes a very brief biographical sketch, bibliography of White's
works, excerpts from book reviews and from press cuttings. The biographical sketch
and the bibliography of criticism should both be expanded. Includes important internal link to the Violet Quill web site and other internal links. Includes external links.

Salon: Books: Edmund White. 19 Mar. 2000, http://www.salonmagazine.com/books/int/
1997/10/15white.html.

Biographies and Criticism

"Edmund White." Riley, *Contemporary Literary Criticism* 110:311-45.
Excerpts of criticism on White from 1980-1995, with an annotated bibliography.

Bibliographies

Bergman, David. "Edmund White Checklist." *Review of Contemporary Fiction* 16
(Fall 1996): 88-89.

Glitsch, Catherine. "White, Edmund." *American Novel Explication, 1991-1995* 267.

McKercher, Pat. "White, Edmund." McCaffery, *Postmodern Fiction: A Bio-
Bibliographical Guide* 542-45.

Diane Glancy, 1941-

Web Site

"Diane Glancy." *Voices from the Gaps: Women Writers of Color*. 19 Mar. 2000,
http://voices.cla.umn.edu/Authors/DianeGlancy.html.

Biographies and Criticism

Abner, Julie LaMay. "Diane Glancy." Roemer, *Native American Writers of the
United States* (*Dictionary of Literary Biography* 175) 105-08.

Simon Ortiz, 1941-

Web Sites

Sand Creek, Poems by Simon Ortiz. 19 Mar. 2000, http://ram.ramlink.net/~napora/
ortiz.htm.

"Simon J. Ortiz." *North American Native Authors Catalog*. 19 Mar. 2000,
http://www.nativeauthors.com/search/bio/bioortiz.html.

Biographies and Criticism

Scarberry-García, Susan. "Simon J. Ortiz." Roemer, *Native American Writers of the United States* (*Dictionary of Literary Biography* 175) 208-21.

Schein, Marie M. "Simon Ortiz." Gwynn, *American Poets since World War II, Third Series* (*Dictionary of Literary Biography* 120) 231-34.

"Simon J. Ortiz." Young, *Poetry Criticism* 17:221-46.
Excerpts of comments and criticism on Ortiz from 1982-1995, with an annotated bibliography.

Bibliographies

Etulain, Richard W., and N. Jill Howard. "Simon Ortiz." *Bibliographical Guide to the Study of Western American Literature* 331.

Leo, John R. "Ortiz, Simon." *Guide to American Poetry Explication* 298.

Ruoff, LaVonne Brown. "Simon Ortiz: A.S.A.I.L. Bibliography 7." *Studies in American Indian Literature* 8 (Summer-Fall 1984): 57-58.

Anne Tyler, 1941-

Web Sites

"Anne Tyler." *Pegasos*. 13 Mar. 2000, http://www.kirjasto.sci.fi/atyler.htm.

Biographies and Criticism

"Anne Tyler." Riley, *Contemporary Literary Criticism* 103:214-78.
Excerpts of criticism on Tyler from 1985-1995, with an annotated bibliography.

Brooks, Mary Ellen. "Anne Tyler." Kibler, *American Novelists since World War II, Second Series* (*Dictionary of Literary Biography* 6) 336-45.

Evans, Elizabeth. *Anne Tyler*. New York: Twayne, 1993.

Petry, Alice Hall. *Understanding Anne Tyler*. Columbia: U of South Carolina P, 1990.

Town, Caren J. "Anne Tyler." Giles and Giles, *American Novelists since World War II, Third Series* (*Dictionary of Literary Biography* 143) 232-49.

Dictionaries, Encyclopedias, and Handbooks

Croft, Robert W. *Anne Tyler Companion*. Westport: Greenwood, 1998.

Bibliographies

Croft, Robert William. *Anne Tyler: A Bio-Bibliography*. Westport: Greenwood, 1995.
Includes a critical biography, brief bibliographic information for Tyler's works, and selective critically annotated entries for about 400 works on her.

Gardiner, Elaine, and Catherine Rainwater. "Bibliography of Writings by Anne Tyler." Catherine Rainwater and William J. Scheick, eds. *Contemporary American Women Writers: Narrative Strategies.* Lexington: UP of Kentucky, 1985. 142-52.

Glitsch, Catherine. "Tyler, Anne." *American Novel Explication, 1991-1995* 249-50.

Nesanovich, Stella. "Anne Tyler Checklist, 1959-1980." *Bulletin of Bibliography* 38 (Apr.-June 1981): 53-64.

Petry, Alice Hall. "Anne Tyler." Bruccoli and Baughman, *Modern Women Writers* 62-66.

Reisman, Rosemary M. Canfield, and Christopher J. Canfield. "Anne Tyler." *Contemporary Southern Women Fiction Writers* [175]-81.
Describes 27 critical works.

Zahlan, Anne R. "Anne Tyler." Flora and Bain, *Contemporary Fiction Writers of the South* [441]-56.

———. "Anne Tyler." Flora and Bain, *Fifty Southern Writers after 1900* 491-504.

John Edgar Wideman, 1941-

Web Sites

"John Edgar Wideman." *Heath Anthology.* 13 Mar. 2000, http://www.georgetown.edu/bassr/heath/syllabuild/iguide/wideman.html.

Salon: John Edgar Wideman. 3 Mar. 2000, http://www.salon.com/nov96/interview961111.html.
Interview article.

Biographies and Criticism

Byerman, Keith E. "John Edgar Wideman." Giles and Giles, *American Novelists since World War II, Third Series* (*Dictionary of Literary Biography* 143) 321-32.

———. *John Edgar Wideman: A Study of the Short Fiction.* New York: Twayne, 1998.

"John Edgar Wideman." Riley, *Contemporary Literary Criticism* 67:369-92.
Excerpts of criticism on Wideman from 1986-1991, with an annotated bibliography.

Samuels, Wilfred D. "John Edgar Wideman." Davis and Harris, *Afro-American Fiction Writers after 1955* (*Dictionary of Literary Biography* 33) 271-78.

Bibliographies

Glitsch, Catherine. "Wideman, John Edgar." *American Novel Explication, 1991-1995* 267-68.

Richard, Jean-Pierre. "John Edgar Wideman: A Bibliography of Primary and Secondary Sources." *Callaloo* 22.3 (1999):750-57.

Samuel R. Delany, 1942-

Web Sites

Samuel R. Delany. 19 Mar. 2000, http://www.eden.com/~prost/delany/.

Samuel R. Delany. 19 Mar. 2000, http://hubcap.clemson.edu/~sparks/sff/delany.html.

Samuel R. Delany Information. Ed. Jay Schuster. 7 Mar. 2000. Physician's Computer Company. 19 Mar. 2000, http://www.pcc.com/~jay/delany/.
Biography; bibliography of works by and about Delany with texts of reviews; and links to other resources (many empty).

Biographies and Criticism

Alterman, Peter S. "Samuel R. Delany." Cowart and Wymer, *Twentieth-Century American Science-Fiction Writers* (*Dictionary of Literary Biography* 8) 119-28.

Govan, Sandra Y. "Samuel R. Delany." Davis and Harris, *Afro-American Fiction Writers after 1955* (*Dictionary of Literary Biography* 33) 52-59.

Bibliographies

Bravard, Robert S., and Michael W. Peplow. "Through a Glass Darkly: Bibliographing Samuel R. Delany." *Black American Literature Forum* 18 (Summer 1984): 69-75.

Cooper, Rebecca. "Samuel R. Delany Checklist." *Review of Contemporary Fiction* 16 (Fall 1996): 170-71.

Glitsch, Catherine. "Delany, Samuel R." *American Novel Explication, 1991-1995* 59-60.

Peplow, Michael W., and Robert S. Bravard. *Samuel R. Delany: A Primary and Secondary Bibliography: 1962-1979.* Boston: G. K. Hall, 1980.
Describes Delany's works and 274 critical studies about him.

Slusser, George. "Delany, Samuel R." McCaffery, *Postmodern Fiction: A Bio-Bibliographical Guide* 320-23.

Barry Hannah, 1942-

Web Sites

"Barry Hannah." *Mississippi Writers Page.* 19 Mar. 2000, http://www.olemiss.edu/depts/english/ms-writers/dir/hannah_barry/.

Biographies and Criticism

"Barry Hannah." Riley, *Contemporary Literary Criticism* 90:124-65.
Excerpts of criticism on Hannah from 1982-1995, with an annotated bibliography.

Charney, Mark J. *Barry Hannah.* New York: Twayne, 1991.

Israel, Charles. "Barry Hannah." Kibler, *American Novelists since World War II, Second Series* (*Dictionary of Literary Biography* 6) 131-33.

Bibliographies

Gilman, Owen W., Jr. "Barry Hannah." Flora and Bain, *Contemporary Fiction Writers of the South* [213]-21.

Israel, Charles. "Hannah, Barry." McCaffery, *Postmodern Fiction: A Bio-Bibliographical Guide* 392-94.

Reisman, Rosemary M. Canfield, and Suzanne Booker-Canfield. "Barry Hannah." *Contemporary Southern Men Fiction Writers* [224]-36.
Describes about 40 critical studies.

Louise Glück, 1943-

Web Sites

"Louise Glück." *Academy of American Poets*. 8 Mar. 2000, http://www.poets.org/lit/poet/lglucfst.htm.

Louise Glück. 19 Mar. 2000, http://members.tripod.com/~oedipa/gluck.html.
Texts of six selections from *Ararat* and nine selections from *The Wild Iris*. Principal link is outdated.

Louise Glück. 19 Mar. 2000, http://www.kingsnet.com/users/monkey/~Brooke~Gluck.htm.
Fulltexts of 15 poems.

Biographies and Criticism

"Louise Glück." Young, *Poetry Criticism* 16:122-74.
Excerpts of comments and criticism on Glück from 1969-1996, with an annotated bibliography.

Trakas, Deno. "Louise Glück." Greiner, *American Poets since World War II, First Series* (*Dictionary of Literary Biography* 5) 290-95.

Bibliographies

Friedman, Paula. "Louise Glück: Primary Source Bibliography (1966-1986)." *Bulletin of Bibliography* 44 (Dec. 1987): 281-85.

Leo, John R. "Glück, Louise." *Guide to American Poetry Explication* 195-96.

Sam Shepard
(Samuel Shepard Rogers, Jr.), 1943-

Web Sites

Sam Shepard. Ed. unknown. 10 Jul. 1998. American Repertory Theatre. 19 Mar. 2000, http://www.fas.harvard.edu/~art/shepard.html.

Sam Shepard Web Site. Ed. Gary M. Grant and Amy Hanson. 21 Feb. 2000. Bucknell U. 19 Mar. 2000, http://www.departments.bucknell.edu/theatre_dance/Shepard/shepard.html.

Well-conceived and organized site with a detailed chronology of Shepard's life and career; extensive classified bibliography of works by and about Shepard (covering plays, screenplays, prose, poetry, newspapers, and magazines) with production and publication information; lists of selected works on specific topics; and links to other information sources.

Biographies and Criticism

Busby, Mark. "Sam Shepard." Cracroft, *Twentieth-Century American Western Writers, Second Series* (*Dictionary of Literary Biography* 212) 259-68.

DeRose, David J. *Sam Shepard*. New York: Twayne, 1992.

Engel, David W. "Sam Shepard." MacNicholas, *Twentieth-Century American Dramatists* (*Dictionary of Literary Biography* 7) 231-38.

"Sam Shepard." Trudeau, *Drama Criticism* 5:338-98.

Excerpts of criticism on Shepard in general and on *The Tooth of Crime*, *Buried Child*, and *Fool for Love* from 1964-1994, with an annotated bibliography.

Bibliographies

Carpenter, Charles A. "Shepard, Sam." *Modern Drama Scholarship and Criticism, 1981-1990* 83-85.

Etulain, Richard W., and N. Jill Howard. "Sam Shepard." *Bibliographical Guide to the Study of Western American Literature* 367-69.

Hart, Lynda. "Sam Shepard." Roudane, *Contemporary Authors: Bibliographical Series: American Dramatists* 325-60.

King, Kimball. "Sam Shepard." King, *Ten Modern American Playwrights* 197-213.

Kleb, William. "Sam Shepard." Kolin, *American Playwrights since 1945* [387]-419.

Luedtke, Luther S. "Shepard: A Bibliographical Guide." Gilbert Debusscher, Henry I. Schvey, and Marc Maufort, eds. *New Essays on American Drama*. Amsterdam: Rodopi, 1989. 167-88.

Alice (Malsenior) Walker, 1944-

Web Sites

"Alice Walker." *Heath Anthology*. 13 Mar. 2000, http://www.georgetown.edu/bassr/heath/syllabuild/iguide/walkera.html.

A disappointing page.

"Alice Walker." *Writing and Resistance*. 19 Mar. 2000, http://www.public.asu.edu/~metro/aflit/walker/link.html.

Brief biography, bibliographies of works by and about Walker, and links to other sources.

Alice Walker. 19 Mar. 2000, http://www.cwrl.utexas.edu/~mmaynard/Walker/walker. htm.
Mainly useful for Walker chronology.

Alice Walker—Womanist Writer. Ed. Melinda Jackson. Jan. 2000. U of Texas at Austin. 19 Mar. 2000, http://wwwvms.utexas.edu/~melindaj/alice.html.
Bibliography, biographical sketch, and links. Includes APA citation for page.

"Anniina's Alice Walker Page." *Luminarium.* 19 Mar. 2000, http://www.luminarium.org/contemporary/alicew/.

Womynlynks!: Alice Walker. 19 Mar. 2000, http://www.netins.net/showcase/slake/women/walker.html.

Biographies and Criticism

"Alice Walker." Harris and Fitzgerald, *Short Story Criticism* 5:400-424.
Excerpts of criticism on Walker from 1974-1988, with an annotated bibliography.

"Alice Walker." Riley, *Contemporary Literary Criticism* 103:354-430.
Excerpts of criticism on Walker from 1981-1996, with an annotated bibliography.

Christian, Barbara T. "Alice Walker." Davis and Harris, *Afro-American Fiction Writers after 1955* (*Dictionary of Literary Biography* 33) 258-71.

Davis, Thadious M. "Alice Walker." Kibler, *American Novelists since World War II, Second Series* (*Dictionary of Literary Biography* 6) 350-58.

Winchell, Donna Haisty. "Alice Walker." Giles and Giles, *American Novelists since World War II, Third Series* (*Dictionary of Literary Biography* 143) 277-93.

———. *Alice Walker.* New York: Twayne, 1992.

Bibliographies

Banks, Erma Davis, and Keith Byerman. *Alice Walker: An Annotated Bibliography: 1968-1986.* New York: Garland, 1989.
Bibliographic information and summaries of Walker's works and annotated entries for about 700 works on her.

Bloxham, Laura J. "Alice [Malsenior] Walker." Flora and Bain, *Contemporary Fiction Writers of the South* [457]-65.

Glitsch, Catherine. "Walker, Alice." *American Novel Explication, 1991-1995* 255-58.

McGowan, Martha J. "Walker, Alice." McCaffery, *Postmodern Fiction: A Bio-Bibliographical Guide* 537-39.

Pratt, Louis H., and Darnell D. Pratt. *Alice Malsenior Walker: An Annotated Bibliography: 1968-1986.* Westport: Meckler, 1988.
Describes about 400 works on Walker.

Reisman, Rosemary M. Canfield, and Christopher J. Canfield. "Alice Walker." *Contemporary Southern Women Fiction Writers* [182]-95.
Describes 46 critical works.

Werner, Craig. "Alice Walker." Bruccoli and Baughman, *Modern African American Writers* 56-62.

Wiedemann, Barbara. "Alice Walker: 'Everydate Use'." Evans, Little, and Wiedemann, *Short Fiction* 256-61.
Describes eight studies.

———. "Alice Walker: 'To Hell With Dying'." Evans, Little, and Wiedemann, *Short Fiction* 262-64.
Describes three studies.

Annie Dillard, 1945-

Web Sites

Annie Dillard World Wide Web Site. Ed. unknown. 22 Jan. 1999. Sponsor unknown. 19 Mar. 2000, http://www.mtsu.edu/~dlavery/dillardtoc.htm.
Site under construction. Includes bibliography of the works of Dillard. Does not yet include brief biography and bibliography of critical works about Dillard.

Biographies and Criticism

"Annie Dillard." Riley, *Contemporary Literary Criticism* 60:69-81.
Excerpts of criticism on Dillard from 1982-1989.

———. Riley, *Contemporary Literary Criticism* 115:159-211.
Excerpts of criticism on Dillard from 1974-1996, with an annotated bibliography.

Smith, Linda L. *Anne Dillard*. New York: Twayne, 1991.

Bibliographies

Etulain, Richard W., and N. Jill Howard. "Annie Dillard." *Bibliographical Guide to the Study of Western American Literature* 215.

Radford, Dawn Evans. "Annie Dillard: A Bibliographical Survey." *Bulletin of Bibliography* 51 (June 1994): 181-94.

August Wilson, 1945-

Web Sites

"August Wilson." *UCL Webliography of Twentieth Century Writers of Color*. 19 Mar. 2000, http://ucl.broward.cc.fl.us/writers/wilsona.htm.

August Wilson. 19 Mar. 2000, http://www.humboldt.edu/~ah/wilson/.

The Hill District: August Wilson. Carnegie Library of Pittsburgh. 19 Mar. 2000, http://www.clpgh.org/exhibit/neighborhoods/hill/hill_n102.html.

Biographies and Criticism

"August Wilson." Riley, *Contemporary Literary Criticism* 63:441-59.
Excerpts of criticism on Wilson from 1988-1990, with an annotated bibliography.

——. Riley, *Contemporary Literary Criticism* 118:370-422.
Excerpts of criticism on Wilson from 1984-1997, with an annotated bibliography.

"August Wilson." Trudeau, *Drama Criticism* 2:469-90.
Excerpts of criticism on Wilson in general and on *Ma Rainey's Black Bottom*, *Fences*, and *Joe Turner's Come and Gone* from 1984-1991, with an annotated bibliography.

Bogumil, Mary L. *Understanding August Wilson.* Columbia: U of South Carolina P, 1999.

Wolfe, Peter. *August Wilson.* New York: Twayne, 1999.

Bibliographies

Carpenter, Charles A. "Wilson, August." *Modern Drama Scholarship and Criticism, 1981-1990* 94.

O'Neill, Michael C. "August Wilson." Kolin, *American Playwrights since 1945* [518]-27.

Shafer, Yvonne. *August Wilson: A Research and Production Sourcebook.* Westport: Greenwood, 1998.

Shannon, Sandra G. "Annotated Bibliography of Works by and about August Wilson." Alan Nadel, ed. *May All Your Fences Have Gates: Essays on the Drama of August Wilson.* Iowa City: U of Iowa P, 1994. 230-66.

Williams, Dana A. "Review Essay of Scholarly Criticism on the Drama of August Wilson." *Bulletin of Bibliography* 55 (June 1998): 53-62.

(William) Tim(othy) O'Brien, 1946-

Web Sites

BoldType: Interview with Tim O'Brien. 19 Mar. 2000, http://www.randomhouse.com/boldtype/0998/obrien/interview.html.

Featured Author: Tim O'Brien. 19 Mar. 2000, http://www.nytimes.com/books/98/09/20/specials/obrien.html.
Containing mostly links to book reviews from the *New York Times* archive; site requires registration.

Tim O'Brien: An Introduction to His Writing. Ed. Ken Lopez. 19 Mar. 2000, http://www.lopezbooks.com/articles/obrien.html.

Tim O'Brien on the WWW. Ed. Jerry Bauer. 4 Mar. 2000. Sponsor unknown. 19 Mar. 2000, http://www.illyria.com/tobsites.html.
Up-to-date bibliographies of works by and about O'Brien, covering interviews, reviews, criticism, and media, with links to other Vietnam War literature sites.

Biographies and Criticism

Herzog, Tobey C. *Tim O'Brien.* New York: Twayne, 1997.

Myers, Thomas. "Tim O'Brien." Giles and Giles, *American Novelists since World War II, Fourth Series* (*Dictionary of Literary Biography* 152) 140-57.

"Tim O'Brien." Riley, *Contemporary Literary Criticism* 103:130-77.
Excerpts of criticism on O'Brien from 1978-1995, with an annotated bibliography.

Bibliographies

Calloway, Catherine. "Tim O'Brien: A Checklist." *Bulletin of Bibliography* 48.1 (Mar. 1991): 6-11.
Lists works by and about O'Brien to 1988.

———. "Tim O'Brien (1946-): A Primary and Secondary Bibliography." *Bulletin of Bibliography* 50 (Sept. 1993): 223-29.

Glitsch, Catherine. "O'Brien, Tim." *American Novel Explication, 1991-1995* 196.

Jason, Philip K. "Tim O'Brien." *Vietnam War in Literature* 136-44.
Describes about 40 studies of *Going after Cacciato, If I Die in a Combat Zone,* and *The Things They Carried.*

Raymond, Michael W. "O'Brien, Tim." McCaffery, *Postmodern Fiction: A Bio-Bibliographical Guide* 477-79.

Stephen King, 1947-

Web Sites

Welcome to Castle Rock. 19 Mar. 2000, http://www.max-net.com/personal/bdobson/king/index.html.

King Sites on the Web. 19 Mar. 2000, http://www.malakoff.com/skc.htm.
Links.

Stephen King: News. Ed. Ed Nomura. 17 Mar. 2000. Sponsor unknown. 19 Mar. 2000, http://www.eddog.com/sk/.
Contains texts of news features, interviews, and reviews; lists King's books and films, with plot and character summaries and FAQs.

Biographies and Criticism

Magistrale, Tony. *Stephen King: The Second Decade, Danse Macabre to The Dark Half.* New York: Twayne, 1992.

Reino, Joseph. *Stephen King: The First Decade, Carrie to Pet Sematary.* Boston: Twayne, 1988.

Senf, Carol A. "Stephen King." Giles and Giles, *American Novelists since World War II, Third Series* (*Dictionary of Literary Biography* 143) 92-110.

"Stephen King." Harris and Fitzgerald, *Short Story Criticism* 17:260-96.
Excerpts of criticism on King from 1978-1993, with an annotated bibliography.

"Stephen King." Riley, *Contemporary Literary Criticism* 61:317-39.
Excerpts of criticism on King from 1986-1989, with an annotated bibliography.

"Stephen King." Riley, *Contemporary Literary Criticism* 113:333-93.
　　Excerpts of criticism on King from 1985-1996, with an annotated bibliography.

Dictionaries, Encyclopedias, and Handbooks

Beahm, George. *Stephen King Companion*. Kansas City: Andrews and McMeel, 1995.
　　Aimed more at fans than scholars.

———. *Stephen King from A to Z: An Encyclopedia of His Life and Work*. Kansas City: Andrews McMeel, 1998.

Bibliographies

Collings, Michael R. *Work of Stephen King: An Annotated Bibliography & Guide*. San Bernardino: Borgo, 1996.
　　Brief bibliographic information and plot summaries for King's works and descriptions of works about him.

Glitsch, Catherine. "King, Stephen." *American Novel Explication, 1991-1995* 143-46.

Ketchum, Marty, Daniel J. H. Levack, and Jeff Levin. "Stephen King: A Bibliography." Tim Underwood and Chuck Miller, eds. *Fear Itself: The Horror Fiction of Stephen King*. San Francisco: Underwood-Miller, 1982. 231-46.

Spignesi, Stephen J. *Shape under the Sheet: The Complete Stephen King Encyclopedia: The Definitive Guide to the Works of America's Master of Horror*. Ann Arbor: Popular Culture, 1991.

David (Alan) Mamet, 1947-

Web Sites

"David Mamet." *Bohemian Ink*. 19 Mar. 2000, http://www.levity.com/corduroy/mamet.htm.

David Mamet. Ed. unknown. 19 Apr. 1999. American Repertory Theatre. 19 Mar. 2000, http://www.fas.harvard.edu/~art/mamet.html.

David Mamet. 3 Mar. 2000, http://www.gigaplex.com/celebs/mamet.htm.

David Mamet Info Page. Ed. Jason Charnick. 3 Sep. 1999. Sponsor unknown. 19 Mar. 2000, http://www.mindspring.com/~jason-charnick/mamet.html.

An Interview with David Mamet. 19 Mar. 2000, http://www.citysearchutah.com/ E/F/SLCUT/0000/06/83/.

Biographies and Criticism

"David Mamet." Trudeau, *Drama Criticism* 4:295-343.
　　Excerpts of criticism on Mamet in general and on *Sexual Perversity in Chicago*, *American Buffalo*, *A Life in the Theater*, *Glengarry Glen Ross*, and *Oleanna* from 1975-1993, with an annotated bibliography.

Lewis, Patricia, and Terry Browne, "David Mamet." MacNicholas, *Twentieth-Century American Dramatists* (*Dictionary of Literary Biography* 7) 63-70.

Journals

David Mamet Review: The Newsletter of the David Mamet Society. Las Vegas: David Mamet Soc., 1994- .
Identifies "New and Forthcoming" productions and publications; includes "David Mamet Bibliography."

Bibliographies

Carpenter, Charles A. "Mamet, David." *Modern Drama Scholarship and Criticism, 1981-1990* 65-66.

Davis, J. Madison, and John Coleman. "David Mamet: A Classified Bibliography." *Studies in American Drama, 1945-Present* 1 (1986): 83-101.

King, Kimball. "David Mamet." King, *Ten Modern American Playwrights* 179-96.

Sauer, Janice A. "Bibliography of Glengarry Glen Ross, 1983-1995." Leslie Kane, ed. *David Mamet's Glengarry Glen Ross: Text and Performance.* New York: Garland, 1996. 263-73.

Schlueter, June. "David Mamet." Roudane, *Contemporary Authors: Bibliographical Series: American Dramatists* 141-69.
Survey of research.

Trigg, Joycelyn. "David Mamet." Kolin, *American Playwrights since 1945* [259]-88.

Wolter, Jurgen. "David Mamet in German-Speaking Countries: A Classified Bibliography." *Studies in American Drama, 1945-Present* 5 (1990): 67-87.

Wendy Rose, 1948-

Web Sites

"Wendy Rose." *North American Native Authors Catalog.* 19 Mar. 2000, http://nativeauthors.com/search/bio/biorose.html.

"Wendy Rose." *Voices from the Gaps: Women Writers of Color.* 19 Mar. 2000, http://voices.cla.umn.edu/authors/WendyRose.html.

Biographies and Criticism

Jaskoski, Helen. "Wendy Rose." Roemer, *Native American Writers of the United States* (*Dictionary of Literary Biography* 175) 259-66.

"Wendy Rose." Riley, *Contemporary Literary Criticism* 85:310-17.
Excerpts of criticism on Rose from 1980-1994, with an annotated bibliography.

"Wendy Rose." Young, *Poetry Criticism* 13:231-42.
Excerpts of comments and criticism on Rose from 1980-1994, with an annotated bibliography.

Ntozake Shange
(Paulette Williams), 1948-

Web Sites

"Ntozake Shange." *Writing and Resistance*. 19 Mar. 2000, http://www.public.asu.edu/
~metro/aflit/shange/link.html.
Brief biography, bibliographies of works by and about Shange, and links to
other sites (many empty).

Ntozake Shange. 19 Mar. 2000, http://www.bridgesweb.com/shange.html.

Biographies and Criticism

Brown, Elizabeth. "Ntozake Shange." Davis and Harris, *Afro-American Writers after
1955: Dramatists and Prose Writers* (*Dictionary of Literary Biography* 38)
240-50.

"Ntozake Shange." Riley, *Contemporary Literary Criticism* 74:290-316.
Excerpts of criticism on Shange from 1978-1991, with an annotated bibliography.

"Ntozake Shange." Trudeau, *Drama Criticism* 3:467-93.
Excerpts of criticism on Shange in general and on *For Colored Girls* and *Spell
#7* from 1976-1990, with an annotated bibliography.

Bibliographies

Carpenter, Charles A. "Shange, Ntozake." *Modern Drama Scholarship and Criticism, 1981-1990* 82-83.

Lee, Catherine Carr. "Ntozake Shange." Roudane, *Contemporary Authors: Bibliographical Series: American Dramatists* 305-24.
Survey of research.

Peterson, Jane T., and Suzanne Bennett. "Ntozake Shange." *Women Playwrights of
Diversity* [302]-306.

Watson, Kenneth. "Ntozake Shange." Kolin, *American Playwrights since 1945*
[379]-86.

Williams, Dana A. "Ntozake Shange." *Contemporary African American Female
Playwrights: An Annotated Bibliography*. 83-94.
Lists about 100 studies.

Leslie Marmon Silko, 1948-

Web Sites

"Leslie Marmon Silko." *Internet Public Library: Native American Authors Project*.
19 Mar. 2000, http://www.ipl.org/cgi/ref/native/browse.pl/A75.

"Leslie Marmon Silko." *Voices from the Gaps: Women Writers of Color*. 19 Mar.
2000, http://voices.cla.umn.edu/authors/LeslieMarmonSilko.html.

Native American Authors—Teacher Resources. 19 Mar. 2000, http://falcon.jmu.edu/
~ramseyil/natauth.htm#2.

Biographies and Criticism

Clements, William M. "Leslie Marmon Silko." Giles and Giles, *American Novelists
since World War II, Third Series* (*Dictionary of Literary Biography* 143)
196-205.

———, and Kenneth M. Roemer. "Leslie Marmon Silko." Roemer, *Native American
Writers of the United States* (*Dictionary of Literary Biography* 175) 276-90.

Jaskoski, Helen. *Leslie Marmon Silko: A Study of the Short Fiction.* New York:
Twayne, 1998.

"Leslie Marmon Silko." Riley, *Contemporary Literary Criticism* 74:317-53.
Excerpts of criticism on Silko from 1980-1992, with an annotated bibliography.

———. Riley, *Contemporary Literary Criticism* 114:282-344.
Excerpts of criticism on Silko from 1988-1996, with an annotated bibliography.

Salyer, Gregory. *Leslie Marmon Silko.* New York: Twayne, 1997.

Bibliographies

Dinome, William. "Laguna Woman: An Annotated Leslie Silko Bibliography."
American Indian Culture and Research Journal 21 (1997): 207-80.

Etulain, Richard W., and N. Jill Howard. "Leslie Marmon Silko." *Bibliographical
Guide to the Study of Western American Literature* 369-71.

Glitsch, Catherine. "Silko, Leslie." *American Novel Explication, 1991-1995* 226-27.

Leo, John R. "Silko, Leslie Marmon." *Guide to American Poetry Explication* 370-71.

Gloria Naylor, 1950-

Web Sites

"Gloria Naylor." *UCL Webliography of Twentieth Century Writers of Color.* 19 Mar.
2000, http://ucl.broward.cc.fl.us/writers/naylor.htm.

"Gloria Naylor." *Writing and Resistance.* 19 Mar. 2000, http://www.public.asu.edu/
~metro/aflit/naylor/index.html.
Brief biography, separate bibliographies of works by Naylor and works about
her, and links to other Naylor sites (many empty).

The Unofficial Gloria Naylor Homepage. 19 Mar. 2000, http://www.lythastudios.com/
gnaylor/.

Biographies and Criticism

Lewis, Vashti Crutcher. "Gloria Naylor." Giles and Giles, *American Novelists since
World War II, Fifth Series* (*Dictionary of Literary Biography* 173) 170-76.

Bibliographies

Brusky, Sarah. "Selective Primary and Secondary Bibliography of Gloria Naylor." *Bulletin of Bibliography* 54 (Sept. 1997): 269-76.

Glitsch, Catherine. "Naylor, Gloria." *American Novel Explication, 1991-1995* 190-93.

Jorie Graham, 1951-

Web Sites

"Jorie Graham." *Academy of American Poets*. 8 Mar. 2000, http://www.poets.org/lit/poet/jgrahfst.htm.
Includes interview from *American Poet* at: http://www.poets.org/LIT/poet/jgrafst2.htm.

Biographies and Criticism

Brien, Peyton. "Jorie Graham." Gwynn, *American Poets since World War II, Third Series* (*Dictionary of Literary Biography* 120) 96-101.

"Jorie Graham." Riley, *Contemporary Literary Criticism* 118:221-64.
Excerpts of criticism on Graham from 1984-1997, with an annotated bibliography.

Joy Harjo, 1951-

Web Sites

"Joy Harjo." *Academy of American Poets*. 8 Mar. 2000, http://www.poets.org/lit/poet/jharjfst.htm.

"Joy Harjo." *North American Native Authors Catalog*. 19 Mar. 2000, http://nativeauthors.com/search/bio/bioharjo.html.

"Joy Harjo." *Storytellers: Native American Authors Online*. Ed. Karen M. Strom. 21 Mar. 2000. Sponsor unknown. 25 Mar. 2000, http://www.hanksville.org/storytellers/joy/.
"Constructed with the assistance and active collaboration of " Harjo. Includes a bibliography of works by and about Harjo, with a brief biography and list of awards; links to fulltexts of selected works and other web sites.

Biographies and Criticism

Field, C. Renee. "Joy Harjo." Gwynn, *American Poets since World War II, Third Series* (*Dictionary of Literary Biography* 120) 114-19.

"Joy Harjo." Riley, *Contemporary Literary Criticism* 83:264-87.
Excerpts of criticism on Harjo from 1985-1993, with an annotated bibliography.

Wilson, Norma C. "Joy Harjo." Roemer, *Native American Writers of the United States* (*Dictionary of Literary Biography* 175) 112-18.

Bibliographies

Etulain, Richard W., and N. Jill Howard. "Joy Harjo." *Bibliographical Guide to the Study of Western American Literature* 250.

Rita Dove, 1952-

Web Sites

"Rita Dove." *Academy of American Poets.* 19 Mar. 2000, http://www.poets.org/lit/poet/rdovefst.htm.

"Rita Dove."*Voices from the Gaps: Women Writers of Color.* 19 Mar. 2000, http://voices.cla.umn.edu/authors/RitaDove.html.

Biographies and Criticism

Jones, Kirkland C. "Rita Dove." Gwynn, *American Poets since World War II, Third Series* (*Dictionary of Literary Biography* 120) 47-51.

"Rita Dove." Young, *Poetry Criticism* 6:103-24.
    Excerpts of comments and criticism on Dove from 1986-1991, with an annotated bibliography.

Bibliographies

Leo, John R. "Dove, Rita." *Guide to American Poetry Explication* 107.

Williams, Dana A. "Dove, Rita." *Contemporary African American Female Playwrights: An Annotated Bibliography* 39-40.

Alberto Rios, 1952-

Web Sites

"Alberto Rios." *Academy of American Poets.* 9 Mar. 2000, http://www.poets.org/lit/poet/ariosfst.htm.

Biographies and Criticism

Saldívar, José David. "Alberto Ríos." Lomelí and Shirley, *Chicano Writers, Second Series* (*Dictionary of Literary Biography* 122) 220-24.

Bibliographies

Leo, John R. "Ríos, Alberto." *Guide to American Poetry Explication* 342-43.

Amy Tan, 1952-

Web Sites

Salon Interview: Amy Tan. 19 Mar. 2000, http://www.salon1999.com/12nov1995/feature/tan.html.

"Anniina's Amy Tan Page." *Luminarium*. 19 Mar. 2000, http://www.luminarium.org/contemporary/amytan/.
Provides the text of "The Chinese Siamese Cat" and list of published criticism of Tan's works; links to several different sources for excerpts of Tan's works, published reviews, interviews, and essays, and biographies in several languages.

Biographies and Criticism

"Amy Tan." Riley, *Contemporary Literary Criticism* 120:361-425.
Excerpts of criticism on Tan from 1989-1996, with an annotated bibliography.

Feng, Pin-chia. "Amy Tan." Giles and Giles, *American Novelists since World War II, Fifth Series* (*Dictionary of Literary Biography* 173) 281-89.

Bibliographies

Etulain, Richard W., and N. Jill Howard. "Amy Tan." *Bibliographical Guide to the Study of Western American Literature* 401.

Glitsch, Catherine. "Tan, Amy." *American Novel Explication, 1991-1995* 238.

Lorna Dee Cervantes, 1954-

Web Sites

"Lorna Dee Cervantes." *Academy of American Poets*. 8 Mar. 2000, http://www.poets.org/lit/poet/ldcerfst.htm.
Does not contain a bibliography.

"Lorna Dee Cervantes." *Heath Anthology*. 13 Mar. 2000, http://www.georgetown.edu/bassr/heath/syllabuild/iguide/cervante.html.

Biographies and Criticism

Fernández, Roberta. "Lorna Dee Cervantes." Lomelí and Shirley, *Chicano Writers, First Series* (*Dictionary of Literary Biography* 82) 74-78.

Bibliographies

Leo, John R. "Cervantes, Lorna Dee." *Guide to American Poetry Explication* 53-54.

Sandra Cisneros, 1954-

Web Sites

"Sandra Cisneros." *Voices from the Gaps: Women Writers of Color*. 19 Mar. 2000, http://voices.cla.umn.edu/authors/SandraCisneros.html.

Sandra Cisneros: Teacher Resource File. 19 Mar. 2000, http://falcon.jmu.edu/schoollibrary/cisneros.htm.
Respectable "annotated bibliography."

Biographies and Criticism

Elías, Eduardo F. "Sandra Cisneros." Lomelí and Shirley, *Chicano Writers, Second Series* (*Dictionary of Literary Biography* 122) 77-81.

"Sandra Cisneros." Riley, *Contemporary Literary Criticism* 69:143-56.
    Excerpts of criticism on Cisneros from 1984-1991, with an annotated bibliography.

———. Riley, *Contemporary Literary Criticism* 118:169-220.
    Excerpts of criticism on Cisneros from 1989-1997, with an annotated bibliography.

Tompkins, Cynthia. "Sandra Cisneros." Giles and Giles, *American Novelists since World War II, Fourth Series* (*Dictionary of Literary Biography* 152) 35-41.

Louise Erdrich, 1954-

Web Sites

"Louise Erdrich." *Internet Public Library: Native American Authors Project.* 19 Mar. 2000, http://www.ipl.org/cgi/ref/native/browse.pl/A30.

The Salon Interview: Louise Erdrich. 19 Mar. 2000, http://www.salon.com/weekly/interview960506.html.

Biographies and Criticism

Beidler, Peter G. "Louise Erdrich." Roemer, *Native American Writers of the United States* (*Dictionary of Literary Biography* 175) 84-100.

Hafen, P. Jane. "Louise Erdrich." Cracroft, *Twentieth-Century American Western Writers, First Series* (*Dictionary of Literary Biography* 206) 85-96.

"Louise Erdrich." Riley, *Contemporary Literary Criticism* 120:131-98.
    Excerpts of criticism on Erdrich from 1984-1996, with an annotated bibliography.

Rosenberg, Ruth. "Louise Erdrich." Giles and Giles, *American Novelists since World War II, Fourth Series* (*Dictionary of Literary Biography* 152) 42-50.

Stookey, Lorena L. *Louise Erdrich: A Critical Companion.* Westport: Greenwood, 1999.

Wong, Hertha D. Sweet. *Louise Erdrich's Love Medicine: A Casebook.* New York: Oxford UP, 2000.

Bibliographies

Beidler, Peter G., and Gay Barton. *Reader's Guide to the Novels of Louise Erdrich.* Columbia: U of Missouri P, 1999.

Burdick, Debra A. "Louise Erdrich's *Love Medicine, The Beet Queen,* and *Tracks*: An Annotated Survey of Criticism through 1994." *American Indian Culture and Research Journal* 20 (1996): 137-66.

Etulain, Richard W., and N. Jill Howard. "Louise Erdrich." *Bibliographical Guide to the Study of Western American Literature* 223-24.

Glitsch, Catherine. "Erdrich, Louise." *American Novel Explication, 1991-1995* 74-75.

"Louise Erdrich: A.S.A.I.L. Bibliography #9." *Studies in American Indian Literatures: The Journal of the Association for the Study of American Indian Literatures* 9 (Winter 1985): 37-41.

Pearlman, Mickey. "Bibliography of Writings by Louise Erdrich"; "Bibliography of Writings about Louise Erdrich." Pearlman, *American Women Writing Fiction* 108-12.

Helena Maria Viramontes, 1954-

Web Sites

"Helena María Viramontes." *Heath Anthology*. 13 Mar. 2000, http://www.georgetown.edu/bassr/heath/syllabuild/iguide/viramontes.html.

"Helena Maria Viramontes." *Voices from the Gaps: Women Writers of Color*. 19 Mar. 2000, http://voices.cla.umn.edu/authors/HelenaMariaViramontes.html.

Biographies and Criticism

Saldívar-Hull, Sonia. "Helena María Viramontes." Lomelí and Shirley, *Chicano Writers, Second Series* (*Dictionary of Literary Biography* 122) 322-25.

Cathy Song, 1955-

Web Sites

"Cathy Song." *Heath Anthology*. 13 Mar. 2000, http://www.georgetown.edu/bassr/heath/syllabuild/iguide/song.html.

Biographies and Criticism

"Cathy Song." Young, *Poetry Criticism* 21:330-51.
    Excerpts of comments and criticism on Song from 1983-1994, with an annotated bibliography.

Schultz, Susan M. "Cathy Song." Conte, *American Poets since World War II, Fifth Series* (*Dictionary of Literary Biography* 169) 267-74.

Li-Young Lee, 1957-

Web Sites

"Li-Young Lee." *Heath Anthology*. 13 Mar. 2000, http://www.georgetown.edu/bassr/heath/syllabuild/iguide/lee.html.
    Page is blank on date of writing, but it is linked to as if it were not blank.

"Poetry of Li-Young Lee." 13 Mar. 2000, http://www.indiana.edu/~primate/lee.html.
    Fulltexts of three poems: "A Story," "Early in the Morning," and "The Gift." Also includes select bibliography and brief biographical sketch.

Biographies and Criticism

Hsu, Ruth Y. "Li-Young Lee." Conte, *American Poets since World War II, Fourth Series* (*Dictionary of Literary Biography* 165) 139-46.

"Li-Young Lee." Young, *Poetry Criticism* 24:239-52.
    Excerpts of comments and criticism on Lee from 1989-1996, with an annotated bibliography.

William T. Vollmann, 1959-

Web Sites

Opening the Book: The William T. Vollmann Homepage. Ed. Chris Sweet. 27 Sept. 1997. Unknown sponsor. 19 Mar. 2000, http://home1.gte.net/csweet/vollmann. htm.
    Intended to promote Vollmann. Lists his works and gives texts of selected interviews and reviews of his works; links to a concise biography and texts of selected articles. "Helpful Links" connects to texts of related background works (described as "Annotations"). Also contains an atlas mapping Vollmann's adventures and photo and art galleries. Some broken links and other parts under construction.

Biographies and Criticism

"William T. Vollman." Riley, *Contemporary Literary Criticism* 89:274-317.
    Excerpts of criticism on Vollman from 1987-1994, with an annotated bibliography.

Bibliographies

Glitsch, Catherine. "Vollmann, William T." *American Novel Explication, 1991-1995* 254-55.

Alphabetical
List of Authors

Adams, Abigail (Smith), 1744-1818, 29
Adams, Henry (Brooks), 1838-1918, 85
Aiken, Conrad (Potter), 1889-1973, 159
Albee, Edward (Franklin), 1928- , 256
Alcott, Louisa May, 1832-1888, 77
(Aldington), H(ilda) D(oolittle),
   1886-1961, 150
Ammons, A(rchie) R(andolph), 1926- ,
   249
Anderson, Sherwood, 1876-1941, 131
Apess, William, 1798-?, 40
Ashbery, John (Lawrence), 1927- , 254
Asimov, Isaac, 1920-1992, 233
Austin, Mary (Hunter), 1868-1934, 110

Baldwin, James, 1924-1987, 243
Bambara, Toni Cade, 1939-1995, 280
Banneker, Benjamin, 1731-1806, 25
Baraka, Imamu Amiri—see Jones, LeRoi
Barlow, Joel, 1754-1812, 31
Barthelme, Donald, 1931-1989, 264
Bartram, John, 1699-1777, 21
Bartram, William, 1739-1823, 27
Bellow, Saul, 1915- , 226
Berryman, John, 1914-1972, 220
Bierce, Ambrose (Gwinett),
   1842-1914?, 86
Bishop, Elizabeth, 1911-1979, 214
Black Elk, (Nicholas), 1863-1950, 109
Bly, Robert (Elwood), 1926- , 249
Bogan, Louise, 1897-1970, 174
Bonnin, Gertrude Simmons (Zitkala-Ša),
   1876-1938, 133
Bontemps, Arna (Wendell), 1902-1973,
   192
Bradbury, Ray (Douglas), 1920- , 234
Bradford, William, 1590-1657, 16

Bradstreet, Anne (Dudley),
   c. 1612-1672, 16
Brent, Linda—see Jacobs, Harriet Ann
   (Linda Brent)
Brooks, Gwendolyn, 1917- , 228
Brown, Charles Brockden, 1771-1810,
   33
Brown, Sterling A(llan), 1901-1989, 190
Brown, William Wells, 1816?-1884, 60
Bryant, William Cullen, 1794-1878, 38
Burroughs, William S(eward),
   1914-1997, 221
Byrd, William, 1674-1744, 20

Cable, George Washington, 1844-1925,
   92
Carver, Raymond, 1939-1989, 281
Cather, Willa (Sibert), 1873-1947, 123
Cervantes, Lorna Dee, 1954- , 301
Cheever, John, 1912-1982, 216
Chesnut, Mary Boykin (Miller),
   1823-1886, 72
Chesnutt, Charles W(addell),
   1858-1932, 102
Child, Lydia Maria, 1802-1880, 40
Chopin, Kate (O'Flaherty), 1851-1904,
   97
Cisneros, Sandra, 1954- , 301
Clemens, Samuel Langhorne (Mark
   Twain), 1835-1910, 79
Cooper, James Fenimore, 1789-1851, 36
Coover, Robert (Lowell), 1932- , 266
Crane, (Harold) Hart, 1899-1932, 181
Crane, Stephen, 1871-1900, 117
Creeley, Robert (White), 1926- , 250
Crèvecoeur, Michel-Guillaume Jean de,
   (J. Hector St. John de Creve
   coeur), 1735-1813, 26